D0518355

A Guide to Information Engineering Using the IEF™

Computer-Aided Planning, Analysis, and Design

Second Edition

A GUIDE TO INFORMATION ENGINEERING USING THE IEF™
Computer-Aided Planning, Analysis, and Design

TI Part Number 2739756-0001
Second Edition: January, 1990

Updates to the information in this document are issued as the need occurs.

Changes are periodically made to the information herein; these changes will be incorporated in new editions of this publication.

Acknowledgements

This document is based upon the Information Engineering concepts expressed by James Martin in his publications, and refined by James Martin Associates.

Normalization techniques in Chapter 16 are based upon principles presented in *An Introduction to Database Systems, Vol. I*, by C. J. Date.

Trademarks

Information Engineering Facility and IEF are trademarks of Texas Instruments Incorporated.

Copyright © 1988 Texas Instruments Incorporated.

All rights reserved. No part of this work covered by the copyright hereon may be reproduced or used in any form or by any means without the written permission of Texas Instruments Incorporated.

Printed in U.S.A.

Table of Contents

CHAPTER 5
DEFINING THE INFORMATION ARCHITECTURE

CHAPTER 8
DEFINING THE TECHNICAL ARCHITECTURE

CHAPTER 13
ACTIVITY ANALYSIS

CHAPTER 15
CURRENT SYSTEMS ANALYSIS

CHAPTER 16
CONFIRMATION

CHAPTER 17
BUSINESS SYSTEM DEFINITION

PART III
A GUIDE TO BUSINESS SYSTEM DESIGN
USING THE INFORMATION ENGINEERING FACILITY

CHAPTER 18
BUSINESS SYSTEM DESIGN OVERVIEW

CHAPTER 19
PREPARING FOR BUSINESS SYSTEM DESIGN

CHAPER 20
PROCEDURE DEFINITION

CHAPTER 21
DIALOG DESIGN

CHAPTER 22
LAYOUT DESIGN

CHAPTER 23
PROCEDURE LOGIC DESIGN

CHAPTER 24
COMPLETING BUSINESS SYSTEM DESIGN

PREFACE

The art of information system development has undergone a difficult and tortuous evolution over the past two and one-half decades. For those of us participating in this software development struggle, it has been frustrating to watch the quantum leaps made in the computing hardware arena, while advances in software quality and productivity have shuffled along at a considerably more modest pace. Now, with the advent of the practices and technologies described in this book, we are stepping across the threshold into a new epoch in the evolution of system development: one in which the right problems are solved, and high-quality solutions are produced very quickly.

One may trace this evolution to two distinct yet parallel paths. One is the **methods** path, which has produced techniques for conceptualizing systems and data: from rudimentary flowcharting through structured programming, design analysis, and data modelling. These emergent methods have enabled developers to deal with problems and their solutions at increasingly higher levels of abstraction in an increasingly higher-quality conceptual framework. The other is the **tools** path, which has created mechanisms to help developers perform tasks more quickly and easily. The products of this path have included programming languages, compilers, debuggers, data base management systems, and code generators.

The Information Engineering Facility (IEF) from Texas Instruments represents a juxtaposition of these two paths. First, it is an automated implementation of James Martin's Information Engineering methodology, widely considered the most advanced and complete development methodology devised to date. Secondly, it is the first fully-integrated set of tools to capture information needs at the highest possible levels of abstraction and successfully transform them into executing application systems using state-of-the-art technology. As such, it is a melding of the latest advances along both the methods and tools paths — a melding that promises to yield a synergistic benefit far greater than the use of tools or methods independently.

Information Engineering is a methodology in seven stages, five of which address various levels of information system development. (The remaining two deal with the transition of developed systems into production and their continued operation.) The IEF currently supports all five development stages, with plans for some level of future support for the remaining two stages. This three-part book deals with the first three development stages: **Information Strategy Planning**, **Business Area Analysis**, and **Business System Design**. Although each part of this book can stand alone, the reader will gain the greatest understanding of the principles involved by reading all three parts in order.

This edition includes extensive revisions to Part II, the Business Area Analysis portion of the book. In particular, I have revised the chapters on Data, Activity, and Interaction Analysis to provide a more complete description of performing those kinds of analysis. This edition also includes a number of minor editorial corrections and revisions.

I would like to thank the teams of Information Engineering consultants at Texas Instruments and James Martin Associates who provided much of the source material without which the writing of this book would have been impossible. Additionally, I would like to thank the IEF development team at Texas Instruments for their technical contribution to this work.

I owe a special debt of gratitude to Doug Conley and Bob Bates of Texas Instruments, and Eric Magnusson, Keith Short, and Bill Dawson of James Martin Associates for their contributions of both technical and methodological expertise; to James Morrison, formerly of Texas Instruments, who was responsible for most of the chapters on Current Systems Analysis and Confirmation; to Sherry Carson Jaco, Mary Hankins, and Mary Orr for their initial work on Business Area Analysis and Laurie Gaines, editor of the first edition; and to Peggy Hester and Mary Jane Fish whose administrative help proved invaluable. Finally, I would like to extend special thanks to Phyllis Moore who edited and formatted the current edition.

Dennis Minium

Plano, TX

1989

OVERVIEW

This guide describes the first three stages of Information Engineering: Information Strategy Planning (ISP), Business Area Analysis (BAA), and Business System Design (BSD), using the Information Engineering Facility™ (IEF™) from Texas Instruments.

Information Engineering methodology includes seven stages, five of which deal with Information Systems development at some level of abstraction. At this writing, the IEF software development group has concentrated on supporting the five development stages of Information Engineering. Of these five, the first three require a good bit of methodological know-how to make the best possible use of the tools, while the remaining two are largely automated by the IEF software. Consequently, the first three development stages are the principal subjects of this guide.

The following pages provide a brief introduction to Information Engineering and give an overview of the structure of this book.

THE SEVEN STAGES OF INFORMATION ENGINEERING

Information Engineering is a comprehensive system development methodology. It provides techniques for identifying and organizing business requirements at the highest possible level. Based on those requirements, it provides tools for building application systems to satisfy them. To this end, Information Engineering is divided into these seven stages:

1. **Information Strategy Planning (ISP)**, in which the developer establishes a broad view of the information requirements of the business.

    The IEF Planning Toolset supports this stage.

2. **Business Area Analysis (BAA)**, in which the developer performs a more detailed analysis on a particular segment of the business called a **business area**.

    The IEF Analysis Toolset supports this stage.

3. **Business System Design (BSD)**, in which the developer describes an application system supporting a segment of a particular business area in detail without regard to the particulars of the target computing environments.

    The IEF Design Toolset supports this stage.

4. **Technical Design (TD)**, in which the developer tailors the results of Business System Design to a specific target computing environment. In this stage, the developer considers the characteristics of the hardware environment, operating system, teleprocessing monitor, and data base management system.

    The IEF Design Toolset supports this stage.

5. **Construction**, in which all of the executable components of a system are created. Included in this process are development of programs, data bases, job control statements, screen formats, transaction definitions – in short, all of the pieces necessary for an application system to run in the selected target environment.

    The IEF Construction Toolset supports this stage.

6. **Transition**, in which a newly constructed application system is installed in a production environment in an orderly manner, possibly replacing existing systems or portions of systems.

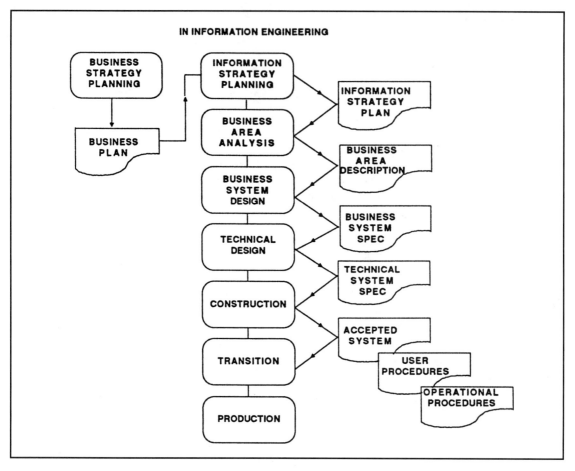

Figure 1-1. The Seven Stages of Information Engineering

7.   **Production**, in which the enterprise realizes the full benefit of the application system as it executes to satisfy some portion of the business requirements identified during ISP.

This broad-brush description of Information Engineering serves to illustrate its top-down nature. Figure 1-1 depicts the relationship between the stages of Information Engineering. From this figure, one might gather that the "pure" practice of Information Engineering is something like sliding down a waterfall, progressing from one stage to the next until the bottom is reached (in fact, Information Engineering is categorized as a "waterfall" methodology.) In practice, though, it is not uncommon to iterate through stages, perhaps taking only a portion of a Business Area Analysis project all the way through to Construction to validate the analytical specifications before continuing the analysis. The effective combination of a waterfall framework with iterative techniques was virtually impossible prior to the automation of Information Engineering.

Note that an additional box entitled "Business Strategy Planning" appears in Figure 1-1. This activity is not one of the formal stages of Information Engineering. Rather, it is the task of building the business plan used by the enterprise to meet its objectives. In some organizations this planning is formal, while in others it is not. In either case, any business plans formulated by the organization are required for the proper execution of the first stage of Information Engineering, Information Strategy Planning.

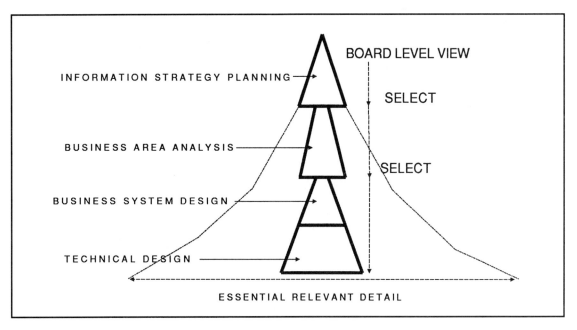

Figure 1-2. The Principal of "Divide and Conquer"

In practice, Information Engineering has proven appropriate for many categories of enterprise. Although some of the terminology may seem slanted towards business concerns, the techniques employed are suitable for use by public agencies and non-profit organizations as well. Generally speaking, any organization that has information processing requirements can benefit from the application of Information Engineering.

At the foundation of Information Engineering lies the principle of "Divide and Conquer." By addressing successively smaller components of the total information requirements of the business as increasing detail is added, each task is reduced to a manageable size. This philosophy is reflected in Figure 1-2.

HOW THIS BOOK IS ORGANIZED

This book is divided into three parts, each of which deals with a separate stage of Information Engineering.

Part I addresses the first stage of Information Engineering, Information Strategy Planning (ISP), and is organized as follows:

- Chapter 1 is an overview of the Information Strategy Planning stage.

- Chapter 2 provides techniques for information gathering that can be used throughout ISP.

- Chapters 3 through 9 present detailed descriptions of each of the major tasks performed during ISP.

Part II deals with the second stage of Information Engineering, Business Area Analysis (BAA), and is organized as follows:

- Chapter 10 is an overview of the Business Area Analysis stage.

- Chapters 11 through 17 present detailed descriptions of the tasks and techniques used during BAA.

Part III explains the Business System Design (BSD) stage, and is organized as follows:

- Chapter 18 is an overview of the Business System Design stage.

- Chapter 19 describes the necessary preparations for undertaking a BSD project.
- Chapters 20 through 24 describe the detailed tasks performed and techniques used throughout BSD.

Appendices summarize important information and explain some of the more esoteric points.

PART I
A GUIDE TO INFORMATION STRATEGY PLANNING USING THE INFORMATION ENGINEERING FACILITY™

1
INFORMATION STRATEGY PLANNING OVERVIEW

This is the first chapter of Part I, which describes the first stage of Information Engineering, **Information Strategy Planning (ISP)**, using the Information Engineering Facility (IEF). Information Strategy Planning is based on two premises:

- Information is a resource
- An organization's opportunities for success are enhanced by effectively using this resource

With its emphasis on supporting business objectives through information technology, Information Strategy Planning provides a way to plan and manage the use of information, just as one might plan and manage the use of any other resource.

During Information Strategy Planning, planners build the framework for satisfying an enterprise's information requirements. Planners use this blueprint in successive stages of Information Engineering to provide the computerized systems needed to manage the information resource.

This chapter introduces the basic concepts that underlie Information Strategy Planning and the support provided by the IEF.

AN OVERVIEW OF INFORMATION STRATEGY PLANNING

The Requirement for Flexibility

In an Information Strategy Planning project, the planner builds a high-level view of the information requirements of an entire enterprise, or a significant portion of an enterprise, and provides a plan for satisfying those requirements. Since such a plan often involves sweeping changes to the information processing environment, the ISP project must have the support of the top management of the company.

Because each enterprise is unique, planners must tailor the framework of each ISP project to the particular enterprise being studied. Planners must be especially sensitive to the corporate culture and political environment; otherwise, the ISP project is doomed to failure. For this reason, the guidelines presented here should be taken as a representative set of suggestions, subject to change based on the constraints within each organization.

For example, if a business has no intention of changing the structure of its Information Systems organization, the ISP task that assesses the current Information Systems organization (Chapter 6) can be given very little emphasis. In another business, management expectations may dictate the use of techniques not described in this book. In all cases, the planners building the Information Strategy Plan must be flexible enough to accommodate the organization's needs.

Despite this requirement for flexibility, a set of rigorous principles rests at the core of the Information Strategy Planning activity. Without a highly structured, soundly developed Information Architecture, for example, there is no firm foundation for future system development.

Thus, the requirements for building a successful Information Strategy Plan include two widely different components. On one hand, the plan must cater to the expectations of management and the realities of the political milieu; otherwise, it will fail to be received and executed. On the other hand, the infrastructure for future systems development must be designed with uncompromising rigor; otherwise, it will fail under the weight of the systems built upon it.

The Three Architectures

Central to Information Strategy Planning is the definition of an architectural framework for future development. The framework devised during an ISP project consists of three major components which, together, address the information requirements of an enterprise. These components are called the Information Architecture, the Business System Architecture, and the Technical Architecture.

- The **Information Architecture** defines the activities performed by the enterprise and the information required to perform them. This high-level view of activities and data provides a basis for the detailed analysis of business segments conducted during the second stage of Information Engineering, **Business Area Analysis**.

- The **Business System Architecture** describes probable **business systems** and **data stores** required to support the Information Architecture. Although a more detailed understanding of information requirements during the BAA stage is needed to determine the actual contents of each business system, the Business System Architecture prepared during the ISP stage provides a high-level initial prediction of the application systems to be developed. During the third stage of Information Engineering, **Business System Design**, the Business System Architecture is used to correctly segment business activities into application systems.

- The **Technical Architecture** describes the hardware and software environment required to support the Business System Architecture. During the fourth stage of Information Engineering, **Technical Design**, the technical support for business systems depends greatly on the definition of the Technical Architecture during the ISP stage.

These three architectures form a blueprint from which the enterprise can build an information environment that addresses its long-term needs. This is the target information environment toward which the enterprise must move to best manage its information resource and support its business objectives.

The Objectives of an ISP Project

The objectives of an ISP project are:

1. To assess the information requirements of the enterprise
2 To construct an Information Architecture that will satisfy those requirements
3. To construct a Business System Architecture to support the implementation of the Information Architecture
4. To identify the Technical Architecture necessary to support the Business System Architecture
5. To present the project's findings in a way top management can readily understand, evaluate, and act upon

The Tasks Performed During an ISP Project

To accomplish the objectives stated above, the planners must perform a number of tasks. While each ISP project is different, the task list presented here and expanded in the following chapters should serve as an appropriate starting point for any ISP project.

1. **Plan the Project**. In this task, the planners determine the project scope, select and train team members, and build a schedule for the remainder of the project.

2. **Make the Initial Assessment**. In this task, planners perform a broad-brush assessment of the organization and its information environment. They elicit facts about the business from a number of sources and analyze them. The results, once reviewed, provide a framework for the remainder of the project.

3. **Define the Information Architecture**. In this task, planners refine the preliminary sketch of the Information Architecture developed during the initial assessment. They record and organize business activities and information usage in more detail.

4. **Assess the Current Environment**. In this task, planners supplement their understanding of the current information environment through further research. They measure these results against the Information Architecture to determine how effectively current systems are satisfying the organization's needs.

5. **Define the Business System Architecture**. During this task, planners group the activities and data described in the Information Architecture to form **natural business systems** and, subsequently, **business areas.** Based on the assessment of the current environment, planners rank the Business Area Analysis projects required for each business area. This forms an implementation plan for the Information Architecture.

6. **Define the Technical Architecture**. During this task, planners forecast the hardware and software facilities required to support the Business System Architecture and compare them against the current technical environment.

7. **Complete the ISP Project**. At this point, planners consider alternative strategies, build the case for the recommended strategy, complete the ISP Report, and present the results to top management.

When considering this list of major tasks, their elaboration throughout Part I, and the summary task list appearing in Appendix A, one must remember that the broad nature of Information Strategy Planning resists the highly structured, cookbook-style approach appropriate to later stages of Information Engineering.

The planners may find that some tasks are iterative in nature. For example, during the initial assessment phase, it may become necessary to interview the same manager more than once in order to completely reconcile his views with those of others.

The planners may also discover a need to execute some tasks or subtasks in a sequence different from the one presented here. For example, the definition of some entity types, part of the "Define the Information Architecture" task, may take place during the "Make the Initial Assessment" task. Likewise, during the "Assess the Current Environment" task, it may become necessary to interview personnel, an activity confined in this task list to the "Make the Initial Assessment" task.

In short, the tasks appearing in the following chapters should not be construed as a rigid, step-by-step approach. Such an approach is inconsistent with the nature of Information Strategy Planning.

AUTOMATED TOOLS AVAILABLE FOR AN ISP PROJECT

The Information Engineering Facility (IEF) from Texas Instruments includes several tools that are useful throughout an ISP project. The following tools are components of the IEF Planning Toolset:

- The **Data Modeling Tool** enables a planner to represent the information used in the business. The **Subject Area Diagram** and the **Entity Relationship Diagram** are built using this tool.

- The **Activity Hierarchy Tool** is used to record high level business activities in a hierarchical fashion. The **Function Decomposition Diagram** is built using this tool.

- The **Activity Dependency Tool** can be used to record the relationships between business activities. The **Function Dependency Diagram** is built using this tool.

- The **Organizational Hierarchy Tool** can be used to record an organizational structure.

- The **Matrix Processor** includes a set of matrices that can be used to perform complex analysis on the many kinds of data required during Information Strategy Planning. Additionally, the planner may create his own matrices to perform whatever additional analyses he might require.[1]

Part I of this guide deals primarily with the Information Strategy Planning methodology, not with a detailed description of the use of the IEF tools. Detailed instructions for using these appear in the *IEF Planning Toolset Guide*.

Some users may experience limited tool usage based on the IEF software version being used. Users should read and thoroughly understand the Release Notes that accompany each version before using the software. These notes clearly document all restrictions applicable to the current version.

---

1. Had the English language been graced with a reasonable gender-neutral prounoun, it would have appeared here. However, since "it" sounds strange in reference to a human being, and since making every personal pronoun reference a "he or she" tends to disrupt continuity, the masculine pronoun is used almost exclusively throughout this text, with apologies. Thus, throughout this book, please understand that references to "he" should be interpreted as "he or she," to "him", "her or him," and so on.

The Author

2
INFORMATION GATHERING TECHNIQUES

OVERVIEW

This chapter describes techniques for gathering data about the organization and the current information environment. The members of the project team use these techniques throughout the project as they gain an increasingly detailed knowledge of the business.

This chapter consists of the following sections:

- **Classes of Information**. This section details the kinds of concepts to be sought by the project team.
- **Review of Written Information**. This section identifies potential sources of written information the project team should consider at different points during the project.
- **Interviewing**. This section presents techniques for effective, structured interviewing.
- **Recording Information in IEF Matrices**. This section presents notes on the effective use of the Matrix Processor in the IEF Planning Toolset.

CLASSES OF INFORMATION

During an ISP project, the goal of gathering raw data is to:

- Assess how well the current information technology environment supports the mission of the enterprise
- Identify an Information Architecture that will improve support for this mission, including aspects of its implementation.

The analysis of raw data, whether gathered through interviews or reading, leads to its organization into meaningful categories. As this categorization takes place, patterns and aggregations emerge which, in some cases, confirm the intuitive views of the project team and, in others, bring new information to light.

The facts collected during an ISP project are organized into the following specific categories:

- Facts about the organization's mission and its plan to accomplish that mission
- Facts about the structure of the organization
- Facts about the activities the business performs and the things about which it may need to hold data
- Facts about the current systems environment
- Facts about the current technological environment.

Each of these categories is further divided into **classes of information**. The following discussion defines and explains each category and provides examples of each class. Some of the examples refer to an imaginary corporation called "Consolidated Implements" that builds and sells farming machinery. Others refer to a fictional non-profit organization devoted to the preservation of endangered species, called the "Wildlife Watchers Foundation" (WWF).

A summary of this classification of business facts appears at the conclusion of this section.

Facts about the Mission

To understand the direction of an enterprise, one must analyze its underlying strategies and plans. This section discusses the facts that support the enterprise's mission and its plan to accomplish that mission.

Most larger organizations have developed, over time, their own set of planning categories and terminology. In such cases, the project team should employ the organization's classification. The following terms should be taken as a representative method of classification:

- Mission
- Objective
- Strategy
- Goal
- Plan
- Critical Success Factor

In some organizations, things defined in this section as objectives might be called goals, goals might be called strategies, plans might be called tactics, and so on. However, the terms listed here are generalizations that cover all aspects of business strategy pertinent to Information Strategy Planning.

An analysis of these facts leads to the identification of two intrinsic categories of information critical to the ISP project. These categories are not subject to differences between organizations:

- Performance Measure
- Information Need

Each of these eight concepts is described below.

Mission   The enterprise's **mission** is a general statement of the purpose and nature of the enterprise. Each enterprise can be characterized by a single mission.

Examples:

The mission of Consolidated Implements might be:

   ◦   To provide the maximum return for investors through the manufacture and distribution of farm machinery.

The mission of the Wildlife Watchers Foundation might be:

   ◦   To raise and employ funds to be used for the identification and preservation of animal species in danger of extinction.

Objective   An **objective** is a broad, longer-term result that the enterprise wishes to achieve to support its mission. The planning horizon for an objective is generally between five and ten years.

Examples:

One of the objectives of Consolidated Implements might be:

   ◦   To become the market leader in farm machinery sales in the southern United States.

An objective of the Wildlife Watchers Foundation might be:

   ◦   To establish wildlife preserves for the protection of raptors indigenous to the Western Hemisphere.

Strategy

A **strategy** is the means by which an objective is achieved. Each objective must be supported by a strategy.

Examples:

A strategy Consolidated Implements might employ to realize its stated objective might be:

◦ Perform market research to determine the types of farming implements most needed in the Southern United States.

WWF, on the other hand, might employ the following strategy to realize its objective:

◦ Establish personal contacts with leaders in both the public and private sector who will assist in fund raising activities.

Goal

A **goal** is a specific target the enterprise wishes to reach at a specific point in time. Each goal of the enterprise supports a single strategy (and, thus, a single objective). A strategy, on the other hand, is likely to be supported by many goals.

Examples:

For the above-stated strategy employed by Consolidated Implements, the following goal might be appropriate:

◦ Complete demographic survey of the farming population in Florida, Georgia and Alabama within six months.

Likewise, the Wildlife Watchers Foundation might establish this goal to support its previously mentioned strategy:

◦ Prepare brochure describing WWF's purpose and needs and send to government and industry leaders by summer.

Critical Success Factor

A **critical success factor (CSF)** is a factor that has a major influence on whether the enterprise will achieve a particular objective or goal. Some planners may prefer to distinguish between positive CSFs (called **facilitators**) and negative CSFs (called **inhibitors**). A goal or objective influenced by a facilitator will be at risk if the facilitator *does not* successfully occur, while a goal or objective influenced by an inhibitor will be at risk if the inhibitor *does* occur.

Examples:

One positive CSF (facilitator) for attaining the previously stated objective of Consolidated Implements might be:

◦ Customer satisfaction

A negative CSF (inhibitor) affecting the realization of the Wildlife Watchers Foundation objective might be:

◦ Non-availability of public lands for wildlife preserves

Plan

A **plan** is a schedule of actions to be taken to implement the strategies and deal with the critical success factors. It constitutes a detailed, step-by-step action list to attain specific goals.

Performance Measure

A **performance measure** is an indicator that shows the progress of an action against the plan. It indicates the extent to which the goal it measures has been reached. Each performance measure monitors a specific goal or objective and may be influenced by many CSFs.

Examples:

Consolidated Implements might use the following performance measure to monitor the success of its previously stated objective:

- Percentage of total farm machinery sales dollars earned by Consolidated Implements each quarter

A performance measure used to monitor WWF's above-stated goal might be:

- Number of Fortune 500 CEOs contacted each month

Information Need

An **information need** is an unstructured statement describing a type of information required by an organizational unit to meet its objectives and support its functions.

When identifying an information need, one should determine the following characteristics:

- A description of the need.

- How the information is used.

- The class of business object it supports (such as a goal, objective, or CSF).

- How well the current or currently planned environment satisfies the need. That is:

  — Is it currently available?

  — If so, how well does it satisfy the need?

  — Is the currently available information provided by a computer system? If so, what is the system's name?

  To this end, each information need must be assigned a relative value between 0 (if the information need is fully supported in the current environment) and 3 (if it is completely unsupported in the current environment). This value is called the information need's **satisfaction rating**.

- What is the relative importance to be assigned to the satisfaction of the information need?

  To determine this relative importance, one may use the following guideline to calculate a **requirement weight**:

  — Assign an **importance factor** to the information need as follows:

    5 - if the information supports a CSF

    4 - if the information is essential for the achievement of a goal or objective

    3 - if the information is essential to carry out a **business activity** (discussed shortly)

    2 - if the information is useful for achievement of a goal or objective

    1 - if the information is useful for any other purpose

  — Multiply the importance factor by the satisfaction rating assigned previously. The resulting requirement weight is a good starting point from which to prioritize the information need. Higher values are assigned to information needs that are more critical.

  For example, if an information need is essential to carry out an objective (thus, importance factor of 4) and is currently supported moderately well (thus, satisfaction rating of 1), the requirement weight is 4*1, or 4.

Note that if the importance factor and satisfaction rating are entered as properties of the information need using the IEF, the requirement weight of the information need will be calculated automatically.

Examples:

Consolidated Implements might have the following information need to support its previously stated objective:

⚬ Total dollars expended in the southern United States on each category of farm implement

This information is currently available to Consolidated Implements through manual means (satisfaction rating of 1) and is essential to achieving an objective (importance factor of 4). Thus, its requirement weight is 4.

The Wildlife Watchers Foundation might have the following information need to support its previously stated objective:

⚬ Estimated number of unprotected, endangered animals, by species, within each region.

This information is currently not available to WWF (satisfaction rating of 3) and would be useful for attaining an objective (importance factor of 2). Thus, its requirement weight is 6.

The following characteristics may also be specified for an information need, although they are not absolutely essential:

• Whether the information which satisfies the need must always be absolutely current or, instead, a "snapshot" is sufficient.

For example, a potential information need in a stock brokerage application might be "current value of stocks." It is likely that, if a broker requests the current value of a particular stock, yesterday's price will not do; the broker needs up-to-the-minute, correct information. Information of this type is identified as requiring **continual update.**

On the other hand, an information need for the business's year-to-date sales figures probably does not require up-to-the-minute information. A snapshot of year-to-date sales (as of, say, last night) is probably close enough. Information of this type is said to require **occasional update.**

• What kind of information fills this need?

That is, is the information a **summary** of other information (as are most counts, totals or averages), is it indicative of an **exception** (as are most requests for a maximum or minimum value), is it a **correlation** of other information (for example, a percentage of suppliers who are also customers), is it **detail** information (like information about specific product in stock) or is it some other kind of information?

Facts about the Organization Structure

The organization's structure reflects its general approach to fulfilling its mission. The following terms are used to classify facts about the organization:

• Organizational Unit

• Organization Structure

• Organizational Role

**Organiza-
tional Unit**

An **organizational unit** is a named collection of people or smaller organizational units used to structure the enterprise or an external body that deals with the enterprise.

Example:

For Consolidated Implements, the following might be numbered among its organizational units:

  ◦ Marketing

  ◦ Manufacturing

  ◦ Information Systems

**Organization
Structure**

An **organization structure** defines the relationship between organizational units.

Example:

For Consolidated Implements:

  ◦ The Information Systems organizational unit reports to the Accounting organizational unit, which reports to the CEO. It is composed of three organizational units: Operations, Development, and Advanced Technology.

Obviously, the representation of an organization structure in this fashion is far less efficient and revealing than use of a hierarchical organization chart. Remember, though, that this discussion focuses on facts about the business, not on their representation.

**Organiza-
tional Role**

An **organizational role** is a type of position that can be allocated to a person or an organizational unit. It defines the kind of job being done.

One may evaluate organizational roles in terms of business activities (defined later). In particular, one may express an organizational unit's involvement in a business activity in terms of one or more of the following types of role:

  • **Responsibility**. The organizational unit or individual is held accountable by management for performing the activity.

  • **Authority**. The organizational unit or individual has the power to make decisions to carry out the activity.

  • **Expertise**. The organizational unit or individual provides knowledge, experience, and the underlying rules for accomplishing an activity.

  • **Work**. The organizational unit actually performs the activity.

Facts about Business Activities and Data

To develop the Information Architecture successfully, the planners must understand the underlying business activities the organization performs and the data affected by these activities.

The following terms describe **business activities** during Information Strategy Planning:

  • Business Function
  • Business Process

The following terms describe **business data** during Information Strategy Planning:

  • Subject Area
  • Entity Type
  • Relationship

Business Function

A **business function** (often referred to simply as a **function**) is a group of business activities that together completely support one aspect of the enterprise. Each function describes something the enterprise does, independent of the structure of the organization.

Functions are higher-level business activities.

The group of activities that comprise a function are generally related because they use similar business data.

Examples:

◦ Manufacturing

◦ Marketing

◦ Sales

◦ Shipping

Business Process

A **business process** (frequently referred to simply as a **process**) is a defined business activity whose executions may be identified in terms of the input and output of **entities** (defined shortly) of specific types.

Processes are lower-level business activities.

A process can be distinguished from a function because it is generally characterized by a verb and a noun.

Examples:

◦ Take An Order

◦ Build A Steering Wheel

◦ Call A Customer

During Information Strategy Planning, processes are not identified unless they are extremely important and deserve special attention. They generally occur at too low a level of detail to be considered during an ISP project.

Subject Area

A **subject area** is an area of interest to the enterprise centered on a major resource, product, or activity. It summarizes things in which the enterprise is interested. As such, it is a rather imprecise description that generally requires further refinement.

The names of subject areas are usually plural nouns.

Examples:

◦ Vendors

◦ Customers

◦ Raw Material

Entity Type

An **entity** is a fundamental thing of relevance to the enterprise about which data may be kept. An **entity type** is the collection of entities that share a common definition. From another perspective, an entity is a single occurrence of an entity type. For example, the entity type EMPLOYEE may describe the entities John Smith, Miles Standish, and David Fremp.

Entity types are refinements of subject areas. Often, close inspection of a subject area will reveal that it is comprised of multiple entity types.

The names of entity types are always singular nouns.

Examples:

- ○ VENDOR SHIPMENT
- ○ CUSTOMER SHIPPING DESTINATION
- ○ CUSTOMER BILLING LOCATION

Relationship   A **relationship** is a reason relevant to the enterprise for associating two entities from one or two entity types.

For example, consider the common business practice of accepting orders for goods from customers. This situation can be represented as two entity types and a relationship:

- ○ Entity type CUSTOMER
- ○ Entity type ORDER
- ○ Relationship *places*

Thus, CUSTOMER *places* ORDER.

In practice, relationships have two names: one for each direction of the relationship. If CUSTOMER *places* ORDER, then ORDER *is placed by* CUSTOMER as well.

Facts about the Current Systems Environment

Facts about the current systems environment are necessary to assess the coverage of business activities by the computer systems already in place. Two terms are used to classify aspects of the current systems environment:

- • Current System
- • Current Data Store

Current Sys-   A **current system** is a collection of automated procedures that already support some aspect
tem   of the enterprise. They are usually fairly easy to identify.

For each system, its name, a short description, and a "system category" are recorded. System category is used to identify, in general terms, the processing characteristics of the system.

A system may belong to one or more of the following categories:

- • STRATEGIC

  Strategic systems tend to be very flexible. The processing characteristics are highly unpredictable and typically support "what-if" analysis.

  The popular terms "Decision Support System" and "Executive Information System" can usually be applied both to Strategic systems and Planning systems.

- • PLANNING

  Planning systems tend to be flexible within an established framework. Generally, there is a good deal of statistical analysis done with this type of system with heavy concentration on "what if" analysis.

- • CONTROLLING

  Controlling systems are those used to monitor and manage operational systems. They feature routine analysis and reporting.

- OPERATIONAL

  Operational systems are the high volume, time-critical systems used in the day-to-day operation of the business. They tend to include pre-defined online transactions and standard batch reports and are primarily dealt with by clerical users.

Examples:

- Marketing Information System (PLANNING)

- In-transit Material Control System (CONTROLLING)

- Order Entry System (OPERATIONAL)

Current Data Store

A **data store** is a repository of data of which users are aware and from which data may be read repeatedly and non-destructively. Thus, **current data stores** are the permanent files and data bases that presently support the enterprise.

The planners should only be concerned with identifying the data store's name and a short description.

Examples:

- Product data base

- Customer Information data base

- Supplier data base

Facts about the Current Technical Environment

Aspects of the current technical environment of interest during Information Strategy Planning fall into two classifications:

- Hardware Item
- Software Product

Hardware Item

A **hardware item** is a physical piece of computing equipment. Included are computer mainframes, terminals, workstations and printers. In general, the ISP project should limit itself to identifying major processing hardware (such as mainframes and minicomputers) and user interface equipment (such as terminals, workstations and printers).

The physical location of the hardware item must be identified.

Examples:

- 236 IBM 3270 terminals at the Peoria, Illinois, site

- Four loosely coupled Amdahl 470 mainframes in the Walla Walla, Washington, plant

- 70 micro-Vax's in the Brussels office

Software Product

A **software product** is a documented and complete collection of statements obtained from a specific supplier. The statements may be executed, directly or indirectly, on a computing device.

Examples:

- DB2 (a DBMS)

- IMS/DC (a teleprocessing monitor)

- MVS/XA (an operating system)

- Smythe's Tractor Problem Logging System (a fictional application software package)

Category	Class	Related Class
Mission	Mission	
Mission	Objective	
Mission	Strategy	Objective
Mission	Goal	Strategy
Mission	Plan	Goal
Mission	CSF	Objective/Goal
Mission	Performance Measure	Objective/Goal/CSF
Mission	Information Need	Objective/Goal/CSF
Organization	Unit	
Organization	Role	Business Function
Organization	Structure	
Activity/Data	Business Function	
Activity/Data	Business Process	Business Function
Activity/Data	Subject Area	
Activity/Data	Entity Type	Subject Area
Activity/Data	Relationship	Entity Type
Systems	Current System	
Systems	Current Data Store	
Technology	Hardware Item	
Technology	Software Product	

Figure 2-1. ISP Information Classes

Summary

The table in Figure 2-1 summarizes the information class structure to be used when categorizing facts collected during Information Strategy Planning. An entry in the Related Class column indicates that a fact in the primary class must be qualified by a fact in the related class.

The project team can use a form like the one in Figures 2-2 and 2-3 to record information while examining a document or conducting an interview.

UNIVERSAL INFORMATION GATHERING FORM			
Source: Date: Page:			
Fact	Class	Related Fact	Class

Figure 2-2. Example of an Information Gathering Form

UNIVERSAL INFORMATION GATHERING FORM			
Source: INTERVIEW w/DAMIEN CASTILLE Date: 02/09			Page: 1
Fact	Class	Related Fact	Class
-Become market leader in Southern U.S.	Objective		
-Build factory in Georgia	Strategy	Become mkt leader	Obj.
-Implement category usage research	Strategy	"	"
-Demographic survey req'd by March	Goal	Cat. Usage research	strat.
-Lou Penhall really handles distribution	Org. Unit		
-3% increase in employee profit sharing rate	Goal	? Imp. Morale	Strat.
-Employee assistance program	Objective	? Imp. Morale	Strat
-Improve productivity by 20%			
-Improve Employee Morale	Strategy	Imp. Productivity	Obj.
-More Automation	Strategy	Imp. Productivity	Obj.

Figure 2-3. Completed Information Gathering Form

Figure 2-3 is a sample of a completed Information Gathering Form after an interview with a member of top management.

The two question marks (?) in the Related Fact column are the result of the interviewee announcing goals before the objectives and strategies they support. As the anomalies were resolved, the question marks were crossed out.

REVIEW OF WRITTEN INFORMATION

The project team must attempt to garner facts from whatever documentation is available. Gaining knowledge about the business and the information environment from documentation familiarizes the project team with the task at hand. It also provides a basis for effective, knowledgeable interviewing later on.

The project team should review all available pertinent documentation. This includes:

- Business documentation
    — Annual reports
    — Business plans and forecasts
    — Organization charts and manuals
    — The corporate chart of accounts
    — Company handbooks and manuals
    — Memoranda dealing with business practices
    — Advertising literature
- Current systems environment documentation
    — System descriptions
    — Data administration guidelines

— System architecture documentation

— System flowcharts and data base specifications

— Memoranda dealing with system architecture

— Information Systems organization planning documents

— Information Systems organization charts

— User manuals

- Current technical environment documentation

— Hardware distribution lists

— Capacity planning documents

— System software lists

— Data network documentation

— Performance statistics

— Hardware and software acquisition plans

In short, the project team members should consider all available written material that describes the business and information environments, and organize the pertinent facts into the information classes enumerated previously. Additionally, they should catalog documents containing important information for future reference.

INTERVIEWING

In addition to perusing available documentation, the project team should conduct a series of interviews with various levels of management in the organization under study. These will yield a significant store of information, particularly in the area of overall business objectives and strategies. Additionally, personal interviews are likely to reveal business characteristics not generally available in company documents, including value judgements and details of the informal organization (as opposed to the one documented on an organization chart).

This section describes a team interviewing technique that has been used successfully in many ISP projects. It also gives some guidelines for dealing with the top management of an organization.

Selecting Interviewees

In general, the project team should interview three categories of individuals during an ISP project:

- **Top Ranking Executives**. These interviews serve both to confirm the project team's understanding of the business and reinforce top management commitment to the project.
- **Middle Managers**. These individuals can provide a greater understanding of specific organizational units.
- **Other Company Personnel**. During interviews or through written documentation, the project team may identify other candidates for interviews who can contribute critical information.

Setting up an Interview

Chapter 3 discusses a Schedule of Interviews to be constructed as part of the Information Strategy Plan. As suggested there, the project team should prepare this tentative schedule well in advance of the interviews, so each interview can be arranged and all scheduling conflicts resolved. Dealing with scheduling problems early eliminates frustration later on.

The actual mechanics for setting up the interview depends, of course, on the culture of the organization. In some organizations, a phone call to the prospective interviewee will suffice. In others, a memorandum to his or her secretary might be necessary. As in all things, the planners must be sensitive to the business environment.

One additional factor that may not be obvious to the inexperienced interviewer deserves consideration. In general, interviews are best conducted in the interviewee's office or, at least, in a location the interviewee considers his or her "home turf." Such a setting usually results in greater openness during the interview.

Structured Interviewing Techniques

The interviewing technique described in this section requires a two-person interviewing team. One project member, who acts as the **interview leader**, is responsible for asking questions and directing the course of the discussion. The other member, who acts as a **notetaker**, is responsible for recording pertinent facts elicited during the interview and maintaining the interview's momentum. The strength of this technique over the use of a single interviewer lies principally in the continuity of the interview. The interview leader is not required to interrupt the discussion to hastily jot a note, while the notetaker is more likely to record the facts correctly and unambiguously than if he were rushing to ask the next question or encourage the next thought.

It might appear that the notetaker could be replaced by a tape recorder. However, the interviewee is much less likely to speak freely if he or she knows that every word is being recorded for posterity. The presence of a human notetaker does not usually elicit this sort of negative response, or at least not to so great a degree. Since the candor of the interviewee is critical to the success of the interview, electronic recording devices should never be used. In addition, the notetaker's responsibilities involve more than a simple recording of information. The notetaker must maintain the momentum of the interview, interjecting questions when the pace of the interview becomes sluggish, requesting elaboration when necessary, and ensuring that the topics considered are fully addressed.

For an interview to be successful, the two team members must follow these steps:

1. Prepare for the interview.
2. Conduct the interview.
3. Analyze the interview results.

Team members should conduct the interview itself in a limited amount of time, usually between one and three hours. Interviews with members of top management should generally take between one and one-and-one-half hours, while other interviews may be scheduled longer.

In general, the total time required to prepare, conduct, and analyze an interview is about one elapsed day for the two-person project team.

Preparing for an Interview

Each interview requires careful preparation. There are three components to this preparation:

1. Research the responsibilities of the interviewee and the structure and function of his or her organization. The project members can glean much of this information from the written documentation available.
2. Prepare a list of discussion topics tailored to the interviewee. The interview leader will use this document to guide the interview. It may take the form of a questionnaire.

   Subsequent chapters in Part I discuss the particular classes of information to be targeted for each category of interviewee. Figure 2-4 offers a sample topic list for a top management interview.

1.	Scope of your responsibility
2.	Your perception of company priorities over the next ten years
3.	The objectives of the business units for which you are responsible over the next ten years
4.	The factors that are critical to the achievement of those objectives
5.	Anticipated changes in your business units (new activities, geographical locations, management structures)
6.	Opportunities you envision for major contributions from information technology
7.	Support required from information systems to assist in the attainment of your objectives and an estimate of the benefits it will yield

Figure 2-4. Example of an Interview Topic List

3.   Present the list of topics to the interviewee in advance of the interview. This gives the interviewee an opportunity to consider and, if necessary, research the issues. Such a briefing can result in a much better interview and may eliminate the need for a follow-up interview.

Conducting the Interview

The actual interview session should include the following elements:

1.   An **introduction**, in which the members of the interview team introduce both themselves and the interviewing technique. Team members restate the objectives of the interview and, if necessary, present the topic list again to the interviewee.

2.   The **discussion**, in which the interview leader walks through the list of topics in the predetermined order as closely as possible. Meanwhile, the notetaker records the pertinent information in the responses. The notetaker may choose to use a form like the one presented in Figure 2-2.

The interview leader must attempt to cover all of the discussion points in the allotted time. However, the interviewee must be given the flexibility to discuss items that do not appear on the agenda. Such side trips often reveal useful information.

As the discussion winds down, the notetaker should take the opportunity to fill any gaps in understanding that remain and to clarify any outstanding issues.

3.   The **conclusion**, in which the team arranges to feed back the results of the interview, through either a follow-up session or a memorandum.

As part of the conclusion, always assure the interviewee that he or she will have the opportunity to approve the resulting interview analysis before it is distributed.

Analyzing the Interview

As soon as possible after completing the interview, the interviewing team reviews and analyzes the results. They should categorize and record the data gathered according to the classes of information presented earlier in this chapter.

INTERVIEWEE: _____	INTERVIEWERS: _____
ORGANIZATION: _____	_____
FUNCTION: _____	DATE/LOCATION _02/09 DC offices_

FACT		CSF	PERFORMANCE MEASURE	CURRENT SUPPORT	COMMENTS
CLASS	DESCRIPTION				
O	improve productivity by 20%				
↓					Talk with personnel
S	Improve employee morale				
↓		Money	% of employees	none	Need to internally
G	Set up profit share	Promotion	with shares		educate
G	Provide internal prog.	People availa-bility	days/year trng	manual/per-sonnel	
G	Automate engine production by Feb. 1989	build new plant train employees	? days/year trng	? all above	no experience:can we do it?
↓	Build new plant	find capital	none	none	?

Figure 2-5. Interview Analysis Form

After analyzing the results, the team can review them with the interviewee either in person or in written form. In some cases, the interviewee's response may lead to a follow-up interview for clarification or augmentation.

Interview notes, often appended with knowledge garnered from other interviews, reading, and follow-ups, can be summarized on a form like the one presented in Figure 2-5.

Some Practical Guidelines for Interviewing

The following guidelines, some of which may appear obvious, will help the inexperienced interviewer to conduct an effective interview.

- Always consider the interviewee's time as being more valuable than your own. In other words:

  — Always be punctual for an interview.

  — Never complain if you must wait for an interviewee.

  This is especially critical for top management interviews.

- Treat company management with respect. Never be casual or presumptuous.

- Be as efficient as possible. Careful preparation will allow you to achieve your mission with the greatest possible speed. Never ramble.

- Never attempt to impress the interviewee with your own knowledge.

- Never crowd or rush the interviewee.

- Assume that there are no secrets and that everything you say will be repeated. Following this guideline will help you refrain from criticizing other company personnel, for example.

In short, the success of an interview depends largely on common sense.

RECORDING INFORMATION IN IEF MATRICES

Much of the information discovered and synthesized during an ISP project is stored in the matrices supported by the Matrix Processor of the IEF Planning Toolset. This section explains the general terminology used in IEF matrix processing. This terminology recurs in descriptions of matrix construction throughout Part I of this guide.

Instructions for operating the facilities of the IEF Planning Toolset are available in the *IEF Planning Toolset Guide*.

The reader should become comfortable with the following terms:

- **Horizontal Axis**. The information represented along the top of the matrix. In Figure 2-6, organization units appear along the horizontal axis.

- **Column**. One entry on the horizontal axis. In Figure 2-6, "Berthold Corporation" is the name of the first column.

- **Vertical Axis**. The information represented along the left side of the matrix. In Figure 2-6, "Information Needs" are listed along the vertical axis.

- **Row**. One entry on the vertical axis. In Figure 2-6, "Daily Sales by Region" is the name of the last row.

- **Cell**. The intersection of a row and column. Each square beneath the horizontal axis and to the right of the vertical axis is a cell.

INFORMATION NEEDS	BERTHOLD_CORPORATION	AUTOMOTIVE_PRODUCTS_G	ECD_PRODUCT_DEVELOPME	EMISSION_CONTROLS_DIV	EXHAUST_SYSTEMS_DEPAR	ESD_MARKETING	ESD_MKT_ORDER_PROCESS	ESD_MKT_CUSTOMER_SERV	ESD_FIELD_SERVICE	ESD_SVC_REPAIR_FACILIT	ESD_SVC_REGIONAL_OFFIC	ESD_SVC_REG_WAREHOUSE	ESD_SVC-REG_REPAIR_SHO	ESD_MANUFACTURING_DEP	ESD_PRODUCTION_PLANNI	ESD_MATERIAL_CONTROL	FUEL_SYSTEMS_DEPARTME	FSD_MARKETING	FSD_MKT_ORDER_PROCESS	FSD_MKT_CUSTOMER_SVC	FSD_FIELD_SERVICE	FSD_SVC_REPAIR_FACILIT	FSD_SVC_REGIONAL_OFFIC	FSD_SVC_REG_WAREHOUSE	FSD_SVC_REG_REPAIR_SHO	FSD_MANUFACTURING_DEP	FSD_PRODUCTION_PLANNI	FSD_MATERIAL_CONTROL
CAPITAL_DEPRECIATION_Y	X													X													X	
SITE_POPULATION_STATS					X													X										
FINISHED_GOODS_AVAILAB						X														X								
60-DAY_HOT_LIST						X									X	X												
RETURNS_BY_PRODUCT_LIN							X													X								
NEW_PRODUCT_RELEASE_SC							X	X		X	X	X		X	X			X	X			X	X	X		X	X	
PRECIOUS_METAL_CONTENT															X	X											X	X
ORG_PROFIT_BY_DIVISION	X	X	X																									
CUSTOMER_ORDERS_>_$50K		X		X		X													X	X								
EMPLOYEE_RECEIVABLES	X			X													X											
MACHINE_LOAD_ON_HI_VAL														X	X											X	X	
HOT_CHECKS	X			X																								
WRITEOFF_CANDIDATES															X	X											X	X
SALES_ORDER_VARIANCE	X	X		X	X													X		X								
DOMESTIC_BACKLOG		X		X														X		X								
DAILY_SALES_BY_REGION	X	X		X														X										

Figure 2-6. Example of an IEF Planning Toolset Matrix

- **Involvement Indicator**. A non-blank entry in a cell. In the cell at the intersection of the "ESD Population" column and the "Customer Orders > $50K" row, the value of the involvement indicator is "X." (In fact, the values of all involvement indicators on the matrix are "X.")

  There are three kinds of involvement indicators. Some matrices support multiple kinds of indicator, but most support only one:

  — **Simple Involvement Indicator**. An "X" or one of the values 1 through 9 may be placed in each cell. The "strength of involvement" signified by each simple involvement indicator is based on its value. Involvement indicators with higher values indicate a greater strength of involvement than those with lower values.

  — **Numeric Involvement Indicator**. Permitted values are the same as for simple involvement indicator, except that the value "X" is not permitted.

  — **CRUD Involvement Indicators**. The only values permitted in each cell are C (Create), R (Read), U (Update), or D (Delete); hence the designation "CRUD." CRUD involvement indicators depict uses of business data or data stores in some matrices. The strength of involvement signified by each CRUD involvement indicator is based on its value. Involvement indicators with values of C or D indicate a greater strength of involvement than those with values of U, which in turn show a greater strength of involvement than those with values of R.

- **User Defined Matrix**. This is a matrix whose definition is created by the planner, in contrast to the IEF-supplied pre-defined matrices. The planner specifies what information will appear along the horizontal and vertical axes and what type of involvement indicators may be placed in cells.

- **User Defined Object**. This refers to information the planner wishes to appear on one of the axes of a matrix which is not known to the IEF. One example (albeit an unlikely one during ISP) might be to record which salesmen are assigned to a geographic region. In this case, SALESMAN and REGION would be user defined objects appearing along the horizontal and vertical axes of a user defined matrix.

- **Cluster Analysis**. This is a mathematical process that orders subjects into groups based on the similarity of certain properties of each subject. The IEF Matrix Processor performs cluster analysis automatically when requested. Appendix B presents a detailed explanation of the techniques for cluster analysis used by the IEF.

The strength of involvement indicated by the values of involvement indicators influences the automatic clustering analysis process.

3
PLANNING THE ISP PROJECT

OVERVIEW

The Information Strategy Plan is a blueprint for developing systems that will satisfy the information requirements of a business. Planning the project is the first task in an ISP project. This chapter addresses the following topics related to project planning:

- Setting the project scope
- Establishing the project organization
- Building the project plan

SETTING THE PROJECT SCOPE

The **scope** of an ISP project can be delimited by three sets of boundaries:

- Organizational boundaries
- Information technology boundaries
- Time boundaries

After determining these boundaries, planners incorporate them into a Statement of Objectives presented to management and used to guide the project. This section presents guidelines for establishing the project scope and discusses the formulation of the Statement of Objectives. Before addressing these areas, the issue of management expectations bears mention.

Determining Management Expectations

The most compelling and often unstated factor in establishing the scope of the project is management expectation. Those who commission an Information Strategy Plan likely have strong preconceived notions about the context and duration of the project. Planners must understand these expectations when establishing formal project boundaries. The primary means for identifying these expectations is the "project champion" (or champions), usually a member of top management or the board of directors, who provides the impetus for the project. More is said about the role of the project champion later in this chapter.

Planners must make clear the relative merits of a full-scale ISP project over a limited one. However, the final determination of project scope is generally made by top management. Any unilateral deviation from this scope by the project team will likely result in the failure of the project.

Establishing Organizational Boundaries

Organizational boundaries dictate which portions of the total enterprise are to be considered during the planning process. Ideally, the scope of an ISP project is wide enough to encompass the enterprise as a whole. However, in some cases, such a broad focus is impossible. The following paragraphs contrast the advantages of full-enterprise planning with those of limited planning.

Full Enterprise Planning

Although an ISP can be performed on a limited scale, its central aim is to set the information strategy for an entire enterprise. An enterprise-wide plan gives top management a blueprint for satisfying the information requirements of the business as a whole. It employs a single, comprehensive strategy. Limiting the scope to particular organizational units can lead to fragmented and competing strategies. Such fragmentation is usually not in the best interests of the enterprise.

The advantages of performing ISP at the enterprise level are twofold:

- A full-scope ISP project addresses the information processing needs of the entire enterprise with a single strategy that embraces all aspects of the business.

- A full-scope ISP project rules out any duplication of effort that might accompany multiple, smaller ISP projects.

Limited Planning

Although the ideal scope encompasses the entire enterprise, there are several distinct advantages to limiting the project scope:

- A limited-scope ISP project is more manageable than a full-scope ISP project, since fewer organization components are considered.

- A limited-scope ISP project can be carried to a greater level of detail than a full-scope ISP project taking place over the same time.

- A limited-scope ISP project will be completed earlier than a full-scope ISP project that achieves the same level of detail.

Establishing Information Technology Boundaries

Information technology boundaries identify that portion of an enterprise's information technology to be addressed by the study. Just as with organizational boundaries, the ideal context for addressing information technology is the entire technology.

In most cases, an ISP project will, in fact, consider all aspects of information technology within the selected organizational boundaries. However, there are situations in which management may limit the scope of the study for a variety of reasons.

The division of information technology into separate components is not an exact science. The following examples illustrate possible categories of information technology that may be studied separately if necessary:

- Office Automation
- Data Processing
- Decision Support
- Telecommunications

Establishing Time Boundaries

The last constraint considered in determining the ISP project scope is its duration. This is the final parameter in determining the level of detail to be achieved.

Any successful ISP project will be completed within a reasonable period of time. If the project is too short, the results will be superficial. If the project is too long, the results will be overly detailed and, perhaps, obsolete. Thus, establishment of the correct project duration is essential.

These are the recommended guidelines:

- Generally, the planners can develop an effective Information Strategy Plan in four to six months, depending on the organizational and technological boundaries established.

- The planners should never schedule the project for less than three months.

- The planners should never schedule the project for more than one year.

General guidelines for estimating project duration appear in the section entitled "Building the Project Plan" at the end of this chapter.

Formulating the Statement of Objectives

Planners document and present the ISP project boundaries to management in a formal Statement of Objectives. This should be a concise document, probably no longer than a page in length. The particular format of the document is largely unimportant, but it must contain the following components to be effective:

- An overall statement of the objective of the project.

- A statement of the organizational scope of the project.

- A statement of the areas of information technology to be addressed.

- A statement of the planned duration of the project.

Additionally, it is useful to include the following components:

- A reference to those members of management commissioning the project.

- A list of deliverables to be presented at the conclusion of the project. These deliverables are derived from the standard task list.

An example of a Statement of Objectives including all of these components appears in Figure 3-1.

ESTABLISHING THE PROJECT ORGANIZATION

The success of an ISP project relies heavily on assembling an effective project organization. The project organization includes the following components:

- A **project sponsor**, a high-ranking executive who champions the project and provides a liaison to top management.

- The **project team**, the collection of planners who actually build the Information Strategy Plan.

- The **reference team**, a group of business experts who can supplement the knowledge of the project team and review detailed deliverables.

- **Administrative and clerical support** for the project team, to keep the project running smoothly. This support includes filing, typing, transcribing interview notes, making travel arrangements, and maintaining the team's calendars. Depending on the geographical scope of the study, translation services may also be required.

In addition, a **steering committee** may exist in many organizations or be established to guide the project.

Statement of Objectives

The objectives of this Information Strategy Planning study are to:

-    Assess the effectiveness of the current information environment
     in supporting the corporate mission;

-    Define the Information Architecture, Business System
     Architecture, and Technical Architecture that will best support
     the corporate mission;

-    Prepare an overall plan for implementing the Information
     Architecture and establishing the correct technical environment.

All present organizational units and locations are included in the scope
of the study. However, the study's technical scope is limited to software
and minor hardware recommendations. The primary computing
infrastructure is to remain in place.

The study will be completed within six months. It has been commissioned
by:

-    Donald Swearinger, Chairman of the Board
-    Albert Schwab, Chief Operating Officer
-    Damien Castille, Executive Director of Marketing Services

The products of the study will include:

-    An analysis of the business and assessment of the current
     information processing environment in satisfying its requirements;

-    A description of the fundamental Information Architecture best
     suited to meet corporate objectives;

-    A Business System Architecture including an implementation plan
     that reflects corporate priorities;

-    A Technical Architecture that defines the hardware and software
     environment required to support the Business System
     Architecture.

Figure 3-1. Example of a Statement of Objectives

The following paragraphs describe the suggested characteristics and responsibilities of each individual in the project organization.

The Project Sponsor

The project sponsor is a high-level executive, preferably a member of top management or the board of directors, who supports the ISP project. The notion of individuals acting as "project champions" was mentioned earlier in this chapter. Project champions can be thought of as the agents of change in top management or the board of directors who commissioned the ISP project in the first place. The project sponsor should be numbered among these.

Although the project sponsor contributes relatively little time to the ISP project, his or her role is absolutely essential to the project's eventual success. The sponsor is responsible for championing the project among top management and for providing high-level guidance to the project team. This individual must:

- Maintain support and visibility for the ISP project within top management.

- Approve and promote the results of major aspects of the study.

- Facilitate the study by:

  — ensuring the availability of manpower and other resources

  — smoothing the way for project team contact with top management.

In a limited-scope ISP project, the project sponsor is also responsible for fostering communication with organizational units outside the scope of the project that may ultimately affect or be affected by its results.

The Project Team

The project team is the group of planners who carry out the detailed construction of the plan on a full-time basis. Because of the potential impact on the organization under study, the participants on this team should be of the highest caliber possible. The ideal project team consists of no more than six members and has the following structure:

- A **project manager**, preferably an experienced manager with a great deal of business acumen and good communication and presentation skills.

- An **Information Strategy Plan expert** who is proficient in the techniques described in this book.

- One or more **business experts** who understand all relevant areas included in the project scope.

- One or more **technical specialists** with a broad range of information systems expertise, particularly in the area of data administration.

Limiting the team size reduces the potential for confusion and miscommunication and maximizes the potential for synergy. In some cases, however, complete coverage of the entire project scope, particularly in the area of business expertise, may be difficult with such a small team. In such cases, the business expertise of the project team can be supplemented by a reference team, described under the next paragraph heading.

In addition to the aforementioned skills, the project team members must possess some less tangible but no less important skills:

- They must be able to interact effectively with top management.

- They must be able to consider issues at several levels of abstraction.

- They must be fully committed to the successful completion of the project.

The Reference Team

The final component of the project organization is the reference team. This team may not be a formal organization or committee at all. In fact, for some projects, such a group may not be necessary. The primary functions of the reference team are to:

- Provide business expertise beyond that available in the project team.

- Review deliverables to ensure that they accurately reflect the business reality.

- Build organizational commitment to the Information Strategy Plan.

Ideally, the reference team is composed of managers who can each be considered a business expert in one or more of the areas addressed in the project scope. The business expertise provided by the full-time members of the project team, supplemented by that of the reference team, should encompass all aspects of the portions of the business to be studied.

BUILDING THE PROJECT PLAN

The Project Schedule

After defining the project scope in the Statement of Objectives and determining the makeup of the project organization, the planners are ready to construct a detailed Project Schedule. To establish this schedule, the planners must first develop a detailed Task List. Appendix A summarizes the list of tasks typically performed for an ISP project.

One may view this Tast List as the project skeleton. To complete the schedule, the project manager must assign team members to each task and predict task durations. From this raw data, the team can chart the detailed schedule using either mechanized techniques (such as a Project Management software product) or manual techniques.

The schedule must include **project checkpoints**. At each checkpoint, the project sponsor must decide between three alternatives:

1.   Approve the continuation of the project to the next major task.

2.   Require additional work on the current task before passing the checkpoint.

3.   Terminate the ISP project.

While one implicitly assumes the sponsor will approve continuation of the project, the use of checkpoints provides an explicit way for management to track its progress. Project checkpoints also serve as appropriate points of review for other management mechanisms (such as a steering committee) within the organization.

Estimating Guidelines

Each project is different. Varying project scopes, emphasis on different tasks, the skill levels of the project team members, and the corporate culture make each ISP project unique. Nevertheless, one may employ the following general guidelines when estimating task durations:

•   A typical interview using the techniques described in Chapter 2 requires one elapsed day for two team members (thus, two man-days per interview). A typical ISP project involves about 40 interviews; thus 80 man-days of effort is a reasonable estimate.

•   ISP practitioners report that specifying the Information Architecture usually requires about 30 man-days for a limited- scope ISP, or about 80 man-days for an enterprise-wide ISP.

•   Again, ISP practitioners report that the tasks of interviewing and specifying the Information Architecture generally consume about one-half of the total elapsed time for a project.

When following this guideline, planners should divide the remaining half of the project time among the other tasks according to their particular emphasis within the ISP project.

The Schedule of Interviews

In addition to the Project Schedule, planners must draw up a tentative Schedule of Interviews at this point. In general, the planners will interview each member of the top management of the organization under study and each member of the layer of management directly beneath top management. The planners must be flexible with this schedule, of course, since it is subject to the availability of the interviewees and since additional interviews may be required (either follow-ups or interviews of additional key people identified in earlier interviews).

REVIEWING THE PROJECT PLAN

The task of planning the ISP project ends with a formal review of the Project Plan by the project sponsor and appropriate members of management (at the sponsor's discretion). This review is the first formal project checkpoint as defined earlier in this chapter.

4
MAKING THE INITIAL ASSESSMENT

OVERVIEW

This chapter presents the activities required to perform an initial assessment of the business. The main goal of this major task is to gain an understanding of the business and, based on that understanding, to sketch a preliminary Information Architecture that will support it. This research is verified and supplemented through interviews with top and middle management.

The task of performing the initial assessment consists of the following subtasks:

1. Identify and record the organization structure
2. Identify and rank objectives and CSFs
3. Formulate a set of information needs and performance measures
4. Determine the possible business impact of the information technology
5. Define a preliminary Information Architecture
6. Interview top management
7. Interview middle management
8. Review results

The discussion of each of these subtasks is organized as follows:

*   Description of the subtask
*   Classes of information involved (based on the classes identified in Chapter 2)
*   Inputs to the subtask
*   Steps required to execute the subtask (including the use of automated tools, if any)
*   Deliverables from the subtask

IDENTIFY AND RECORD THE ORGANIZATION STRUCTURE

During this subtask, planners determine the structure of the organization to the greatest extent possible from available documentation. An understanding of the organization is important for two reasons:

*   It helps the planner to identify the individuals in the organization who must be interviewed.
*   It provides a basis for determining responsibilities for the business activities of the enterprise.

During an ISP project, it is not necessary to document the entire organization structure. The planners must use their discretion in determining a level of major functional responsibility beyond which organizational details are irrelevant.

Classes of Information

Planners seek the following classes of information during this subtask:

- Organizational Unit
- Organization Structure

Inputs

The input to this subtask is the written documentation available to the project team, particularly:

- Organization charts
- Organization handbooks or manuals
- Policy and procedure manuals
- Reports from organization files or data bases

Steps

The steps required for this subtask are as follows:

1. Represent the organization structure as a hierarchy using the Organizational Hierarchy Diagram in the IEF Planning Toolset. An example of a portion of an organization structure represented in this way appears in Figure 4-1. Note that the three dots in the upper right corner of some of the boxes indicate that the organizations represented have had subordinate organizations defined which are not shown (that is, are "contracted") on the diagram.

    An alternative representation, the indented list format, can be used to show more information in less space (Figure 4-2). The IEF's *redraw* feature, fully described in the *IEF Planning Toolset Guide*, can be used to "flip" the diagram.

    In enterprises of great size and complexity, the organization structure recorded here can actually be a model of a representative structure. However, the IEF does not support the mapping of such a model to particular organizational units.

2. Record the following information for each organization unit considered:

    a. Name

    b. Name and title of individual responsible for the organization unit

    c. The mission of the organization unit

    d. Special relationships the organizational unit may have with other organizational units. This includes any relationship that is not depicted in the formal organization hierarchy (for example, "dotted line" responsibilities or matrix management participation).

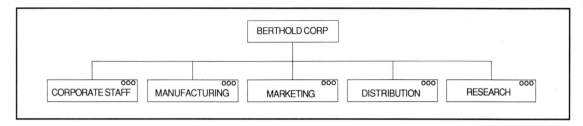

Figure 4-1. Organization Hierarchy

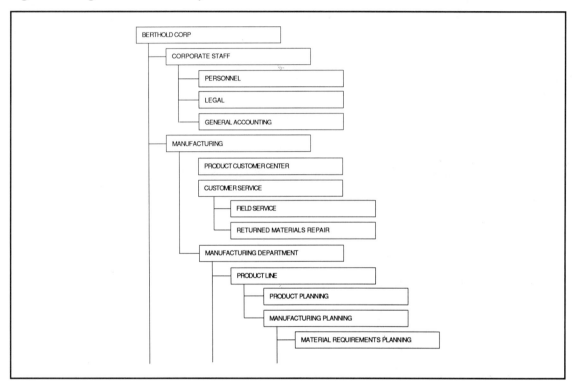

Figure 4-2. Organizational Hierarchy, Indented List Format

Deliverables

The deliverables of this subtask are:

• Organization Hierarchy Diagram

• Supportive text recorded in step 2, above

IDENTIFY AND RANK BUSINESS OBJECTIVES

In this subtask, planners extract important facts about the business from written documentation. Planners discover objectives and CSFs and rank them according to perceived importance.

Classes of Information

Planners seek the following classes of information during this subtask:

- Mission
- Objective
- Strategy
- Critical Success Factor (CSF)

This subtask may also reveal information from these classes:

- Goal
- Plan

This discussion assumes the definitions for each of these classes are those presented in Chapter 2. Organizations that use different terminology must alter the identification of classes accordingly.

Finally, the objectives and CSFs are decomposed based on information of a different class:

- Organization Structure

Inputs

The inputs to this subtask are:

- Written documentation available to the planning team, particularly:
    — Formal business plans (at multiple organizational levels)
    — Annual reports
    — Strategic memoranda
- Organization Hierarchy Diagram

Steps

The steps required for this subtask are as follows:

1. By reviewing available documentation, identify and list the mission, objectives, and strategies of the enterprise. For each objective, list its critical success factors.

2. Organize the mission, objectives, and critical success factors into a Mission Statement. This brief document communicates the planners' understanding of the business to top management without inundating them with irrelevant detail. An example of a Mission Statement appears in Figure 4-3.

    While seeking these classes of information, the planners will likely stumble onto statements of goals, their critical success factors, and plans. These should be recorded for later use.

3. Record the objectives, strategies, and critical success factors of each major organizational unit. Limit this analysis to the first layer organization within the organization under study. In other words, include those organizational units that are directly connected to the enterprise in the Organization Hierarchy Diagram.

```
┌─────────────────────────────────────────────────────────┐
│                                                         │
│   Mission                                               │
│                                                         │
│   To provide the maximum return for investors through the│
│   manufacture and distribution of farm machinery.       │
│                                                         │
│   Objectives                                            │
│                                                         │
│   1.  35% market share in the southern United States.   │
│   2.  Sales growth of at least 8% per year.             │
│   3.  ROI of 12% per year.                              │
│   4.  Grow and maintain small machinery business at 20% of│
│       total sales.                                      │
│   5.  Grow and maintain aerospace business at 6% of total sales.│
│                                                         │
│   Critical Success Factors                              │
│                                                         │
│   1.  Effective management of physical distribution channels.│
│   2.  Selection of high quality supplies.               │
│   3.  Awarding of space station contract.               │
│   4.  Adequate information support.                     │
│   5.  Customer satisfaction.                            │
│   6.  Employee productivity.                            │
│   7.  Successful integration of robotics.               │
│                                                         │
│                                                         │
└─────────────────────────────────────────────────────────┘
```

Figure 4-3. Example of a Mission Statement

4. Relate the enterprise's objectives to those of its major organizational units. This step verifies the planners' understanding of the organization.

Planners can use the Enterprise/Organizational Unit Objectives Matrix for this purpose. An example appears in Figure 4-4. Prepare it manually as follows:

a. Place the corporate objectives on the horizontal axis.

b. Place the objectives of each major organizational unit on the vertical axis.

c. At each intersection:

  (1) Place a D if the organizational unit's objective directly satisfies the enterprise's objective.

  (2) Place an I if the organizational unit's objective is indirectly related to the enterprise's objective.

After completing this matrix, each objective of an organizational unit should relate to at least one enterprise objective and vice versa. If not, there is most likely an error in the planners' analysis. It can, however, reflect an anomalous business condition where no organizational unit is supporting one of the enterprise's objectives or an organizational unit has its own agenda.

It is possible to simulate this matrix using the IEF. One can add a user defined matrix, add a user defined object called "Organizational Objective," and specify a numeric involvement indicator using, for example, "3" to correspond to "D", "2" to correspond to "I", and "1" to correspond to the question marks (?) appearing in Figure 4-4. However, be forewarned that, in this case, each organizational objective name will have to include the name of the organization, making it difficult to describe the organizational objective completely on the axis.

	Become market leader in USA for Farm Equipment	Provide Min 10% ROI	Grow Sales at 8% P.A. for 5 years	Open European Market by 1989
Marketing				
- Grow sales in Southern States by 12% over 18 months	D		D	
- Reduce service costs		I	I	
- Increase QA: Reduce failure rates to < 5%	I	I	I	
Operations				
- Reduce # of options by 50%	?	I	I	
- Improve stock of standard items	?			
- Automate engine production		I?		
Distribution				
- Set up 3rd party US distributors	I			
- Open European distribution network				D
Finance				
- Reduce financial liability to investors				
- Issue stock for plant capitalization	I			
Personnel/Staff				
- Decrease absenteeism by 50%		I?		
- Cross train ops staff for auto plant and reduce by 10%	I	D		
- Setup European offices				D

Figure 4-4. Enterprise/Organizational Unit Objectives Matrix

5.   Finally, assemble the objectives of the enterprise and each major organizational unit in priority sequence based on the available documentation. The result, a preliminary Ranked List of Objectives, is a summary of the planners' perceptions and provides a framework for their understanding of the business. The true priorities and conflicts are later clarified through interviews with top management.

Deliverables

The deliverables of this subtask are:

• Mission Statement

• List of Objectives, Strategies, and CSFs by Organizational Unit

• Enterprise/Organizational Unit Objectives Matrix

• Preliminary Ranked List of Objectives for the enterprise and each major business unit

FORMULATE INFORMATION NEEDS AND PERFORMANCE MEASURES

Based on the objectives, strategies, and CSFs identified in previous tasks, the planners must identify the information required to support each objective and critical success factor (called **information needs**) and ways to assess accomplishment of each objective (called **performance measures**). Information needs and performance measures are two of the classes of information presented in Chapter 2.

Planners must recognize that the information recorded during this subtask is likely to be radically affected by later interviews. Expect that this subtask will yield no more than a skeleton of information needs and performance measures subject to refinement later.

Classes of Information

Planners seek the following classes of information during this subtask:

- Information Need
- Performance Measure

That information subsequently relates to the following class of information:

- Organizational Unit

Inputs

The inputs to the formulation of information needs and performance measures are:

- Written documentation available to the planning team; largely the same set of documents used during the "Identify and Prioritize Business Objectives" subtask
- Mission Statement
- List of Objectives, Strategies, and CSFs by Organizational Unit
- Enterprise/Organizational Unit Objectives Matrix
- Preliminary Ranked List of Objectives for the enterprise and each major business unit
- Organization Hierarchy Diagram

Steps

The steps required for this subtask are as follows:

1. Identify and record information needs. As explained in Chapter 2, an **information need** is an unstructured statement describing a type of information required by an organizational unit to meet its objectives and support its functions.

   Planners need not record all of the characteristics of information needs as presented in Chapter 2 at this point. The characteristics critical during the initial assessment are:

   a. A description of the need
   b. How the information is or should be used
   c. The objective or critical success factor it supports
   d. The importance factor of the information need (a relative measure of its importance)
   e. Whether snapshot (occasionally updated) information can satisfy the need or current (continually updated) information is required.

f. Whether the information satisfying the need is summary, exception, detail, a correlation, or some other kind of information is required.

These characteristics can be recorded as properties of the information need in the IEF.

Planners can postpone identifying current systems that supply this information and assigning the satisfaction rating until the "Assess the Current Environment" task. However, if this information happens to be discovered as a by-product of identifying the need, it should be recorded here.

If any of the terminology in the above discussion appears unfamiliar, please review the description of information needs in Chapter 2.

Planners can list information needs and their characteristics on a form similar to the one in Figure 4-4. Alternatively, they can be entered directly into the IEF as in step (2).

INFORMATION NEED	USAGE	OBJECTIVE SUPPORTED BY NEED	SYSTEMS SUPORTING NEED	IMP FACTOR	SAT RATING	REQMT WEIGHT
RETURNS BY PRODUCT LINE	QUALITY CONTROL	OBJ- IMPROVE CUSTOMER SATISFACTION	INVENTORY SYSTEM	4	2	8
SITE POPULATION STATISTICS	MARKET RESEARCH	OBJ- IDENTIFY NEW MARKETS		2		
FINISHED GOODS AVAILABLE	SALES PRE- ORDER CHECK	CSF- CUSTOMER DISSATISFACTION WITH LEAD TIMES	NONE	5	3	15
DAILY SALES BY REGION	PROGRESS AGAINST PLAN	GOAL- INCREASE SALES BY 3% BY 4Q	ORDER PROCESSING	4	1	4

Figure 4-5. Information Needs List

2. List information needs on the vertical axis of the Information Needs/Organization Matrix using the IEF Planning Toolset. The horizontal axis, representing organizational units, is pre-populated from the organization structure represented earlier in the Organizational Hierarchy Diagram.

3. Relate each information need to the organization unit whose objectives or CSFs require the information using the Information Needs/Organization Matrix. Place a simple involvement indicator in each cell that represents an information need by an organization. (If this terminology seems unfamiliar, review the section entitled "Recording Information in IEF Matrices" in Chapter 2.)

An example of an Information Needs/Organization Matrix appears in Figure 4-6.

4. Identify the performance measures used to assess each objective and record them on the vertical axis of the Performance Measure/Organization Matrix in the IEF Planning Toolset. The horizontal axis of this matrix, representing organizational units, is pre-populated based on the Organization Hierarchy Diagram.

Performance measures are described in Chapter 2.

5. Relate the organization unit to the performance measures that monitor its objectives using the Performance Measure/Organization Matrix in the IEF Planning Toolset. Place a simple involvement indicator in each cell that represents an organization's monitoring by a performance measure.

INFORMATION NEEDS (ORGANIZATION UNIT)	BERTHOLD_CORPORATION	AUTOMOTIVE_PRODUCTS_G	ECD_PRODUCT_DEVELOPME	EMISSION_CONTROLS_DIV	EXHAUST_SYSTEMS_DEPAR	ESD_MARKETING	ESD_MKT_ORDER_PROCESS	ESD_MKT_CUSTOMER_SERV	ESD_FIELD_SERVICE	ESD_SVC_REPAIR_FACILIT	ESD_SVC_REGIONAL_OFFIC	ESD_SVC_REG_WAREHOUSE	ESD_SVC-REG_REPAIR_SHO	ESD_MANUFACTURING_DEP	ESD_PRODUCTION_PLANNI	ESD_MATERIAL_CONTROL	FUEL_SYSTEMS_DEPARTME	FSD_MARKETING	FSD_MKT_ORDER_PROCESS	FSD_MKT_CUSTOMER_SVC	FSD_FIELD_SERVICE	FSD_SVC_REPAIR_FACILIT	FSD_SVC_REGIONAL_OFFIC	FSD_SVC_REG_WAREHOUSE	FSD_SVC_REG_REPAIR_SHO	FSD_MANUFACTURING_DEP	FSD_PRODUCTION_PLANNI	FSD_MATERIAL_CONTROL
CAPITAL_DEPRECIATION_Y	X													X												X		
SITE_POPULATION_STATS						X												X										
FINISHED_GOODS_AVAILAB							X												X									
60-DAY_HOT_LIST							X								X	X												
RETURNS_BY_PRODUCT_LIN								X												X								
NEW_PRODUCT_RELEASE_SC							X	X		X	X	X		X	X			X	X			X	X	X		X	X	
PRECIOUS_METAL_CONTENT															X	X											X	X
ORG_PROFIT_BY_DIVISION	X	X	X																									
CUSTOMER_ORDERS_>_$50K		X		X		X												X	X									
EMPLOYEE_RECEIVABLES	X			X													X											
MACHINE_LOAD_ON_HI_VAL															X	X											X	X
HOT_CHECKS	X			X																								
WRITEOFF_CANDIDATES															X	X											X	X
SALES_ORDER_VARIANCE	X	X		X		X												X		X								
DOMESTIC_BACKLOG			X			X												X		X								
DAILY_SALES_BY_REGION	X	X		X														X										

Figure 4-6. Information Needs/Organization Matrix

Deliverables

The deliverables of this subtask are:

- Information Needs List
- Information Needs/Organization Matrix
- Performance Measure/Organization Matrix

DETERMINE POTENTIAL IMPACT OF INFORMATION TECHNOLOGY

In this subtask, the planners identify potential uses of information technology to further the mission of the enterprise. **Information technology** in this context refers to computing hardware and software that can be used to create new business opportunities.

Since the planners have not yet formally assessed the current technical environment, this is only a broad-brush view of ways in which information technology can benefit the business. The effectiveness of this subtask depends greatly on the project team's understanding of information technology.

Classes of Information

The information derived during this subtask falls into the following classes of information:

- Hardware Item
- Software Product

Inputs

The inputs to this subtask are:

- Publications (such as articles and product announcements) about the emergence and application of information technologies. For many industries, planners can easily find periodicals with related articles about the use of hardware and software technology.

- Business documentation that addresses the current technical environment.

- Business strategies that may rely on information technology.

Steps

The steps required for this subtask are as follows:

1. Review the available technical documentation to determine the extent of information technology usage within the enterprise.

2. List technologies from which the business might benefit based on the planners' experience and information found in publications. These technologies include four categories:

    a. Those that can become a product or service, or part of a product or service. For Consolidated Implements (the fictional farm machinery firm used in previous examples), the use of microprocessors to monitor engine performance falls into this category.

    b. Those that deliver a product or service. For a banking concern, the introduction of Automated Teller Machines falls into this category.

    c. Those that can be used as marketing tools. For Consolidated Implements, providing large customers a means to enter orders online falls into this category.

    d. Those that can be used to increase the organization's competitive advantage. This covers a wide range of alternatives, since any use of information technology that improves the creation or delivery of a product or service falls into this category. For Consolidated Implements, this might include the use of Just-In-Time inventory control software or an Engineering Revisions System that allows quick modification of components.

Deliverables

The single deliverable from this subtask is a brief statement of the areas in which new uses of information technology can create or enhance business opportunities. It is called a Statement of Potential Information Technology Impact.

DEFINE A PRELIMINARY INFORMATION ARCHITECTURE

In this subtask, the planners construct a high-level Information Architecture that reflects the needs of the business. Once verified, this preliminary architecture will become the foundation for developing the overall Information Architecture for the enterprise.

Classes of Information

Planners seek the following classes of information during this subtask:

- Business Function
- Subject Area

Inputs

Inputs to this subtask include:

- Company's annual report
- Any models of the enterprise previously developed
- Organization Hierarchy Diagram

Steps

The steps required for this subtask are as follows:

1. Identify the subject areas with which the business deals. As defined in Chapter 2, a **subject area** is a summary of things in which the enterprise is interested. Each subject area can potentially be decomposed into elementary data objects, but the planners should only attempt to identify large groupings of concepts at this point.

   Planners should record a name and brief description for each subject area. An example of a Subject Area List for Consolidated Implements appears in Figure 4-7.

   The name of each subject area should be a plural noun.

2. Describe the associations between the various subject areas in a Subject Area Diagram using the IEF Data Modeling tool. An association between two subject areas indicates a business relationship between one or more of their components. For example, one might associate a subject area called Customers, representing people or companies who buy the goods produced by an enterprise, with the subject area Products, representing the goods produced.

Subject Area	Description
CUSTOMERS	Information about all persons or organizations who purchase Products. Includes delivery and billing locations.
PRODUCTS	All goods manufactured and sold.
RAW MATERIALS	Components used to manufacture Products. While some are actually "raw " materials, others are pre-assembled parts.
VENDORS	Suppliers of Raw Materials.
BUYERS	Company personnel responsible for purchasing Raw Materials from Vendors.

Figure 4-7. Example of a Subject Area List

The Subject Area Diagram uses two symbols, one to represent a subject area and one to represent the association between two subject areas:

a. A double-bordered box containing the name of a subject area represents that subject area.

b. A line connecting two subject area boxes represents an association between those respective subject areas. (In the IEF, in order to cause a line to appear on the subject area diagram, *entity types* from the two subject areas being associated must be connected via a *relationship*; there is no facility to allow the direct addition of lines between subject areas.)

Figure 4-8 shows a sample Subject Area Diagram based on the partial Subject Area List in Figure 4-7.

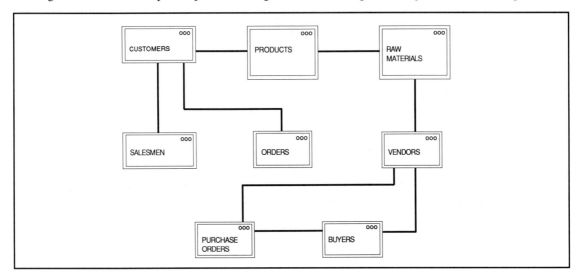

Figure 4-8. Subject Area Diagram

3.   Identify the highest-level business functions. The highest-level business functions are groupings of activities that deal with the major areas of interest (that is, subject areas) in the enterprise.

Initially, the difference between a high-level business function and a high-level organization unit may be difficult to see, since organizations often attempt to organize themselves into functional units. However, the planners must learn to divorce the organizational structure from the structure of business functions. The organizational structure reflects an aspect of the business's strategy in carrying out its mission, while business functions reflect the actual activities performed.

The list of high-level business functions must occur at the proper level of detail. In most organizations, major activities can be grouped into five to ten top-level business functions.

For each top-level business function, give the following information:

a.   The function's name.

b.   A brief description. This should describe *what* the function does and, perhaps, *why* it is done. It should never describe who, when, where, or how because such information is not fundamental to the function's existence. Rather, those aspects reflect the business's approach to executing the activities that make up the function.

c.   A list of the subject areas involved with the function.

Planners can record this information as the first level of a Function Hierarchy Diagram (sometimes called a Function *Decomposition* Diagram) using the Activity Hierarchy Diagramming Tool in the IEF Planning Toolset. In this diagram, each top-level business function appears as a cyan (light blue) cushion (a box with rounded edges) with its name in the center. These functions are joined to an even higher-level cushion representing all activities performed by the enterprise.

In the Function Hierarchy Diagram, planners can give each function a long textual description. For the set of top-level functions, the textual description can refer to the subject areas affected by the function.

A Function Hierarchy Diagram representing only top-level functions appears in Figure 4-9. A report prepared by the IEF, with a description of the Product Research function, appears in Figure 4-10.

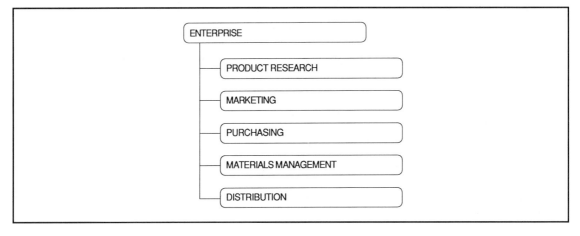

Figure 4-9. Top Level Function Hierarchy Diagram

4. Decompose the top-level business functions into lower-level business functions. This step employs the "divide and conquer" principle mentioned in Chapter 1. Each business function is broken into smaller, more detailed business functions. Although the level of decomposition required for this step is quite shallow, the division of business activities into successively smaller components continues throughout both the ISP and BAA stages of Information Engineering until the lowest-level, fundamental activities (called **elementary processes**) are identified.

Activity Definition

Name:	PRODUCT_RESEARCH
Description:	Research and Development of new Products and major refinements to existing products.
	This function is primarily concerned with the Subject Areas PRODUCTS and RAW MATERIALS.
Type:	Function
Subordinate of:	ENTERPRISE

Figure 4-10. Report of Top-Level Function Definitions

At this point, the planners take the first steps in fully decomposing business activities by dividing the top-level business functions into one or two levels of subordinate function. Planners add these results to the Function Hierarchy Diagram begun in step 3, using the Activity Hierarchy Diagramming Tool.

The principal technique used to decompose a business function is to analyze its use of subject areas. The decomposition can take place based on the life cycle of a subject area component or any other useful distinction between subject areas. For example, Materials Management might decompose into Materials Acquisition, Component Manufacture, Assembly, and Quality Assurance, reflecting the life cycle of the Products subject area.

In any event, the organization hierarchy should not influence decomposition. The task at hand involves a pure division of business functions into components and should not be contaminated by existing organizational constraints.

The decomposition of each function will usually yield between three and seven subordinate functions. It must yield at least two. Any function whose decomposition results in more than seven direct subordinates should be examined closely. More than likely, the diagram reflects too great a level of detail.

Figure 4-11 depicts a portion of the completed Function Hierarchy Diagram for Consolidated Implements' preliminary Information Architecture.

Deliverables

The deliverables of this subtask are:

- Subject Area List
- Subject Area Diagram
- Initial Function Hierarchy Diagram

INTERVIEW TOP MANAGEMENT

During this subtask, the project team interviews members of top management to verify and supplement their findings to date. An additional purpose is to provide a forum for increasing management commitment to the ISP project.

This subtask usually involves from five to ten interviews.

Chapter 2 presented techniques for conducting interviews. This section assumes the use of those techniques.

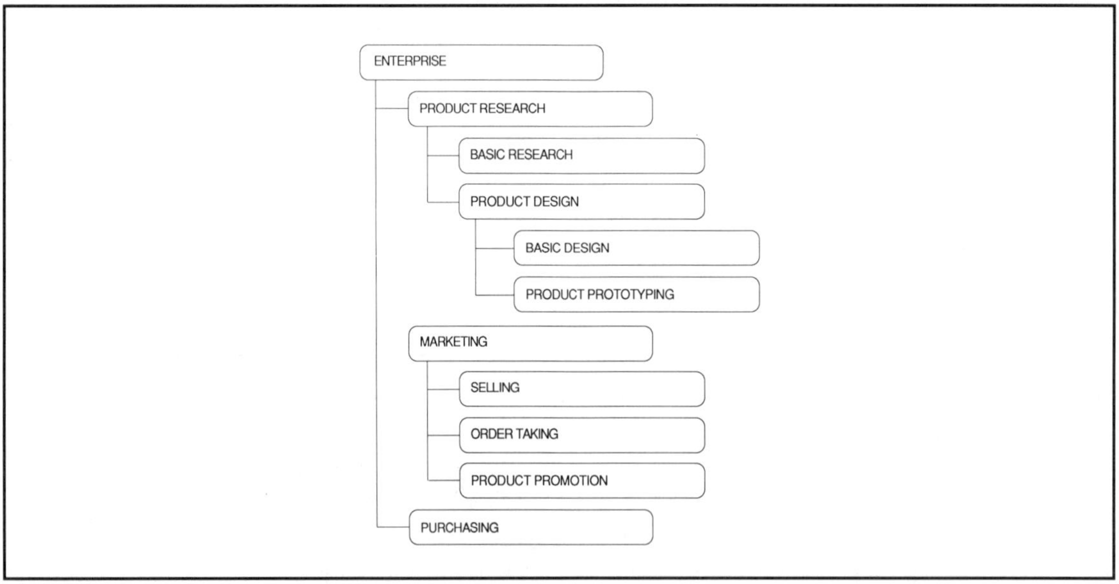

Figure 4-11. Three Levels of Function Decomposition

Classes of Information

The planners attempt to verify information gleaned in these classes:

- Mission
- Objective
- Strategy
- Critical Success Factor
- Information Need
- Performance Measure

They try to improve their understanding of the organization by expanding their knowledge about these classes:

- Organizational Unit
- Organization Structure

They listen for references to information in these categories:

- Business Function
- Subject Area

Finally, they attempt to inform management of the potential uses of information technology by describing information in these classes:

- Hardware Unit
- Software Product

Inputs

All of the deliverables from the preceding subtasks contribute to this subtask. They include:

- Organizational Hierarchy Diagram and supportive text
- Mission Statement
- List of Objectives, Strategies, and CSFs by Organizational Unit
- Enterprise/Organizational Unit Objectives Matrix
- Preliminary Ranked Lists of Objectives
- Statement of Potential Information Technology Impact
- Subject Area List
- Subject Area Diagram
- Initial Function Hierarchy Diagram

Steps

As with any interview, the three steps required for each of these interviews are to prepare for the interview, conduct the interview, and analyze the results.

1. Prepare the topic list for the interview. Each topic should focus on one of these issues:

    a. The interviewee's understanding of the mission, objectives, strategies, and critical success factors for both the enterprise as a whole and the organizational unit for which the interviewee is responsible.

    b. The interviewee's perception of the priorities of business objectives.

    c. The interviewee's perception of the future direction of the enterprise.

    d. The impact of information technology, present and future, on the enterprise.

    An interview that targets these issues will normally also reveal facts about business functions, subject areas, and the structure of the organization.

2. Conduct the interview. The interview may reveal facts in a variety of categories, but the notetaker must be especially sensitive to those mentioned in "Classes of Information" for this subtask.

3. Analyze the results. Each interview has the potential of adjusting and increasing the project team's knowledge. The deliverables produced to this point must be adjusted to reflect new information.

4. After collecting all the data, the project team may find discrepancies. Team members must resolve these, either through memoranda, phone calls, or follow-up personal interviews. They should incorporate the results into the adjusted set of deliverables before conducting the middle management interviews.

Deliverables

The deliverables from this subtask are simply verifications to, corrections of, or refinements to its inputs. These are restated here:

*   Organization Hierarchy Diagram and supportive text

*   Mission Statement

*   List of Objectives, Strategies, and CSFs by Organizational Unit

*   Enterprise/Organizational Unit Objective Association Matrix

*   Ranked Lists of Objectives

*   Statement of Potential Information Technology Impact

*   Subject Area List

*   Subject Area Diagram

*   Initial Function Hierarchy Diagram

INTERVIEW MIDDLE MANAGEMENT

During this subtask, the project team conducts a series of interviews with middle management to further refine the information gleaned earlier and verified, to some degree, by top management.

Depending on the scope of the project, the number of middle management interviews required will range from 15 to 40.

The classes of information, inputs, and steps required for this subtask are the same as for the "Interview Top Management" subtask. The deliverables from this subtask are further refinements of those produced in that subtask.

REVIEW THE INITIAL ASSESSMENT

The initial assessment ends with a formal review of the project team's findings by the project sponsor, appropriate members of management (at the sponsor's discretion), and selected members of the reference team, if one exists.

The project team should pay particular attention to the emerging Information Architecture during this review. They should attempt to gain a consensus on their initial understanding of the required information infrastructure before proceeding.

Just as in an interview, the review may reveal a number of facts belonging to a variety of classes of information. One member of the project team should act as notetaker to ensure that all facts are recorded.

This review constitutes a project checkpoint as described in Chapter 3.

ADDITIONAL MATRICES USEFUL DURING THIS TASK

The IEF provides additional matrices beyond those mentioned in the preceding list of tasks which may prove useful to the planner while conducting the initial assessment. For instance, it is possible to plot objectives against strategies, information needs against objectives, critical success factors against organizational units, and so on. These matrices can be used to verify the initial assessment in fairly obvious ways (for example, every objective should be supported by one or more strategies) and to provide additional insight into the enterprise.

For a complete list of IEF-supplied matrices useful during the initial assessment, see the *IEF Planning Toolset Guide*.

5
DEFINING THE INFORMATION ARCHITECTURE

OVERVIEW

This chapter presents the activities required to define the Information Architecture, which governs the construction and integration of future systems development. The goal of this major task is to refine in more detail the preliminary Information Architecture built during the initial assessment.

The task of defining the Information Architecture is composed of the following subtasks:

1. Complete the function decomposition
2. Analyze function dependencies
3. Map functions to organizations
4. Build the Entity Relationship Diagram
5. Map entity types to information needs
6. Record usage of entity types by function
7. Review results

The discussion of each of these subtasks is organized in the same way as in Chapter 4:

- Description of the subtask
- Classes of information involved (based on the classes identified in Chapter 2)
- Inputs to the subtask
- Steps required to execute the subtask (including the use of automated tools, if any)
- Deliverables from the subtask

COMPLETE THE FUNCTION DECOMPOSITION

During this task, the planners continue decomposing the business functions defined while constructing the preliminary Information Architecture. At this point, planners decompose business functions as far as possible, even, in some cases, into top-level business processes.

Planners should already have verified the function decomposition up to this point to the greatest extent possible from their reading and interviewing. Since the initial function decomposition is the foundation of the activity side of the Information Architecture, it must accurately reflect the business. If any anomalies or gray areas exist, the planners should make every attempt to resolve them before continuing into this subtask.

As a very general guideline, this subtask typically results in the identification of from 50 to 100 functions and processes.

Classes of Information

During this subtask, the planners refine information belonging to the following classes:

- Business Function
- Business Process

Inputs

The inputs to this subtask are:

- Initial Function Hierarchy Diagram
- Additional, detailed information regarding business activities discovered during the initial assessment

Steps

The steps employed in completing the function decomposition are really a single step executed repeatedly: decompose each business function into component functions or processes and document them in a Function Hierarchy Diagram using the Activity Hierarchy Diagramming Tool in the IEF Planning Toolset. As mentioned earlier, functions appear in this diagram as cyan cushions with their names in the center. Processes appear as dark blue cushions with their names in the center.

The technique for performing this decomposition follows the same basic form as the first attempt at decomposition (see step 4 of the "Define a Preliminary Information Architecture" task in Chapter 4).

The following rules and guidelines for function decomposition elaborate on those presented informally in Chapter 4. Some apply to all decomposition of business activities while others are specific to Information Strategy Planning.

The rules of function decomposition are as follows:

- Each function must decompose into at least two subordinate functions or processes.
- Siblings (activities at the same level of hierarchy beneath a single higher-level function) must all be of the same type. That is, they must either all be functions or they must all be processes. The same higher-level function must never decompose directly into both a function and a process.
- The same function must not appear twice in the same decomposition.
- The subordinate functions or processes that compose a higher-level function must reflect all aspects of that higher-level function. For example if function A decomposes into functions W, X, Y, and Z, the statement $A = W + X + Y + Z$ must be true.

The above rules must never be violated. In fact, the IEF Activity Hierarchy Diagramming Tool will not allow specification of a structure that does not comply with the first three rules.

In addition, follow these guidelines closely when performing function decomposition. They are less stringent but no less important to the proper decomposition of functions.

- Functions should decompose into between three and seven subordinates. If the decomposition yields a number of subordinates outside these boundaries, the results should be reviewed.
- Function decomposition should never proceed beyond top-level processes. That is, during Information Strategy Planning, the planners should never decompose processes.
- Siblings should have some kind of interdependence.

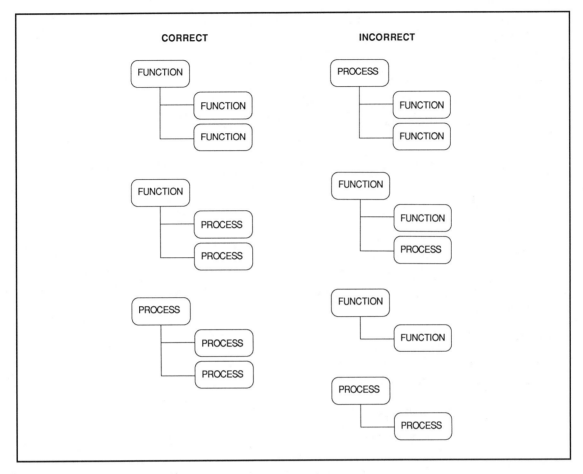

Figure 5-1. Examples of Correct and Incorrect Decompositions

Some examples of correct decomposition as well as some violations appear in Figure 5-1.

As mentioned in Chapter 2, business functions are major groupings of activities. Business processes are also groupings of activities, but they occur at a lower level. The difference is that the execution of a process has meaning; it is an activity with a beginning and an end and reflects a set of executable steps. A function, on the other hand, is defined at too high a level of abstraction for its execution to have meaning.

The two concepts dovetail in this way: in a Function Hierarchy, functions decompose from the top-level functions to the lowest-level functions. Lowest-level functions decompose into top-level processes. During Business Area Analysis, these top-level processes eventually decompose into lowest-level (elementary) processes.

The distinction between functions and processes at either end of the spectrum is usually fairly obvious. For example, Purchasing is definitely a function, while Order Raw Materials is definitely a process. The demarcation between low-level functions and high- level processes is not always so clear. In such cases, the planners must use their own judgement in deciding whether or not an activity is executable.

Naming conventions help emphasize the difference between functions and processes during function decomposition. A function is always named by a single noun, often the noun form of a verb. The examples presented in Chapter 2 are restated here:

- Marketing
- Manufacturing
- Sales (or, alternatively, Selling)
- Shipping

Each process, on the other hand, is named using a verb-noun combination that summarizes the steps in its execution. For example:

- Take Order
- Assemble Part
- Bill Customer

Additionally, a process has a discrete set of inputs that is used to create a discrete set of outputs. The process Take Order, for example, probably requires details about customers and the products being ordered to produce an order with order lines.

Deliverables

The single deliverable produced by this subtask is the complete Function Hierarchy Diagram (including all of its supportive descriptive documentation).

ANALYZE FUNCTION DEPENDENCIES

In the preceding subtask, one of the guidelines for function decomposition was that siblings should have some kind of interdependence.

In this subtask, planners verify the function decomposition by identifying the dependencies between functions or processes subordinate to a common function. The analysis performed here may result in a restructuring of the Function Hierarchy Diagram.

In the context of Information Engineering, the term **dependency** is strictly defined as an association between two business activities that exists because information provided by one is required by the other.

In the following discussion, the dependency analysis of a function refers to the analysis of dependencies between its subordinate activities. Similarly, a dependency diagram for a function shows that function's subordinates and the dependencies between them.

For example, if function A decomposes into functions W, X, Y, and Z, the dependency analysis of A identifies the dependencies between W, X, Y, and Z. Likewise, the dependency diagram for A shows the dependencies between W, X, Y, and Z.

Classes of Information

Planners seek no new information during this analysis. Rather, they concentrate on verifying the information assembled previously. This information falls into two classes:

- Business Function
- Business Process

Inputs

The inputs to this subtask are:

- Function Hierarchy Diagram
- Written documentation that may reveal interdependencies between activities

Steps

The steps required for this subtask are as follows:

1. Identify the functions for which dependency analysis is to be performed. At this point, dependency analysis is used only to validate the function decomposition previously performed. Since dependency analysis can be time consuming, limit the scope as follows:

   a. Limit dependency analysis to those functions at the next-to-lowest level of decomposition. In other words, identify dependencies between activities at the lowest-level of decomposition only.

   b. In large projects, only perform dependency analysis on functions of great complexity.

2. Construct a Function Dependency Diagram for each selected function using the Activity Dependency Diagramming Tool in the IEF Planning Toolset.

   The following symbols are used when building a Function Dependency Diagram:

   a. A cyan (light blue) cushion (a box with rounded edges) represents a function.

   b. A dark blue cushion represents a process.

   c. A directed line (a line with an arrowhead indicating its direction) connects two cushions and depicts a dependency between the activities they represent.

   Figure 5-2 is an example of a simple Dependency Diagram for a function named Order Processing. It shows that the processes Change Order and Cancel Order both depend on the process Take Order.

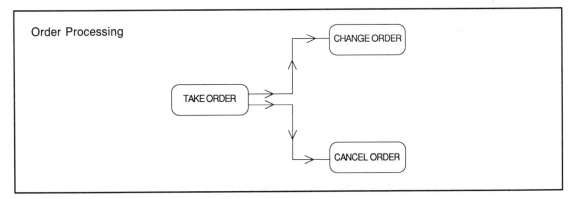

Figure 5-2. Dependency Diagram for the ORDER PROCESSING Function

If, after performing dependency analysis on a function, one or more of its components have no dependencies identified for them, the decomposition itself must be questioned. In this case, revisit the Function Hierarchy Diagram and devise a new decomposition that results in an interdependent grouping.

Deliverables

The deliverables of this subtask are:

- Function Dependency Diagrams
- A revised Function Hierarchy Diagram

MAP FUNCTIONS TO ORGANIZATIONS

In this subtask, the functions identified during function decomposition are related to organizational units. This mapping serves three purposes:

- It improves the project team's general understanding of the enterprise's current strategy for accomplishing its mission.
- It verifies the function decomposition. If an organizational unit is not involved with any function, the planners may have overlooked some functions performed by the business. On the other hand, if a function is not involved with any organizational unit, the decomposition may be faulty or the planners may have misunderstood the organizational unit.
- It provides a basis for a more in-depth assessment of the organization later on.

Classes of Information

The following classes of information relate to this subtask:

- Business Function
- Organizational Unit

Inputs

The inputs to this subtask are:

- Function Hierarchy Diagram
- Organization Hierarchy Indented List

Steps

There is only a single step required for this subtask.

Record the involvement of an organizational unit in a business function using the Business Function/Organization Matrix in the IEF Planning Toolset. The vertical axis of this matrix is pre-populated based on the business functions specified on the Function Hierarchy Diagram and the horizontal axis is pre-populated based on the organization hierarchy defined during the initial assessment.

Place a simple involvement indicator in each cell that represents an organizational unit's involvement in a business function. (If this terminology seems unfamiliar, review the section entitled "Recording Information in IEF Matrices" in Chapter 2.)

An example of a Business Function/Organization Matrix appears in Figure 5-3.

Planners may choose to use values that reflect the relative degree of involvement of the organizational unit in the business function. This can simplify the task of assessing the organization later on. In this case, it is generally sufficient to use the following values for the involvement indicator:

ORGANIZATION UNIT

BUSINESS FUNCTIONS	BERTHOLD_CORPORATION	AUTOMOTIVE_PRODUCTS_G	ECD_PRODUCT_DEVELOPME	EMISSION_CONTROLS_DIV	EXHAUST_SYSTEMS_DEPAR	ESD_MARKETING	ESD_MKT_ORDER_PROCESS	ESD_MKT_CUSTOMER_SERV	ESD_FIELD_SERVICE	ESD_SVC_REPAIR_FACILIT	ESD_SVC_REGIONAL_OFFIC	ESD_SVC_REG_WAREHOUSE	ESD_SVC_REG_REPAIR_SHO	ESD_MANUFACTURING_DEP	ESD_PRODUCTION_PLANNI	ESD_MATERIAL_CONTROL	FUEL_SYSTEMS_DEPARTME	FSD_MARKETING	FSD_MKT_ORDER_PROCESS	FSD_FIELD_SERVICE	FSD_SVC_REPAIR_FACILIT	FSD_SVC_REGIONAL_OFFIC	FSD_SVC_REG_WAREHOUSE	FSD_SVC_REG_REPAIR_SHO	FSD_MANUFACTURING_DEP	FSD_PRODUCTION_PLANNI	FSD_MATERIAL_CONTROL	FSD_MKT_CUSTOMER_SVC
BASIC_RESEARCH	X																											
PRODUCT_DESIGN		X																										
METHODS_ENGINEERING			X													X												
MARKETING						X												X										
ORDER_PROCESSING							X												X									
PURCHASING									X					X														
RECEIVING										X		X			X				X						X			
WAREHOUSING												X			X							X		X				X
SCRAP_DISPOSAL											X													X				X
DISTRIBUTION_CENTER_OP												X											X					
PACKING												X														X		
SHIPPING											X	X														X		
TRAFFIC_MANAGEMENT																										X	X	
GENERAL_ACCOUNTING	X																											
COST_ACCOUNTGING			X														X											
LEGAL_SERVICES	X																											

Figure 5-3. Business Function/Organization Matrix

3 - High level of involvement

2 - Moderate level of involvement

1 - Low level of involvement

Ordering from high to low is suggested because of the clustering technique used in the IEF Matrix Processor (see Chapter 2).

Deliverables

The single deliverable from this task is the Business Function/Organization Matrix.

BUILD THE ENTITY RELATIONSHIP DIAGRAM

This subtask refines the portion of the preliminary Information Architecture that depicts business data on which business functions operate. This refinement results in the creation of a diagram similar to the Subject Area Diagram described in Chapter 4, but carried to a greater level of detail. This diagram is called the Entity Relationship Diagram.

The Entity Relationship Diagram is a simple, straightforward representation of the things of interest to the business. During Information Strategy Planning, planners use this diagram to present a sketch of business requirements. They do not carry it to the level of detail required during Business Area Analysis.

As a general guideline, this subtask should result in the analysis of from 30 to 60 entity types.

The reader familiar with Entity Relationship Diagramming may notice that some familiar concepts are missing from this discussion. For example, no mention is made of attributes, identifiers, relationship optionality or entity subtypes. Since the level of detail required during Information Strategy Planning is very high, these and other concepts have been purposely omitted because they are too detailed for an ISP project.

Classes of Information

During this subtask, planners seek out and record the following classes of information:

- Entity Type
- Relationship

Inputs

The inputs to this subtask are:

- Subject Area Diagram
- Interview results
- Written documentation

Steps

The steps required for this subtask are as follows:

1. Identify entity types and record them using the Data Modeling tool in the IEF Planning Toolset.

    As defined in Chapter 2, an **entity type** is a fundamental thing of relevance to the enterprise about which data may be kept. These fundamental things of relevance can be discovered in a number of ways. In particular:

    a. By refining the understanding of broad subject areas defined in the preliminary Information Architecture. For example, an examination of the subject area Customers may yield the individual fundamental concepts CUSTOMER, DELIVERY POINT, BILLING LOCATION, and so on.

    b. By evaluating the results of interviews. For example, the simple statement:

       "Most of these customers are big guys. Some of 'em have ten or eleven different locations we end up having to deliver to."

       reveals the existence of an entity type CUSTOMER and another entity type DELIVERY LOCATION. (It also reveals a relationship between the two, such that CUSTOMER *receives delivery at* DELIVERY LOCATION.)

    c. By analyzing written business documentation in the same way as interview results.

    When an entity type is discovered, record the following information for it:

    a. Its name. Unlike subject area names, each entity type name is a singular noun which, if possible, has meaning to company personnel. For example, PRODUCT, ORDER, and ORDER LINE are valid entity type names.

    b. A definition, usually in one or two sentences.

    During Information Strategy Planning, these are the only characteristics recorded for entity types. Both may be captured in the Entity Relationship Diagram.

    On an Entity Relationship Diagram built using the IEF Data Modeling tool, the symbol for entity type is a single bordered box with the entity type's name in the center.

Assuming the construction of a Subject Area Diagram during the initial assessment, the IEF Data Modeling tool allows the planner to add entity types *inside* of the subject area to which they belong.

2. Define the relationships between the entity types and record them using the Data Modeling tool in the IEF Planning Toolset.

As defined in Chapter 2, a **relationship** is a reason relevant to the enterprise for associating two entities from one or two entity types. In other words, any reason two entities might be related to one another is characterized by a relationship. Consider, for example, two entity types named CUSTOMER (people who buy products) and ORDER (a request from a customer for products). Since each CUSTOMER can place ORDERs, there is a relationship between entities of the type CUSTOMER and those of the type ORDER.

Further consideration of this example reveals an interesting property of relationships. Each relationship can be described from two viewpoints, one for each entity type. For example, CUSTOMER *places* ORDER describes the relationship from the viewpoint of entities of the type CUSTOMER. On the other hand, from the viewpoint of entities of the type ORDER, the relationship might be stated as ORDER *is placed by* CUSTOMER. Each of these two viewpoints is called a **relationship membership**. Each relationship is composed of two relationship memberships.

The definition of a relationship, then, is really a definition of its two relationship memberships. For each relationship membership, planners should identify the following information during Information Strategy Planning:

a. Its name. The name of a relationship membership is a verb or verb phrase that joins the names of the two participating entity types. The name of the first entity type presented dictates the relationship viewpoint under consideration. The construction of the phrase should be such that it makes sense when presented as follows:

(entity-type-1) (relationship-membership-name) (entity-type-2)

Examples include:

CUSTOMER *places* ORDER

ORDER *is placed by* CUSTOMER

b. Its **cardinality**. Cardinality is a property that identifies the number of **pairings** in which an entity may participate within a relationship membership. During Information Strategy Planning, it is sufficient to establish whether the cardinality of a relationship membership is "only one" or "one or more."

For example, when considered from the standpoint of CUSTOMER:

Each CUSTOMER places *one or more* ORDERs

However, when considered from the standpoint of ORDER:

Each ORDER is placed by *only one* CUSTOMER

On an Entity Relationship Diagram, a relationship is depicted as a single line joining two entity types. The line is labeled with the names of one or both of its relationship memberships. At either end of the line, the cardinality of the relationship membership is depicted as follows:

a. A bar that crosses the line perpendicularly indicates "only one."

b. A crow's foot at the end of the line indicates "one or more."

Although it may not be immediately obvious, only three combinations of relationship membership cardinalities can exist:

a. **One-to-one**, in which each entity participating in the relationship can be related to only one entity of the other type.

b.   **One-to-many**, in which a single entity of one type participating in the relationship can be related to one or more entities of the other type, but not vice versa.

c.   **Many-to-many**, in which a single entity of either type participating in the relationship can be related to one or more entities of the other type.

Examples of each of these three kinds of relationships using the symbols of the Entity Relationship Diagram appear in Figure 5-4.

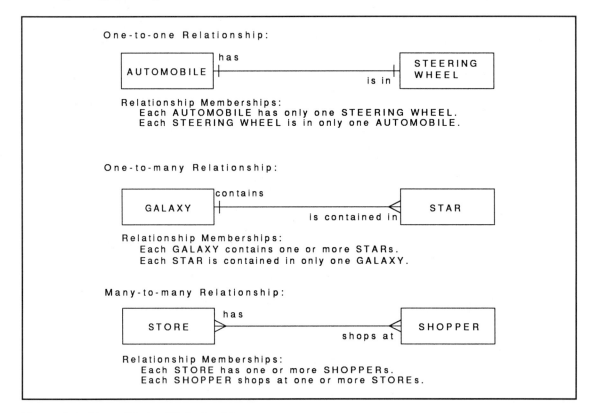

Figure 5-4. Three Kinds of Relationships

A portion of a completed Entity Relationship Diagram appears in Figure 5-5. Note that the entity types are *contained within* the subject areas from which they were refined.

Deliverables

The single deliverable from this subtask is the Entity Relationship Diagram.

MAP ENTITY TYPES TO INFORMATION NEEDS

During the initial assessment, the planners assembled a list of information needs for the support of objectives and CSFs. In this subtask, planners compare the list of entity types defined in the preceding subtask against this list of information needs to ensure the completeness of each. In particular, the planners should be alert for information needs not satisfied by entities from one or more types. Such cases typically indicate that the list of entity types is incomplete.

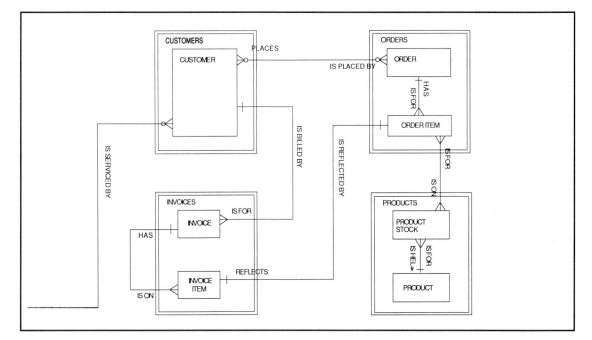

Figure 5-5. Entity Relationship Diagram

Classes of Information

During this subtask, planners consider two classes of information:

• Information Need

• Entity Type

Inputs

The inputs to this subtask are:

• Information Needs List

• Entity Relationship Diagram

• Written documentation/interview results that will help the planners to relate the two

Steps

There is only one step required for this subtask.

Record the contribution of an entity type to the satisfaction of each information need using the Entity Type/Information Needs Matrix in the IEF Planning Toolset. The vertical axis of this matrix is pre-populated based on the entity types defined using the Data Modeling Tool and the horizontal axis is pre-populated based on the Information Needs List recorded during construction of the Information Needs/Organization Matrix in the initial assessment.

Place a simple involvement indicator (defined in Chapter 2) in each cell that represents an entity type's contribution to the satisfaction of an information need.

ENTITY TYPES	CAPITAL_DEPRECIATION_Y	SITE_POPULATION_STATS	FINISHED_GOODS_AVAILAB	SALES_ORDER_VARIANCE	DOMESTIC_BACKLOG	DAILY_SALES_BY_REGION	ABSENTEES	EMPLOYEE_BY_SKILL	BAD_LOTS	FAB_MACHINE_MBTF	30-60-90-CUSTOMER-DELI	DRAWING_CHANGES	INSTALLED_BASE_BY_ECN	CONVEYOR_SPEED	BIN_QUANTITY_BY_PART_	OPEN_COMMITMENTS	60-DAY_HOT_LIST	RETURNS_BY_PRODUCT_LI	NEW_PRODUCT_RELEASE_S	ORG_PROFIT_BY_DIVISION	PRECIOUS_METAL_CONTEN	CUSTOMER_ORDERS_>_$50K	EMPLOYEE_RECEIVABLES	MACHINE_LOAD_ON_HI_VA	HOT_CHECKS	WRITEOFF_CANDIDATES	WAREHOUSE_LOAD_FACTOR	SALES_BY_ZIP_AREA
SALES_REGION						X							X															X
CUSTOMER				X	X	X																X						X
CUSTOMER_ORDER											X		X					X	X	X		X						X
CUSTOMER_ORDER_ITEM				X	X	X					X		X															X
ACKNOWLEDGEMENT																												
INVOICE											X																	
PAYMENT											X														X			
LEDGER_ENTRY	X																											
SUPPLIER									X									X	X									
PURCHASE_ORDER	X								X									X	X							X		
PURCHASE_ORDER_ITEM									X									X	X							X		
TERMS_AND_AGREEMENTS																										X		
BLANKET_ORDER_AGREEMEN																										X		
SUPPLIER_DRAWING												X																
PURCHASED_PART												X						X	X							X	X	
RAW_MATERIAL												X						X	X							X	X	

Figure 5-6. Entity Type/Information Needs Matrix

An example of the Entity Type/Information Needs Matrix appears in Figure 5-6.

Deliverables

The single deliverable from this subtask is the Entity Type/Information Needs Matrix.

RECORD USAGE OF ENTITY TYPES BY BUSINESS FUNCTION

During this subtask, the planners record the expected effects of business functions on entity types. This validates both the Function Hierarchy Diagram and the Entity Relationship Diagram.

Classes of Information

During this subtask, planners consider the following classes of information:

- Entity Type
- Business Function

Inputs

The inputs to this subtask are:

- List of functions stored in the IEF Planning Toolset
- List of entity types stored in the IEF Planning Toolset

Steps

The steps required for this subtask are as follows:

1. Record the effect of each business function on entities of each entity type using the Entity Type/Business Function Matrix in the IEF Planning Toolset. The vertical axis of this matrix is pre-populated with the previously identified entity types, and the horizontal axis is pre-populated with the previously identified business functions.

    At each cell, consider whether the column's business function has any effect on the row's entity type. If it does, specify a CRUD involvement indicator (as described in Chapter 2). In some cases, a single business function may produce multiple effects on entities of a certain type. In such cases, the value of the involvement indicator should reflect the most significant of those effects using the following priority list:

    a. 1st — C(reate)
    b. 2nd — D(elete)
    c. 3rd — U(pdate)
    d. 4th — R(ead)

2. Analyze the resulting matrix for its validity. In particular, the matrix should conform to this set of rules:

    a. Each function must be involved with at least one entity type. Otherwise, the function serves no useful purpose.
    b. Each entity type must have exactly one Create (C) to be valid (unless, in a limited-scope ISP project, it is created in some other area). If entities of a given type are Created by more than one function, it often indicates that the function decomposition has been done along *organizational* lines, rather than along true *business function* lines.
    c. Each entity type should generally be involved with at least two functions: one that creates (C) it and one that uses (D, U, R) it.

    Violations of these guidelines generally indicate one of three conditions:

    a. Business functions are missing and should be added.
    b. Entity types are missing and should be added.
    c. The involvement indicators are incorrect.

    In any event, planners must correct or explain the anomalies before continuing.

Deliverables

The single deliverable from this subtask is the Entity Type/Business Function Matrix.

REVIEW THE INFORMATION ARCHITECTURE

The task of defining the Information Architecture concludes with a formal review of the project team's findings by the project sponsor and selected members of the reference team. This review consists primarily of a presentation of the Function Hierarchy Diagram and the Entity Relationship Diagram, with the additional deliverables from the subtasks used as supporting information.

Since the review may reveal additional facts important to the Information Architecture, one member of the project team should act as notetaker to ensure that all facts are recorded.

This review constitutes a project checkpoint as described in Chapter 3.

6
ASSESSING THE CURRENT ENVIRONMENT

OVERVIEW

The Information Architecture, properly constructed, constitutes the ideal framework for the enterprise's information environment. In this chapter, planners examine current systems to determine how much of the ideal framework they cover and how well they cover it.

To support this assessment, planners also review the Information Systems organization responsible for current systems and the technical environment in which they operate.

The subtasks performed when assessing the current environment are:

1. Inventory current systems and data stores
2. Determine Information Architecture coverage
3. Complete the Information Needs List
4. Analyze the Information Systems organization
5. Analyze the current technical environment
6. Review results

The format for presenting these subtasks is the same as in Chapters 4 and 5:

- Description of the subtask
- Classes of information involved (based on the classes identified in Chapter 2)
- Inputs to the subtask
- Steps required to execute the subtask (including the use of automated tools, if any)
- Deliverables from the subtask

INVENTORY CURRENT SYSTEMS AND DATA STORES

During this subtask, planners compile a list of the major current systems in place and the major current data stores that support them. (The terms **current system** and **current data store** are defined in Chapter 2.) Planners use the resulting inventory later to assess the coverage of business needs by the existing Information Systems environment.

As in all ISP-related activities, the planners must be wary of carrying their analysis to too great a level of detail. There is no strict guideline for determining the proper level of detail. As an informal gauge, however, planners should usually identify between 40 and 70 systems, and between 50 and 100 data stores.

Classes of Information

During this subtask planners identify information in two classes:

- Current System

- Current Data Store

Inputs

The input to this subtask is written systems documentation, including system descriptions, data base descriptions, procedural manuals, and user manuals.

Steps

The steps required for this subtask are as follows:

1. Identify and list the current systems, either operational or under development. For each, record the following information:

   a. Its name

   b. A short description (one or two sentences)

   c. Its status (operational or planned)

   In some cases, major areas of concern may not be supported by automated systems. If so, document their status as manual systems.

   The resulting list of current systems is called the Current Systems Inventory, an example of which appears in Figure 6-1.

2. Identify and list the current data stores either in use or under development. For each, record the following information:

SYSTEM	DESCRIPTION	STATUS
Personnel	Tracks Employee and subcontractor History.	Operational
Shipping	Tracks picking, packing and delivery of products at each warehouse location.	Operational
Engineering Information System	Maintenance of product bills-of-materials. Includes tracking of product specs and engineering revisions.	Operational
G/L	Tracks activity against the General Ledger using the corporate chart of accounts.	Operational
Marketing Information System	Provides results of market research and customer profiles including sales history. Also used by salesmen to track customer needs.	Planned
Finished Goods Inventory	Maintains finished goods inventory at each warehouse location. Supports cycle inventory.	Operational

Figure 6-1. Current Systems Inventory

a. Its name

b. A short description (one or two sentences)

c. Its status (in use or planned)

As with current systems, major areas of concern may be supported by non-computerized data stores (such as paper records or microfiche). If so, document their status as manual data stores.

The resulting list of current data stores is called the Current Data Stores Inventory. It is similar to the Current Systems Inventory that appears in Figure 6-1.

3. Record the names of all current systems along the vertical axis of the Current System/Data Store Matrix in the IEF Planning Toolset. Each current system may also be given a description and an indication of its status (currently operational, or planned).

4. Record the names of all current data stores along the horizontal axis of the Current System/Data Store Matrix in the IEF Planning Toolset. Each current data store may also be given a description.

5. Relate each current system to the current data stores with which it is involved using the Current System/Data Store Matrix. This matrix, whose purpose is to verify the inventory of current systems and current data stores, supports the CRUD involvement indicator introduced in Chapter 2.

An example of a Current System/Data Store Matrix appears in Figure 6-2.

Key: (Enter highest classification only)
C = Create
D = Delete
U = Update
R = Read only

CURRENT SYSTEMS	CUSTOMER_MASTER	CUSTOMER_ORDER	PRODUCT_MASTER	PRODUCT_STRUCTURE	STORES	SHOP_ORDER	PROCESS_ROUTINGS	INTRANSIT	CARRIER_ROUTINGS	VENDOR_MASTER	OPEN_COMMITMENTS	PERSONNEL	PAYROLL	GENERAL_LEDGER	CAPITAL_EQUIPMENT	COST_MANAGEMENT	FACILITIES	EDUCATION_DATA_BASE	CONTRACTS	OPERATING_TRANSFER_PRI	MASTER_PRODUCTION_SCH	MASTER_PARTS_FILE	PARTS_STANDARDS	DRAWING_CONTROL_DATAB	NC_PROGRAM_MASTER	PCB_LAYOUT_MASTER	PARAMETRIC_NOMENCLATU	LITIGATION_ARCHIVE
LABORATORY_MGT_SYS														R								R	R		U			
PRODUCT_ENGINEERING_SY			c	c		U									U	U						U	c	c	c		c	
MARKETING	c	U	R		R														c		R		R					
SALES_AND_BILLINGS	U	c	R		U	R		R	R										U	R	R							
MATL_RQT_PLANNING_SYS		R	R	R	R	U	R			U						U						c	R	R			R	
CAPACITY_RQTS_PLANNING		R	R	R	c	c										U									c	R		
PURCHASING_RECEIVING		R	R	R	U	U		U	R	c	c					U			R			c	c	R			U	
STORES_CONTROL					c	R		R								U												
TRAFFIC_MANAGEMENT	R							c	c	R																		
PERSONNEL_RECORDS												c	R	U		U		c										
PAYROLL												U	c	U		U												
GENERAL_LEDGER		R			R	R		R					R	R	c	R	R	R			R							
SHOP_FLOOR_CONTROL			R	R	U	U	U	U		R					R	U						R	R	R	R	U	R	R
COST_MANAGEMENT		R			R	R		R					R	R		c												
LEGAL	R	R						R											c									c
FACILITIES															U	U	U	c										

Figure 6-2. Current System/Data Store Matrix

6. Analyze the results. In particular, be alert for data stores not involved in any systems (indicated by any column with no involvement indicators) and systems that do not use any data stores (indicated by any row with no involvement indicators). Further, ensure that each data store has its components created by at least one current system. Anomalies may point out deficiencies in the current systems and current data stores inventories.

    For example, when a system appears to interact with no data stores, this may actually reveal a data store missed by the planners. On the other hand, it may simply reveal that an involvement indicator was overlooked when preparing the matrix. In either case, planners must resolve any discrepancies before using the information in this matrix.

Deliverables

The deliverables from this subtask are as follows:

*   Current Systems Inventory List
*   Current Data Stores Inventory List
*   Current System/Data Store Matrix

DETERMINE INFORMATION ARCHITECTURE COVERAGE

During this subtask, planners use matrix analysis to determine how well existing systems and data stores support the ideal Information Architecture. The techniques employed here also serve to further verify the correctness of the Information Architecture.

Classes of Information

This subtask deals with information in the following classes:

*   Business Function
*   Entity Type
*   Current System
*   Current Data Store

Inputs

Planners should previously have captured the following inputs to this subtask in the IEF Planning Toolset while defining the Information Architecture (see Chapter 5):

*   Business Functions
*   Entity Types

Planners should have recorded the following inputs in the IEF Planning Toolset as part of the previous subtask:

*   Current Systems
*   Current Data Stores

Additional inputs include:

*   Supporting documentation, including:
    — Function Hierarchy Diagram

— Function Dependency Diagrams

— Entity Relationship Diagram

— Current System/Data Stores Inventory Lists

— Matrices

Steps

The steps required for this subtask are as follows:

1. Relate the business functions to the current systems that support them using the Business Function/Current System Matrix in the IEF Planning Toolset. The horizontal axis of this matrix is pre-populated with the names of previously specified current systems. The vertical axis is pre-populated with the names of previously specified business functions.

    Place a simple involvement indicator (as described in Chapter 2) in each cell that represents business function support by a current system. The planners may choose to use different values for involvement indicators to reflect different strengths of involvement. (For example, 3 = function supported well, 2 = function supported moderately, 1 = function supported poorly.) This yields a more meaningful matrix, but requires a greater depth of analysis on the part of the project team. Base the decision on which value to use on the emphasis accorded this subtask in the Project Plan.

    An example of a Business Function/Current System Matrix that uses a single value ("X") for its involvement indicators appears in Figure 6-3.

BUSINESS FUNCTIONS	LABORATORY_MGT_SYS	PRODUCT_ENGINEERING_S	MARKETING	SALES_AND_BILLINGS	MATL_RQT_PLANNING_SY	CAPACITY_RQTS_PLANNIN	PURCHASING_RECEIVING	STORES_CONTROL	TRAFFIC_MANAGEMENT	PERSONNEL_RECORDS	PAYROLL	GENERAL_LEDGER	SHOP_FLOOR_CONTROL	COST_MANAGEMENT	LEGAL	FACILITIES	REAL_ESTATE	EMPLOYEE_EDUC_SYS	AVIATION_MGT	GOVERNMENT_CONTRACTS	FOOD_SERVICE
BASIC_RESEARCH	X	X																			
PRODUCT_DESIGN		X																			
METHODS_ENGINEERING		X																			
MARKETING			X	X																	
ORDER_PROCESSING				X										X							
PURCHASING						X	X	X	X					X							
RECEIVING							X	X	X					X							
WAREHOUSING								X						X							
SCRAP_DISPOSAL								X						X							
DISTRIBUTION_CENTER_OP								X	X												
PACKING								X													
SHIPPING								X	X												
TRAFFIC_MANAGEMENT									X												
GENERAL_ACCOUNTING				X							X	X		X							
COST_ACCOUNTING				X	X	X	X	X	X		X	X	X	X		X					
LEGAL_SERVICES															X		X			X	

Figure 6-3. Business Function/Current System Matrix

ENTITY TYPES	CUSTOMER_MASTER	CUSTOMER_ORDER	PRODUCT_MASTER	PRODUCT_STRUCTURE	STORES	SHOP_ORDER	PROCESS_ROUTINGS	INTRANSIT	CARRIER_ROUTINGS	VENDOR_MASTER	OPEN_COMMITMENTS	PERSONNEL	PAYROLL	GENERAL_LEDGER	CAPITTAL_EQUIPMENT	COST_MANAGEMENT	FACILITIES	EDUCATION_DATA_BASE	CONTRACTS	OPERATTING_TRANSER_PRI	MASTER_PRODUCTION_SCH	MASTER_PARTS_FILE	PARTS_STANDARDS	DRAWING_CONTROL_DATAB	NC_PROGRAM_MASTER	PCB_LAYOUT_MASTER	PARAMETRIC_NOMENCLATU	LITIGATION_ARCHIVE
SALES_REGION	X																											
CUSTOMER	X																											
CUSTOMER_ORDER		X																										
CUSTOMER_ORDER_ITEM		X																										
ACKNOWLEDGEMENT		X																										
INVOICE														X														
PAYMENT														X														
LEDGER_ENTRY														X														
SUPPLIER										X																		
PURCHASE_ORDER											X																	
PURCHASE_ORDER_ITEM											X																	
TERMS_AND_AGREEMENTS											X																	
BLANKET_ORDER_AGREEMEN											X																	
SUPPLIER_DRAWING																								X				
PURCHASED_PART																							X					
RAW_MATERIAL			X																									

Figure 6-4. Entity Type/Current Data Store Matrix

2.   Relate entity types to the current data stores that support them using the Entity Type/Current Data Store Matrix in the IEF Planning Toolset. The horizontal axis of this matrix is pre-populated with the names of previously specified current data stores. The vertical axis is pre-populated with the names of previously specified entity types.

The techniques described in step 1 for specifying the involvement indicator apply to this step as well.

An example of an Entity Type/Current Data Store Matrix appears in Figure 6-4.

3.   Analyze the results. These matrices, assuming that their cell entries are correct, can indicate the existence of a variety of anomalous conditions. In particular, be alert for rows and columns in which no involvement indicators appear.

On the Business Function/Current System Matrix, an empty column (indicating a current system that supports no business function) probably represents one of the following conditions:

a.   A business function has been left out of the Information Architecture.

b.   The planners do not fully understand what the system does.

An empty row on the matrix (indicating a function not supported by a current system) probably indicates that:

c.   The business function is unsupported in the current information environment.

d.   The planners have not understood how the various systems support the business function.

Of the four alternatives mentioned, only one (c) reflects a true condition in the business. The remainder are simply mistakes of the planners that must be rectified.

Perform the same kind of analysis on the Entity Type/Current Data Store Matrix, addressing the same sorts of anomalous conditions. At the end of this subtask, the only remaining anomalies should be in those areas where a business need identified in the Information Architecture is not addressed by a current system or data store.

If the planners specified different values for the involvement indicator during steps 1 and 2, they can perform a more detailed analysis. This will help determine whether a business function or entity type is supported well, moderately, or poorly by the related current system or data store.

The planners may wish to accompany the matrices with a short statement of evaluation summarizing the problems uncovered.

Deliverables

The deliverables of this subtask are:

- Business Function/Current System Matrix
- Entity Type/Current Data Store Matrix
- Evaluation of Results

COMPLETE THE INFORMATION NEEDS LIST

During the initial assessment, planners created the initial Information Needs List. At this point, planners rate the coverage by current systems in order to determine the requirement weight (see Chapter 2) of each information need. Planners subsequently use this information to rank projects when constructing the Implementation Plan.

Calculation of the requirement weight requires two components: the importance factor (a measure of the relative priority of the information need to the business, determined during the initial assessment) and the satisfaction rating (a measure of how well the information need is fulfilled in the current environment). This subtask deals with the recording of the satisfaction rating.

Classes of Information

Planners evaluate the following classes of information during this subtask:

- Information Need
- Current System

Inputs

The inputs to this subtask are:

- Information Needs List
- Current System Inventory

Steps

1. Determine the satisfaction rating for each information need on the Information Needs List. As described in Chapter 2, the value of the satisfaction rating is a whole number between zero and three, as follows:

   0 = Information need is fully supported in the current environment

   1 = Information need is moderately supported in the current environment

2 = Information need is poorly supported in the current environment

3 = Information need is completely unsupported in the current environment

While making this assessment, record the name of the current system that presently satisfies the need (if the satisfaction rating is 0, 1 or 2).

2. Calculate the requirement weight by multiplying the importance factor by the newly determined satisfaction rating. Since importance factors are integers between one and five and satisfaction rating is an integer between zero and three, the range of values for the requirement weight is between zero and 15. The higher the value, the higher the combined priority and lack of satisfaction. A value of 15 represents an extremely important information need that is completely unsupported in the current environment.

3. Record the requirement weight on the Information Needs List.

Deliverables

The single deliverable from this subtask is the updated Information Needs List.

ASSESS THE INFORMATION SYSTEMS ORGANIZATION

Information is a valuable corporate resource. This subtask is concerned with determining whether the current Information Systems organization is suited to properly administer that resource. Planners should make no explicit attempt to judge the effectiveness of Information Systems management or the performance of project teams. Rather, they should focus on determining whether the Information Systems organization is properly positioned to implement the new order imposed by the Information Architecture.

Classes of Information

Planners consider the following classes of information during this assessment:

*   Business Function
*   Organization Structure
*   Organizational Unit
*   Organizational Role

Inputs

The following inputs are required for this subtask:

*   Organization Hierarchy Diagram
*   Function Hierarchy Diagram
*   Written documentation that describes the Information Systems organization and responsibilities

Steps

The steps required for this subtask are as follows:

1. Identify Information Systems organizational units and business functions. At this point, the planners may require additional detail concerning the Information Systems organization to carry out their assessment. If so, they should extend the Organization Hierarchy Diagram and the Function Hierarchy Diagram as appropriate (at most, one or two levels) in the areas that directly affect Information Systems.

2. Prepare an RAEW matrix for the Information Systems organization. This technique is used to depict the type of involvement each organizational unit has with each specific business function.

    On this matrix, the business functions specific to Information Systems are listed along the vertical axis, and Information Systems organizational units are listed along the horizontal axis. Each cell is divided into four components, each of which can contain one of the following values:

    R - Responsibility. The organizational unit is held accountable for carrying out the business function.

    A - Authority. The organizational unit has the power to carry out the business function.

    E - Expertise. The organizational unit provides the knowledge and experience required to carry out the business function.

    W - Work. The organizational unit actually performs the business function.

    This analysis may highlight some anomalies in the organization. For example, an organizational unit with either authority or responsibility for a business function but not both should be examined closely, as should an organizational unit that does the work but has no expertise. A sample RAEW matrix appears in Figure 6-5.

3. Consider the possibility of new roles required within the Information Systems organization to accommodate business needs. Examples of such roles include, but are not limited to:

    a. **Information Management**, the planning and coordination of the information environment as a whole.

    b. **Data Administration**, the caretakers of the organization's data resources.

    c. **Development Support**, which provides methodology and tools support for system developers.

    d. **Information Center**, providing support to those who wish to access information over end-user oriented query facilities.

    e. **Communications Management**, controlling the integrated communications environment.

    The Information Architecture defined in Chapter 5 is likely to require a high level of integration. If organizational roles like the ones listed here are not represented in the current organization structure, they should be added to implement it properly.

4. Define an organizational structure that includes the newly defined roles but remains in step with the enterprise's policies and directions. For each new or changed organizational unit, define its responsibilities.

5. Prepare a target RAEW matrix that shows the involvement of the newly defined organization structure in the various Information Systems functions.

    A sample target RAEW matrix appears in Figure 6-6.

Deliverables

The deliverables of this subtask are:

*   Current Information Systems Organization RAEW Matrix

*   Proposed Information Systems Organization Roles

*   Proposed Information Systems Organization Structure

*   Proposed Information Systems RAEW Matrix

LEGEND		ORGANIZATION UNIT								
R = Responsibility / E = Expertise	A = Authority / W = Work	BOARD OF DIR.	VP I.S.	IS DEPT HQ.	IS PRODUCTION	IS MARKTG	INTERNAL CONSUL. GROUP	MAINTENANCE GROUP	NETWORK GROUP	OPERATIONS
PLANNING LONG TERM		R A	R							
			E W	E W	E W	E W				
TACTICAL PLANNING				R A	R	R				
				E W	E W	E W				
SYSTEMS DEVELOPMENT					R A			E W		
					E W					
DEVELOPMENT COORDINATION					R A					
					E W					
SYSTEMS PACKAGIING						R A				
						E			E W	
MARKETING SALES				R		R A				
						E W				
NETWORK MANAGEMENT									R A	
									E W	
DOCUMENT/OFFICE MANAGEMENT				A	R					
					W	W		W	E	
USER TRAINING						R	R A			
						E W	E W			
USER SUPPORT							R A			
						E W	E W			
OPERATIONS/ NETWORK									R A	R A
									E W	E W
DISTRIBUTION SUPPORT				R A						
				E W	E W					
FACILITIES MANAGEMENT		A	R	R						
				E W						

Figure 6-5. Initial RAEW Matrix for Information Systems

ANALYZE THE CURRENT TECHNICAL ENVIRONMENT

The final aspect of the current environment for study is the technical environment. In this subtask, planners examine and assess the current hardware and software infrastructure.

Classes of Information

This subtask deals with the following classes of information:

- Hardware Unit
- Software Product

FUNCTION	BOARD OF DIR.		VP I.S.		IS DEPT HQ.		IS PRODUCTION		IS MARKTG		INTERNAL CONSUL. GROUP		MAINTENANCE GROUP		NETWORK GROUP		OPERATIONS	
PLANNING LONG TERM		A	R	A														
			E	W	E	W												
TACTICAL PLANNING				A	R													
					E	W												
SYSTEMS DEVELOPMENT						A	R							E	W			
							E	W										
DEVELOPMENT COORDINATION					R	A												
							E	W										
SYSTEMS PACKAGIING						A									R			
									E						E	W		
MARKETING SALES						A	R											
							E	W	E	W								
NETWORK MANAGEMENT															R	A		
															E	W		
DOCUMENT/OFFICE MANAGEMENT						A	R											
								W		W				W	E			
USER TRAINING											R	A						
							E	W	E	W	E	W						
USER SUPPORT											R	A						
							E	W	E	W	E	W			E	W		
OPERATIONS/ NETWORK													R	A	R	A		
													E	W	E	W		
DISTRIBUTION SUPPORT						R	A											
							E	W										
FACILITIES MANAGEMENT		A	R														
					E	W												

Figure 6-6. Target RAEW Matrix for Information Systems

Inputs

The inputs to this subtask are:

- Written documentation describing computer hardware and software products used within the enterprise
- Written documentation describing business policies that may affect the technical environment

Steps

The steps required for this subtask are as follows:

1. Compile an inventory of the hardware items and software products used within the enterprise. The following list of technical categories can provide a convenient way to organize this inventory:

   a. Processing facilities (such as computers, peripherals, operating systems, and support software)

b.   Workstations and terminals

c.   Communications facilities (such as teleprocessing monitors like CICS or IMS/DC, network protocols, concentrators, and modems)

d.   Data Base Management software (such as data base management systems and data dictionaries)

e.   System Development facilities (such as CASE tools, compilers, debuggers, and code animators)

f.   Office Support software (such as word processing facilities and electronic mail)

g.   Decision Support software (such as spreadsheets and statistical software)

h.   External resources (such as time sharing services, service bureaus, and facilities management)

Record the following information for each type of hardware or software inventoried:

a.   Its name

b.   Its location (or locations)

c.   For each location, the quantity used by the enterprise

d.   The date of acquisition

e.   Whether it is owned or rented

f.   Comments about performance and usage

Planners can assemble this information into a Technical Inventory List. An example appears in Figure 6-7.

PRODUCT	LOCATION	QUANTITY	STATUS	ACQ. DATE	COMMENTS
Processing: IBM 3083	Los Angeles	2	Rented	1984	Slow throughput
	San Diego	1	Rented	1985	
IBM 4341	Los Angeles	1	Owned	1987	Development only No excess capacity
IBM S/38	New York	1	Rented	1984	
Workstations: IBM 3270	Los Angeles	200	Owned	1979- 1985	
	San Diego	30	Owned	"	
	New York	2	Owned	1987	Electronic mail
	Washington	1	Owned	1987	"
	Minneapolis	2	Owned	1987	"
IBM PC	Los Angeles	50	Rented	1986	Mostly LOTUS; some DB applications
IBM PC	San Diego	15	Owned	1987	Word Processing
DBMS: DL/1	All MF sites	4	Rented	1978	Phasing out.
DB2	San Diego	1	Rented	1987	
dBASE III	Los Angeles	10	Owned	1986	

Figure 6-7. Sample Technical Inventory List

In organizations with a highly decentralized or distributed technical environment, matrices can sometimes be used to effectively present some components of this inventory. Examples might include:

a. A matrix that maps hardware items to the organizations that use them. (This matrix can easily be supported as an IEF user defined matrix.)

b. A terminal distribution matrix that maps various types of terminals and workstations to the locations in which they are used. In this matrix, the cell entries can contain the number of terminals of the given type at each location.

c. A technical category distribution matrix. Each cell contains the items in each category used at each location.

2. Identify non-technical constraints on the technical environment. These cover all internal and external influences. For example:

a. Government contract requires specific class of operating system

b. Corporation does not want to fund plumbing for computer coolant

c. No increases in personnel allowed for the current fiscal year

Simply note these on a Statement of Non-Technical Constraint. Planners will use this document later to influence the forecast of the required technical environment (see Chapter 8).

3. Assess the organization's technical position. The primary focus in this step is to measure the maturity of the technical environment with two yardsticks:

a. The first yardstick is the current state of the art in general. The use of this yardstick depends largely on the technical breadth and experience of the project team. In each of the categories mentioned above, the team must determine whether the organization is making the best use of the currently available technology.

Clearly, this assessment relies a great deal on the judgement of the planners.

b. The second yardstick is the use of technology in the organization's principal field of endeavor. In a corporate environment, for example, the planners will attempt to measure the organization's use of technology with that of other organizations in the same industry.

Data about a competitor's technical environment is not often easy to obtain, rendering such comparisons difficult. However, if any such information is available, it helps gauge the effectiveness of the organization's use of information technology.

Planners can summarize the results of this analysis in a Technical Environment Assessment document.

Deliverables

The deliverables of this subtask are:

- Technical Inventory List
- Various matrices (optional)
- Statement of Non-Technical Constraint
- Technical Environment Assessment

REVIEW THE ASSESSMENT

The task of assessing the current environment ends with a formal review of the project team's findings by the project sponsor and selected members of the reference team. Because of the technical nature of some of this material, the project team may elect to include members of the Information Systems management organization as well.

This review considers all of the deliverables from this task, with particular attention to areas that most heavily exercise the planners' judgement.

Since the review may reveal additional facts important to a full understanding of the current environment, one member of the project team should act as notetaker to ensure that all facts are recorded.

This review constitutes a project checkpoint as described in Chapter 3.

ADDITIONAL MATRICES USEFUL DURING THIS TASK

The IEF provides some additional matrices beyond those mentioned in the preceding task list which may prove useful to the planner while conducting the current environment assessment. For a complete list, see the *IEF Planning Toolset Guide*.

7
DEFINING THE BUSINESS SYSTEM ARCHITECTURE

OVERVIEW

During this task, planners analyze the Information Architecture to reveal the existence of certain clusters of business functions and entity types referred to as **business areas**. Following the principle of "divide and conquer" advanced in Chapter 1, each of these business areas can be analyzed in detail in a Business Area Analysis project.

In order to identify business areas, planners group business functions and entity types into **natural business systems** and **natural data stores**. These fundamental elements of the Business System Architecture help verify the division of business areas into **business systems** in preparation for the Business System Design stage. Additionally, since senior management tends to be interested in the *systems* that will result from the implementation of the Information Strategy Plan, this early prediction of business systems plays an important role in gaining acceptance of the ISP as a whole.

After defining business areas, planners use the results of both the initial assessment and the assessment of the current environment to help prioritize the projects required to support them. The resulting prioritized list of potential Business Area Analysis projects is called the Implementation Plan.

This task is composed of the following subtasks:

1. Identify and record natural data stores
2. Identify and record natural business systems
3. Build the Business System Architecture diagram
4. Record and validate business areas
5. Record impact of business functions on performance measures
6. Rank Business Areas Analysis projects

The discussion of each of these subtasks relies on the same structure as in preceding chapters:

- Description of the subtask
- Classes of information involved (based on the classes identified in Chapter 2)
- Inputs to the subtask
- Steps required to execute the subtask (including the use of automated tools, if any)
- Deliverables from the subtask

IDENTIFY AND RECORD NATURAL DATA STORES

Previous tasks frequently used the term **current data store** to identify existing repositories of data. During this task, planners analyze the newly defined Information Architecture to discover **natural data stores**, hypothetical repositories of data that are geared to support the Information Architecture.

Classes of Information

Planners use information in these classes to synthesize natural data stores:

- Business Function
- Entity Type

Inputs

The single input to this subtask is the Entity Type/Business Function Matrix.

Steps

The steps required for this subtask are as follows:

1. Identify groupings of business functions and entity types based on their involvement with one another. Previously a time-consuming manual task, the automated clustering facilities of the IEF Planning Toolset have rendered this task nearly trivial.

   Using the Entity Type/Business Function Matrix in the IEF Planning Toolset, invoke the clustering function to reveal the naturally occurring groupings of functions and entity types. An example of this matrix after clustering appears in Figure 7-1. The IEF has automatically rearranged the horizontal and vertical axes to place groupings of entity types near groupings of business functions that use them.

Key: (Enter Highest classification only)
C = Create
D = Delete
U = Update
R = Read only

BUSINESS FUNCTIONS

ENTITY TYPES	PURCHASING	RECEIVING	SCRAP_DISPOSAL	WAREHOUSING	DISTRIBUTION_CENTER_O	SHIPPING	PACKING	TRAFFIC_MANAGEMENT	MARKETING	ORDER_PROCESSING	GOVERNMENT_CONTRACTS	GENERAL_ACCOUNTING	COST_ACCOUNTING	RELEASE_PLANNING	FINITE_CAPACITY_SCHEDU	FACTORY_MONITORING_AN	MASTER_PRODUCTION_SCH	MATERIAL_REQUIREMENTS	METHODS_ENGINEERING	PRODUCT_DESIGN	BASIC_RESEARCH	FACILITIES_MAINTENANC	EMPLOYEE_TRAINING	PAYROLL_AND_BENEFITS	FOOD_SERVICE	REAL_ESTATE_OPERATIONS	SECURITY	AVIATION_SERVICES
PURCHASE_ORDER	C	U	R	R	C	U	U	U	U	U	C	R	R	R	R	R	U	R	C									
PURCHASE_ORDER_ITEM	C	U	R	R	U	U	U	U	U	U	U	R	R	R	R			R										
SUPPLIER	C	U	R	R	U	R	R	U	U	U	U	R	R														R	R
SUPPLIER_SALES_ORDER	C	U	R	R	R	R	R	R	R	R	R	R	R	R													R	R
SUPPLIER_SALES_ORDER_I	C	U	R	R	R	R	R	R	R	R	R	R	R	R													R	R
LEDGER_ENTRY	U	U	U	U								R	R			U												
PURCHASED_PART	C	R	U	R									R			R	R	R	R									
RAW_MATERIAL	C	R	U	R									R			R	R	R	R									
SHOP_SUPPLY	C	R	U	R									R			R	R	R	R				R					
CHEMICAL	U	R	U	R						U						R	R	R	R			C	R					
BLANKET_ORDER_AGREEMEN	U	U	R	R																								
STOCK_REQUISITION	R	R	R	C										R	C		R						R					
BIN	R	R	R	C	U	U	U	R						U	R		R						R					
WAREHOUSE	R	R	R	C	U	U	U	R						U			R	R					R					
CUSTOMER					C	C	C	R	R	R	C	C	R	R					R	U								
CUSTOMER_ORDER_ITEM					U	U	U	R	R	R	R	C	U	R	R				R	R								

Figure 7-1. Business Function/Entity Type Usage Matrix after Clustering

As with any automated analysis technique, the result of automatic clustering may not agree with the planners's intended groupings. In this case, the planners may refine the automatically clustered matrix by moving rows or columns as they see fit.

2. Identify entity type clusters by inspecting the Entity Type/Entity Type Affinity Matrix in the IEF Planning Toolset. This matrix maps entity types to entity types based on their common usage by the business functions that reference them. An example of the Entity Type/Entity Type Affinity Matrix appears in Figure 7-2.

   The IEF automatically generates the values of the involvement indicators on this matrix when the Business Function/Entity Type Usage Matrix is clustered. A "9" in a cell indicates a high degree of similarity between the sets of business functions that refer to the entity types represented in both its column and row, using the same priority CRUD involvement indicator (see Chapter 2) in each case. A blank cell indicates that the two entity types are referenced by few or no common business functions. All other values represent a degree of affinity between none (blank) and total (9).

3. Identify natural data stores. During this step, planners analyze the results of the previous steps and define boundaries for the entity type groupings that constitute natural data stores. As a general guideline, planners should set these boundaries so as to identify from 20 to 40 natural data stores.

   The technique employed in this step is to determine the affinity boundaries based on the Entity Type/Entity Type Affinity Matrix. Planners then use their own judgement in rounding out the clusters.

   An **affinity boundary** is a cut-off point for the affinity values calculated in step 2. It specifies the smallest involvement indicator value to be considered when identifying natural data stores. For example, in Figure 7-2, the planner might choose an affinity boundary of "7." In this case, only entity types with affinity

ENTITY TYPES	PURCHASE_ORDER	PURCHASE_ORDER_ITEM	SUPPLIER	SUPPLIER_SALES_ORDER	SUPPLIER_SALES_ORDER_I	LEDGER_ENTRY	PURCHASED_PART	RAW_MATERIAL	SHOP_SUPPLY	CHEMICAL	BLANKET_ORDER_AGREEME	STOCK_REQUISITION	BIN	WAREHOUSE	CUSTOMER	CUSTOMER_ORDER_ITEM	INVOICE	TERMS_AND_AGREEMENTS	CUSTOMER_ORDER	ACKNOWLEDGEMENT	SALES_REGION	FINISHED_GOODS	FABRICATED_PART	PACKING_MATERIAL	PACKING_LIST	FACTORY	WAYBILL	SUPPLIER_DRAWING
PURCHASE_ORDER	9	9	8	8	8	5	5	5	4	4	3	1																
PURCHASE_ORDER_ITEM	9	9	9	8	8	5	6	6	5	4	1	4	2															
SUPPLIER	8	9	9	9	7	2																						
SUPPLIER_SALES_ORDER	8	8	9	9	9	3																						
SUPPLIER_SALES_ORDER_I	8	8	7	9	9	6																						
LEDGER_ENTRY	5	5	2	3	6	9	6	5	4	4		3					4											
PURCHASED_PART	5	6				6	9	9	8	7		4	2										4					5
RAW_MATERIAL	5	6				5	9	9	9	7		3	2										3					
SHOP_SUPPLY	4	5				4	8	9	9	7		2	1										1					
CHEMICAL	4	4				4	7	7	7	9	3	2	1										1					
BLANKET_ORDER_AGREEMEN	3	1								3	9	2																
STOCK_REQUISITION	1	4				3	4	3	2	2	2	9	9	7			2						2	2				
BIN		2						2	2	1	1	9	9	9									2	2	1			
WAREHOUSE												7	9	9	6								4	1	2			
CUSTOMER														6	9	9	8	7	8	5	2	1						
CUSTOMER_ORDER_ITEM														9	9	9	5	8	6	1		1						

Figure 7-2. Entity Type/Entity Type Affinity Matrix

values of "7," "8," or "9" are considered for mutual inclusion in a grouping. Within the Entity Type/Entity Type Affinity Matrix, planners can adjust parameters so that only entity types with involvement indicators within the affinity boundary appear in the matrix. This greatly simplifies the task.

Despite the assistance of automated techniques, this step relies on the judgement of the planners for its final completion. The project team must determine the correct composition of natural data stores, based on their understanding of the business and their intuitive groupings of entity types. Even if the mathematical techniques employed during automatic clustering are accepted unquestioningly, the planners must still use their own judgement to establish cut-off points and to assign non-conforming entity types into clusters. Non-conforming entity types are those that do not have a high enough affinity with any other entity type to be automatically included in a cluster.

4. Record the final groupings of entity types into natural data stores using the Data Cluster/Entity Type Matrix in the IEF Planning Toolset. The horizontal axis of this matrix is pre-populated with the previously defined entity types, ordered in the same way as the Entity Type/Entity Type Affinity Matrix. The vertical axis, labeled "Data Clusters", must then be populated with one entry for each of the groupings of entity types (natural data stores) identified in the previous step. The planners must invent a meaningful name for each of these groupings.

An example of a Data Cluster/Entity Type Matrix appears in Figure 7-3.

DATA CLUSTERS	PURCHASE_ORDER	PURCHASE_ORDER_IITEM	SUPPLIER	SUPPLIER_SALES_ORDER	SUPPLIER_SALES_ORDER_I	LEDGER_ENTRY	PURCHASED_PART	RAW_MATERIAL	SHOP_SUPPLY	CHEMICAL	BLANKET_ORDER_AGREEMENT	STOCK_REQUISITION	BIN	WAREHOUSE	CUSTOMER	CUSTOMER_ORDER_ITEM	INVOICE	TERMS_AND_AGREEMENTS	CUSTOMER_ORDER	ACKNOWLEDGEMENTG	SALES_REGION	FINISHED_GOODS	FABRICATED_PART	PACKING_MATERIAL	PACKING_LIST	FACTORY	WAYBILL	SUPPLIER_DRAWING
OPEN_COMMITMENTS	x	x																										
SUPPLIER			x																									
GENERAL_LEDGER						x																						
PARTS							x	x		x																		
ORDER_AGREEMENTS											x										x							
STORES												x	x	x														
CUSTOMER															x													
SALES_AND_BILLINGS																x	x		x	x								
PRODUCTS																						x	x					
SUPPLIES									x																			
SHIPPING																									x		x	
ACCOUNTS_PAYABLE				x	x													x										
ACCOUNTS_RECEIVABLE																												
SHOP_ORDER																										x		
CAPITAL																												
MFG_CONTROL																												

(Horizontal axis category label: ENTITY TYPES)

Figure 7-3. Data Cluster/Entity Type Matrix

Deliverables

The deliverables from this subtask include:

*   Clustered Business Function/Entity Type Matrix

*   Data Cluster/Entity Type Matrix

The other matrices prepared during this subtask are simply intermediate results that culminate in the creation of the Data Cluster/Entity Type Matrix.

IDENTIFY AND RECORD NATURAL BUSINESS SYSTEMS

This subtask is very similar to the previous one. Here, planners group business functions into natural business systems, in the same way entity types were previously grouped into natural data stores. While the term **current systems** refers to existing business systems, **natural business systems** refer to hypothetical groupings of business functions to address the business needs represented in the Information Architecture.

Classes of Information

Planners use information in these classes to synthesize natural business systems:

*   Business Function

*   Entity Type

Inputs

The single input to this subtask is the Business Function/Entity Type Matrix.

Steps

The steps required for this subtask are as follows:

1. Identify business function clusters using the Business Function/Business Function Affinity Matrix in the IEF Planning Toolset. This matrix maps business functions to business functions based on their usage of common entity types. An example of the Business Function/Business Function Affinity Matrix appears in Figure 7-4.

    The IEF automatically generates the values of the involvement indicators on this matrix when the Business Function/Entity Type Usage Matrix is clustered. A "9" in a cell indicates a high degree of similarity between the sets of entity types referenced by the business functions represented in both its column and row, using the same priority CRUD involvement indicator in each case. A blank cell indicates that the two business functions reference few or no common entity types. All other values represent a degree of affinity between none (blank) and total (9).

2. Identify natural business systems. In this step, planners analyze the results of the previous steps and define boundaries for the business function groupings that constitute natural business systems. As a general guideline, planners should set these boundaries so as to identify from 25 to 50 natural business systems.

    The technique employed in this step is to determine the affinity boundaries based on the Business Function/Business Function Affinity Matrix. Planners then use their own judgement in rounding out the clusters. The same technique used during step 3 of the previous subtask ("Identify and Record Natural Data Stores") is appropriate here. Please refer to that section for a complete discussion of this technique, bearing in mind that "business system" must be substituted for "data store" and "business function" must be substituted for "entity type."

Business Functions	PURCHASING	RECEIVING	SCRAP_DISPOSAL	WAREHOUSING	DISTRIBUTION_CENTER_O	SHIPPING	PACKING	TRAFFIC_MANAGEMENT	MARKETING	ORDER_PROCESSING	GOVERNMENT_CONTRACTS	GENERAL_ACCOUNTING	COST_ACCOUNTING	RELEASE_PLANNING	FINITE_CAPACITY_SCHEDU	FACTORY_MONITORING_AN	MASTER_PRODUCTION_SCH	MATERIAL_REQUIREMENTS	METHODS_ENGINEERING	PRODUCT_DESIGN	BASIC_RESEARCH	FACILITIES_MAINTENANC	EMPLOYEE_TRAINING	PAYROLL_AND_BENEFITS	FOOD_SERVICE	REAL_ESTATE_OPERATION	SECURITY	AVIATION_SERVICES
PURCHASING	9	9	6	8	6	3	3	1			1								1									
RECEIVING	9	9	5	5	4	2	1	2																				
SCRAP_DISPOSAL	6	5	9	7		1							1															
WAREHOUSING	8	5	7	9	9	8	8	3					2			2												
DISTRIBUTION_CENTER_OP	6	4		9	9	8	8	3					1			1												
SHIPPING	3	2		8	8	9	9	6					2			1												
PACKING	3	1	1	8	8	9	9	8																				
TRAFFIC_MANAGEMENT	1	2		3	3	6	8	9	5	2						3												
MARKETING								5	9	9	9	5					7	4										
GOVERNMENT_CONTRACTS_A							2		2	9	9	9	6				2	4										
ORDER_PROCESSING	1								9	9	9	7					1	1										
GENERAL_ACCOUNTING									5	6	7	9	9	5										4		7	2	
COST_ACCOUNTING			1	2	1	1						9	9	4			2	1	3									
RELEASE_PLANNING												5	4	9	9	8	8	8	7									
FINITE_CAPACITY_SCHEDU														9	9	9	7	7	8									
FACTORY_MONITORING_AND				2	1			3					2	9	9	9	9	5	7									

Figure 7-4. Business Function/Business Function Affinity Matrix

3.   Record the final groupings of business functions into natural business systems using the Activity Cluster/Business Function Matrix in the IEF Planning Toolset. The horizontal axis of this matrix is pre-populated with the previously defined business functions, ordered in the same way as the Business Function/Business Function Affinity Matrix. The vertical axis, labeled "Activity Cluster," must then be populated with one entry for each of the groupings of business functions (natural business systems) identified in step 2. The planners must invent a meaningful name for each of these groupings.

Alternatively, the planners may choose to define *actual* business systems at this time. That is, it is possible to specify the business systems that will be used during the Business System Design stage during ISP with the understanding that the list of systems might change as the result of further analysis. In order to specify actual business systems, the planner must specify an IEF user defined matrix plotting Business Functions against Business Systems. The technique of assigning Business System names and cell values is exactly the same as for the Activity Cluster/Business Function Matrix.

The advantage to specifying actual Business Systems at this point is that they need not be re-entered later on at the conclusion of the various Business Area Analysis projects resulting from the ISP. The disadvantage is that when the model is refined after the Business Area Analysis projects, there will be no record in the model of the configuration of systems originally predicted by the planners.

An example of an Activity Cluster/Business Function Matrix appears in Figure 7-5.

ACTIVITY CLUSTERS	PURCHASING	RECEIVING	SCRAP_DISPOSAL	WAREHOUSING	DISTRIBUTION_CENTER_O	SHIPPING	PACKING	TRAFFIC_MANAGEMENT	MARKETING	ORDER_PROCESSING	GOVERNMENT_CONTRACTS	GENERAL_ACCOUNTING	COST_ACCOUNTING	RELEASE_PLANNING	FINITE_CAPACITY_SCHEDU	FACTORY_MONITORING_AN	MASTER_PRODUCTION_SCH	MATERIAL_REQUIREMENTS	METHODS_ENGINEERING	PRODUCT_DESIGN	BASIC_RESEARCH	FACILITIES_MAINTENANC	EMPLOYEE_TRAINING	PAYROLL_AND_BENEFITS	FOOD_SERVICE	REAL_ESTATE_OPERATION	SECURITY	AVIATION_SERVICES
PROCUREMENT	X	X																										
STORES			X	X	X																							
SHIPPING						X	X																					
TRAFFIC MANAGEMENT								X																				
MARKETING									X	X																		
CONTRACT_ADMINISTRATIO											X																	
GENERAL_ACCOUNTING												X																
COST_ACCOUNTING													X															
MANUFACTURING_PLANNING														X	X	X												
MATERIALS_PLANNING																	X	X										
METHODS_MANAGEMENT																			X									
ENGINEERING																				X	X							
FACILITIES																						X				X		
PERSONNEL_RECORDS																							X					
PAYROLL																								X				
PLANT_SECURITY_MANAGEM																											X	

Figure 7-5. Activity Cluster/Business Function Matrix

Deliverables

The single deliverable from this subtask is either the Activity Cluster/Business Function Matrix or the Business System/Business Function Matrix. The other matrices prepared during this subtask are simply intermediate results that culminate in the creation of this deliverable.

BUILD THE BUSINESS SYSTEM ARCHITECTURE DIAGRAM

During this task, planners categorize business systems based on their anticipated processing characteristics, identify probable information flows between systems, and record the results on a Business System Architecture diagram, a manually prepared graphical representation of planned system coverage.

Classes of Information

Planners consider the following classes during this subtask:

- Business Function
- Entity Type

Inputs

The inputs to this subtask are:

- Business Function/Entity Type Usage Matrix
- Activity Cluster/Business Function Matrix or Business System/Business Function Matrix

Steps

The steps required for this subtask are as follows:

1. Categorize each predicted business systems (whether they were recorded as "natural" or "actual" business systems during the previous subtask) into one or more of the following categories (originally defined in Chapter 2):

   a. STRATEGIC

   Strategic systems tend to be very flexible. The processing characteristics are highly unpredictable and typically support "what-if" analysis.

   The popular terms "Decision Support System" and "Executive Information System" can usually be applied both to Strategic systems and Planning systems.

   b. PLANNING

   Planning systems tend to be flexible within an established framework. Generally, there is a good deal of statistical analysis done with this type of system with heavy concentration on "what if" analysis.

   c. CONTROLLING

   Controlling systems are those used to monitor and manage operational systems. They feature routine analysis and reporting.

   d. OPERATIONAL

   Operational systems are the high volume, time-critical systems used in the day-to-day operation of the business. They tend to include pre-defined online transactions and standard batch reports and are primarily dealt with by clerical users.

   One convenient way to record this categorization is to build a user defined matrix mapping each system to the categories to which it belongs, as in Figure 7-6. In this figure, Activity Clusters represent natural business systems with the names S1 through S15.

2. Identify likely information flows between systems. For example, given an "Order Entry System" and a "Billing System," it is likely that the orders recorded in the order entry system will become the basis for invoices prepared by the billing system. Since the billing system uses information created using the order entry system, it is convenient to imagine the information "flowing" from one system to the next.

   The identification of information flows is not an exact science; the existence of one merely indicates that it is likely that information used by one system will be used in another. However, when the Business System Architecture diagram is presented to management the presence of these flows will help them to grasp the interfaces between predicted systems.

   The Business Function/Entity Type Usage Matrix is a good place to begin to identify possible flows. Any two systems that include functions that reference entities of the same type have the potential for a flow. The planner must decide whether a flow exists and, if one does, in which direction the information flows.

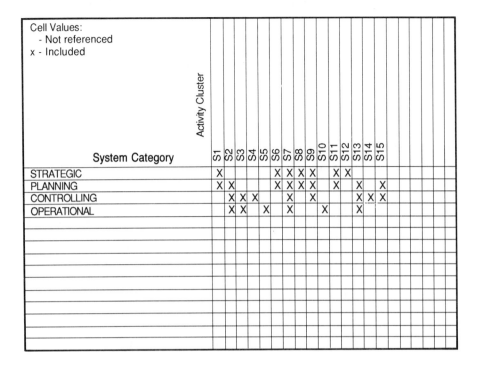

Cell Values:
 - Not referenced
 x - Included

System Category	Activity Cluster	S1	S2	S3	S4	S5	S6	S7	S8	S9	S10	S11	S12	S13	S14	S15
STRATEGIC		X					X	X	X	X		X	X			
PLANNING		X	X				X	X	X	X		X		X		X
CONTROLLING			X	X	X		X		X				X	X	X	
OPERATIONAL			X	X		X	X			X			X			

Figure 7-6. Mapping Systems to System Categories

One way the information flows can initially be recorded is by building an IEF user defined matrix which has the probable business systems (either Business Systems or Activity Clusters) plotted along both axes. The systems along the horizontal axis represent **providers** of information, and the systems along the vertical axis represent **receivers** of information. An "X" in a cell value indicates the system in the column provides information to the system in the associated row. For example, in Figure 7-7, system S1 is shown to provide information to systems S2 and S7.

3.   Draw the Business System Architecture diagram.

The Business System Architecture diagram is something like a graphical matrix. Highest level functions are placed along one axis and system categories are placed along the other.

After the axes are established, systems are represented as variably shaped objects that "stretch" as needed to encompass each of the functions they are to implement and each of the categories to which they belong. For example, in Figure 7-8, system S1 implements elements of business functions F1 and F2. (For this example, assume the categorizations in Figure 7-6 and the flows in Figure 7-7, and the Activity Cluster/Business Function Matrix in Figure 7-5.)   For F2, S1 acts as a strategic system, while for F1 it acts both as a strategic and a planning system. System S2 provides planning, controlling and operational support for function F1.

Cell Values:
- Not referenced
x - Included

Activity Cluster	S1	S2	S3	S4	S5	S6	S7	S8	S9	S10	S11	S12	S13	S14	S15
S1		X		X											
S2	X		X	X											
S3					X										
S4															
S5			X	X											
S6				X											
S7	X														
S8									X						
S9								X							
S10							X		X			X			
S11									X						
S12									X						
S13											X	X		X	
S14															
S15											X				

Figure 7-7. Mapping Information Flows Between Systems

Clearly, the functions have to be specified in the sequence most conducive to the creation of a single box per system. For example, if functions F2 and F3 had not appeared next to each other on the horizontal axis, it would have been impossible to draw system S4 as a contiguous shape. It is conceivable that in some situations the drawing of a single box to represent a system might be impossible (a system that is strategic and operational, but neither planning nor controlling, perhaps), but in practice such a thing rarely happens.

After the boxes have been laid out, the potential information flows identified in step 2 are drawn as directed lines between the systems involved. In Figure 7-8, system S4 provides information to systems S1, S2, S5 and S6. As the bidirectional arrow connecting systems S1 and S2 illustrate, it is possible for two systems to both provide information to and receive information from each other.

4.   Finally, any anomalies in the Business System Architecture diagram should either be corrected or explained.

The following conditions do not necessarily constitute an error, but are unusual conditions that should at least be regarded with suspicion:

a.   Business functions that are lacking systems coverage in one or more categories. It is unusual to discover a high level business function for which strategic, planning, controlling and operational systems are not desirable, especially over the planning horizon served by an Information Strategy Plan. In Figure 7-8, function F2 lacks planning systems coverage; the planners must either establish a good reason for this condition or add more system coverage.

b.   System boxes that have more than four sides. It is not unusual to find systems that fall into multiple categories (as do systems S2, S3, S6, S7, S8, S9 and S11). Less frequently, one may find systems

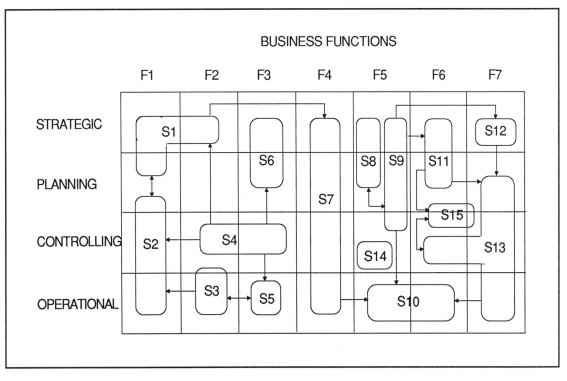

Figure 7-8. Business System Architecture Diagram

that cross function boundaries (as do systems S4 and S10). Still less frequently, a system may be discovered that addresses multiple categories for more than one business function (as does system S15.)

However, all of the systems mentioned above have been drawn as four sided objects of differing dimensions. It is unusual in the extreme to find a system which performs in different categories for multiple functions, thus leading to non-rectangular shapes. Systems S1 and S13, then, deserve closer inspection before the Business System Architecture is declared complete.

c. Systems which have no flows. In an integrated environment where systems exist to further the goals and objectives of the organization, it is indeed unusual to find a system which has no interaction with data used by other systems. Thus, system S14 should be examined more closely to ensure that it does not really have any information flows.

RECORD AND VALIDATE BUSINESS AREAS

During this task, planners synthesize business areas from the results of the preceding subtasks and verify them. Each business area represents a collection of functions and entity types to be analyzed during a single Business Area Analysis project. Thus, the boundary is likely to be larger than that of the natural business systems and data stores previously defined.

The business areas identified here are based on the natural business systems and natural data stores they encompass.

Classes of Information

Planners consider information in the following classes during this subtask:

- Business Function
- Entity Type

Inputs

The inputs to this subtask are:

- Data Cluster/Entity Type Matrix
- Activity Cluster/Business Function Matrix or Business System/Business Function Matrix
- Entity Type/Business Function Matrix

Steps

The steps required for this subtask are as follows:

1. From the input matrices, develop a list of business areas that includes all natural business systems and natural data stores. Generally speaking, planners should identify between 8 and 15 business areas.

    It is not unusual for some business areas to consist of few business functions referencing many entity types, while others consist of many business functions referencing few entity types. Business areas in the first category tend to reflect the information infrastructure of the business: the set of corporate data bases and their maintenance activities. Those in the second category usually represent groupings of user-oriented information systems.

2. Record the business areas on the Business Area/Activity Cluster Matrix (or the Business Area/Business System Matrix if the "actual" business system option was adopted earlier) in the IEF Planning Toolset. The vertical axis of either matrix is pre-populated with the list of predicted business systems developed in the preceding subtask.

3. Relate the business area to the predicted business systems it includes by placing a simple involvement indicator (as defined in Chapter 2) in each appropriate cell of the matrix. During this activity, each predicted business system must be assigned to one and only one business area.

    An example of a Business Area/Activity Cluster Matrix appears in Figure 7-9.

4. Relate the business area to the natural data stores it includes using the Business Area/Data Cluster Matrix in the IEF Planning Toolset. Again, place a simple involvement indicator in each appropriate cell. At this point, planners should consider the Entity Type/Business Function Matrix and the Data Cluster/Entity Type Matrix to ensure that relationships are reasonable in light of the natural business systems each business area includes.

    The involvement of natural data stores with business areas in this matrix represents *ownership* of the natural data store rather than simple usage. During this step, each natural data store is associated with the business area that has *responsibility* for it. This requires the use of judgement on the planners' part and must result in each natural data store being associated to one and only one business area.

    An example of a Business Area/Data Cluster Matrix appears in Figure 7-10.

BUSINESS AREA	ACTIVITY CLUSTER	PROCUREMENT	STORES	SHIPPING	TRAFFIC MANAGEMENT	MARKETING	CONTRACT_ADMINISTRATIO	GENERAL_ACCOUNTING	COST_ACCOUNTING	MANUFACTURING_PLANNING	MATERIALS_PLANNING	METHODS_MANAGEMENT	ENGINEERING	FACILITIES	PERSONNEL_RECORDS	PAYROLL	PLANT_SECURITY_MANAGEM
PURCHASING		X															
STORES			X														
TRAFFIC _MANAGEMENT				X	X												
MARKETING						X	X										
FINANCIAL								X	X								
MANUFACTURING										X	X						
ENGINEERING												X	X				
HUMAN_RESOURCES															X	X	
FACILITIES														X			X

Figure 7-9. Business Area/Activity Cluster Matrix

5. Relate business areas to the functions they include based on each function's planned implementation by a predicted business system. Given that the planner has specified which predicted business systems will be included in each business area (using either the Business Area/Activity Cluster or the Business Area/Business System matrix), and which functions will be implemented by each predicted business system (using either the Activity Cluster/Business Function or Business System/Business Function matrix), he can easily derive the relationship between each business area and its included functions.

    The inclusion of functions in business areas can be specified either by highlighting clusters of functions in the Business Function/Business Function Affinity Matrix using the "Define Business Area" feature or by relating business areas to business functions with simple involvement indicators using the Business Area/Business Function matrix. The IEF ensures the synchronization of these two matrices so that changes made in one of them are automatically reflected in the other. Details for using either of these techniques are presented in the *IEF Planning Toolset Guide*.

6. Relate business areas to the entity types they include based on each entity type's planned implementation in a predicted data store. Given that the planner has specified which predicted data stores will be included in each business area (using the Business Area/Data Cluster matrix), and which entity types will be implemented by each predicted data store (using the Data Cluster/Entity Type Matrix), he can easily derive the relationship between each business area and its included entity types.

BUSINESS AREA	DATA CLUSTER																		
	GENERAL_LEDGER	SUPPLIER	OPEN_COMMITMENTS	PARTS	STORES	ORDER_AGREEMENTS	CUSTOMER	SALES_AND_BILLINGS	PRODUCTS	SUPPLIES	SHIPPING	ACCOUNTS_PAYABLE	ACCOUNTS_RECEIVABLE	SHOP_ORDER	CAPITAL	MFG_CONTROL	PERSONNEL_RECORDS	PAYROLL	ORGANIZATION
PURCHASING		x	x			x													
STORES					x														
TRAFFIC _MANAGEMENT											x								
MARKETING							x	x											
FINANCIAL	x											x	x						
MANUFACTURING									x					x		x			
ENGINEERING			x				x												
HUMAN_RESOURCES																	x	x	x
FACILITIES															x				

Figure 7-10. Business Area/Data Cluster Matrix

The inclusion of entity types in business areas can be specified either by highlighting clusters of entity types in the Entity Type/Entity Type Affinity Matrix using the "Define Business Area" feature or by relating business areas to entity types with simple involvement indicators using the Business Area/Entity Type Matrix. The IEF ensures the synchronization of these two matrices so that changes made in one of them are automatically reflected in the other. Details for using either of these techniques are presented in the *IEF Planning Toolset Guide*.

Deliverables

The deliverables from this subtask are:

1. Business Area/Activity Cluster Matrix or Business Area/Business System Matrix
2. Business Area/Data Cluster Matrix
3. Business Area/Business Function Matrix
4. Business Area/Entity Type Matrix

RECORD IMPACT ON PERFORMANCE MEASURES

With business area boundaries established and verified, the final subtasks for completing the Implementation Plan involve ranking the business areas. The first criterion measured during this ranking process is the impact of business functions on performance measures (and thus, indirectly, on the objectives they measure).

Classes of Information

This subtask involves associating information in two classes:

- Business Function
- Performance Measure

Inputs

The inputs to this subtask are:

- Written documentation and interview results that reveal relationships between business functions and performance measures
- List of performance measures previously recorded in the IEF Planning Toolset (see Chapter 4)
- List of business functions previously recorded in the IEF Planning Toolset (see Chapter 5)

Steps

The steps required for this subtask are as follows:

1. Review the written documentation and interview results to determine the potential impact on each performance measure of improving support for each identified business function. This measurement is largely subjective.

2. Record the potential impact using the Performance Measure/Business Function Matrix in the IEF Planning Toolset. The vertical axis of this matrix is pre-populated with the previously defined business functions. The horizontal axis is pre-populated with the previously defined performance measures.

   Record the potential impact as a simple involvement indicator (see Chapter 2) whose values are restricted to 1, 2, 3, 4, or blank as follows:

   4 = The function has great impact on the performance measure.

   3 = The function has significant impact on the performance measure.

   2 = The function has moderate impact on the performance measure.

   1 = The function has slight impact on the performance measure.

   Blank = The function has no impact on the performance measure.

Deliverables

The single deliverable from this subtask is the Performance Measure/Business Function Matrix.

RANK BUSINESS AREA ANALYSIS PROJECTS

During this subtask, planners finish ranking the Business Area Analysis projects. The ranking performed during Information Strategy Planning takes place at such a high level that it is often difficult to quantify the benefits of each business area. Thus, a correct ranking relies heavily on the business understanding derived by the project team from written documentation and interviews.

Classes of Information

Planners specifically consider information in the following classes during this subtask:

- Performance Measure

- Information Need

- Business Function

Additionally, information in virtually any of the remaining classes can influence the ranking.

Inputs

The inputs to this subtask are:

- Information Needs List

- Performance Measure/Business Function Matrix

- Business Area/Business Function Matrix

- Business Area/Entity Type Matrix

- Entity Type/Information Needs Matrix

Steps

The steps required for this subtask are as follows:

1. Review the Performance Measure/Business Function Matrix in conjunction with the Business Area/Business Function Matrix to assess which business areas, when implemented, will have the greatest impact on the recorded performance measures.

2. Review the Entity Type/Information Needs Matrix in conjunction with the Business Area/Entity Type Matrix and the Information Needs List to assess which business areas, when implemented, will provide the greatest increase in the satisfaction of information needs (based on their current satisfaction rating as defined in Chapter 2).

3. Hold a ranking session that includes all members of the project team and selected members of the reference team. Combine the information collected in steps 1 and 2 with the business expertise and experience of the participants in this session to produce a ranked list of Business Area Analysis projects.

   The rationale used for assigning different priorities to each of the business areas must accompany the ranked list.

Deliverables

The single deliverable from this subtask is the Ranked List of Business Area Analysis Projects, including a description of the rationale used in the ranking process.

REVIEW THE BUSINESS SYSTEM ARCHITECTURE

Construction of the Business System Architecture formally ends with a review of the project team's findings by the project sponsor, selected members of management (at the sponsor's discretion), and selected members of the reference team, if one exists. During this session, the participants should discuss techniques and results of the definition of business areas, (including the definition of natural business systems and data stores). However, they should put the greatest emphasis on ranking Business Area Analysis projects. A great deal of input on this ranking is likely to come forth during this review, along with additional facts important to the proper formulation of the Business System Architecture and Implementation Plan. One member of the project team should act as notetaker to ensure that all these facts are recorded.

This review constitutes a project checkpoint as described in Chapter 3.

8
DEFINING THE TECHNICAL ARCHITECTURE

OVERVIEW

The purpose of this task is to define the hardware and software environment, or Technical Architecture, required to support the Information and Business System Architectures previously constructed.

This task consists of the following subtasks:

1. Perform business area distribution analysis
2. Analyze performance requirements
3. Analyze technical distribution requirements
4. Define and evaluate architectural options
5. Review results

The discussion of each of these subtasks employs the same structure as in preceding chapters:

- Description of the subtask
- Classes of information involved (based on the classes identified in Chapter 2)
- Inputs to the subtask
- Steps required to execute the subtask (including the use of automated tools, if any)
- Deliverables from the subtask

PERFORM BUSINESS AREA DISTRIBUTION ANALYSIS

During this subtask, the planners analyze each business area to determine characteristics vital to its adequate technical support. In particular, planners assess the level of distribution of the various business functions and entity types required for the business area. This analysis points out local (one site) versus global (multiple site) support requirements for each natural business system and natural data store.

Note that the term **location** used throughout this chapter can refer either to a specific location (the Williamsburg office) or a type of location that occurs frequently in the organization (such as a sales office or warehouse).

Classes of Information

The categories of information dealt with during this analysis do not belong to the primary classes of information but are synthesized from them. For example, business areas, natural business systems, and natural data stores are synthesized categories. Thus, this subtask deals with information in the following classes indirectly:

- Organizational Unit
- Business Function
- Entity Type

Inputs

The inputs to this subtask are as follows:

- Organization Hierarchy Indented List and supportive text (in particular, data about the locations in which each organization operates)

- Business Function/Organizational Unit Matrix

- Activity Cluster/Business Function Matrix or Business System/Business Function Matrix

- Data Cluster/Entity Type Matrix

- Business Area/Activity Cluster Matrix or Business Area/Business System Matrix

- Business Area/Data Cluster Matrix

Steps

The steps required for this subtask are as follows:

1. Determine the requirement for support of each predicted business system by location. In particular:

   a. Identify which organizations appear at which locations. This information can be recorded using the Organizational Unit/Location Matrix in the IEF Planning Toolset.

   b. Identify which functions are used at each location based on the contents of the Business Function/Organizational Unit Matrix.

   c. Determine which predicted business systems are required at each location. Do this by assigning the business system planned to support each function to the locations at which it is used. Planners can use the Activity Cluster/Business Function Matrix to help in this effort.

   Planners must temper the results of this analysis with their knowledge of the organization. For example, just because an organization does business at a specific location does not necessarily mean it performs all the business functions required by the organization at that location.

   Planners may record the results in the Activity Cluster/Location Matrix in the IEF Planning toolset, an example of which appears in Figure 8-1. Alternatively, if the planners earlier decided to record *actual* business systems rather than "natural" ones, they may record the results in a user defined matrix plotting Business Systems against Locations.

2. Determine the requirement for support of each natural data store by location. In particular:

   a. Identify which organizations appear at which locations (this information should be available from step 1a, above).

   b. Identify which entity types are used at each location based on the results of (a) plus the contents of the Business Function/Organizational Unit Matrix combined with the Entity Type/Business Function Matrix.

   c. Determine which natural data stores are accessed at each location. Do this by assigning the natural data store to which each entity type belongs to the locations at which it is used. Planners can derive this information by combining the results of (b) with the Data Cluster/Entity Type Matrix.

   Planners may record the results in a Data Cluster/Location Matrix, an example of which appears in Figure 8-2.

ACTIVITY CLUSTER	LOCATION	SEATTLE	SAN FRANCISCO	LOS ANTGELES	SAN DIEGO	ATLANTA	NEW YORK	LONDON	BRUSSELLS	TAIPEI	TOKYO	MANILA
PROCUREMENT		X		X			X	X		X		
SHIPPING		X	X	X	X	X	X	X	X	X	X	X
STORES		X	X	X	X		X		X			X
TRAFFIC MANAGEMENT			X									
MARKETING			X					X				
CONTRACT ADMINISTRATION			X					X				
GENERAL ACCOUNTING		X	X	X	X	X	X	X	X	X	X	X
COST-ACCOUNTING		X	X		X				X			X
MANUFACTURING PLANNING			X									
MATERIALS PLANNING			X							X		
ENGINEERING			X	X								

Figure 8-1. Activity Cluster/Location Matrix

DATA CLUSTER	LOCATION	SEATTLE	SAN FRANCISCO	LOS ANTGELES	SAN DIEGO	ATLANTA	NEW YORK	LONDON	BRUSSELLS	TAIPEI	TOKYO	MANILA
OPEN COMMITMENTS			X	X				X			X	
SUPPLIER		X		X			X	X		X		
GENERAL LEDGER		X	X	X	X	X	X	X	X	X	X	X
PARTS			X		X			X			X	
ORDER AGREEMENTS		X	X	X	X	X	X	X	X	X	X	X
STORES		X	X	X	X		X		X		X	
CUSTOMER		X	X	X	X	X	X	X	X	X	X	X
SALES AND BILLINGS		X	X	X	X	X	X	X	X	X	X	X
PRODUCTS		X	X	X	X	X	X	X	X	X	X	X
SUPPLIES		X	X	X	X	X	X	X	X	X	X	X

Figure 8-2. Data Cluster/Location Matrix

Deliverables

The deliverables of this subtask are:

- Organizational Unit/Location Matrix

- Activity Cluster/Location Matrix or Business System/Location Matrix

- Data Cluster/Location Matrix

ANALYZE PERFORMANCE REQUIREMENTS

In this subtask, planners estimate the performance requirements for each natural business system. Planners can combine this information with business area distribution information to determine the kind of technical support needed throughout the organization.

Classes of Information

Along with synthesized categories of information like business areas, natural business systems, and natural data stores, this subtask deals with the following classes of information:

- Current System

- Current Data Store

- Business Function

- Entity Type

Inputs

The inputs to this subtask are:

- Assessment of Current Systems

- Technology Inventory

- Business Function/Current System Matrix

- Entity Type/Current Data Store Matrix

- Activity Cluster/Business Function Matrix or Business System/Business Function Matrix

- Written documentation that addresses performance levels (for example, some organizations have published standards for online response times)

Steps

The steps required for this subtask are as follows:

1. For each predicted business system, review applicable information gathered previously in an effort to identify performance criteria. This includes:

   a. The assessment of current systems that at least partially support the natural business system (Chapter 6)

   b. The portion of the initial assessment that describes the potential impact of information technology (Chapter 4)

   c. The analysis of the current technical environment (Chapter 6)

Performance criteria in this step include:

a. Current and projected throughput requirements (average and peak volumes)

b. Availability requirements. For example, must online components be available 24 hours? Is a nightly batch run required? If so, how long is its window?

c. Response requirements. For example, is sub-second response required for online transactions? Is two-hour turnaround acceptable for batch jobs?

d. Security requirements for both business functions and entities

Planners may have difficulty obtaining this detailed information. Members of the Information Systems organization may be able to contribute to this effort by helping to summarize requirements. In any event, the planners must not become embroiled in detail at this point. General statements about performance criteria are acceptable.

2. Synthesize a Statement of Technical Requirement that identifies the performance criteria associated with each business system. This document should make broad statements about performance requirements. For example:

a. Online systems must be available for at least 22 hours per day.

b. Sub-second response time is required for all Order Processing transactions.

Deliverables

The only deliverable from this task is the Statement of Technical Requirement.

ANALYZE TECHNICAL DISTRIBUTION REQUIREMENTS

In this subtask, planners determine the requirements for the technical support of each predicted business system and data store (and, by implication, business area) based on the following:

*   The distribution of business areas over various geographical locations

*   The performance requirements for the natural business systems that make up each business area

Classes of Information

During this subtask, planners consider information in the following classes:

*   Hardware Item

*   Software Product

Inputs

The inputs to this subtask are:

*   Statement of Technical Requirement

*   Activity Cluster/Location Matrix or Business System/Location Matrix

*   Data Cluster/Location Matrix

*   Written documentation, including articles and advertising information from hardware and software vendors

*   Statement of Non-technical Constraint

Steps

The steps required for this subtask are as follows:

1. Assess integration requirements. In this step, planners consider predicted business systems and data stores to determine whether they should be highly integrated (implemented at a central facility), moderately integrated (using some form of distributed processing), or can stand alone (via local processing at a single site or workstation).

    Planners may apply the following criteria to each business system and data store to aid in this assessment:

    a. If supported functions and entity types are only used in one location, the business system/data store can stand alone.

    b. If real-time accuracy of data is required, a high degree of integration is necessary.

    c. If functions and entities are dealt with at many locations, a high degree of integration is also necessary.

    d. If faster response time is necessary than that available through centralized means, moderate integration may be satisfactory.

2. Determine the level of technology required to satisfy the requirements of each business area based on the following:

    a. The distribution of business systems and data stores

    b. The performance requirements of each business system

    c. The level of integration required between this business area and others

    d. The non-technical constraints on the technical environment

    This step requires both technical knowledge and creativity on the part of the project team. Based on very high-level information, the project team must attempt to forecast some very specific technical requirements. This endeavor is often quite difficult.

    Planners can summarize the results of this step on a manually prepared Technical Facility/Location Matrix. On such a matrix, the locations in which the business requires technical facilities appear on one axis, and the categories of hardware unit and software product initially presented in Chapter 6 appear on the other. Each cell is a free-form description of the particular types of technical facilities required at the corresponding locations in as much detail as possible.

Deliverables

The only deliverable from this task is the Technical Facility/Location Matrix.

DEFINE AND EVALUATE ARCHITECTURAL OPTIONS

Planners should define and evaluate at least two and preferably three options for the Technical Architecture. This will give management a yardstick with which to judge the final recommended Technical Architecture.

Classes of Information

Planners develop alternatives based on information in the following classes:

-   Hardware Unit
-   Software Product

Inputs

The inputs to this subtask are:

- Technical Facility/Location Matrix
- Current Technical Inventory
- Written documentation describing hardware units and software products differing from those included in the Technical Facility/Location Matrix

Steps

The steps required for this subtask are as follows:

1. Invent some alternatives. Despite the creation of the Technical Facility/Location Matrix, planners must resist the temptation to build straw men to enhance their initial recommendation. Each alternative must be feasible from the technical, financial, and organizational viewpoints.

   The alternatives should include:

   a. A low profile option, easy to implement (probably making the best use of existing facilities) and easy to control

   b. A high profile option, which yields the highest benefit but at a greater cost

   c. A middle-of-the-road option, in which benefits are maximized while costs are minimized

2. Evaluate the alternatives from the standpoints of:

   a. Relative cost of each alternative

   b. Relative flexibility of each alternative with respect to changes in either the organization or technology

   a. Relative impact on success or failure of business operations

   b. Business opportunities provided

   c. Technical expertise required

   d. Relative risk incurred

   At this high level, there is no need to attempt to estimate actual cost figures. Planners should limit the evaluation of an alternative to a comparison with other alternatives.

3. Document the recommended architecture. As a result of building and evaluating alternatives, the project team may have changed its position on the selection of hardware units and software products required at different locations. In such a case, the planners must update the Technical Facility/Location Matrix to reflect the new recommendation.

   The recommendation may also have some policy implications. Any policies not considered sancrosanct by management (that is, any policies not part of the Statement of Non-technical Constraint) are fair game for modification at this point. Planners can document the modified policies along with those that remain unchanged in a Statement of Technical Direction.

Deliverables

The deliverables of this subtask are:

- Technical Facility/Location Matrix
- Descriptions of Technical Alternatives
- Statement of Technical Direction

REVIEW THE TECHNICAL ARCHITECTURE

The forecasting of technical requirements formally ends with a review of the project team's findings by the project sponsor, members of the Information Systems organization, and selected members of management. The project team members must be prepared to defend their recommendation and prove the viability of all alternatives.

This review may reveal additional facts that have bearing on the technical environment. One member of the project team should act as notetaker to ensure that all facts are recorded.

This review constitutes a project checkpoint as described in Chapter 3.

ADDITIONAL MATRICES USEFUL DURING THIS TASK

The IEF provides some additional matrices beyond those mentioned in the preceding task list which may prove useful to the planner while constructing the technical architecture. For a complete list, see the *IEF Planning Toolset Guide*.

9
COMPLETING THE ISP PROJECT

OVERVIEW

This chapter presents techniques for summarizing the results of the ISP project and presenting them to top management. This is easily the single most important task in the ISP project. No matter how brilliant the assessments and suggestions formulated during the previous tasks, the Information Strategy Plan will have no impact unless it is accepted by the organization's top management. To be accepted, it must first be understood. Either the Information Strategy Plan is adopted as an active and vital part of the corporate culture, or the results of the project become 100-page doorstops. The difference between success and failure rests largely on the production and presentation of the ISP Report.

To complete this task, the project team must perform the following subtasks:

1. Complete the plan
2. Prepare the ISP Report
3. Present the Information Strategy Plan
4. Prepare models for Business Area Analysis

COMPLETE THE PLAN

At this point, the planners bring together some of the previously defined elements to formulate a three- to five-year plan that will bring the organization in line with its newly defined Information Architecture.

In particular, the planners must merge the Implementation Plan developed as part of the Business System Architecture (Chapter 7) and the Technical Architecture (Chapter 8) to present a complete picture of the Information Strategy Plan. Planners calculate task durations and hardware acquisition lead times, estimate staffing requirements, and establish task interdependencies. Planners also correlate the timing of hardware acquisitions with their need by Business Area Analysis projects.

Each project identified in this final plan belongs to one of three categories:

*   **Business Area Analysis Projects**. These, of course, should already have been defined (see Chapter 7).

*   **Technical Projects**. Each of these implements some aspect of the target Technical Architecture. Planners have already enumerated the requirements for change in the technical environment (Chapter 8), but have not yet grouped them into projects. Typically (but certainly not always), a technical project supports a particular business area.

*   **Organizational Projects**. These projects will implement the proposed Information Systems organizational structure (see Chapter 6). Depending on the ISP project scope and the current state of the Information Systems organization, the list of projects might address a variety of issues, including recruiting, education, establishment of standards and procedures, and introduction of new organizational units (such as data administration or development coordination).

The resulting plan must be a concise road map showing the juxtaposition of all these major projects. The road map must conclude with the organization well on its way to the successful management of its information resource. Many project management software products can help in the assembly of a PERT or Gantt chart that will clearly depict the interrelationship of the various projects over the planning period. As an alternative, the number of projects will generally be small enough for a PERT chart to be manually drawn.

Before considering the plan complete, the project team must identify some alternative strategies for satisfying the business needs of the enterprise over the long term, and compare and contrast their respective benefits. Up to this point, the project has involved defining an Information Architecture to satisfy the business needs and a Business System Architecture and Technical Architecture to support it. Now the planners must prepare to answer a number of oft-posed questions like these:

- What parts of this do we really need?
- What will it cost to do these things in a different order?
- How can I get it done faster?
- How can I get it done more cheaply?
- What if I don't want to buy new hardware after all?

The planners will probably find it distasteful to view elements of the plan as bargaining chips. If management is serious about implementing changes in their organization, however, they will likely want to know what trade-offs they can make without sabotaging the whole plan. For this reason, the planners should be sure to understand ahead of time the kinds of changes that can be made without severely undermining the plan's intent.

In cases where the planners have some indication of particular biases in the ranks of management, they may choose to anticipate them by developing alternative plans. In that way, if the bias should become an issue, the project team will be able to demonstrate their foresight in addressing it.

In short, the plan distilled from the information collected to this point must reflect a reasonable and flexible approach, one that can be tailored by management as needed. If the plan appears rigid and unyielding, the likelihood of adopting it is greatly reduced.

PREPARE THE ISP REPORT

As suggested in the overview to this chapter, proper preparation of the ISP Report is absolutely critical to the success of the project. A flawlessly executed ISP project is worthless if management fails to get the point, and the vehicle for making the point is the ISP Report.

Intended Audience

The ISP Report must be tailored to its audience. Since the audience is the top management of an organization, planners must write the report in terms that managers understand. The most common mistake is to treat the report as a technical rather than a management document. Do not misunderstand: the technical basis for the ISP Report must be impeccable. However, the technical detail required to support the project team's findings must be summarized in terms meaningful to management.

From a presentation standpoint, the project team must prepare graphs and figures that are easy to understand. While a matrix is an excellent analytical device, its use for presenting information to a high-level audience is questionable. Instead, represent data in more traditional formats likely to be recognized and quickly understood by management. For example, use pie charts and histograms to depict coverage of information needs by current systems. Use line graphs to show trends. Use annotated maps of the world to show the distribution of technical facilities. Always use the techniques prevalent in the corporate culture for depicting whatever conditions are deemed important. Do not use formats fraught with abstruse symbols and hidden meaning: they will simply be ignored.

Do not attempt to justify the conclusions of the report by burying the reader in technical detail. Do not attempt to demonstrate the technical prowess of the project team in the report. Although the conclusions must be supportable and the project team should be judged capable, writing an ISP Report with such motives will inevitably lead to disaster. Instead, concentrate on making the important points in a way managers can understand, if not outright enjoy.

In short, the language of the report should be terse and business-like. The appearance of the report should be professional. The message of the report should be stated clearly and concisely with as little technical jargon as possible.

Report Format

As suggested in Chapter 1, each Information Strategy Planning project is different. The unique characteristics of each project are nowhere more evident than in the report. This section mentions some guidelines for report size and content. Bear in mind, however, that the planners must be sensitive to their audience and prepare a document that "presses the right buttons" with the right language. For this reason, the guidelines presented here are only suggestions, not regulations. Based on the organizational milieu and the attitudes of top management, the project team may decide to add topics, delete topics, or rearrange topics. Such variations from the format suggested here are acceptable and to be expected.

An ISP Report usually consists of three major sections:

- An **Executive Summary**, which concisely summarizes the results of the project.
- The **Information Strategy Plan**, which presents the plan and its rationale more completely.
- A set of **Appendices**, which contain supporting information.

The Executive Summary

The Executive Summary extracts the high points from the main body of the Information Strategy Plan. It must be written in hard- hitting, brief prose with an aim toward capturing the interest of management. A manager who wishes only a cursory understanding of the project's results should be able to gain it here. A more interested manager should be encouraged by the summary to continue.

The Executive Summary should generally be no longer than five pages. A typical Executive Summary will touch on the following points:

- The project scope
- Business objectives and priorities
- Business impact of information technology
- Assessment of current environment (including the Information Systems organization, use of information technology and systems support for business activities)
- Recommended systems strategy (a summary of the Information Architecture and Business System Architecture, accompanied by a brief review of the alternatives considered)
- Recommended technical strategy (a summary of the Technical Architecture accompanied by a brief review of the alternatives considered)

- Recommended organizational strategy (a summary of the changes recommended to the Information Systems organization)

- Recommended Action Plan (distilled from the plan described earlier in this chapter)

Information Strategy Plan

The Information Strategy Plan constitutes the main body of the ISP Report. Its purpose is to elaborate on and clarify the points briefly touched on in the management summary. Planners should use charts, graphs, and figures liberally to convey important information.

This section of the ISP Report should be in the neighborhood of 40 pages in length. Never write over 70 pages. Many people are more intimidated than impressed by a thick document.

As suggested earlier, there is no strict format for an ISP Report. The planners must carefully judge what to include and exclude. However, the following general approach seems to work well:

1. Summarize the project (for example, its scope, who commissioned it, and the composition of the project team).

2. Describe the business environment (including, for example, the mission, objectives, CSF's, information needs, and organization structure).

3. Define the problem (assessment of the strengths and weaknesses of the current information environment in satisfying the needs of the business environment).

4. Define the solution (presentation of alternative and recommended Information Architecture, Business System Architecture, Technical Architecture and the respective benefits of each).

5. Present the recommended Action Plan.

This, of course, is a very broad framework within which the planners enjoy considerable latitude. For those readers disappointed that a more rigid formula for this report is not offered, it bears repeating that intended recipients of the ISP Report are *people*, often tough-minded ones, who must act based on the report's content. A strict outline is simply not appropriate given the diversity of organizational cultures and individuals who shape and live by those cultures.

Appendices

Place the bulk of the detailed information supporting the report in a set of appendices. Organize the deliverables from each task and include them here.

The appendices may be quite large, outweighing the remainder of the report. In such cases, planners should consider creating a separate document to contain the technical information (sometimes called the **ISP Technical Report**), leaving only the bare essentials in the appendices of the primary ISP Report. Preparing an ISP Technical Report serves two related purposes: it reduces the chances of intimidating management by the size and technical content of the report, and yet reassures them that the report has a firm technical basis.

PRESENT THE RESULTS

The ISP project team should typically report its findings to top management in a formal presentation. Depending on the outcome of this presentation, the results can then be published throughout the organization as appropriate, either through additional presentations or through distribution of ISP Reports.

Management Presentation

Planners should report their findings to top management in a formal presentation at which the ISP Report is initially distributed. The presentation should generally last for about one hour.

The aim of this presentation is to make management aware of the team's findings and convince them that the findings are valid. For this reason, management must not become distracted from the main points by presentation mechanics. Careful attention to the following guidelines will help to minimize this risk:

- **Presentation Materials**. In some organizational environments a particular presentation medium may be preferred to others. The planners should respect that preference and not use, for example, 35mm slides when the audience expects overhead transparencies.

  Regardless of the medium selected, the presentation materials should be professionally prepared. They should employ color liberally but tastefully. They must be easily read, using few words, many pictures (mostly borrowed from the graphs and figures in the ISP Report), large letters, and a great deal of blank space. As mentioned earlier, matrices do not usually make good presentation vehicles. Planners should generally avoid using them.

- **Presentation Environment**. It goes almost without saying that planners must carefully choose the time and place of the presentation, respectfully invite managers, and make arrangements for technical facilities (like overhead projectors and flip charts). These details are mentioned here only to re-emphasize the point that the presentation is *critical*. Near certain doom awaits the ISP project whose participants consider the presentation a last minute formality instead of the project's climax.

- **Rehearsal**. Planners should rehearse the presentation so that it appears smooth and professional. If more than one speaker presents, the transitions between them should be comfortable for the audience. If possible, the rehearsal should take place in the same location as the real presentation to give the team an opportunity to determine a suitable arrangement for any physical equipment required.

  Even experienced, confident speakers can benefit from a critique by other team members. Some aspects of timing, transition, and phrasing can be effectively addressed by no other means than rehearsal.

As for the presentation content, it should highlight the salient points from the ISP Report, often following the outline of the Executive Summary. Planners should follow the same guidelines for level of technical detail used in preparing the ISP Report.

If major points of disagreement arise during the presentation between the perceptions of top management and the findings of the project team, the team's findings and recommendations may need to be re-evaluated. In general, such disagreement should be anticipated and avoided based on the results of interviews with top management and the insight of the project sponsor. However, in cases where a problem goes undetected to this point, the project team must be flexible enough to adapt the report to the newly emerged requirements.

General Publication

Assuming that top management accepts and adopts the Information Strategy Plan, the team should publish the project results throughout the organization. The project sponsor should establish general guidelines for identifying recipients of the report, but in most cases they will include:

- All members of top management
- All interviewees
- Additional selected members of middle management
- Information Systems management

In some cases, the planners may elect to omit a presentation and simply send out copies of the ISP Report and, selectively, the Appendices or ISP Technical Report. The delivery of the report is likely to have more impact, however, if it is accompanied by a presentation.

PART II

A GUIDE TO BUSINESS AREA ANALYSIS USING THE INFORMATION ENGINEERING FACILITY™

10
BUSINESS AREA ANALYSIS OVERVIEW

This is the first chapter of Part II, which describes the practice of the second stage of Information Engineering, **Business Area Analysis** (BAA), using the Information Engineering Facility (IEF) from Texas Instruments.

AN OVERVIEW OF BUSINESS AREA ANALYSIS

Planners generally establish the boundaries of a Business Area Analysis project as part of the first stage of Information Engineering, Information Strategy Planning. During a Business Area Analysis project, analysts perform a detailed analysis of a selected area of the business. Developers use the results of Business Area Analysis in successive stages of Information Engineering to provide the computerized systems needed to manage the enterprise's information resource.

Business Area Analysis involves the definition and refinement of the activities a business performs (called **business functions** and **business processes**), the things with which it deals (called **entities**) and the interaction between the two. A Business Area Analysis project, then, is a refinement of a specific subset of the Information Architecture initially developed during Information Strategy Planning. This subset is called a **business area.**

Business Area Analysis does not deal with *ad hoc* solutions for immediate problems. Rather, it defines a foundation for developing integrated information systems.

Since the scope of a BAA project normally includes more than one information system, this type of analysis requires more initial resources and investment than traditional analysis projects. However, BAA leads to better, more effective systems.

The Objectives of a BAA Project

The objectives of a BAA project are:

1. To fully identify and define the type of data required
2. To identify and define the business activities that make up each business function
3. To define the data required for each business activity
4. To identify the necessary sequence of business activities
5. To define how business activities affect the data
6. To produce a plan for Business System Design (BSD) within a prioritized sequence of business systems. Normally, several business systems will be defined to support a single business area.

In short, the principle objective of a BAA project is to refine in detail a specific portion of the Information Architecture established during ISP. (Of course, it is possible to perform Business Area Analysis without having first built a comprehensive Information Strategy Plan, as will be discussed later.) In any case, the elements dealt with by analysts during BAA are precisely those dealt with by planners while defining the Information Architecture: data, activities and the interaction between them.

The Tasks Performed During a BAA Project

Analysts perform the following major tasks during a BAA project:

1. **Prepare for Business Area Analysis.** In this task, analysts identify business needs by conducting interviews and reviewing written documentation.

2. **Data Analysis.** In this task, analysts define the data used to represent fundamental things of relevance to the business (called **entities**) and their interrelationships. The result of this task is a **data model** of the business area.

3. **Activity Analysis.** In this task, analysts examine business functions to determine the business processes they comprise. The result of this task is an **activity model** of the business area.

4. **Interaction Analysis.** In this task, analysts fully define the effect of activities on data. The result of this task is an **interaction model** of the business area.

The data model, activity model and interaction model are referred to collectively as the **business model** of the business area being analyzed.

5. **Current Systems Analysis.** During this task, analysts examine the existing systems that support the business area to insure the completeness of the data, activity, and interaction analyses.

6. **Confirmation.** During the execution of this task, the results of Business Area Analysis are verified for completeness and consistency.

7. **Business System Definition.** In this task, analysts group the activities defined during Business Area Analysis into potential **business systems**, each of which can be subsequently addressed in a Business System Design (BSD) project.

During a Business Area Analysis project, analysts concentrate their greatest efforts on data analysis, activity analysis, and interaction analysis. When these tasks are completed, the result is a complete model of the selected business area. This model has three components (Figure 10-1).

Two of the remaining tasks (current systems analysis and confirmation) serve to verify this model. The last task (business system definition) prepares for the next stage of Information Engineering, Business System Design.

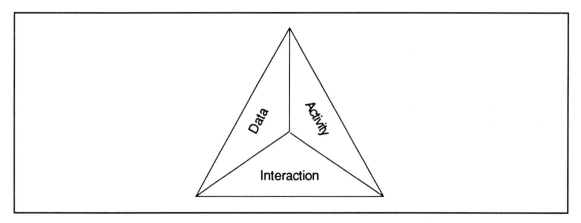

Figure 10-1. The Business Area Analysis Model

AUTOMATED TOOLS AVAILABLE FOR A BAA PROJECT

The Information Engineering Facility (IEF) from Texas Instruments provides several tools that are useful throughout a BAA project:

- During BAA, data about the business is modeled by building an Entity Relationship Diagram (ERD). Entity Relationship Diagrams are built using the IEF Data Modeling Tool.

- Data about business activities are represented in hierarchical fashion on a Process Hierarchy Diagram. Process Hierarchy Diagrams are built using the IEF Activity Hierarchy Tool.

- Dependencies between business activities are recorded on Proces Dependency Diagrams. Process Dependency Diagrams are built using the IEF Activity Dependency Tool.

- The detailed logic of a business process is specified in a Process Action Diagram. Process Action Diagrams are built using the IEF Action Diagramming Tool.

- Processes can be clustered together to help identify business systems using the IEF Matrix Processor.

Part II of this guide deals primarily with the Business Area Analysis portion of the Information Engineering methodology, not with a detailed description of the use of the IEF tools. Detailed instructions for using these appear in the *IEF Analysis Toolset Guide*.

Some users may experience limited tool usage based on the IEF software version being used. Users should read and thoroughly understand the Release Notes that accompany each version before using the software. These notes clearly document all restrictions applicable to the current version.

11
PREPARING FOR A BAA PROJECT

OVERVIEW

This chapter discusses the steps for preparing a BAA project. The topics presented include:

- Setting the project scope (with or without an ISP)
- Establishing the project team
- Building the project plan
- Gathering information during BAA

SETTING THE PROJECT SCOPE

BAA project scope determination depends on whether it is a stand-alone project or based on an ISP project. In the latter case, the planners will already have established the BAA project scope, since part of an ISP project involves identifying business areas. In either case, the typical BAA project should last no longer than six months.

It is quite common to perform a BAA project without the benefit of an Information Architecture derived from an ISP. Although analysts do not realize the benefits of establishing a corporate information strategy, they can still reap significant rewards for performing a thorough analysis on a single segment of the business. The results of the BAA project provide the necessary conceptual understanding of the area under study. This understanding, in turn, will translate into systems that solve business needs, whether or not they are based on an enterprise- wide Information Architecture.

To adequately prepare for a stand-alone BAA project, analysts must do some of the work normally done during the ISP stage. This "mini-ISP" will help provide a feeling of project continuity and insure that the scope of the BAA project is correctly set. In particular, scaled-down versions of the ISP tasks "Making the Initial Assessment," "Defining the Information Architecture," and "Defining the Business System Architecture" may prove helpful. Part I of this book describes these tasks.

In practice, the scope of a stand-alone BAA project is often predetermined based on management expectations. Even in such cases, it is wise to sketch out a skeletal Information Architecture early in the BAA project to ensure that the project scope does not encompass too great an area of the business.

ESTABLISHING THE PROJECT ORGANIZATION

As in an ISP project, the success of a BAA project relies heavily on assembling an effective project organization. In a BAA project, the project organization includes the following components:

- A **project sponsor**, a senior executive within the business area under study who has authority and responsibility for the BAA project.
- The **project team**, the collection of full-time analysts who actually perform the Business Area Analysis.
- An assortment of other individuals who can provide expertise at various times during the project.

In addition, a **steering committee** may exist in many organizations or be established to provide management direction for the project.

The Project Sponsor

During an ISP project, the role of project sponsor is critical. The same holds true during a BAA project. Since a BAA project deals with a smaller segment of the enterprise, the BAA project sponsor need not be positioned at as high a level in the company as in an ISP project. Still, the sponsor should be a senior executive within the context of the business area.

The project sponsor provides the focus for the BAA project and has the final responsibility and authority for all aspects of it. As during an ISP, the project sponsor is expected to contribute relatively little time to the BAA project. However, the role of project sponsor is very important to the project's eventual success. By championing the project to management, ensuring the availability of manpower and resources as required, and eliminating political obstacles, the project sponsor facilitates the timely and orderly completion of the project.

The Project Team

The project team is the group of analysts who carry out the detailed analysis of the business area under study on a full-time basis. The size of the project team varies according to the scope of the business area being analyzed. The composition of the project team includes:

- A **project manager** who understands the business and possesses good communication and presentation skills.
- Several **business analysts**, members of the user community who are familiar with the business area under study.
- A **Business Area Analysis expert** (possibly a consultant) who is proficient in the techniques used in Business Area Analysis.

Occasional Contributors

In addition to the full-time project team members, a number of other individuals may be required to contribute on an as-needed basis. These might include:

- End users
- Specialists in the current systems used within the business area
- Data administration personnel
- Standards personnel

Additional Resources

In addition to the right people, it is important to establish the right environment for the project team. This environment should include:

- The necessary software environment (the IEF, Project Management tools, and so forth)
- The necessary computing hardware for the team (workstations, plotters, mainframe connections, and so on)
- Additional equipment such as white boards, bulletin boards, and flip charts

- If possible, a project room. A common room for all team members, this room should serve as an informal meeting place during a BAA project. The walls of such a room will often be festooned with printed or plotted diagrams to facilitate team discussion.

BUILDING THE PROJECT PLAN

Based on the project scope and the set of BAA tasks presented in the rest of Part II, the analysts establish a Project Schedule. Analysts list detailed tasks associated with data analysis, activity analysis, interaction analysis, current systems analysis, model confirmation and business system definition and construct a schedule using either mechanized or manual techniques.

In order to build the task list, analysts must make some decisions about alternative courses of action available during a BAA project. These alternatives, identified in later chapters, include such examples as:

- Will current systems analysis be performed?
- To what level of detail will Process Action Diagrams be carried?
- Will expected effects be defined for all elementary processes?

Obviously, the decisions implied by these questions will affect the project duration and, thus, the Project Schedule.

A summary of the tasks performed during a Business Area Analysis project is available in Appendix B.

GATHERING INFORMATION DURING BAA

In BAA, the project team members are expected to be individuals familiar with the business area under study. Thus, the technique of conducting interviews, central to the gathering of information during ISP, plays only a minor role during BAA. Instead, the members of the project team use their own knowledge of the business area, augmented by documentation and informal interviews, to build the details of the Information Architecture.

When a formal interview is required, the interviewing techniques described in Part I are appropriate during BAA as well.

12
DATA ANALYSIS

OVERVIEW

As mentioned in earlier chapters, the business model to be constructed during a Business Area Analysis project has three major components:

- The data model, which describes the things of interest to the business and the relationships between them.
- The activity model, which records the things the business does (or should do).
- The interaction model, which details how the things the business does (activities) affect the things of interest to the business (data).

This chapter describes the techniques used to build the data model. It presents data analysis, which was introduced in Chapters 4 and 5 of Part I, in much greater detail. Those chapters explained data modeling using Entity Relationship Diagramming methods in just enough depth to allow planners to construct an overall sketch of business data during ISP. This chapter, on the other hand, shows the analyst how to develop a detailed data model for a particular segment of the business during BAA. When this data analysis is complete, the resulting Entity Relationship Diagram and supporting information will depict in a detailed, abstract way the information used within the business.

The data analysis techniques described in this chapter are associated with **top-down** data modeling. Analysts can use a second set of techniques which reflect **bottom-up** data modeling to help verify the top-down data model. Bottom-up data modeling techniques are described in Chapter 15, "Current Systems Analysis."

This chapter contains the following major sections:

- **Basic Concepts**. This section defines some fundamental terms essential to the detailed modeling of data.
- **Building the Entity Relationship Model**. This long section discusses top-down entity analysis, relationship analysis and attribute analysis. It deals with the details of modeling data using the IEF.
- **Notes on Drawing Entity Relationship Diagrams.** This short section briefly discusses some of the aesthetics of drawing ERDs.
- **A Summary of Data Modeling Rules.** This section briefly describes data-oriented consistency and completeness checks.
- **A Summary of Data Analysis Deliverables.** This short section itemizes the outputs resulting from data analysis.

BASIC CONCEPTS

Before building a detailed data model, the analyst must fully understand some key underlying concepts. This section presents some precise terminology to help the analyst understand these concepts.

First, one must realize that the business of data modeling is only distantly related to database design. Although it is possible to design a database after establishing a data model (in fact, the IEF performs this transformation automatically), the goal of data modeling is to accurately depict the things with which the business deals and their interrelationships. To do so, one must recognize the fundamental elements of business data. They are:

- The things with which the business deals.

- The associations which may exist between those things.

- The detailed characteristics each thing may possess.

Second, one must realize that two different levels of generalization exist for each of these three fundamental elements. One is the type level while the other is the occurrence level. A **type** is a description of some collection of fundamental elements which share similar traits. An **occurrence** is a single instance of one of those elements.

Given this definition of the central concepts of data modeling, Figure 12-1 summarizes the nomenclature used for each concept at each level of generalization.

Concept	Type	Occurrence
Thing	Entity Type	Entity
Association between Things	Relationship	Pairing
Characteristic of a Thing	Attribute	Value

Figure 12-1. Basic Data Modeling Nomenclature

The following discussion defines and gives examples of the six terms presented in Figure 12-1 (entity type, entity, relationship, pairing, attribute and value).

Entity and Entity Type

As illustrated in Figure 12-1, an entity is an occurrence of an entity type and an entity type describes a collection of entities. For example, consider a company whose business is one in which (typically enough) customers buy products. Assume that this firm sells two kinds of products: left-handed smoke shifters and bacon stretchers. Further assume that the firm has three customers: Elwyn Dobson, Bilbo Baggins and Lord Baden-Powell. In this example, CUSTOMER and PRODUCT are both entity types, while the specific instances of CUSTOMER and PRODUCT are entities, as illustrated in Figure 12-2.

Entity Type	Entities
CUSTOMER	Elwyn Dobson
	Bilbo Baggins
	Lord Baden-Powell
PRODUCT	left-handed smoke shifter
	bacon stretcher

Figure 12-2. Entity Types and Entities

The formal definitions of entity and entity type are:

Entity A fundamental thing of relevance to the enterprise about which data may be kept.

Entity Type The description of all the entities to which a common definition and common predicates (defined later) apply.

Pairing and Relationship

In the previous example, it was stated that "customers buy products." That is, an entity belonging to the entity type CUSTOMER can purchase an entity belonging to the entity type PRODUCT. This reason for associating customers and products (that is, *buy*) is called a **relationship.**

An instance of an association between two entities for the reason described by a relationship is called a **pairing.** Thus, if Elwyn Dobson (a customer) buys a bacon stretcher (a product), the entities "Elwyn Dobson" and "bacon stretcher" are said to be paired based on the relationship *buys*. In other words, a relationship is a *type* of association between two entity types, while a pairing is an *occurrence* of an association between two entities.

The formal definitions of pairing and relationship are:

Pairing   Two entities of one or two entity types associated by virtue of a defined relationship.

Relationship   A reason of relevance to the enterprise for associating entities from one or two entity types.

Attribute Value and Attribute

In our fictitious example, the company will more than likely need to know certain characteristics about each entity with which it deals. One typically needs to know the same kinds of characteristics about each entity of the same entity type. One characteristic of entities of the entity type CUSTOMER was already mentioned (but not identified as such): each CUSTOMER has a Name. Other characteristics of a CUSTOMER of interest to the business might be Address, Phone Number and Credit Rating. Each of these possible characteristics of entities of the entity type CUSTOMER is called an **attribute.** Each entity type may be detailed by a set of attributes.

Each entity may have an **attribute value** for each of its attributes. For instance, in the previous example, one of the entities of the entity type CUSTOMER has "Elwyn Dobson" as an attribute value for its Name attribute. (For the sake of convenience, the term "attribute value" will be abbreviated as "value" for the remainder of the data modeling discussion.)

The formal definitions for value and attribute are:

Value   A quantitative or descriptive characteristic of an entity.

Attribute   A descriptor whose values are associated with individual entities of a specific entity type.

Types and Occurrences

The process of data modeling (and, in fact, modeling in general) can be characterized as the definition of *types* that can faithfully represent all the real world *occurrences* of interest to the business. As implied, this general statement applies across all aspects of the modeling effort. During activity analysis, for example, the type **process** (defined in Chapter 5) is used to describe the possible occurrences (or *executions*) of that process.

It goes without saying that all the diagrams used to build business models deal with types, not occurrences. Sometimes, however, one can use an **occurrence diagram** to illustrate the application of a type diagram to a real world example. Examples of some entity occurrence diagrams based on an Entity Relationship Diagram appear later in this chapter.

BUILDING THE ENTITY RELATIONSHIP MODEL

The products of data analysis are a detailed Entity Relationship Diagram (ERD) and supporting documentation. This information is collectively referred to as an **entity relationship (ER) model** of the business area or, alternatively, the **data model** of the business area.

Analysts previously involved in data base definitions must avoid the temptation to define a data base when building the ER model. The emphasis during BAA is on modeling business data, not on constructing optimal data structures. The analyst must ignore implementation details in order to accurately model business data. Later, during the Technical Design stage, the designer may take steps to optimize the physical implementation derived from the ER model.

In addition, analysts must bear in mind that the process of data analysis is not an exact one. A business model (of which a data model makes up a significant part) is based largely on the business practitioners' subjective understanding of the business. Thus, if two analysts were to study the same business area independently, they would likely develop models with significant differences. Some representations of the underlying business reality are certainly better than others. The real success of the data modeling effort, however, lies in depicting the business environment in a thorough and workable way that is generally understood by and sensible to the business organizations involved.

Entity Types and Their Detail

Categories of Entity Type

This section discusses the various kinds of detailed information captured for each entity type. First, however, the concept of entity type requires some refinement.

The definition of entity ("a thing of fundamental relevance to the enterprise about which data may be kept") might lead one to believe that an entity type can only describe physical objects. This is not the case. The "thing" referred to in the definition can be either tangible or intangible, as long as it is of interest to the business.

Three categories of entity type have, in fact, been identified. Entity types that describe physical objects (like CUSTOMER and PRODUCT) are called **tangible** entity types. Entity types used to capture data about less tangible concepts of interest to the business are called **conceptual** entity types. Examples include COST CENTER and LEDGER ENTRY. Finally, entity types used to represent information about events that take place are called **active** entity types. Examples include LECTURE ATTENDANCE and EQUIPMENT BREAKDOWN. For obvious reasons, active and conceptual entity types are more difficult to identify than tangible entity types, but are no less important in creating an accurate model of the business.

In practice, the distinction between these categories of entity types is seldom explicitly made. In fact, the IEF provides no facility to capture the category of an entity type. Analysts simply need to bear in mind that an entity type need not represent a set of purely physical things.

Entity Type Detail

The IEF allows analysts to specify a number of details about entity types, most of which remain hidden behind the entity type's graphical representation on the diagram. In particular, the IEF captures the following details:

- Name
- Description
- Properties

— Expected Number of Occurrences

— Expected Growth Rate

- Predicates
- Identifiers
- Mutually Exclusive Relationship Memberships
- Aliases

Each of these concepts is described in the following paragraphs.

Name

The name of an entity type is a short classification of the type of entities it describes. It should take the form of a singular noun (such as CUSTOMER, not CUSTOMERS) and must be unique within the enterprise (For example, there may not be two entity types named DELIVERY POINT representing two different things.) In the IEF, an entity type name may not exceed 32 characters.

Sometimes an analyst may wish for an entity type to have multiple names, or synonyms. For example, an entity type called CUSTOMER by one department might be known as CLIENT by another. In such cases, the analyst must decide on the most commonly used alternative as the name and record the remaining synonyms as aliases (described below).

A more insidious and, happily, less frequent situation occurs when an analyst inadvertently uses the same name to reference two different entity types (homonyms). In order to build a sensible model, entity type names must be unique (in fact, the IEF insists on it). As a result, the analyst must modify one of the homonyms to some degree. If necessary, the analyst may store the original name as a synonym in the entity type description.

Description

The entity type **description** is a block of text that describes the entities collected by the entity type. In particular, analysts can specify the following kinds of information in the entity type description:

- Its definition, preferably in terminology commonly used in the business. This should include an indication of exactly what the entities are (called the **scope**) and how they are distinguished from one another (called the **qualification**). The names of relationships and other entity types will probably appear in the definition, but the analyst should avoid the temptation to merely respecify the Entity Relationship Diagram in words.

  The definition of the entity type CUSTOMER might be:

  "An individual or organization (scope) who purchases (qualifying relationship) products (qualifying entity type) marketed by (qualifying relationship) a division (qualifying entity type)."

  A definition should never include a layout of the detailed data recorded for each entity.

- Some examples of the entity type, if desired.
- Any integrity conditions associated with entities of the type being described. Integrity conditions are discussed under the heading entitled "Some Additional Concepts" at the end of this section.

Properties

Entity type **properties** describe the estimated number of entities and the anticipated increase (or decrease) in that number over time. This statistical information is captured during the BAA stage simply because the analyst is in an excellent position to furnish it. During the Technical Design stage, the IEF uses these volume and activity measurements to influence the technical design of the data base.

Predicates

The collection of attributes and relationship memberships that describe an entity type are called its **predicates.** Each attribute or relationship membership, then, is a predicate of its associated entity type. The details of attributes and relationships are discussed in more depth later. These predicates constitute an extremely important set of details concerning an entity type.

Identifiers

An **identifier** is a predicate or collection of predicates that uniquely identifies an entity of the type under consideration. For example, assume that the entity type CUSTOMER has an attribute called Number. If no two CUSTOMER entities have the same value for their Number attribute, the value of the predicate Number can be used to uniquely identify one and only one CUSTOMER entity.

This leads to another important point: each entity type must have at least one identifier. In other words, each entity must be distinguishable from all other entities based on some combination of values and pairings. A detailed discussion of identifiers appears under the heading entitled "Some Additional Concepts" at the end of this section.

Mutually Exclusive Relationship Memberships

A discussion of this item of detail is deferred to the end of this section, where it appears under the heading entitled "Some Additional Concepts."

Aliases

Each entity type may actually be known by a number of different names in different business contexts. For example, the entity type CUSTOMER might be known variously as CLIENT, CUST, COOB (obviously an abbreviation for Customer Of Our Business) or CONSUMER. Each of these synonyms should be recorded as an alias of the entity type.

Each alias may be identified as being either an **acronym** (like COOB), an **abbreviation** (like CUST), or neither (like CLIENT and CONSUMER). Additionally, a **long name** of up to 50 characters can be recorded for the entity type. The long name is typically used only to provide compatibility with data dictionary products which support names longer than the 32-character IEF standard.

Relationships and Their Detail

Relationships and Relationship Memberships

As mentioned in Chapter 5, each relationship actually consists of two memberships, one for each entity type participating in the relationship. Each of these relationship memberships is a predicate of the entity type to which it belongs.

For instance, consider a company in which customers place orders. The fragment of Entity Relationship Diagram which represents the fact that a customer can place an order appears in Figure 12-3. (The basic set of symbols for Entity Relationship Diagramming was introduced in Chapter 5).

Figure 12-3. An Entity Relationship Diagram Fragment

The relationship shown between CUSTOMER and ORDER actually consists of two separate relationship memberships:

CUSTOMER *places* ORDER

and

ORDER *is placed by* CUSTOMER

Each membership has its own set of characteristics. Figure 12-4 depicts the division of this relationship into its two component memberships.

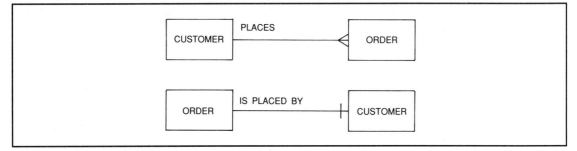

Figure 12-4. Two Relationship Memberships

As it turns out, there are no details unique to the entire relationship. The relationship is fully described by the properties of its component relationship memberships.

In the IEF, each piece of detail associated with a relationship membership contributes to the construction of a sentence describing that membership (with the exception of the *description* detail). In addition, some of the details become part of the graphical representation of the Entity Relationship Diagram.

The details captured for each relationship membership include the following:

- Name
- Cardinality
- Optionality
- Percentage of entities participating in pairings based on this relationship (for optional relationship memberships only)
- Expected number of pairings per entity type (for relationship memberships with a cardinality of *many*)
- Transferability
- Description

Name

The **name** of a relationship membership describes the reason for joining two entities of the types participating in the relationship. It should be a verb (either active or passive) which connects one entity type (the subject of a sentence) to another (the object of a sentence.)

In the previous example, the two relationship membership names used to describe the relationship in Figure 12-3 were *places* and *is placed by*, respectively. Always construct a complete verb phrase. For example, use *is placed by*, not just *placed by*. It not only makes a better sentence here, but reads well in the syntax of the Process Action Diagram defined during interaction analysis.

With just the relationship membership names in place, then, the two sentences which describe the relationship in Figure 12-3 look like this:

CUSTOMER *places* ORDER

ORDER *is placed by* CUSTOMER

The IEF makes an arbitrary distinction between relationship memberships, based on the order in which the analyst chooses the entity types participating in the relationship. The relationship membership associated with the entity type chosen first is called the **source** membership, while the other is called the **destination** membership. This distinction merely provides a means for selecting individual memberships when using the IEF. It does not imply a *direction* to a relationship.

Cardinality

The **cardinality** of a relationship membership determines the number of entities on one side of the relationship which may be joined to a single entity on the other side. As mentioned in Chapter 5, each relationship can be one-to-one (1:1), one-to-many (1:M) or many-to-many (M:N). The cardinality of each relationship membership is either *one* or *many* (sometimes *many* is characterized as *one or more*).

The relationship depicted in Figure 12-3 is a 1:M relationship. It shows that each customer can place one or more orders, but that each order is placed by only one customer. Based on the cardinality of each relationship membership, the sentences begun earlier can be expanded as follows:

Each CUSTOMER *places* one or more ORDERs.

Each ORDER *is placed by* one CUSTOMER.

The most common cardinality for relationships is 1:M. (Although 1:1 and M:N relationships sometimes occur naturally, they often appear as the result of inaccurate analysis. This topic is addressed in some detail in another section of this chapter under the heading "Data Modeling Anomalies.") The frequency of occurrence of 1:M relationships has led to the development of some specialized terminology:

- Each entity of the entity type on the *one* side of the 1:M relationship is called a **single member.** In Figure 12-3, entities of the type CUSTOMER are single members of CUSTOMER *places* ORDER.

- Each entity of the entity type on the *many* side of the 1:M relationship is called a **plural member.** In Figure 12-3, entities of the type ORDER are plural members of CUSTOMER *places* ORDER.

- The term **grouping** refers to the set of entities that includes a single member and all of its plural members based on a specific relationship. In the example shown in Figure 12-3, a single CUSTOMER and all the ORDERS it *places* constitute a grouping.

Optionality

During data analysis, the analyst must determine whether entities of types joined by a relationship must participate in pairings. This characteristic, called the **optionality** of a relationship membership, is very important in understanding the business reality being modelled.

Consider for a moment the example in Figure 12-3. Assuming that neither relationship membership is optional (which is, in fact, represented in Figure 12-3), one can infer the following:

Each ORDER must be *placed by* a CUSTOMER.

Each CUSTOMER must *place* at least one ORDER.

The first statement makes sense. It is unlikely that the business will accept an order for its products without a customer having placed it. Likewise, if the customer placing the order ceases to be a customer, it is reasonable for all of the orders for that customer to be eliminated. If this is true, the relationship membership ORDER *is placed by* CUSTOMER is said to be **mandatory.**

On the other hand, the truth of the second statement is doubtful. Assume for the moment that CUSTOMER entities include information about the customer's address, phone number and credit rating. Further assume that an ORDER entity is deleted once an order is successfully filled or cancelled. In this case, the business loses all knowledge of a customer whenever its last order is filled. It is unlikely that this condition reflects the business reality. Rather, the business probably wants to retain knowledge of a customer whether or not the CUSTOMER has an active pairing with an ORDER. If this is true, the relationship membership CUSTOMER *places* ORDER is said to be **optional.**

Optional relationship memberships are represented diagrammatically as a circle on the relationship line next to the cardinality symbol. Figure 12-5 depicts CUSTOMER *places* ORDER as an optional relationship membership.

Figure 12-5. Figure 12-3 with Optionality Specified

One may now expand the sentences that describe the relationship membership to reflect optionality as follows:

Each CUSTOMER sometimes *places* one or more ORDERs.

Each ORDER always *is placed by* exactly one CUSTOMER.

Some analysts prefer to consider optionality a special case of cardinality that permits zero pairings. The distinction between optionality and **zero cardinality** (as the other alternative is called) is actually academic. However, the analyst should note that the two sentences showing optionality (above) are exactly equivalent to the following sentences showing zero cardinality:

Each CUSTOMER *places* zero, one or more ORDERs.

Each ORDER *is placed by* exactly one CUSTOMER.

This book (and, coincidentally, the IEF) uses the optionality alternative exclusively rather than the zero cardinality alternative.

Entity types whose relationship memberships are all optional are said to be **independent entity types**, meaning that entities of this type do not depend on other entities for their existence. Independent entity types tend to be the more important ones in the model. In our example, CUSTOMER is an independent entity type, while ORDER is a dependent entity type (an ORDER cannot exist without a related CUSTOMER.)

The optionality of a relationship can be fully mandatory (both memberships are mandatory), fully optional (both memberships are optional) or partly optional (one membership mandatory, one optional). Figure 12-5 shows a partly optional relationship. Figure 12-6 shows examples of both a fully mandatory relationship and a fully optional relationship. An ORDER cannot exist without ORDER LINES, nor an ORDER LINE without an ORDER. On the other hand, a CAR can exist whether or not anybody is driving it, and a PERSON, contrary to the belief of American teenagers, can exist without having a CAR to drive.

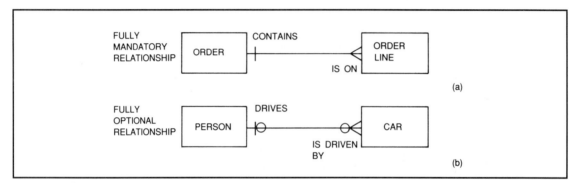

Figure 12-6. Fully Mandatory and Fully Optional Relationships

In practice, the majority of relationships are partly optional. Some cardinality/optionality combinations are very unusual and should be viewed with suspicion. These are covered in some depth under the heading entitled "Data Modeling Anomalies" later in this chapter.

Often, the existence of a pairing for an optional relationship membership depends on some combination of predicate values. This combination is called an **optionality condition.** There are three types of conditions, the **required** condition (a pairing must exist if the condition is true), the **forbidden** condition (a pairing may *not* exist if the condition is true) and the **don't care** condition (the pairing can exist regardless of other predicate values). This last kind of condition requires no explicit definition.

For example, consider Figure 12-6b (the PERSON/CAR relationship). Assume that the entity type PERSON has one attribute called Job Title and another called Age. Assume also that if a PERSON has a value of "chauffeur" for the attribute Job Title, he/she must have a pairing with a CAR. This optionality condition for the relationship membership PERSON *drives* CAR can be represented as follows:

> Required when PERSON Job Title is equal to "chauffeur"

Likewise, assume that a PERSON cannot drive a CAR if his/her Age is less than the legal driving age (say, 16). This optionality condition for the relationship membership PERSON *drives* CAR can be represented as follows:

> Forbidden when PERSON Age is less than 16

(Note the implied constraint that a PERSON under 16 cannot be a chauffeur.)

Analysts should record these optionality conditions in the description of the affected relationship membership. Later, during interaction analysis, analysts can incorporate them into process specifications.

Pairing Percentage

For an optional relationship membership, the percentage of time that at least one pairing is likely to exist for a given entity will be useful during data base design. It is captured here because the analyst should have the information available as the result of his or her analysis.

In the example in Figure 12-5, if one assumes that 200 customers will exist and 190 of them will have an outstanding order, one can say that the probability of a CUSTOMER being paired with an ORDER based on the *places* relationship membership is 95%. One can include this fact in the sentences being built by showing the percentage in parentheses, as follows:

> Each CUSTOMER sometimes (95%) *places* one or more ORDERs.

> Each ORDER always *is placed by* exactly one CUSTOMER.

The second membership is mandatory, thus it remains unchanged.

Number of Pairings

Another piece of information useful during data base design but available in BAA is the estimated number of pairings in a *many* relationship membership for a single entity. In the case of Figure 12-5, there is only one *many* relationship membership: CUSTOMER *places* one or more ORDERs. Thus, the number of pairings of interest represents the potential number of orders to be placed by a single customer.

One may specify the following information for the number of pairings:

- The minimum number of pairings for an entity and whether that minimum is estimated or absolute. In the case of an optional membership the minimum is obviously zero. However, the value specified here presupposes the existence of at least one pairing. Thus, it might better be thought of as "the minimum number of pairings if any exist."

- The maximum number of pairings for an entity, and whether that maximum is estimated or absolute.

- The average number of pairings for an entity.

For example, assume that experience teaches that each customer who has any orders outstanding has at least two, and that no customer is ever expected to have more than ten orders outstanding simultaneously. Most have three. These numbers are estimates; a customer who wishes to place an eleventh order will not be turned away based on a technicality. Given these assumptions, one may modify the sentences as follows:

> Each CUSTOMER sometimes (95%) *places* at least 2 (estimated), at most 10 (estimated) and on average 3 ORDERs.

> Each ORDER always *is placed by* exactly one CUSTOMER.

The second membership remains the same because it is neither optional nor *many*.

A relationship membership in which the minimum, maximum and average are equal and for which the minimum and maximum are absolute is said to have **fixed cardinality.**

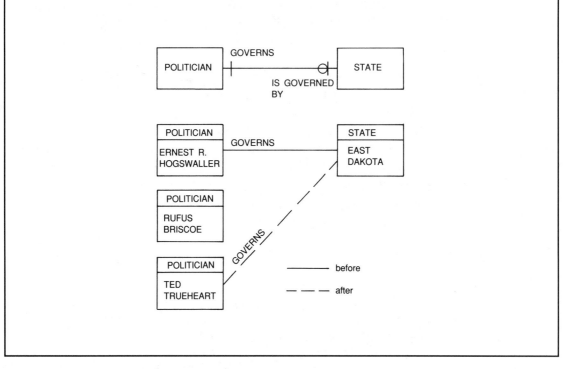

Figure 12-7. A Transferable Relationship

There are cases where the allowable number of pairings can vary based on combinations of predicate values. For example, a customer whose credit rating indicates that he or she is a questionable risk might be allowed one outstanding order at a time, while one with a more favorable rating might be allowed many. The analyst can document a rare situation such as this as a cardinality condition in the description of the affected relationship membership.

Transferability

In some cases, one must be able to move a pairing from one entity type to another. For example, consider Figure 12-7, which shows the two relationship memberships:

> Each POLITICIAN sometimes *governs* exactly one STATE.

> Each STATE always *is governed by* exactly one POLITICIAN.

This model, finely tailored to state government in the U.S., represents a highly volatile situation. The sad truth is that a state is always governed by a politician. However, at election time the identity of the politician might change. In other words, when the governor gets the "boot," the pairing between a STATE entity and a POLITICIAN entity based on the *governs* relationship must be transferred from one POLITICIAN entity to another. An occurrence diagram depicting this state of events appears in the lower portion of Figure 12-7. Here, Ted Trueheart has wrested the Governor's mansion of the great state of East Dakota from the incumbent, Ernest R. Hogswaller. As a result, the pairing "East Dakota *is governed by* Ernest R. Hogswaller" must be transferred from Ernest to Ted Trueheart (another entity of type POLITICIAN.)

This example points out a characteristic of relationship memberships called **permanence of membership.** Some memberships are permanent: once a pairing is established, it relates the same two entities until the entities are **disassociated.** Others, as in the gubernatorial example above, are temporary: a pairing can move from entity to entity as needed. A relationship membership whose pairings are permanent is called a **fixed** membership, and one whose pairings are temporary is called a **transferable** membership. In practice, fixed memberships are much more common than transferable ones.

In the CUSTOMER/ORDER example (Figure 12-5), it is unlikely, after a customer places an order, for the order to be transferred to a different customer. Thus, the membership ORDER *is placed by* CUSTOMER is not transferable. The converse (transferring a customer between orders) is difficult to imagine. To complete the sentences, one can append these facts to the end as follows:

Each CUSTOMER sometimes (95%) *places* at least 2 (estimated), at most 10 (estimated) and on average 3 ORDERs and is not transferable.

Each ORDER always *is placed by* exactly one CUSTOMER and is not transferable.

Description

The final characteristic of each relationship membership is its **description.** In general, the sort of information captured as part of the relationship membership description should reflect the two types of integrity conditions that pertain to relationship memberships: cardinality conditions and optionality conditions.

Alternative Relationship Representations

For those who have been exposed to other ER modeling techniques, Information Engineering's manner of handling relationships bears mention.

First, in Information Engineering, only entity types can have attributes. Relationship memberships are considered predicates of entity types, not as objects in their own right. Thus, a relationship can never have an attribute. In the Information Engineering world, if one feels the need to add an attribute to a relationship, one has likely discovered a new entity type (probably a conceptual or active one).

Second, in Information Engineering, a relationship has exactly two memberships; two and only two entities can participate in a single pairing. ER models with this constraint are said to depict **binary** relationships. Other modeling styles allow the appearance of three or more entities in a single relationship occurrence (the term "pairing" makes no sense in this context). This style of model is said to support **n-ary** relationships. In Information Engineering, a relationship that appears to require more than two memberships should be replaced by an entity type. An entity type introduced for this reason is called an **associative entity type.** Consider figure 12-8, for example. It shows a ternary (three membership) relationship between PERSON, MATERIAL and BUILDING which represents a leasing arrangement. Since Information Engineering modeling rules do not allow three memberships in a relationship, a fourth entity type, LEASE, and some new relationships must be added to model the business reality. The resulting binary model is shown in Figure 12-9.

Although the Information Engineering style of representing relationships (binary with no attributes) might initially appear somewhat restrictive, it greatly simplifies the operations on relationships specified during interaction analysis. Since one can model the same set of real world instances using either style of modeling, and since operations on model objects are much less complex using Information Engineering, the binary/no-attribute style of relationship modeling is superior in the context of Business Area Analysis.

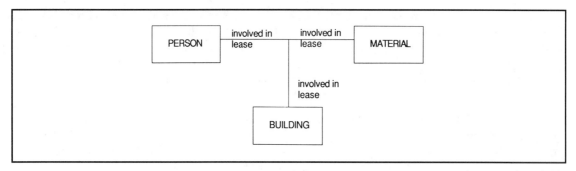

Figure 12-8. A Relationship with Three Memberships

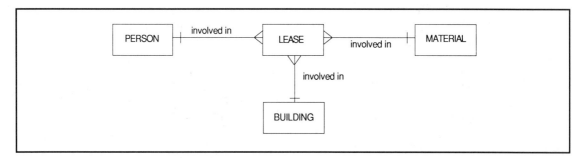

Figure 12-9. An Equivalent Model Using Binary Relationships

Attributes and Their Detail

For each attribute of an entity type, one may capture the following detailed information:

- Name
- Description
- Optionality
- Source category (basic, derived, designed)
- Primitive domain (number, text, date, time)
- Length
- Number of decimal places (numbers only)
- Case sensitivity (text attributes only)
- Permitted values
- Default value or algorithm
- Derivation algorithm (derived attributes only)
- Aliases

The following paragraphs describe each of these characteristics in detail.

Name

The **name** of an attribute is a noun or noun phrase describing the purpose or content of the attribute, preferably using terminology prevalent in the business.

Previous examples presented a list of attributes with the CUSTOMER entity type. Figure 12-10 presents those attributes again along with some new ones to illustrate attribute naming:

Attributes of Entity Type CUSTOMER
NUMBER
NAME
ADDRESS
PHONE NUMBER
STATUS
CREDIT RATING
DATE KNOWN
VALUE OF OUTSTANDING ORDERS

Figure 12-10. Attributes of CUSTOMER

Note that none of the attribute names shown here include the name of the entity type. Since each attribute is associated with exactly one entity type, repeating the entity type name in the attribute name is redundant. In addition, including the entity type name in the attribute name makes the Action Diagram built during activity analysis read strangely. In the Action Diagram, references to attributes are usually immediately qualified by their entity type names. The setting of an attribute of CUSTOMER named Number would read "SET CUSTOMER Number TO *xxx*," while the setting of an attribute of CUSTOMER named Customer Number would read "SET CUSTOMER Customer Number TO *xxx*."

Description

The **description** of an attribute may include any textual information the analyst deems useful. In general, there are two optional components of an attribute description:

- The attribute's definition, which elaborates on the information about the attribute's role available from its name.

- Any optionality conditions (described shortly), if the attribute is optional.

Optionality

The **optionality** of an attribute indicates whether each entity of the type described by the attribute must have a value for the attribute under consideration. Attributes for which each entity must have a value are called **mandatory,** while attributes for which each entity need not have a value are called **optional.**

Consider the attributes of CUSTOMER from Figure 12-10. It is reasonable to assume that each customer with which our business deals must have a Name, Number and Address. Likewise, each customer will always have a Status, whose value is automatically assigned when the business is made aware of the customer. Date Known, the date on which the business became aware of the customer, will always be present as well. Finally, the Value of Outstanding Orders for a customer always has some value, even if it is zero.

This leaves Phone Number and Credit Rating. It is conceivable (although unlikely) that a customer has no telephone. If, in our business, we accept customers who have no telephones, then some CUSTOMER entities will exist with no value for their Phone Number attribute. Likewise, it is possible that some customers require no credit and prefer to pay cash for all purchases. Assume that in such a case the attribute Credit Rating will not have a value.

Given all of the above assumptions, the entity type CUSTOMER has six mandatory attributes and two optional attributes as follows:

Mandatory Attributes of CUSTOMER
NUMBER NAME ADDRESS STATUS DATE KNOWN VALUE OF OUTSTANDING ORDERS

Optional Attributes of CUSTOMER
PHONE NUMBER CREDIT RATING

Just as with relationship memberships, the optionality of an attribute can sometimes be affected by a combination of values of other predicates. In this case, one can represent the combination as an optionality condition. The cases Required, Forbidden and Don't Care also apply here. For example, assume that the attribute Status can have a value of "cash only" and that only CUSTOMERS with that Status are allowed to have no Credit Rating. In such a case, the following optionality condition applies to Credit Rating:

> Required when Status is not equal to "cash only"

The Forbidden case is not nearly as common as the Required one but is likewise possible. Consider the case where another possible value of Status is "wealthy mogul." Assume that we want to avoid offending such CUSTOMERS with mundane queries about their credit worthiness and thus forbid the inclusion of a value for Credit Rating for them. Further assume that the previous "cash only" optionality condition is true. The new optionality conditions applicable to Credit Rating are:

> Required when Status is not equal to "cash only" and Status is not equal to "wealthy mogul"
>
> Forbidden when Status is equal to "wealthy mogul"

The analyst specifies optionality conditions for an attribute as part of its description.

Source Category

An attribute may fall into one of three **source categories**:

- **Basic**, in which the attribute's values are intrinsic to entities of the type being described and cannot be deduced from the values of other predicates.

- **Derived**, in which the attribute's values are always deduced or calculated from the values of other predicates.

- **Designed**, in which the attribute is invented to overcome some sort of business constraint or to simplify a system operation.

In practice, the IEF treats basic and designed attributes the same way. While the distinction is interesting, there is little to be gained from debating whether a particular attribute belongs to one or the other of these two categories. Derived attributes, however, are treated very differently. Values are never merely set to some value. Rather, they are derived using a calculation called a **derivation algorithm** assigned to the attribute as part of its definition.

The CUSTOMER entity type (Figure 12-10) contains examples of attributes belonging to each source category. The likely assignment of source category to these attributes is:

Attribute	Source Category
NUMBER	Designed
NAME	Basic
ADDRESS	Basic
PHONE NUMBER	Basic
STATUS	Basic Or Designed
CREDIT RATING	Basic Or Designed
DATE KNOWN	Basic
VALUE OF OUTSTANDING ORDERS	Derived

Notes:

1. As indicated above, one might consider Status and Credit Rating to be either basic or designed, under differing conditions. The distinction is relatively unimportant.

2. Value of Outstanding Orders for a particular CUSTOMER entity is assumed to be the sum of the Amounts (an attribute) of all ORDERs (an entity type) which are *placed by* (a relationship membership) that CUSTOMER. Thus, its value depends wholly on the values of other predicates. If the customer places a new order (causing a new pairing based on *places/is placed by*) the value of Value of Outstanding Orders is likely to change. Likewise, if the Amount of any order placed by the customer is modified, the value of Value of Outstanding Orders will change. Thus, Value of Outstanding Orders is a derived attribute.

Domains

The term **domain** refers to the collection of possible values for an attribute or set of attributes. Put another way, the attribute's domain must include each value actually assigned an attribute.

The IEF requires that each attribute be assigned to one of four basic domains, called **primitive domains.** These primitive domains can be used as the basis for forming other domains, called **complex domains** or **user-defined domains.** A discussion of user-defined domains appears later.

The four primitive domains to which an attribute may belong are:

- **Text**, in which each value is a string of characters.

- **Number,** in which each value is a number (positive or negative, integer or real).

- **Date,** in which each value represents a date (including century).

- **Time,** in which each value represents an hour, minute and second.

(Some analysts may consider the domains Date and Time to be complex domains based on the primitive domain Number. However, dates and times are so universally important and uniquely configured that they are regarded as primitive domains in this discussion.)

The values of attributes from different primitive domains usually cannot be compared or used together in calculations. For example, it makes no sense to compare CUSTOMER Number with CUSTOMER Address. Neither does it make sense to multiply ORDER Quantity by Current Date.

The attributes of the CUSTOMER entity belong to the following primitive domains:

Attribute	Primitive Domain
NUMBER	Number
NAME	Text
ADDRESS	Text
PHONE NUMBER	Text
STATUS	Text
CREDIT RATING	Text
DATE KNOWN	Date
VALUE OF OUTSTANDING ORDERS	Number

(Assume that Phone Number includes parentheses and hyphens for readability.)

Length

The **length** of an attribute indicates the maximum number of characters or digits for each of its values. One may consider this to be a subset of the domain of an attribute, since the number of characters or digits restricts the possible set of values for the attribute.

Using the IEF, the maximum length of an attribute varies based on the primitive domain to which it belongs. Figure 12-11 lists the possible lengths of attributes which belong to each of the four primitive domains.

Domain	Possible Attribute Length
Text	1 - 9999
Number	1 - 18
Date	8
Time	6

Figure 12-11. Attribute Lengths by Domain

Note that no range of lengths is available for attributes belonging to the domains Date and Time. This is because the format of Date and Time attributes is fixed. Each Date includes four digits for the year, two for the month and two for the day. Each Time includes two digits for the hour, two for the minute and two for the second. The IEF automatically sets the length property of Date and Time attributes and prohibits their modification.

Analysts must first specify the length of an attribute before establishing its permitted values.

Number of Decimal Places

This property is only available for attributes belonging to the Number domain. It reflects the number of digits of the attribute's total length which fall to the right of the decimal point. Figure 12-12 illustrates the relationship between length and number of decimal places:

Format of Number	Length	Decimal Places
9999	4	0
999.9	4	1
99.99	4	2
9.999	4	3
.9999	4	4

Figure 12-12. The Relationship Between Length and Number of Decimal Places

Case Sensitivity

For text attributes, the analyst can specify whether the attribute is to contain both upper and lower case characters or only upper case characters. If an attribute is defined as upper case sensitive, all characters in any views of the attribute will be translated to upper case before any operations are performed on them.

Permitted Values

The analyst can use **permitted values** to further restrict the domain of certain kinds of attributes. The set of permitted values for an attribute exhaustively describes the potential values of the attribute. If the analyst specifies no permitted values for an attribute, the IEF considers any value consistent with the attribute's primitive domain and length to be a legal value.

One may specify permitted values for any attribute that is either basic or designed and either text or a number. Permitted values for text attributes are restricted to discrete values, while permitted values for number attributes may include ranges as well as discrete values.

Each permitted value may be given a detailed description in the IEF.

Default Value or Algorithm

For each attribute which may contain permitted values (basic or designed, text or number), one may specify either a default value or default algorithm (but not both).

The **default value** is a single value for the attribute that must be among its permitted values. When creating an entity, the IEF automatically assigns default values to all attributes for which default values were specified, unless another value is explicitly set. For example, imagine that CUSTOMER Status (from Figure 12-10) has a default value of "cash only." In such a case, whenever a CUSTOMER is created, Status will automatically be set to "cash only" unless it is explicitly overridden.

The **default algorithm** is a calculation whose result is used to initialize attribute values. When the entity which contains the attribute is created, the attribute is assigned its value based on the result of the default algorithm. For example, imagine that CUSTOMER Numbers are assigned sequentially. As a new CUSTOMER is created, its Number attribute receives the value of the previously created CUSTOMER Number plus one. The rule that states that

(CUSTOMER Number = previous CUSTOMER Number + 1)

is a default algorithm.

The actual construction of default algorithms requires the use of the Action Diagramming Tool. As a result, the details of building a default algorithm are deferred to Chapter 14, "Interaction Analysis."

Derivation Algorithm

One may only specify **derivation algorithms** for derived attributes. Conceptually, every time the value of a derived attribute is requested, the derivation algorithm executes.

Some analysts might wonder about performance implications associated with derived attributes. In practice, designers must make a performance-oriented detailed design decision during Technical Design to determine whether a derived attribute should actually be *calculated* or *stored*. If calculated, the value of the derived attribute is recalculated every time it is requested. If stored, the value of the derived attribute is recalculated only when one of the predicates on which it depends is modified. Since the distinction between calculation and storage is irrelevant during Business Area Analysis, it is deferred until Technical Design.

The actual construction of derivation algorithms requires the use of the Action Diagramming Tool. As a result, the details of building a derivation algorithm are deferred to Chapter 14, "Interaction Analysis."

Aliases

Just as for entity types, each attribute may be known by a number of different names. For example, the attribute Number of the entity type CUSTOMER might be known variously as NUM, NO, CN (short for Customer Number) or NUMERIC_MONICKER. Each of these synonyms should be recorded as an alias of the attribute.

Each alias may be identified as being either an **acronym** (like CN), an **abbreviation** (like NUM or NO), or neither (like NUMERIC_MONICKER). Additionally, a **long name** of up to 50 characters can be recorded for the attribute. The long name is typically used only to provide compatibility with data dictionary products which support names longer than the 32 character IEF standard.

Some Additional Concepts

Previous subsections explained the basic characteristics of the three primary components of ER modeling: entity types, attributes and relationships. This subsection deals with some of the less obvious concepts in more detail.

Identifiers

Each **identifier** of an entity type is a combination of predicates whose values uniquely identify an entity. Analysts familiar with data base terminology might recognize that the concept of an identifier is similar to that of a unique key in some kinds of database management facilities. Each entity type must have at least one identifier and, in fact, most have only one. The IEF allows specification of up to five separate identifiers for each entity type.

Analysts need not specify the predicates that comprise an identifier in any particular order, because an identifier insures *uniqueness*, not *sequence*. For analysts familiar with data base concepts, this reveals an important distinction between the concept of a data base key and an entity identifier. Where data base keys generally imply sequence, identifiers of entity types do not. Likewise, a data base management system that allows specification of a primary key and multiple secondary keys generally only requires the primary key to be unique. With IEF, each identifier of an entity type *must* uniquely identify an entity.

Figure 12-13 shows part of an Entity Relationship Diagram that expands on the diagram shown in Figure 12-5. Here, a new entity type, ORDER LINE, has been added. Although attribute names do not normally appear on Entity Relationship Diagrams, they appear in this example to help clarify the notion of identifiers.

Beginning with the entity type CUSTOMER, assume that the attribute Number is an identifier. In other words, no two CUSTOMERS have the same value for Number. Further assume that while two CUSTOMERS can have the same name, and two CUSTOMERS can live at the same address, no two CUSTOMERS can have both the same name and live at the same address. Thus, the combination of Name and Address can also be an identifier. The entity type CUSTOMER, then, has two identifiers:

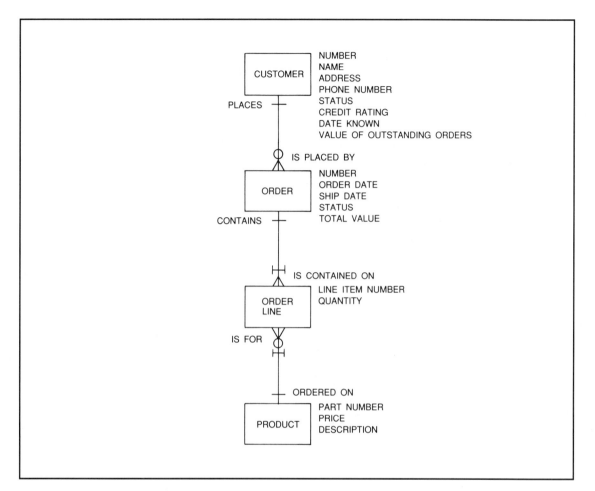

Figure 12-13. An ERD Fragment

Identifiers of CUSTOMER	
Identifier 1	NUMBER
Identifier 2	NAME ADDRESS

(In reality, there is little benefit to be gained from specifying the second identifier in this example. In fact, it might actually impose an artificial restriction — one American television comedy show features two brothers both named Darryl who live at the same address. However, since cases where multiple identifiers occur naturally are relatively rare, we will accept this slightly questionable situation as an example of an entity type with two identifiers.)

Next, consider the entity type ORDER. Assuming that no two ORDERS have the same values for Number, Number is an identifier of ORDER. Likewise, the entity type PRODUCT has an identifier which is an attribute called Part Number.

ORDER LINE is slightly different. Assuming that the attribute Line Item Number is unique only within an ORDER, no combination of attributes of ORDER LINE can be used to uniquely identify each of its

ORDER NUMBER 125607

DATE: XX/YY/ZZ

NO.	PART NO.	DESCRIPTION	QTY.	PRICE	TOTAL
001	5ZA96	BLINDERS	4	2.50	10.00
002	36B92	ROSE GLASSES	1	15.00	15.00
003	1A462	BACON STRETCHER	30	1.00	30.00
TOTAL					55.00

ORDER NUMBER 111572

DATE: XX/YY/ZZ

NO.	PART NO.	DESCRIPTION	QTY.	PRICE	TOTAL
001	1A462	BACON STRETCHER	3	1.00	3.00
002	2Z329	SKYHOOK	20	.30	6.00
003	1B4AN	WRENCH	1	400.00	400.00
004	Q3333	VITAMINS	2	6.00	12.00
005	1A463	CRUISE MISSILE	1	25.00	25.00
TOTAL					446.00

Figure 12-14. Two ORDERS with Similarly Numbered ORDER LINES

occurrences. Figure 12-14, for example, shows two ORDERS, each with ORDER LINE Line Item Numbers of 001, 002 and 003.

However, since the value of ORDER LINE is unique for a given ORDER, one can uniquely identify each ORDER LINE entity by the combination of its pairing with a particular ORDER and its Line Item Number. Thus, the combination of predicates involved includes one relationship membership and one attribute, as follows:

Identifiers of ORDER LINE	
Identifier 1	*is contained on* ORDER LINE ITEM NUMBER

Finally, if we impose a constraint that each PRODUCT can only appear once on an ORDER (that is, that no two ORDER LINES on any one ORDER will reference the same PRODUCT), another identifier emerges which requires no attributes at all. One can uniquely identify an ORDER LINE by the combination of its pairing with a specific ORDER and a specific PRODUCT. Thus, the identifier is composed entirely of relationship memberships. As a result, the set of identifiers for ORDER LINE becomes:

Identifiers of ORDER LINE	
Identifier 1	*is contained on* ORDER LINE ITEM NUMBER
Identifier 2	*is contained on* ORDER *is for* PRODUCT

In the IEF, relationship memberships which participate in identifiers are highlighted on the Entity Relationship Diagram with a red "I" superimposed over the end of the relationship nearest the entity type it identifies. Figure 12-15 illustrates this convention for a portion of the ERD fragment appearing in Figure 12-13, assuming that both *is contained on* ORDER and *is for* PRODUCT participate in identifiers.

Analysts familiar with data base design should take note that a relationship membership should always be preferred as an identifier to using an attribute as a foreign key.

For example, instead of using *is contained on* ORDER as an identifier of ORDER LINE, one could have added the identifier of ORDER (in this case, Number) as an attribute of ORDER LINE, so that each ORDER LINE contains the Number of the ORDER on which it appears. Since Number is not really an attribute of ORDER LINE but exists only to facilitate access to ORDER, it is called a **foreign key.** A foreign key serves the same purpose as a relationship: to relate two entities. However, while a relationship explicitly defines a possible pairing, the use of a foreign key actually obscures the fact that entities of the two affected types can be related.

Mutually Exclusive Relationships

Consider the case where PRODUCT entities are either manufactured by an internal manufacturing department or purchased from a supplier (Figure 12-16). Assume that each PRODUCT can be acquired from only one source. In other words, each PRODUCT entity either *is supplied by* a SUPPLIER or *is made by* a DEPARTMENT, but never both. In this case, the existence of a pairing based on one of the relationships precludes the existence of one based on the other. For a given entity type, relationship memberships whose occurrences preclude the existence of occurrences of other relationship memberships are said to be **mutually exclusive** of one another.

More than two relationship memberships can be mutually exclusive. For example, one could add another relationship membership to PRODUCT (*is conjured by* SORCERER, perhaps) that is mutually exclusive with the other two.

In the IEF, one records the mutual exclusivity of a set of relationship memberships when detailing the entity type to which the relationship memberships belong. One may specify up to five different sets of mutually exclusive relationship memberships for each entity type. The IEF provides no graphical way to represent mutually exclusive relationships.

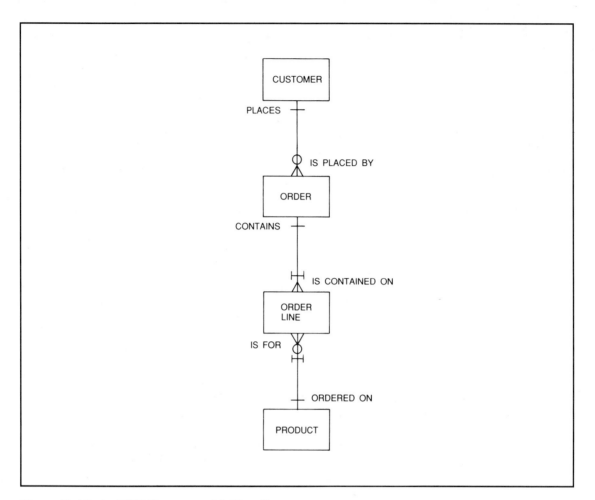

Figure 12-15. An ERD Fragment with Identifiers

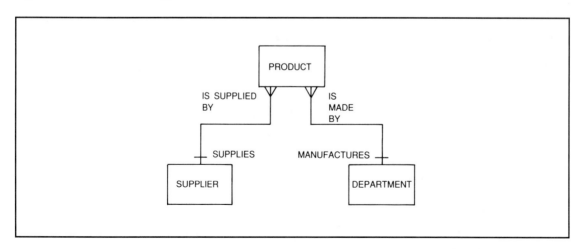

Figure 12-16. Mutual Exclusivity

General Integrity Constraints

In some cases, certain combinations of predicate values can be invalid for entities of a given type. Conditions that determine the validity of entities of a given type are called **integrity constraints.**

One may be surprised to learn that a number of kinds of integrity constraint have already been introduced in different guises. Optionality conditions for relationship memberships and attributes, cardinality conditions for relationship memberships, permitted values for attributes and the mutual exclusivity of relationship memberships are all examples of special kinds of integrity constraints. However, these specifications do not exhaustively address all issues that can determine an entity's validity. To do so, one must specify a general integrity constraint.

In the IEF, integrity constraints not otherwise addressed are captured as part of an entity type's description. During activity analysis, the analyst must insure that the integrity constraints documented during the data modeling activity are enacted in the detailed process definition.

Two examples of conditions addressed by general integrity constraints include:

- Complex permitted values, where certain permitted values of an attribute are valid only when other attributes have specific values or specific pairings exist. For example, imagine that for a CUSTOMER to have the Status "preferred," he or she must have a Credit Rating of "impeccable" and at least one outstanding ORDER.

   One might record this in the description of the entity type CUSTOMER as:

   > Valid when Status is equal to "preferred," Credit Rating is equal to "impeccable" and *places* ORDER.

- Mutually inclusive relationships, where one pairing can exist only if another exists. For example, assume that a PRODUCT can only appear on an ORDER LINE if it *is supplied by* a SUPPLIER or *is made by* a DEPARTMENT (see Figures 12-15 and 12-16.)

   One might record this condition in the description of the entity type PRODUCT as:

   > Invalid when *ordered on* ORDER LINE and not *supplied by* SUPPLIER and not *made by* a DEPARTMENT.

One could formulate countless other examples, but these two exemplify the variety of conditions for which one should specify integrity constraints.

User-Defined Domains

The concept of complex or user-defined domains was mentioned earlier in the discussion of primitive domains. User-defined domains define sets of possible values that may be shared by multiple attributes.

For example, consider the case where PRODUCTS are available in a limited number of colors. In some other business area, there might be an entity type EMPLOYEE whose security badge can be one of a number of badge colors. If we assume a fairly standard list of colors (no taupe or mauve), it is possible to imagine a common definition for both the attribute PRODUCT Color and EMPLOYEE Badge Color, called simply Color, which has the same:

- Primitive domain
- Length
- List of permitted values

Such a definition is called a **user-defined domain.** The specification of the user-defined domain Color might be:

User-Defined Domain COLOR	
Primitive Domain	Text
Length	25 characters
Permitted Values	RED
	BLUE
	YELLOW
	SILVER
	GOLD
	GREEN
	GREEN FLECKED WITH GOLD

The use of domains provides some benefits over the use of discrete attribute definitions. First, domain definitions are shared. Thus, if the domain changes (a new permitted value is added), the change is reflected in all of the separate attribute definitions. Second, operations involving attributes from different domains can be restricted to avoid illogical conditions. For example, if there exists one domain called Price and another called Quantity, it is reasonable to allow multiplication of attributes belonging to the two domains, as in:

(ORDER LINE Amount = PRODUCT Price * ORDER LINE Quantity)

but it is probably not reasonable to allow them to be compared (If PRODUCT Price is greater than ORDER LINE Quantity,...) or added together.

The IEF currently provides no direct support for user-defined domain definitions. However, the analyst can still realize some of the benefits of user-defined domain support by observing the following guidelines:

1. Use the name of the domain as the name of the attribute wherever possible. For example:

Domain QUANTITY	Attributes
	Entity Type ORDER LINE
	Attribute QUANTITY
	Entity Type INVOICE ITEM
	Attribute QUANTITY
	Entity Type PRODUCT STOCK
	Attribute QUANTITY

In cases where one cannot easily follow this convention, the analyst should at least include the domain name as part of the attribute name. For example:

Domain COLOR	Attributes
	Entity Type PRODUCT Attribute COLOR Entity Type EMPLOYEE Attribute BADGE COLOR Entity Type BUILDING Attribute EXTERIOR COLOR Attribute INTERIOR COLOR

In the case of EMPLOYEE, the use of the domain name without qualification is misleading and potentially offensive. In the case of BUILDING, two attributes belong to the Color domain; therefore, some additional qualification is needed to distinguish between them.

In practice, this convention almost implements itself, given reasonable domain names. In the preceding examples, for example, the attribute names naturally contain the name of the domain to which they belong. In fact, it is difficult to imagine a sensible formation of those attribute names which does not include the domain name (EMPLOYEE Badge Hue? INVOICE Number of Things?).

2. Copy the attribute's definition. To help manipulate attributes, the IEF includes a COPY command that allows an attribute's definition to be copied to a different entity type. Through judicious use of this command, analysts can use an attribute in a particular domain as a basis for defining other attributes in the same domain. For example, given the existence of the attribute ORDER LINE Quantity, one could create the attribute Quantity of entity type INVOICE ITEM by copying the definition of Quantity from the entity type ORDER LINE to the entity type INVOICE ITEM.

Composite Attributes

Information Engineering includes the concept of **composite attributes**. A composite attribute is one that is actually made up of other attributes. Attributes of the sort previously defined in this chapter are sometimes called **elementary attributes** to distinguish them from composite attributes.

An example of a composite attribute might be the attribute Phone Number of the entity type CUSTOMER:

Entity Type CUSTOMER

Composite Attribute PHONE NUMBER
    Elementary Attribute AREA CODE
    Elementary Attribute EXCHANGE
    Elementary Attribute STATION

The intent here is to allow the attribute Phone Number to be treated as a single attribute in some cases, while still making it possible to inspect and modify its components individually whenever necessary.

The IEF does not currently support the concept of composite attributes directly. In general, the absence of composite attribute support causes few problems. In the previous example, for instance, the decomposition of Phone Number into its components is unnecessary in most business situations. If, however, the business happens to be a telephone company, the need for Phone Number to be a composite attribute is probably quite acute. In such a situation, the composite attribute can easily be simulated by using a derivation algorithm. The use of derivation algorithms to support composite attributes is discussed in the section entitled "Notes on SET. . .USING, Default and Derivation Algorithms" in Chapter 14.

The Modeling of Hierarchies and Networks

Recall the definition of relationship ("A reason relevant to the enterprise for associating entities from one or two entity types"). Up to now, this book has presented examples of relationships between two separate entity types. However, it is clear from the definition that entities from the same entity type can also be paired based on a relationship. The most frequent use of such a relationship is to represent either a hierarchy or a network of entities.

Consider Figure 12-17. This occurrence diagram represents a situation where one EMPLOYEE can supervise one or more other EMPLOYEES who can, in turn, supervise one or more other EMPLOYEES. Such a hierarchy of EMPLOYEE entities can be modelled as shown in Figure 12-18.

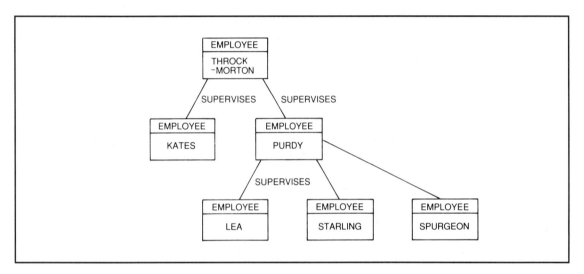

Figure 12-17. An Occurrence Diagram Representing a Hierarchy

A relationship which joins an entity type to itself, as in Figure 12-18, is called an **involuted** relationship or, more simply, a **looped** relationship. Note that the relationship must be fully optional to avoid a situation in which the hierarchy continues forever. The EMPLOYEE at the top of the hierarchy has no pairing based on its *is supervised by* relationship membership and the ones at the bottom have no pairings based on their *supervises* relationship membership.

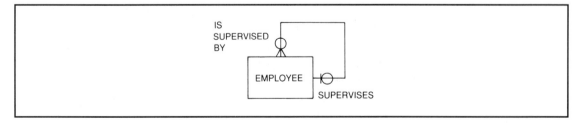

Figure 12-18. ER Model Fragment Supporting Figure 12-17

The model fragment in Figure 12-18 models a true hierarchy. Each EMPLOYEE *is supervised by* at most one EMPLOYEE. (By implication, it is also true that each EMPLOYEE entity can only appear once in the hierarchy.) Now, however, consider the situation in Figure 12-19. This occurrence diagram shows a less desirable (but more realistic) business condition in which a single individual (named "Sam") has multiple bosses. In this situation, EMPLOYEE entities do not participate in a true hierarchy. Rather, they are arranged in a **network.**

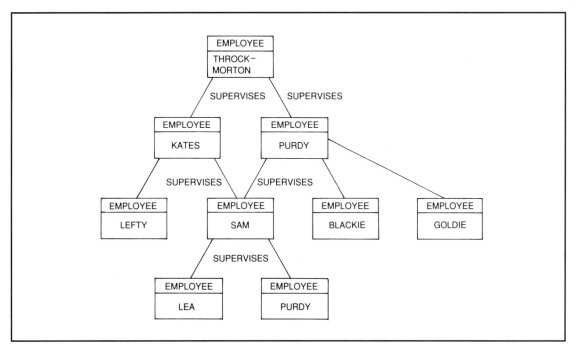

Figure 12-19. An Occurrence Diagram Representing a Network

In a network, an entity can participate in multiple pairings based on either membership of its involuted relationship. Obviously, the model fragment presented in Figure 12-18 is too restrictive to allow for such a condition. Figure 12-20, however, will support a network.

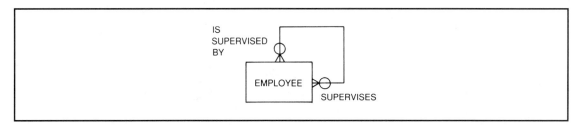

Figure 12-20. An ER Model Fragment Supporting Figure 12-19

The style of involuted, fully optional, M:N relationship shown in Figure 12-20 can be used to support any sort of general network.

Finally, consider a Bill of Materials structure. A Bill of Materials structure is generally shown as a hierarchy. In reality, however, it is a network, since a single PART can appear multiple times, as shown in Figure 12-21.

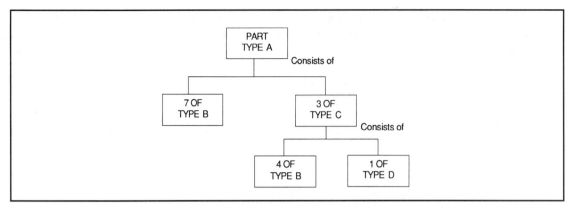

Figure 12-21. An Occurrence Diagram Representing a Bill of Materials Structure

This sort of structure is slightly different from the general network previously presented. Here, each time a PART appears in the structure, it is accompanied by a piece of related information, namely Quantity Used. For example, in Figure 12-21, 7 PARTS of type B are required for a single PART of type A, while 4 PARTS of type B are required for a single PART of type C (of which 3 are required for each type A PART).

Obviously, Quantity Used is an attribute of something besides the entity type PART. Otherwise, each PART, with all of its attendant predicates, would have to be repeated each time it appeared in the structure, with the only difference being the value of Quantity Used. In order to solve this problem, one can introduce an entity type whose sole function is to hold Quantity Used (and any other attributes associated with the specific usage of a PART in the structure.) Figure 12-22 shows a model fragment that uses this technique and the set of occurrences that support Figure 12-22.

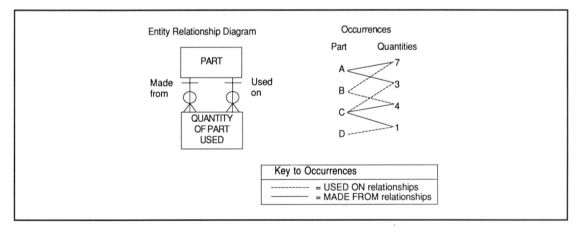

Figure 12-22. Modelling a Bill of Materials Structure

Partitionings and Their Detail

In some cases, entities of the same type may have differing characteristics. For example, consider the expanded definition of entity type CUSTOMER presented in Figure 12-23.

Attributes of Entity Type CUSTOMER
NUMBER
NAME
ADDRESS
PHONE NUMBER
STATUS
CREDIT RATING
VALUE OF OUTSTANDING ORDERS
NATIONALITY (Foreign or Domestic)
COUNTRY CODE
IMPORT LICENSE NUMBER
CURRENCY
TAX ID NUMBER
STATE OF INCORPORATION
TYPE (Commercial or Government)
GOVERNMENT AGENCY NAME
INTERESTED POLITICIAN NAME

Figure 12-23. Extended Attribute List for CUSTOMER

Given this set of attributes, assume the following to be true:

- The attributes Country Code, Import License Number and Currency have values only for FOREIGN CUSTOMERS.

- The attributes Tax ID Number and State of Incorporation may only have values for DOMESTIC CUSTOMERS.

- The attributes Government Agency Name and Interested Politician Name are valid for either FOREIGN or DOMESTIC CUSTOMERS, but only when the CUSTOMER is a GOVERNMENT CUSTOMER, not a COMMERCIAL one.

One could record these facts as a set of integrity constraints on CUSTOMER. However, in Information Engineering, this sort of situation is recognized as a special one and is handled using a concept known as **subtyping.**

Entity Subtypes

One can infer from the above assumptions that entities of the type CUSTOMER fall into two mutually exclusive groups: FOREIGN and DOMESTIC. Although all CUSTOMERS share a set of predicates, some CUSTOMERS (FOREIGN ones) have predicates beyond those in the common set and others (DOMESTIC ones) have *different* predicates in addition to the common set. One can define these mutually exclusive groups of entities of the same type as **entity subtypes.**

The formal definition of an entity subtype is:

Entity Sub-   A description of entities of the same type that is more restrictive than that of the entity type
type   and to which additional common predicates may apply.

Figure 12-24 shows an Entity Relationship Diagram in which the entity type CUSTOMER (Figure 12-23) has been separated into subtypes FOREIGN CUSTOMER and DOMESTIC CUSTOMER, annotated with attributes.

The following observations are important:

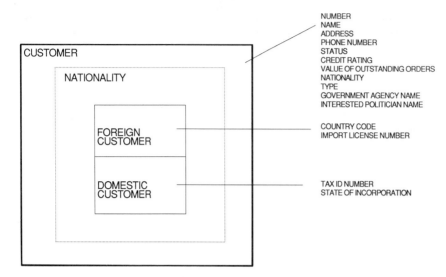

Figure 12-24. ERD for CUSTOMER with Two Subtypes

- The entity type CUSTOMER is a supertype in relation to FOREIGN CUSTOMER and DOMESTIC CUSTOMER.

- The entity types FOREIGN CUSTOMER and DOMESTIC CUSTOMER are subtypes of the entity type CUSTOMER.

- The dashed box inside CUSTOMER containing FOREIGN CUSTOMER and DOMESTIC CUSTOMER represents a **partitioning** of the entity type CUSTOMER into subtypes. The name appearing inside the dashed box, NATIONALITY, is the name of the **classifying attribute** of the partitioning. Classifying attributes are discussed later in this section.

- Predicates of subtypes are mutually exclusive with predicates of other subtypes on the same partitioning. A FOREIGN CUSTOMER may not have values for Tax ID Number and State of Incorporation, while a DOMESTIC CUSTOMER may not have values for Country Code or Import License Number.

Subtypes are said to **inherit** the predicates of their supertypes. For example, every FOREIGN CUSTOMER can have values for all of the predicates defined for the supertype CUSTOMER as well as those defined specifically for FOREIGN CUSTOMER. Since each CUSTOMER must have a value for the attribute Number (it is a mandatory attribute), each FOREIGN CUSTOMER must have a Number as well. Similarly, since each CUSTOMER may *place* ORDERS, each FOREIGN CUSTOMER may also *place* ORDERS.

The optionality of predicates of a subtype depends, of course, on whether a given entity belongs to that subtype. In Figure 12-24, for example, assume that Country Code is defined as a mandatory attribute of the subtype FOREIGN CUSTOMER. In this case, every FOREIGN CUSTOMER must have a value for Country Code. A DOMESTIC CUSTOMER will not and, in fact, cannot have a value for Country Code.

Partitionings

The formal definition of a **partitioning** is:

Partitioning   A basis for subdividing the entities of one type into subtypes.

Figure 12-24 shows the entity type CUSTOMER partitioned into two subtypes along a single partitioning. However, there is no limit to the number of subtypes one can define along a partitioning. For example, after the UFO's land, there might be three subtypes of CUSTOMER along the same partitioning: FOREIGN CUSTOMER, DOMESTIC CUSTOMER and EXTRATERRESTRIAL CUSTOMER (Figure 12-25).

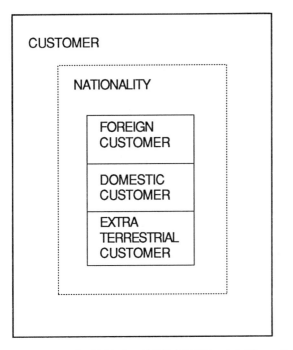

Figure 12-25. ERD for CUSTOMER with Three Subtypes

A subtype can also have partitionings of its own. For example, the subtype FOREIGN CUSTOMER might have different predicates, depending on whether the CUSTOMER resides in a Warsaw Pact nation, as shown in Figure 12-26.

One may divide each entity type into multiple partitionings, where each partitioning is a different reason for having subtypes. For example, a review of Figure 12-23 and the integrity constraints that resulted in the first partitioning reveals the potential for a second partitioning: GOVERNMENT CUSTOMERS have predicates not shared by COMMERCIAL CUSTOMERS. Since a GOVERNMENT CUSTOMER can be either a DOMESTIC CUSTOMER or a FOREIGN CUSTOMER (that is, GOVERNMENT CUSTOMERS are not mutually exclusive with DOMESTIC or FOREIGN CUSTOMERS), GOVERNMENT and COMMERCIAL CUSTOMERS may be broken into their own partitioning, as in Figure 12-27.

Subtypes within a partitioning are mutually exclusive with each other but not with subtypes in other partitionings. Thus, Figure 12-27 reveals the possibility of at least four flavors of CUSTOMER:

FOREIGN, GOVERNMENT

DOMESTIC, GOVERNMENT

FOREIGN, COMMERCIAL

DOMESTIC, COMMERCIAL

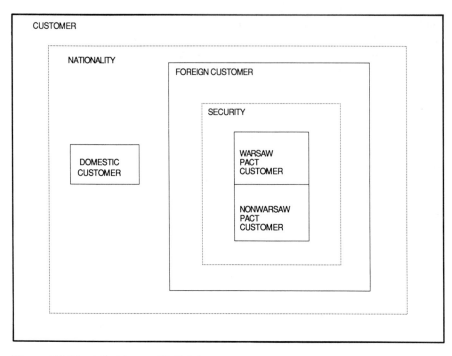

Figure 12-26. A Subtype with Subtypes

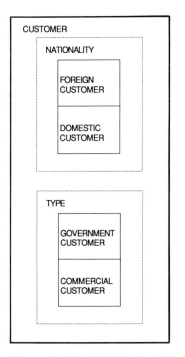

Figure 12-27. Multiple Partitionings

Some situations may require cross-partitioning restrictions to accurately reflect the needs of the business. For example, business rules may dictate that the company does not deal with FOREIGN, GOVERNMENT CUSTOMERS. One should record such a restriction as an integrity constraint of the entity type being partitioned.

One may specify the following detailed information for each partitioning:

- Description
- Enumeration
- Whether the partitioning is the life cycle partitioning
- Classifying attribute
- Classifying values (one for each subtype)

Description

Analysts can use the partitioning **description** to elaborate on the reason for the partitioning's existence.

Enumeration

If a partitioning is **fully enumerated**, every entity belonging to the entity type it divides must belong to one of the subtypes along the partitioning.

For example, consider Figure 12-27 again. Assuming that every CUSTOMER is either foreign or domestic, the partitioning that divides CUSTOMER into FOREIGN and DOMESTIC must be fully enumerated. Likewise, assuming that every CUSTOMER is either a GOVERNMENT CUSTOMER or a COMMERCIAL CUSTOMER, that partitioning is also fully enumerated.

However, a review of Figure 12-23 reveals that there are really no predicates unique to a commercial customer. While government customers require some additional attributes, non-government customers do not. As a result, the subtype COMMERCIAL CUSTOMER is really unnecessary. A more accurate depiction of the situation is that some customers are government customers while others simply are not. By specifying that the partitioning that identifies GOVERNMENT CUSTOMERS is **not fully enumerated**, some CUSTOMER entities may be government customers while others are not, without adding the superfluous COMMERCIAL CUSTOMER subtype. This alternative representation is shown as Figure 12-28.

It should be obvious that a partitioning with only one subtype cannot be fully enumerated.

Life Cycle Partitioning

The **life cycle partitioning** is a special partitioning that identifies the states through which an entity can pass. The movement of an entity from state to state during its life is an important aspect of interaction analysis.

In the life cycle partitioning, each subtype reflects a specific entity state. Consider, for example, Figure 12-29.

Each entity type can have one life cycle partitioning and that partitioning must be fully enumerated. In other words, an entity must always be in some state. Refer to Chapter 14, "Interaction Analysis," for a detailed discussion of entity life cycle analysis.

Classifying Attribute and Classifying Values

The classification of a particular entity along a partitioning is based on the value of a specific attribute of the entity being partitioned. This attribute is called the **classifying attribute.** For example, in Figures 12-23 and

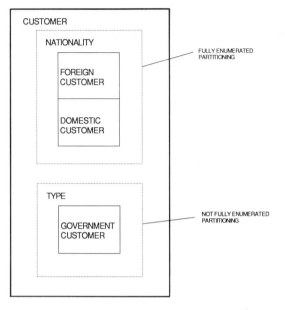

Figure 12-28. Fully Enumerated Versus Not Fully Enumerated Partitionings

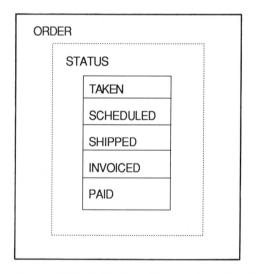

Figure 12-29. Life Cycle Partitioning of Entity Type ORDER

12-24, the distinction between a FOREIGN CUSTOMER and a DOMESTIC CUSTOMER depends on the value of the attribute Nationality of the entity type CUSTOMER. A CUSTOMER for whom the value of Nationality is "foreign" is a FOREIGN CUSTOMER, while one for whom the value of Nationality is "domestic" is a DOMESTIC CUSTOMER. In this case, the values "foreign" and "domestic" are **classifying values** of the classifying attribute Nationality.

Each partitioning must be associated with a classifying attribute, which, in turn, must be an attribute of the entity type being partitioned. Additionally, each subtype in the partitioning must be associated with a classifying value for the partitioning's classifying attribute.

Data Modeling Anomalies

This section deals with some of the more questionable, unusual, or impossible situations that might arise when developing the ER model.

Redundant Relationships

A relationship conveying no information that cannot be deduced from other relationships is said to be **redundant.** For example, consider the ER model fragment shown in Figure 12-30. The M:N relationship between PRODUCT and WAREHOUSE records the fact that a PRODUCT *is stocked in* a particular WAREHOUSE. Assume that if a product is stocked at one or more warehouses, the Quantity of product at a particular warehouse is held as an attribute of the entity type STOCK. If this is true, one can deduce the fact that a product is stored at a warehouse from the PRODUCT's pairing with STOCK which, in turn, is paired with a WAREHOUSE. The relationship PRODUCT *is stocked in* WAREHOUSE conveys no new information and is, thus, redundant.

Analysts should eliminate redundant relationships. Besides being completely superfluous, such relationships require duplicate operations to properly record the information reflected in the model. For example, each time a product is to be stocked in a new warehouse, the PRODUCT must be paired both with a WAREHOUSE and with a STOCK entity. When the product's stock is exhausted, two pairings must be deleted instead of just one.

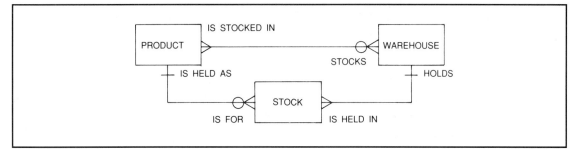

Figure 12-30. A Redundant Relationship

However, one must exercise caution when removing apparently redundant relationships. Imagine, for example, a situation only slightly different from the one pictured in Figure 12-30. Assume that certain warehouses are equipped to handle certain products and that the ability of a warehouse to stock a particular product, whether or not it actually carries it, is of interest to the business. Figure 12-31 models this situation, which looks remarkably similar to Figure 12-30. In this case, the relationship between PRODUCT and WAREHOUSE is not redundant, although at first glance it might appear to be.

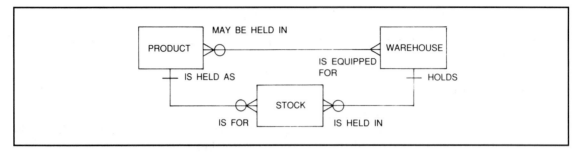

Figure 12-31. A Non-Redundant Relationship

Relationships with Multiple Meanings

Each relationship reflects a reason for associating two entities. Sometimes there are multiple reasons for joining two entities of the same two types. If so, the model should contain one relationship for each reason.

For example, consider the example in Figure 12-32. In this case, the M:N relationship between PERSON and CAR has two distinct meanings:

- A PERSON can *own* one or more CARS which can, in turn, *be owned by* just one PERSON, and

- A PERSON can *drive* one or more CARS which can, in turn, *be driven by* many PERSONS.

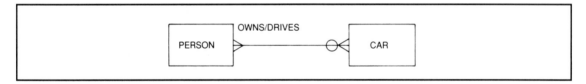

Figure 12-32. A Relationship with Two Meanings

The single M:N relationship in Figure 12-32 hides an important fact and should be expanded into two relationships, as shown in Figure 12-33.

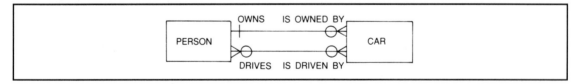

Figure 12-33. Two Relationships, Each with a Single Meaning

Two or more relationships that join the same entity types (as in Figure 12-33) are called **parallel** relationships.

Information Loss in an M:N Relationship

The injudicious use of M:N relationships can sometimes lead to the loss of important information. Although M:N relationships sometimes occur naturally, there is often information of interest hidden by the relationship itself. Figure 12-34, for example, shows that an ORDER can *be for* one or more PRODUCTS and that a PRODUCT can *appear on* one or more ORDERS. While this is true enough, some important details have been omitted. For example, what is the quantity of each PRODUCT appearing on a given ORDER? One cannot extract this information from the example in Figure 12-34.

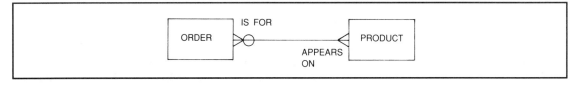

Figure 12-34. Information Loss in an M:N Relationship

Useful information of this sort that appears at the juncture of an M:N relationship is called **intersection data.** The presence of intersection data calls for the addition of an entity type to hold that data as attributes. By adding an associative entity type and replacing the M:N relationship with two 1:M relationships, one can retain all of the information conveyed by the original M:N, and also represent additional facts about the intersection. In Figure 12-35, entity type ORDER LINE has been added to hold the attribute Quantity for a given PRODUCT on a given ORDER.

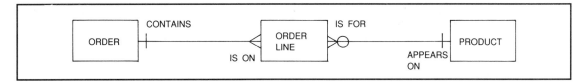

Figure 12-35. Addition of an Associative Entity Type

As a matter of course, analysts should carefully evaluate each M:N relationship appearing in a data model to insure that it results in no information loss.

1:1 Fully Mandatory Relationships

Analysts should be wary of any 1:1 relationship defined as fully mandatory (that is, with both relationship memberships mandatory). Unless there is a good, solid business reason for identifying the entity types separately, they should probably be combined into a single entity type.

Isolated Entity Types

An **isolated** entity type is one with no relationships. In such cases, the entity type definition is probably incorrect. Most things of value to a business relate to some other aspects of the business. If, after careful consideration, one determines that an entity type has no relationships, it should probably be removed from the model.

Solitary Entity Types

An entity type which has only one entity by definition is called a **solitary** entity type. The existence of solitary entity types often indicates incorrect analysis of some kind.

For example, a model that depends on there being only one occurrence of some entity type, say, FACTORY, is **time dependent.** If more factories are added in the future, the model will require modification.

In other cases, where there actually is and will be only one occurrence of an entity type, one should make sure it is not a special instance of another, more general, entity type. For example, an entity type representing the entire ENTERPRISE which has only one occurrence might well fit into an entity type called ORGANIZATION UNIT.

In any event, one should evaluate solitary entity types carefully whenever they appear.

Multi-Valued Attributes

Occasionally, an attribute seems to need to hold multiple values simultaneously. For example, consider an entity type called POLYGLOT which has Language Spoken as one of its attributes. The central distinguishing characteristic of a polyglot is, of course, that he or she speaks many languages. Thus, the attribute Language Spoken would seem to require multiple values for each POLYGLOT entity. An attribute that seems to require multiple values simultaneously is called a **multi-valued** attribute.

The IEF does not provide for multi-valued attributes, nor should it. Rather, one should remove an apparently multi-valued attribute to its own entity type and relate it to the original entity type via a 1:M relationship as shown in Figure 12-36.

Figure 12-36. Correct Handling of a Multi-Valued Attribute

Entity Types with Too Few Predicates

Sometimes an analyst may describe an entity type that contains too few predicates. Each entity type must have either:

* One attribute and one relationship membership, or
* Two relationship memberships

This is a hard and fast rule in data modeling. It makes sense because an entity type with only one relationship membership and no attributes can convey no additional information. Another inviolable rule relates to isolated entity types. Each entity type must have at least one relationship membership, regardless of the number of attributes it contains. Certain other combinations of predicates, though not strictly prohibited, should be regarded with suspicion. These include:

* Entity types with no attributes (and, by implication, two or more relationships). One should evaluate these carefully to insure there are really no values associated with them. One should also make sure that the pairings in which they participate are truly of interest to the business.

  One case where an entity type with no attributes should *not* be eliminated is when an associative entity type resolves a many-to-many relationship. There is always the possibility of discovering some attributes later on. Adding an entity type and its relationship memberships has a much greater impact on other portions of the model (such as the Process Action Diagram, the Screen Designs built during Business System Design and the Data Structure Diagram in Technical Design) than adding an attribute to an entity type. Hence, the existence of an associative entity type without attributes can improve the model's stability.

• Entity types with only one attribute. These are very rare. Occasionally they are valid (as in the case of the multi-valued attribute mentioned earlier), but the analyst should always insure that the sole attribute does not, in fact, belong to some other entity type.

NOTES ON DRAWING ENTITY RELATIONSHIP DIAGRAMS

Since the Entity Relationship Diagram is primarily a vehicle for communication, some attention should be given to the actual layout of the diagram. The IEF Data Modeling Tool provides a good deal of flexibility to support the construction of meaningful diagrams. In particular, the IEF supports **variable-sized boxes** to represent entity types and **subject areas** to provide for the hiding of detail.

Using Variable-Sized Boxes

The IEF allows the resizing of entity type boxes appearing on the Entity Relationship Diagram. This allows the analyst to change the shape of an entity type box to virtually any size of rectangle. This feature can be used to emphasize an important entity type by making it larger, or to de-emphasize an unimportant entity type to make it smaller. Additionally, the shape of an entity type can be changed simply to enhance the aesthetics of the diagram.

Figure 12-37 illustrates the use of variable-sized boxes.

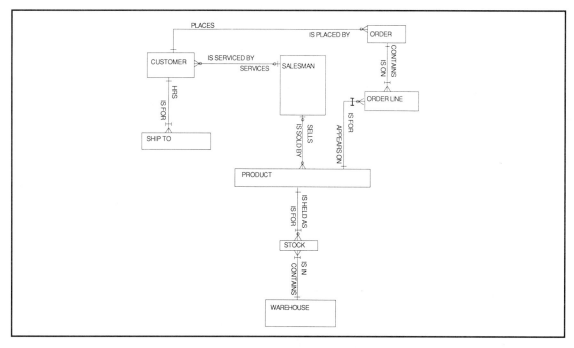

Figure 12-37. An ERD with Variable Sized Boxes

Hiding Unnecessary Detail

In larger Entity Relationship Diagrams, it is sometimes desirable to look at a small portion of the diagram in great detail while hiding much of the surrounding diagram. This is done in the IEF Data Modeling Tool through the use of **subject areas.**

Subject areas were introduced in Chapter 4 as high-level views of business data which are eventually decomposed into entity types. As it turns out, entity types can be collected together into smaller subject areas during BAA in order to provide a higher-level view of the Entity Relationship Diagram as well.

In figure 12-38, the Entity Relationship Diagram shown in figure 12-37 has been revised to include subject areas. In this example, the subject area CUSTOMERS includes the entity types CUSTOMER and SHIP TO, the subject area ORDERS includes ORDERS and ORDER LINES, the subject area INVENTORY includes PRODUCT, STOCK and WAREHOUSE. Additionally, the subject area SALES includes both the subject areas ORDERS and CUSTOMERS and the entity type SALESMAN.

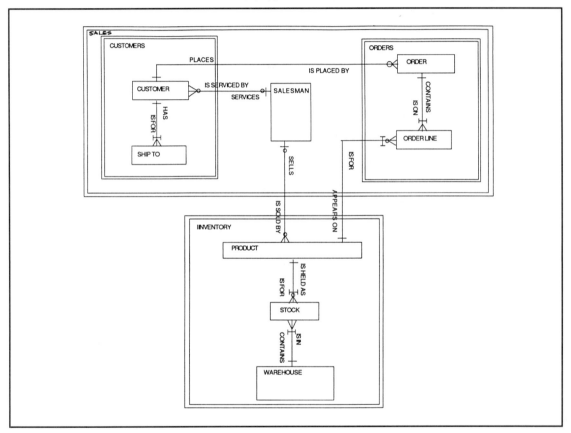

Figure 12-38. An ERD with Subject Areas

The IEF supports the contraction of all components of a subject area into a single box. Thus, in order to produce a version of the diagram which emphasizes the entity type SALESMAN, the underlying details of CUSTOMERS, ORDERS and INVENTORY can be hidden by contracting those subject areas, as in Figure 12-39.

Likewise, in order to produce a version of the diagram featuring elements of the INVENTORY subject area, one need only contract the SALES subject area, as in Figure 12-40.

SUMMARY OF DATA MODELING RULES

The preceding discussions have revealed a number of data modeling rules, some explicitly and others by implication. These rules are summarized in the following paragraphs.

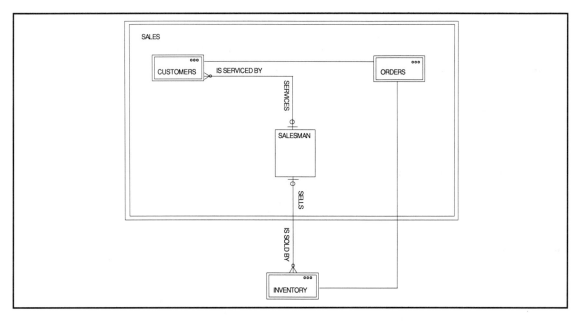

Figure 12-39. SALES Subject Area with Enclosed Subject Areas Contracted

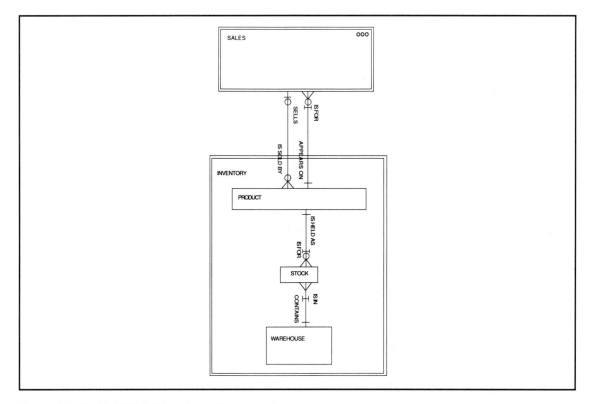

Figure 12-40. SALES Subject Area Contracted

Rules for Entity Types

- Each entity described by an entity type must be uniquely identifiable.

- An entity type must have at least one attribute or two relationship memberships.

- An entity type must participate in at least one relationship.

- An entity type is part of one and only one subject area.

Rules for Relationships

- Each relationship associates one or two entity types and depicts a pairing between exactly two entities.

- A relationship must not have attributes.

- An optional relationship membership may not participate in an identifier.

Rules for Attributes

- An attribute describes exactly one entity type.

- An attribute must have at most one value for any entity of the type it describes.

- An attribute must not have attributes of its own.

- An optional attribute may not participate in an identifier.

- A derived attribute may not participate in an identifier.

Rules for Partitionings and Subtypes

- Each subtype belongs to exactly one partitioning.

- Each partitioning must be associated with a classifying attribute that belongs to the entity type it partitions.

- Each subtype must be identifiable by a classifying value or range of classifying values.

- A fully enumerated partitioning must divide the entity type it partitions into two or more subtypes.

One can verify these rules automatically by running the IEF's Consistency Check facility. In addition, the Consistency Check software points out a number of the *suspect* conditions mentioned earlier. Those situations that must be addressed before the data model can be considered complete are flagged as **errors**. Any questionable situations with no definite errors are flagged as **warnings**. The IEF will not permit data modeling objects that contain errors to be used during Business System Design, the next stage of Information Engineering.

For a complete list of Consistency Check Rules for a particular release of the IEF, consult the *IEF Analysis Toolset Guide* and the Release Notes that accompany the IEF software.

SUMMARY OF DATA MODELING DELIVERABLES

Top-down data modeling results in the following deliverables:

- An Entity Relationship Diagram describing the data requirements of the entire business area.

- Supporting documentation (stored as details of the objects appearing on the Entity Relationship Diagram).

This combined set of deliverables is called the business area's **data model** or **ER model.**

13
ACTIVITY ANALYSIS

OVERVIEW

To review, the business model to be constructed during a Business Area Analysis project has three major components:

- The data model, which describes the things of interest to the business and the relationships between them.

- The activity model, which records the things the business does (or should do).

- The interaction model, which details how the things the business does (activities) affect the things of interest to the business (data).

This chapter describes the techniques used to build the activity model. Construction of the activity model for a business area involves the continued decomposition of the function/process hierarchy until the analyst has identified the lowest level processes of interest to the business. Part I dealt with the task of performing decomposition in some detail. The analyst may wish to refer there for a discussion of the rules and techniques of activity decomposition and definitions of functions and processes.

After process decomposition, the analyst verifies the results and augments them by creating Process Dependency Diagrams. The concept of **process dependency** is very similar to that of **function dependency** as presented in Chapter 5 of Part I. The analyst may wish to refer to that discussion for an explanation of the concept of **dependency** and an introduction to Dependency Diagrams.

The relatively short length of this chapter testifies to the fact that activity modeling, by itself, is not terribly complex. Nevertheless, an extremely important concept lies at the core of activity modeling: that of the **elementary process.** This chapter deals primarily with identifying the elementary processes that terminate decomposition. Since most of the work involved in process detailing centers around their interaction with the data model, that topic is deferred until Chapter 14, "Interaction Analysis."

This chapter contains the following major sections:

- **Basic Concepts**. This section reviews the concept of a business function and a business process and presents a more detailed definition of processes.

- **Process Decomposition**. This section describes techniques for decomposing a function or process into its lowest level components, with particular attention given to the discovery of elementary processes.

- **Dependency Analysis**. This section explains techniques for verifying process decomposition by specifying process dependencies.

- **External Objects**. This section describes objects outside the business area with which a process can exchange information.

- **Events**. This section covers objects that trigger execution of a process.

- **A Summary of Activity Modeling Rules**. This section combines the rules for activity modeling presented in Part I with those explained in this chapter. The result is a complete set of rules for activity analysis during BAA.

- **A Summary of Deliverables from Activity Analysis.** This short section itemizes the outputs resulting from activity analysis.

BASIC CONCEPTS

As mentioned in Part I, Information Engineering recognizes two kinds of business activities. Higher level activities are called **functions** and lower level ones are called **processes.** The goal of activity analysis is to identify the lowest level processes of interest to the business through continued decomposition.

This section describes processes in greater detail than in Part I. The properties of processes discussed here are optional for all but elementary processes.

Functions and Their Detail

Chapter 4 of Part I explained the details of functions. Since BAA deals primarily with processes rather than functions, no further refinement of the definition of functions is necessary. However, analysts should note that the IEF supports two types of function details not previously mentioned: information views and expected effects. While the IEF supports the recording of this data, in practice there is rarely a reason for specifying them at the function level. The analyst may choose to record them if he or she sees some benefit in doing so. Generally, however, analysts only record expected effects and information views for processes and, most frequently, for elementary processes. As a result, the discussion of both of these concepts is deferred.

Processes and Their Detail

Earlier, processes were described as activities for which one can actually imagine a start and an end. That is, a process is something that can be said to be **executable.** Using the terminology introduced in Chapter 12, a process is a **type** of activity. An occurrence of a process is called a process **execution.**

The formal definition of a process, initially presented in Chapter 2, is:

Process   A defined business activity whose executions may be identified in terms of the input and output of specific entities or of data about specific entities.

For example, a single execution of a process called Take Order deals with the input of certain information about a particular ORDER and results in the creation of that ORDER.

The IEF captures the following details about a process:

- Name
- Description
- Expected Effects
- Definition Properties
- Usage Properties
- Information Views

Name

As described previously, the **name** of a process should consist of a verb-noun combination. The noun is typically the name of an entity type or attribute. For example:

- Take Order

- Create Invoice
- Terminate Contract
- Calculate Account Balance

ORDER, INVOICE and CONTRACT are likely to be the names of entity types whose occurrences are manipulated during process execution. ACCOUNT is likely to be an entity type for which an entity will have its Balance attribute modified.

Description

The definition of a process, stored as part of its **description** on the IEF, should explain *what* the process does and, perhaps, *why* it does it. It should never describe who performs the process, when it is performed, or how it is performed. Such information is not fundamental to the existence of the process. It merely reflects the business's approach to implementing the process. Additionally, the definition should reflect a single execution of the process.

A process called Take Order, for example, might be defined as follows:

"An ORDER is created based on a CUSTOMER request, along with an ORDER LINE for each different type of PRODUCT requested."

The definition should be both precise and concise.

Expected Effects

Expected effects define, at a high level, the effect a process can have on the data model. For each entity type with which the process deals, the analyst may specify whether entities will be read, created, updated or deleted.

Analysts record expected effects in tabular fashion. For example, consider the process Take Order. It probably affects entities of the following types:

- CUSTOMER (since a customer places an order)
- ORDER (since the order is created)
- ORDER LINE (since each order likely contains multiple lines)
- PRODUCT (since the order is for particular products)
- PRODUCT STOCK (since the stock level of a product must be reduced to reflect the number of items appearing on an order line)

The expected effects, then, appear as follows:

	Create	Read	Update	Delete
CUSTOMER		x		
ORDER	x			
ORDER LINE	x			
PRODUCT		x		
PRODUCT STOCK			x	

Figure 13-1 Expected Effects of TAKE ORDER

When recording expected effects using the IEF, the analyst must have previously defined related entity types on the Entity Relationship Diagram. This is one instance where activity modeling encroaches on the boundaries of interaction analysis.

Definition Properties

The analyst may record the following **definition properties** for a process:

• Whether or not it is an **elementary** process. A discussion of the unique characteristics of an elementary process appears in the next section.

• Whether or not the process is **repetitive**; that is, whether it is likely to execute multiple times whenever executed. This property simply reminds the analyst that the detailed logic associated with the process (defined during interaction analysis) should allow for repetition.

For example, suppose the process Take Order is divided into two subordinate processes, Record Order Header and Record Order Line, as shown in Figure 13-2. Whenever an order is taken, Record Order Header executes once (and is, thus, not repetitive), but Record Order Line executes once per order line added to the order (and is, thus, repetitive).

A repetitive process is indicated by a horizontal bar within the process cushion (as is Record Order Line in Figure 13-2).

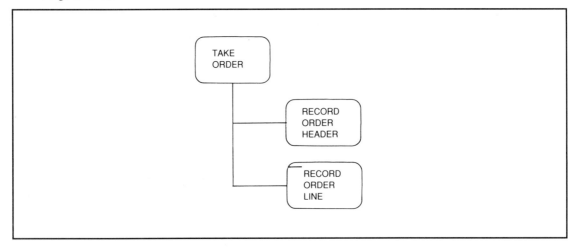

Figure 13-2. Process Hierarchy Diagram for the Process TAKE ORDER

• The suggested mechanism for implementing the process. Technically speaking, this decision belongs to the Business System Design stage. When defining a process during BAA, however, the analyst may have a feel for the eventual implementation and can record it here.

The alternatives for suggested mechanism are:

— Online (a terminal operator will carry out the process, interacting with some sort of terminal device)

— Batch (a computerized batch job will carry out the process, non-interactively)

— Manual (the process will not be computerized)

— Other (the process will be computerized, but will use some alternative other than online or batch. This classification of process is very rare in business situations. Examples include Real Time Systems and Process Control Systems.)

This property is typically recorded only for elementary processes.

Usage Properties

Usage properties include the estimated number of executions of a process in a given time period, and the anticipated change to that number of executions over time. This information is useful in later stages (when defining data bases during Technical Design, for example).

Usage properties are typically recorded only for elementary processes.

Information Views

The **information views** of a process describe in detail which entities and attributes may be referenced or manipulated during execution of the process. Chapter 14 presents a detailed discussion of information views.

Information views are typically recorded only for elementary processes.

PROCESS DECOMPOSITION

Process decomposition is merely a continuation of the function decomposition described in Chapters 4 and 5 of Part I. The same techniques and guidelines presented there are used in process decomposition. Whereas function decomposition involves decomposing functions until lowest-level functions or highest-level processes are discovered, process decomposition continues until the lowest-level, or **elementary,** processes are identified.

Process decomposition is recorded by building a Process Hierarchy Diagram (PHD) using the IEF Activity Hierarchy Tool. If the BAA project is using the Information Architecture established in ISP as a starting point, the creation of the Process Hierarchy Diagram is really a refinement of the Function Hierarchy Diagram built earlier.

General Nomenclature for Hierarchies

A general nomenclature for describing any hierarchical or **tree** structure is useful when discussing process decomposition. Some terms have fairly obvious meanings and have already been used. Others that are not so obvious are defined in the following discussion.

All definitions are expressed in terms of the sample Process Hierarchy Diagram shown in Figure 13-3.

Root	The **root** of a hierarchy is its highest level object. In Figure 13-3, A is the single root.
Leaf	The **leaves** of a hierarchy are its lowest level objects. C, D, F, and G are leaves.
Parent	Any object to which other objects are subordinate is called the **parent** of the subordinate objects. A is the parent of B and E, B is the parent of C and D, and E is the parent of F and G.
	Any object that is not a leaf is the parent of some object.
Child	Any object subordinate to another object is called the **child** of that object. C and D are children of B, F and G are children of E, and B and E are children of A.
	Any object that is not the root is the child of some object.
Sibling	Two or more objects that share an immediate parentage are called **siblings** of one another. C and D are siblings, F and G are siblings, and B and E are siblings.

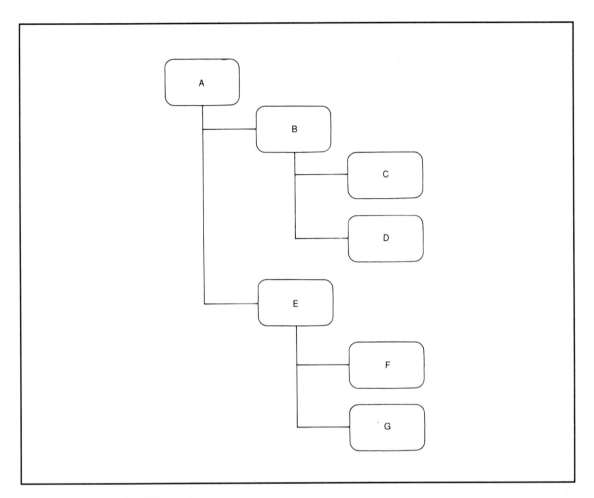

Figure 13-3. A Typical Hierarchy

Ancestor	Any object to which other objects are subordinate is called the **ancestor** of those objects, plus all objects of which they are ancestors. A is the ancestor of B, C, D, E, F, and G.
Progeny	The **progeny** of an object is the set of objects for which it is the ancestor. The progeny of A is B, C, D, E, F, and G.
Ancestry	The **ancestry** of an object is the set of ancestors of the object. The ancestry of C is B and A.

Identifying Elementary Processes

The main challenge during process decomposition lies in correctly identifying the **elementary processes** that terminate the decomposition. As might be expected, a process that is described as elementary cannot be further decomposed (at least not into subordinate processes using the Process Hierarchy Diagram.) Thus, each elementary process is a leaf in the hierarchy. When the Process Hierarchy Diagram is complete for a business area, all leaves are elementary processes.

The formal definition of elementary process is:

Elementary Process   A process which is the smallest unit of business activity of meaning to the business and which, when complete, leaves the business in a consistent state.

Identifying elementary processes is, to a large degree, subjective and frequently difficult (in fact, the elementary process has sometimes been called the "Holy Grail" of activity analysis). However, the analyst must identify elementary processes properly, because they form the basis for implementation during Business System Design.

The following guidelines are useful in deciding whether a process is, indeed, elementary. The analyst should apply these guidelines as a yardstick to each process suspected of being elementary, to insure that it falls neither above nor below the elementary process level.

- Each execution must leave the business data in a consistent state.

- Each execution must produce a result that is complete and meaningful to the user in itself.

- Each execution should take place, from beginning to end, at a single point in time.

- Each execution should take place, from beginning to end, at a single location.

- None of its components can be executed individually.

A process that violates the first or second rule is below the elementary process level, indicating that decomposition has progressed to too much detail. Such a process is called a **sub-elementary process** and has an ancestor that is an elementary process. A process that violates one of the last three rules is above the elementary process level, indicating that the process is not yet fully decomposed. Such a process is called a **super-elementary process** and has elementary processes among its progeny.

Take, for example, the Process Hierarchy Diagram presented in Figure 13-4 (another flavor of the Take Order process presented earlier). Assume that all of the activities appearing are processes. Further assume that the ERD fragment presented in Figure 13-5 has already been described in the data model. Finally, assume that the following descriptions of the business are true:

- When a customer places an order, all of the header information for the order is recorded, after which an order line is established for each different type of product ordered.

- When an order is corrected (or amended), a correction is normally made either to the header (for example, the requested date of shipment might be changed by the customer) or to a single line item (for example, the customer may request a change to the quantity of product ordered). It is unlikely that a change to both the header and a line item or to multiple line items is necessary.

First, one may consider whether Record Order Header is an elementary process. Record Order Header is a process that captures the details of an ORDER entity, but none of its ORDER LINES. Applying the guidelines mentioned above results in the following observations:

- An execution of Record Order Header by itself does *not* leave business data in a consistent state. Figure 13-5 shows clearly that an ORDER cannot exist without ORDER LINES (the relationship is fully mandatory.)

- An execution of Record Order Header is unlikely to produce a meaningful result. More likely, the creation of an entire order and all of its order lines constitutes a result meaningful to the individual taking the order.

- An execution of Record Order Header *will* take place at a single point in time.

- An execution of Record Order Header *does t*ake place at a single location.

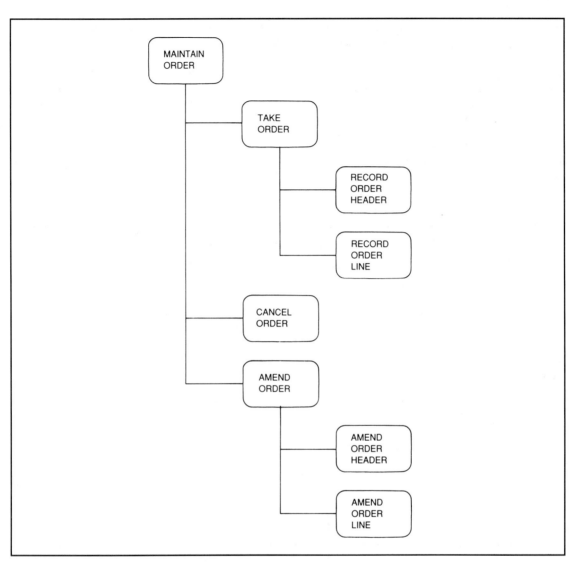

Figure 13-4. Process Decomposition of MAINTAIN ORDER

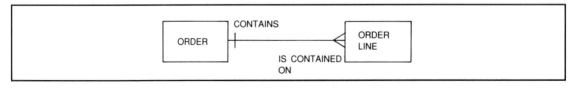

Figure 13-5. ERD Fragment for ORDER and ORDER LINE

- Record Order Header has no components that are individually executable. (One can imagine a decomposition of Record Order Header resulting in such subordinates as Identify Customer, Check Customer Credit, and Record Date Requested, but it is difficult to imagine the execution of those components independently of one another.)

Because it fails to satisfy the first two guidelines, Record Order Header is clearly not an elementary process. Neither is Record Order Line (it is left to the reader to determine why). Since the first two guidelines are the ones violated, the process is sub-elementary. One must search for an elementary process among its ancestry.

Now consider the process Maintain Order. Application of the guidelines yields the following results:

- Each execution of Maintain Order leaves business data in a consistent state (at least as far as the ERD fragment in Figure 13-4 is concerned).

- Each execution of Maintain Order will likely produce either a newly taken order, an order cancellation notice, or an amended order, each of which are complete and meaningful to the user.

- Each execution of Maintain Order takes place at a single point in time.

- Each execution of Maintain Order takes place at a single location.

- The components of Maintain Order *can* be executed individually. For example, it is sensible to take an order without cancelling one in the same execution.

Since Maintain Order fails to comply with the last guideline, it is a process above the level of elementary. (In practice, of course, if the analyst had considered Maintain Order to be an elementary process, he or she would not have decomposed it into the children shown in Figure 13-4.) This failure would trigger the analyst to continue decomposition of Maintain Order until an elementary process was found.

Since Maintain Order is at too high a level of detail, while Record Order Header is at too low a level, Take Order is likely to be an elementary process. Application of the guidelines reveals that:

- Each execution of Take Order leaves the business data in a consistent state (since both an order and its order lines are accepted in "one fell swoop").

- Each execution of Take Order produces a result (that is, an order) which is complete and meaningful to the user in itself.

- Each execution of Take Order takes place from beginning to end at a single point in time.

- Each execution of Take Order takes place at a single location.

- Neither component of Take Order (neither Record Order Header nor Record Order Line) can be executed independently of one another, as demonstrated earlier.

Since Take Order complies with each and every one of the guidelines, it measures up: it is an elementary process.

Consider the Amend Order process shown in Figure 13-4. It decomposes similarly to Take Order, which was determined to be an elementary process. However, based on the underlying set of assumptions, Amend Order Header and Amend Order Line can be executed independently of one another. Given that Amend Order Header and Amend Order Line each produce an amended version of the order, they are elementary processes (each produces meaningful results and leaves the business in a consistent state) even though Record Order Header and Record Order Line were not. This example illustrates that even when decomposition is similar, the designation of elementary processes may be different.

Given the results of all of the foregoing analysis, the corrected Process Hierarchy Diagram appears in Figure 13-6, with the decomposition of Maintain Order terminating at the elementary processes Take Order, Cancel Order, Amend Order Header, and Amend Order Line. Since process decomposition stops at the elementary process level, the sub-elementary processes appearing in Figure 13-4 (Record Order Header and Record Order Line) have been removed.

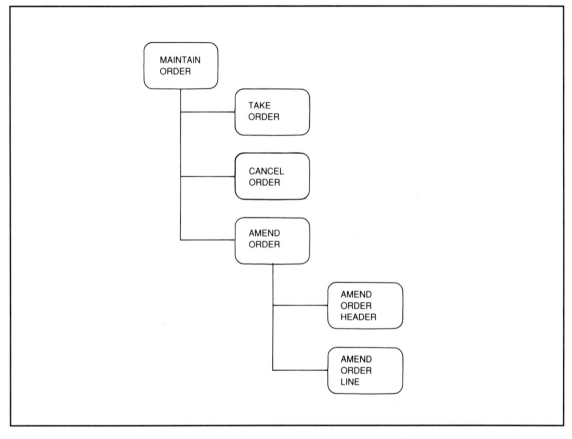

Figure 13-6. Corrected Process Hierarchy Diagram

Before leaving the subject of elementary processes, one should consider the case where none of the processes in the decomposition qualify as elementary processes. Suppose, for example, that an execution of Take Order need not take place at a single point in time. In such a case, the decomposition appears to proceed directly from super-elementary processes to sub- elementary processes without an elementary process between them.

When such an anomaly occurs, either the guidelines have been misapplied, there is a flaw somewhere in the business model, or both. For instance, the problem might be that the ERD appearing in Figure 13-5 was wrong. If it were really valid for an ORDER to exist without pairings to any ORDER LINES (as in Figure 13-7), an execution of Record Order Header would leave the business data in a consistent state. If the resulting stand-alone ORDER had meaning, in and of itself, to the user, Record Order Header would be an elementary process.

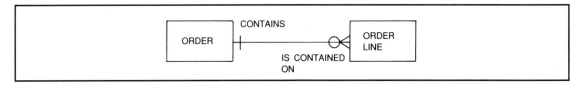

Figure 13-7. Alternate ERD Fragment for ORDER and ORDER LINE

DEPENDENCY ANALYSIS

Chapter 5 of Part I first introduced the concept of dependency analysis. Analysts identify and record dependencies between processes by building Process Dependency Diagrams using the IEF Activity Dependency Tool.

Basic Terminology

Some of the terminology used in dependency analysis was introduced in Chapter 5. This subsection reviews that terminology and introduces some new terms.

In Figure 13-8, assume that A, B, and C are processes.

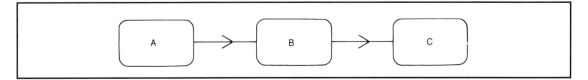

Figure 13-8. A Simple Process Dependency Diagram

- The directed line (line with an arrowhead) from A to B represents a **dependency** of B on A. Likewise the directed line from B to C represents a dependency of C on B.
- A, B and C are **interdependent** because they are joined by a network of dependencies.
- A and B are **immediately interdependent** because they are joined by a dependency. Likewise, B and C are immediately interdependent.
- A is **prerequisite** to B. Likewise, B is prerequisite to C.
- B is **dependent** on A. Likewise, C is dependent on B.

This terminology is used extensively in the following discussion.

The Purpose of Dependency Analysis

The principle role of dependency analysis is to verify activity decomposition in general and, in the case of BAA, to verify the correct decomposition of processes into elementary processes. Dependency analysis during BAA serves a secondary role as well. Analysts can identify providers of information that facilitate the execution of processes, receivers of information the process produces, and events that trigger processes.

Analysts verify decomposition by insuring that all sibling processes are interdependent. If they are not, this strongly indicates that the decomposition is invalid in one of two ways: either the analyst has incorrectly grouped processes that do not belong together, or the analyst has erroneously identified an object as a process. In a few cases, siblings may not actually be interdependent, but one must regard such cases with suspicion.

In any event, analysts must resolve or explain any anomalies to insure that elementary processes are correctly identified. Only then can designers correctly implement systems in later stages of Information Engineering.

Selecting Processes to be Analyzed

One can construct a Dependency Diagram for any process in the business area except for elementary processes (recall that a Dependency Diagram for process X shows the interdependence of the children of X). However, since dependency analysis tends to be time consuming, and since its chief purpose is to verify decomposition, it is normally adequate to build Dependency Diagrams only for parents of elementary processes.

Using that criterion against Figure 13-6, two Dependency Diagrams are required: one for Maintain Order and one for Amend Order. The Maintain Order diagram should depict the interdependency between Take Order and Cancel Order, two elementary processes, and Amend Order, their non-elementary sibling. The Amend Order diagram should depict the interdependency between the elementary processes Amend Order Header and Amend Order Line. The Dependency Diagram for Maintain Order appears in Figure 13-9. The Dependency Diagram for Amend Order represents a possible anomaly and will be discussed later.

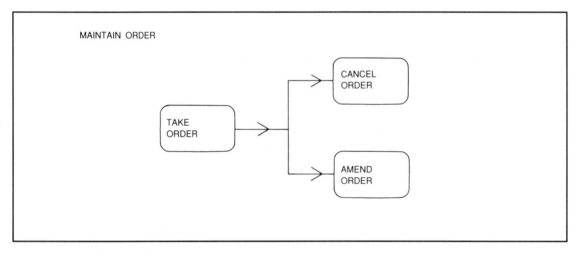

Figure 13-9. Dependency Diagram for MAINTAIN ORDER

The True Meaning of Dependency

Dependencies do not imply that a set of steps must be executed in order to execute the parent process. Rather, they reflect a business state that allows execution of dependent processes.

In Figure 13-9, for example, the execution of Maintain Order does not mean that an execution of Take Order must be followed by an execution of Cancel Order or Amend Order. Rather, the diagram shows that Take Order can leave the business in a state that permits execution of Cancel Order or Amend Order. In this situation, Take Order is considered prerequisite to Cancel Order and Amend Order, while Cancel Order and Amend Order are dependent on Take Order.

Take Order, then, has a **post condition** which, when true, satisfies the **pre-conditions** for either Cancel Order or Amend Order. Given this understanding, one can consider the dependency line as a matching of a post-condition of the prerequisite process to the pre-condition of the dependent process. In the case of Figure 13-9, order creation is probably the post-condition of Take Order that matches the pre-condition of Amend Order or Cancel Order. Thus, if an execution of Take Order completes successfully (resulting in creation of an ORDER entity and its attendant ORDER LINE entities), it becomes possible for the ORDER to be affected by Cancel Order or Amend Order.

Dependencies and Their Detail

Dependencies have only two properties: name and description.

Name

The **name** of a dependency is purely optional. If one is specified, it should reflect the post- and pre-conditions it matches. In Figure 13-9, "order is created" is a suitable name for the dependency.

Description

The analyst should specify the post- and pre-conditions represented by a dependency in its **description.** This description should be both concise and precise. The analyst should avoid referencing the processes involved, because one can add or delete processes from a dependency without actually affecting the post- or pre-condition.

In the example in Figure 13-9, one might simply state the condition as "an ORDER is created." The description "an ORDER is created by Take Order which can subsequently be either cancelled by Cancel Order or changed by Amend Order" is overly wordy. It also happens to be a verbal restatement of the Dependency Diagram, with the condition thrown in. If the analyst should later discover an additional elementary process called Verify Order (see Figure 13-10) that is dependent on Take Order and prerequisite to Amend Order, the post- and pre-conditions for the dependency would remain the same ("an ORDER is created"). Had the analyst included the names of the processes involved in the dependency's description, it would require modification.

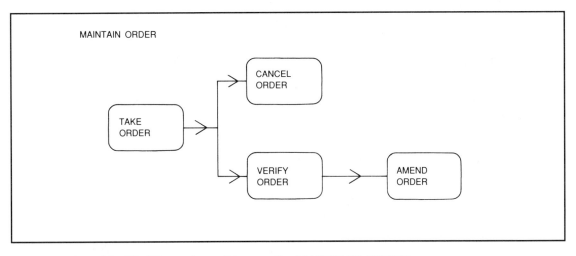

Figure 13-10. A Modified Dependency Diagram for MAINTAIN ORDER

Types of Dependency

Analysts can clarify the meanings of dependencies on a Dependency Diagram by using certain constructs that depict different types of dependency. One can distinguish three primary types of dependency on a Dependency Diagram:

- Sequential dependency
- Parallel dependency
- Mutually Exclusive dependency

The following paragraphs describe each in turn, followed by a discussion of some of the less obvious characteristics of dependencies.

Sequential Dependency

A **sequential dependency** involves two processes, one of which is dependent on the other. When the prerequisite process executes, it fulfills its post-condition and satisfies a pre-condition that will allow the dependent process to execute.

Figure 13-11 illustrates a sequential dependency between two processes: Pick Goods and Pack Goods. Pick Goods, if it completes successfully, satisfies the post-condition "goods have been picked" which is, in turn, a pre-condition of Pack Goods. In other words, one cannot pack goods until they have been picked from stock.

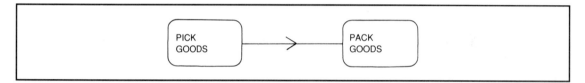

Figure 13-11. A Sequential Dependency

The structure in Figure 13-11 reads as follows:

> Pick Goods may be followed by Pack Goods if goods have been picked.

Parallel Dependency

A **parallel dependency** involves three or more processes, one a prerequisite process and the rest dependent processes. When the prerequisite process executes, it fulfills its post-condition and satisfies the pre-condition of each dependent process.

Consider Figure 13-12. Receive Goods, if it executes successfully, satisfies the condition "goods received" which is a pre-condition of both dependent processes Count Goods and Inspect Goods.

The structure in Figure 13-12 reads as follows:

> Receive Goods may be followed by Count Goods and Inspect Goods if goods are received.

Mutually Exclusive Dependency

A **mutually exclusive dependency** involves three or more processes, one a prerequisite process and the rest dependent processes. When the prerequisite process executes, it satisfies one of a number of alternative (mutually exclusive) post-conditions, each of which is a pre-condition of exactly one dependent process.

This kind of dependency is quite different from those previously described because it is associated with multiple alternative conditions.

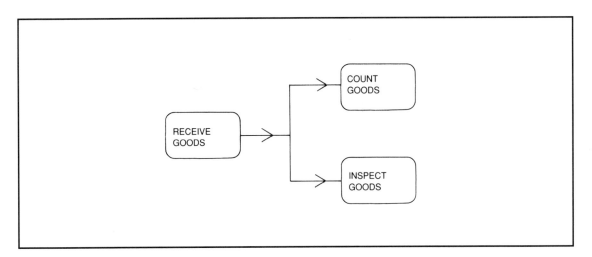

Figure 13-12. A Parallel Dependency

Consider the example in Figure 13-13. In the diagram, a darkened circle where the dependency diverges indicates a mutually exclusive dependency. Interview Candidate, if it completes successfully, satisfies either the condition "candidate accepted" or "candidate not accepted," but not both. Hire Candidate has "candidate accepted" as a pre-condition and Reject Candidate has "candidate not accepted" as a pre-condition.

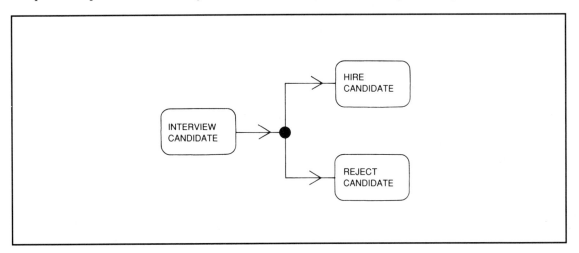

Figure 13-13. A Mutually Exclusive Dependency

The structure in Figure 13-13 reads as follows:

> Interview Candidate may be followed by Hire Candidate if candidate is accepted or Reject Candidate if candidate is not accepted.

Mutually exclusive dependencies also differ from other dependencies in that they can be **closed.** Closure of a mutually exclusive dependency takes place when two or more dependent processes are prerequisite to a common process. For example, based on the dependency shown in Figure 13-13, suppose that one wants to record the candidate's reaction, regardless of whether he or she is accepted or rejected. One can model this situation by adding a new process, Record Reaction, which is dependent on either Hire Candidate or Reject Candidate, as in Figure 13-14.

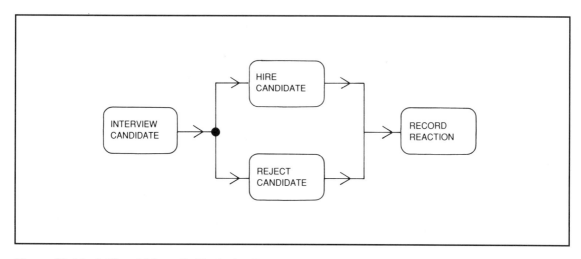

Figure 13-14. A Closed Mutually Exclusive Dependency

An execution of either Hire Candidate or Reject Candidate can satisfy a post-condition ("candidate informed of decision") that is a pre-condition of Record Reaction. The new dependency (depicted by two lines converging and entering Record Reaction as a single line) closes the mutually exclusive dependency.

The closing dependency shown in Figure 13-14 reads as follows:

> Either Hire Candidate or Reject Candidate may be followed by Record Reaction if the candidate is informed of the decision.

Note that one cannot describe the post- and pre-conditions of a mutually exclusive dependency meaningfully without including the name of each process associated with a particular condition, thus violating the guideline for descriptions suggested earlier. In this case, clarity is more important than avoiding mention of process names. For example, rather than:

> "candidate is accepted or candidate is rejected"

the condition recorded on the dependency should be:

> "candidate is accepted, enabling Hire Candidate, or candidate is rejected, enabling Reject Candidate"

Some Additional Concepts

This subsection deals with some of the less obvious concepts involved in dependency analysis.

First, a single process can be prerequisite to multiple dependencies, based on different post-conditions. Consider, for example, the Dependency Diagram for the process Take Inventory, shown in Figure 13-15. Assume that Count Stock may satisfy two post-conditions. Assume further that Record Stock Level has the post-condition "stock has been counted" as its pre-condition, while Analyze Deviation has as its pre-condition the post- condition "stock has been counted and the actual quantity on hand deviated from the recorded quantity on hand by more than two percent." Since multiple non-mutually exclusive conditions are present, multiple dependencies must appear in the diagram.

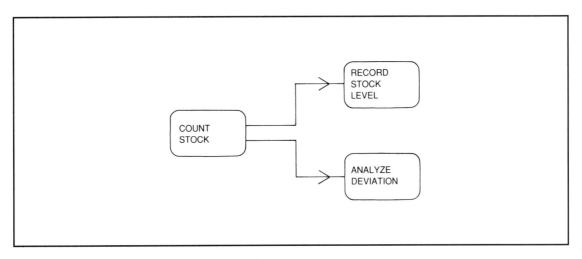

Figure 13-15. Multiple Enabling Dependencies

When a process is prerequisite to multiple dependencies, those dependencies are sometimes collectively called **multiple-enabling dependencies**.

Second, if the dependent process in a dependency is a repetitive process, the dependency is called a **repetitive dependency.** This means that when the prerequisite process executes, its resulting post-condition can satisfy the pre-condition of multiple executions of the dependent process. An example of this situation appears in Figure 13-16.

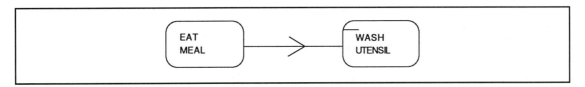

Figure 13-16. Repetitive Dependency

A single execution of Eat Meal satisfies the post-condition "meal consumed." Multiple executions of Wash Utensil (one for each article of silverware used during the meal's consumption) can be executed based on Wash Utensil's pre-condition "meal is consumed." (This example does not strain reality. Recall that the setting of the appropriate post-condition by the prerequisite process only *enables* execution of the dependent process; it does not require it. Thus, there is no requirement that utensils be washed after eating a meal.)

Third, a process that is a prerequisite based on one dependency can be dependent on a process for which it is a prerequisite, based on a separate dependency. Figure 13-17 illustrates this somewhat confusing declaration, which expands the example appearing in Figure 13-16.

In this case, assume that Set Table can result in one of two mutually exclusive conditions; either there is clean silverware available or there is not. Eat Meal has a precondition of "clean silverware is available," while Wash Utensil has a pre-condition of "clean silverware is not available." This describes the mutually exclusive dependency labelled *a*. Further assume that Wash Utensil can satisfy a post-condition "enough silverware has been washed," which, in turn, is a possible pre-condition of Set Table. This describes the sequential dependency labelled *b*.

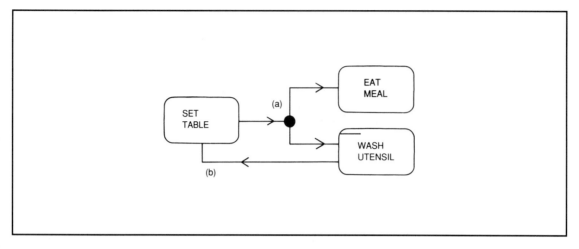

Figure 13-17. Two Processes Dependent on Each Other

If enough clean silverware is available when trying to set the table, it is possible to Eat Meal. If there is not (assuming that the diners are even moderately fastidious), Wash Utensils must be executed repeatedly until enough silverware is clean. When enough silverware has been washed, it is possible to try to set the table again.

In one situation, then, Wash Utensil is dependent on Set Table, while in another situation, Set Table is dependent on Wash Utensil.

Finally, one can specify a sequential dependency in which a process is dependent upon itself, as in Figure 13-18. Such a dependency is called a **recursive dependency.** This indicates that one execution of the process satisfies a post-condition that is a pre-condition of a subsequent execution of the process. Assume that Decompose Bill of Materials is a process that decomposes one level of a bill of material structure (bill of material structures were discussed in Chapter 12). To decompose the entire bill of materials, Decompose Bill of Materials must execute one (or more) times for each level of the structure.

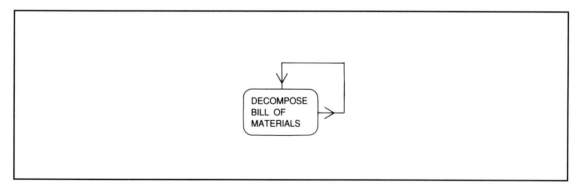

Figure 13-18. A Recursive Dependency

EXTERNAL OBJECTS

The IEF allows analysts to define types of objects from which a process can receive information and to which a process may send information. Such objects, called **external objects**, are depicted on the Process Dependency Diagram as two stacked red boxes (see Figure 13-19).

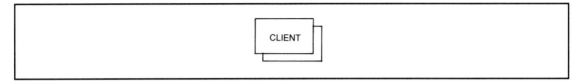

Figure 13-19. An External Object

External objects are rather loosely defined. Analysts can use them to show virtually any source of information required by a process, or consumer of information produced by the process. Sometimes they represent entities and sometimes business systems external to the business area. In most cases, external objects are considered to be outside the business area to which the process belongs; hence, the designation "external."

The interaction of an external object with a process is diagrammed as a directed line connecting the two. One should not confuse this line with a dependency; rather, it indicates an **information flow.** In the IEF Process Dependency Diagram, information flows are colored cyan (light blue) to distinguish them from dependencies (which are colored white.) Figure 13-20 depicts the fact that a CUSTOMER sends the Take Order process the order details it requires, and gets back order number information produced by the Take Order process.

External objects should only be associated with elementary processes.

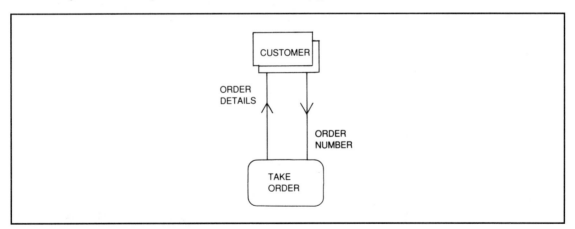

Figure 13-20. Information Flows Between a Process and an External Object

External Objects and Their Detail

Analysts must give each external object a name. Optionally, they may specify a description.

The **name** of the external object is any short textual description. As external objects are loosely defined concepts, there are no explicit rules for their definition. However, it is not unusual for an external object to have the same name as an entity type.

The **description** of an external object may contain any textual information needed to elaborate on its definition beyond that available in its name.

Information Flows and Their Detail

The IEF can capture the following details for each information flow:

- Name
- Description
- Optionality
- Associated Views

Name

The **name** of an information flow, when specified, is a free form description of the information presented to or received from a process by an external object, depending on the direction of flow. For example, the flow from CUSTOMER to Take Order in Figure 13-20 is named "order details" and the one returning from Take Order to CUSTOMER is named "order number."

Description

Analysts can use the **description** of an information flow to record any additional information deemed useful. One should not, however, use it to record the detail of the information passed between the external object and process. If that information is considered important, one should record it as **associated views,** described below.

If an information flow is optional, one may record the conditions under which it is required or forbidden in the flow's description (much as one records the optionality conditions for relationships).

Optionality

The **optionality** of an information flow indicates whether information passes between the external object and process at every execution of the process. An open circle near the destination of the line identifies an information flow as optional in a Dependency Diagram.

Figure 13-21 shows examples of four information flows associated with the process Apply For Loan. The flows which run between CLIENT and Apply For Loan are mandatory. For each execution of Apply For Loan, credit information must be received from a CLIENT and a decision must be produced for the CLIENT. The other two flows are optional. A letter of approval is required from the CLIENT'S MOTHER in some cases (the optionality condition is left to the reader's imagination), but not in others. Assuming that each loan application is routinely compared against the FBI's Most Wanted List, the name and address of each client discovered to be a dangerous criminal is reported to the FBI.

The conditions under which Apply For Loan requires a letter of approval from the CLIENT'S MOTHER and Apply For Loan produces the client whereabouts for the FBI may be documented as part of each information view's description.

Associated Views

One can specify exactly which components of the information required or produced by the process pass along the information flow. This level of detail is only recommended when two or more external objects provide

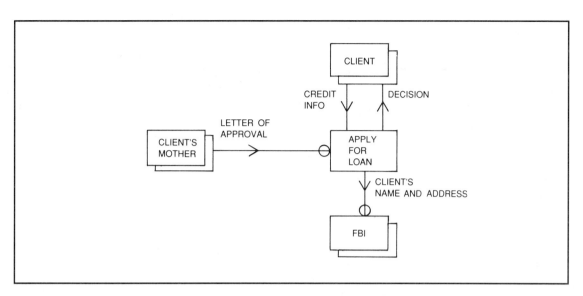

Figure 13-21. Optional Information Flows

information to the process, or two or more external objects receive information from the process. In such cases, **associated views** help identify the providers and receivers of information unambiguously.

Associated views for an information flow depend on the information views of the associated process. Consequently, a detailed discussion of associated views is deferred to Chapter 14, "Interaction Analysis."

EVENTS

If something must happen in order for a process to execute, that something is called an **event**. Events appear as large red arrows on the IEF Process Dependency Diagram, connected to a dependent process by a dependency line. An event can occur arbitrarily (for example, Customer Calls might be an event that triggers the famous Take Order process). It can also depict some cyclical occurrence (for example, End of Month).

In Figure 13-22, the process Count Stock is triggered at End of Year.

Each event must have a name and may have a description if needed.

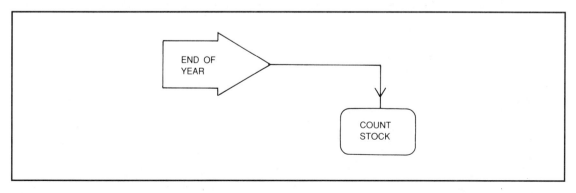

Figure 13-22. An Event

SUMMARY OF ACTIVITY MODELING RULES

This section presents all the rules associated with constructing an activity model. Some were explicitly stated in this chapter, others were presented implicitly, and still others appeared in Part I.

Rules for Activities

The following rules must never be violated:

- Each activity must be uniquely named.
- Each activity that is not an elementary process must decompose into at least two subordinate activities.
- Siblings must all be either functions or processes.
- The same function may not appear twice in the decomposition.
- An elementary process may not be decomposed.
- Each leaf of the hierarchy must be an elementary process.
- The subordinates of an activity must completely describe the activity. For example, if process A decomposes into processes W, X, Y, and Z, then the following statement must be true:

  $A = W + X + Y + Z$

Guidelines for Processes

Violations of the following guidelines may indicate some problem in process decomposition or dependency analysis:

- An activity should decompose into between three and seven subordinate activities.
- Siblings should have some interdependence.

Rule for Dependencies

Each dependency must be described by a condition or set of conditions that represent post-conditions of the prerequisite process and pre-conditions of the dependent process(es).

Rules for External Objects and Events

- Each external object must be associated with at least one process via an information flow.
- Each event must be associated with exactly one process.

Guideline for External Objects and Events

External objects and events should only be associated with elementary processes.

SUMMARY OF ACTIVITY MODELING DELIVERABLES

Top-down activity analysis results in the following deliverables:

- A Process Hierarchy Diagram depicting the decomposition of processes to the elementary process level.
- A Process Dependency Diagram for each parent with an elementary process as a child.

- Supporting documentation (captured as details of the processes, dependencies, external objects and events appearing on the Process Hierarchy and Process Dependency Diagrams).

This combined set of deliverables constitutes the activity model of the business area being analyzed.

14
INTERACTION ANALYSIS

OVERVIEW

Previous chapters have described two of the three major components of the business model built during a Business Area Analysis project: data analysis and activity analysis. This chapter deals with the remaining component: interaction analysis. To recap the general objectives of each of these components:

- The data model describes the things of interest to the business and the relationships between them.

- The activity model records the things the business does (or should do).

- The interaction model details how the things the business does (activities) affect the things of interest to the business (data).

When constructing the interaction model, the analyst specifically represents the effects of elementary processes on entity types and their predicates. To represent this information, the analyst performs two distinct types of analysis: **entity life cycle analysis** and **process logic analysis**. Entity life cycle analysis approaches interactions from the point of view of an entity type. In other words, which processes affect entities of this type? Process logic analysis approaches interactions from the point of view of a process. In other words, how are entities used in this particular process? Analysts consider only elementary processes during interaction analysis.

This chapter contains the following major sections:

- **Entity Life Cycle Analysis.** This section presents a manual method of recording the effects of elementary processes on entities of a single type using the Entity Life Cycle Diagram.

- **Introduction to Process Logic Analysis.** This section contrasts the central concepts of process logic analysis with entity life cycle analysis. The remaining sections in this chapter explain various details of process logic analysis.

- **Information Views.** This section presents techniques used for associating elements of the data model with those of the process model during process logic analysis.

- **Formulating Process Logic.** This section suggests a technique for sketching the detailed logic of a process before building an action diagram.

- **Process Action Diagramming Nomenclature**. This section presents several important definitions.

- **Process Action Statements.** This section describes the building blocks for specifying the details of process logic: action statements. Analysts combine these fundamental elements to describe an entire process in a Process Action Diagram.

- **Considerations for Process Action Diagramming.** This section presents some additional considerations for building Process Action Diagrams and Process Action Blocks.

- **Advanced Topics.** This section includes discussions of a number of more complex action diagramming topics including:

    — Action Diagram Functions

— Expression handling

— Advanced Repeating Group handling

— Notes on SET...USING, Default and Derivation Algorithms

— Exception Conditions

— Implications of sharing Action Blocks between BAA and BSD

• **A Summary of Interaction Analysis Deliverables.** This short section itemizes the outputs resulting from interaction analysis.

ENTITY LIFE CYCLE ANALYSIS

The discussion of entity subtypes in Chapter 12 described a special partitioning of an entity type called **life cycle partitioning.** The subtypes appearing along the life cycle partitioning represented discrete states of entities of a given type at different times during their "lives."

Given this life cycle partitioning of an entity type, one may use life cycle analysis to show how process executions can cause an entity to change from one state to another. This analysis helps insure that each entity state is addressed.

The Life of an Entity and the Life Cycle of an Entity Type

As usual during business modeling, the issue of types versus occurrences is present during life cycle analysis. Each entity type's life cycle is a description of the possible "lives" entities of that type may lead. On the other hand, each entity occurrence leads a life that is compatible with the entity life cycle of its type.

The formal definition of an entity life is:

Entity Life A description of what happens to an entity from the time it becomes of interest to an enterprise to the time it ceases to be of interest to an enterprise.

Note that an entity is not considered to exist until the business becomes interested in it. Thus, the person Fred Smith, though 45 years old, may be created as a new CUSTOMER entity because the business ignored the first 44 years and some months of his life. Likewise, though Fred may live to a ripe old age, as soon as the business is no longer interested in him as an entity, he ceases to exist for business purposes. (This is similar to the "falling-tree-makes-no-sound-if-there-is-nobody-to-hear-it" philosophy.)

The formal definition of entity type life cycle is:

Entity Type
Life Cycle A description of what can happen during lives of entities of one type.

As it turns out, the lives of different entities of the same type can vary greatly from one another, based on the complexity of their entity life cycle. While every entity type has a life cycle, some are so simple that they do not require explicit definition. This topic will be revisited after the following discussion of entity states.

Entity States

The entity life cycle consists of a series of **entity states**, defined as subtypes along the life cycle partitioning. An entity can exist in four different types of states: a creation state, a termination state, the null state, and some kind of intermediate state.

The Creation State

The **creation state** is the initial state of an entity after the business becomes interested in it. An entity type might have multiple possible creation states in its life cycle.

Each entity type must have at least one creation state in its life cycle.

The Termination State

The **termination state** is the final state in the life of an entity. As with creation states, an entity type may have multiple termination states and must have at least one.

In some cases, the entity may still be of interest to the business when it is in a termination state. In such cases, the termination state is said to be **indefinite** and the entity is not deleted. In other cases, the entity is truly no longer of interest to the business and may be deleted. In such cases, the termination state is said to be **definite**.

In either case, an entity in a termination state, by definition, cannot be changed to another state, although it can be referenced (read).

The Null State

An entity is in the **null state** if it does not exist. This might seem silly at first, but it is very convenient to visualize the creation of an entity as involving a transition from its null state to a creation state. For example, the Add Customer process might change the state of an entity of type CUSTOMER from the null state to a creation state. The null state may also be a termination state of the "definite" variety.

The null state never explicitly appears as an entity state subtype along the life cycle partitioning in an Entity Relationship Diagram.

Intermediate States

Any state that is not a creation, termination, or null state is called an **intermediate state**.

Notes on States

Until an entity reaches a termination state, it may move from state to state without restriction. An entity may return to a previous state or skip a state, as long as the life cycle of its entity type supports such behavior. Thus, although one may view an entity as passing from its creation state to its termination state, it need not pass through all the intermediate states sequentially and may, in fact, take quite a complex and tortuous path.

While the life cycles of some entity types can be extremely complex, others can be quite simple. The simplest entity life cycle has only one explicit state indicating its existence. When an entity of this type is created, it moves from the null state to the creation state EXISTS. When it is deleted, it returns to the null state as its termination state. Entity types with this simplest of possible life cycles are never explicitly partitioned by a life cycle partitioning.

Every entity is in one and only one state at a given point in time. Every entity type has at least one creation and one termination state. Since the termination state may be null, it may not be explicitly specified.

Life Cycle and State Rules

The preceding text has implied or explicitly stated the following set of rules:

- Each entity has a life that must pass through at least two states: the creation state and the termination state.

- Each entity type has a life cycle that contains at least two states: the creation state and the termination state.

- The null state is never shown as an entity state subtype along the life cycle partitioning.

- An entity may only change states as the result of a process execution.

- Each entity must, at any point in time, be in one and only one state.

The Entity Life Cycle Diagram

Analysts can represent entity states and their transitions on an Entity Life Cycle Diagram. Since the IEF does not directly support this diagram, it is recommended that analysts construct it manually for entity types with non-trivial life cycles.

The purpose of an Entity Life Cycle Diagram is to depict the possible state changes for entities of a single type. This style of diagram, called a **fencepost** diagram, is often used to represent state transitions. In fact, the Entity Life Cycle Diagram is sometimes called the Entity State Transition Diagram.

The Entity Life Cycle Diagram uses two symbols. A horizontal bar appears for each state specified on the life cycle partitioning. A vertical arrow represents a process that can cause an entity in an initial state to move to a destination state.

The Entity Relationship Diagram fragment in Figure 14-1 presents a rather complex life cycle with ten discrete entity states possible. The Entity Life Cycle Diagram in Figure 14-2 depicts this life cycle by showing the possible movement of an entity between states.

Note that each of the horizontal bars in Figure 14-2 corresponds to a subtype in Figure 14-1. Had a Process Hierarchy Diagram been prepared for this example, all the names appearing on the vertical arrows would have appeared as names of elementary processes in the PHD.

In the example given, notice that:

- There is one creation state: TAKEN. the process Take Order moves an ORDER from the null state to the TAKEN state. Any horizontal bar that is the target of an arrow leading from the null state is a creation state.

- There are four possible termination states: the null state, PAID, CANCELLED and RETURNED. The null state is always a termination state when used as the destination of an arrow, because this implies deletion of the entity (the ultimate in termination). The other three are easily recognizable as termination states because no vertical arrows issue from them. Hence, no changes of entity state are possible once any of those states is entered.

- The horizontal bars from which arrows emerge constrain the processes represented by those arrows. For example, Erase Order is only valid for ORDERS in the TAKEN state. An ORDER that is SCHEDULED may not be operated upon by Erase Order. Likewise, Cancel Order may only be executed against ORDERS in either the TAKEN or SCHEDULED state.

- Some processes may act on an entity type without changing its state. In this example, MODIFY ORDER changes the contents of an ORDER without changing its state and is thus shown as an involuted arrow.

- The Entity Life Cycle Diagram only shows processes from the viewpoint of the entity type under consideration. For example, the process Bill Customer is likely to create an entity of type INVOICE as

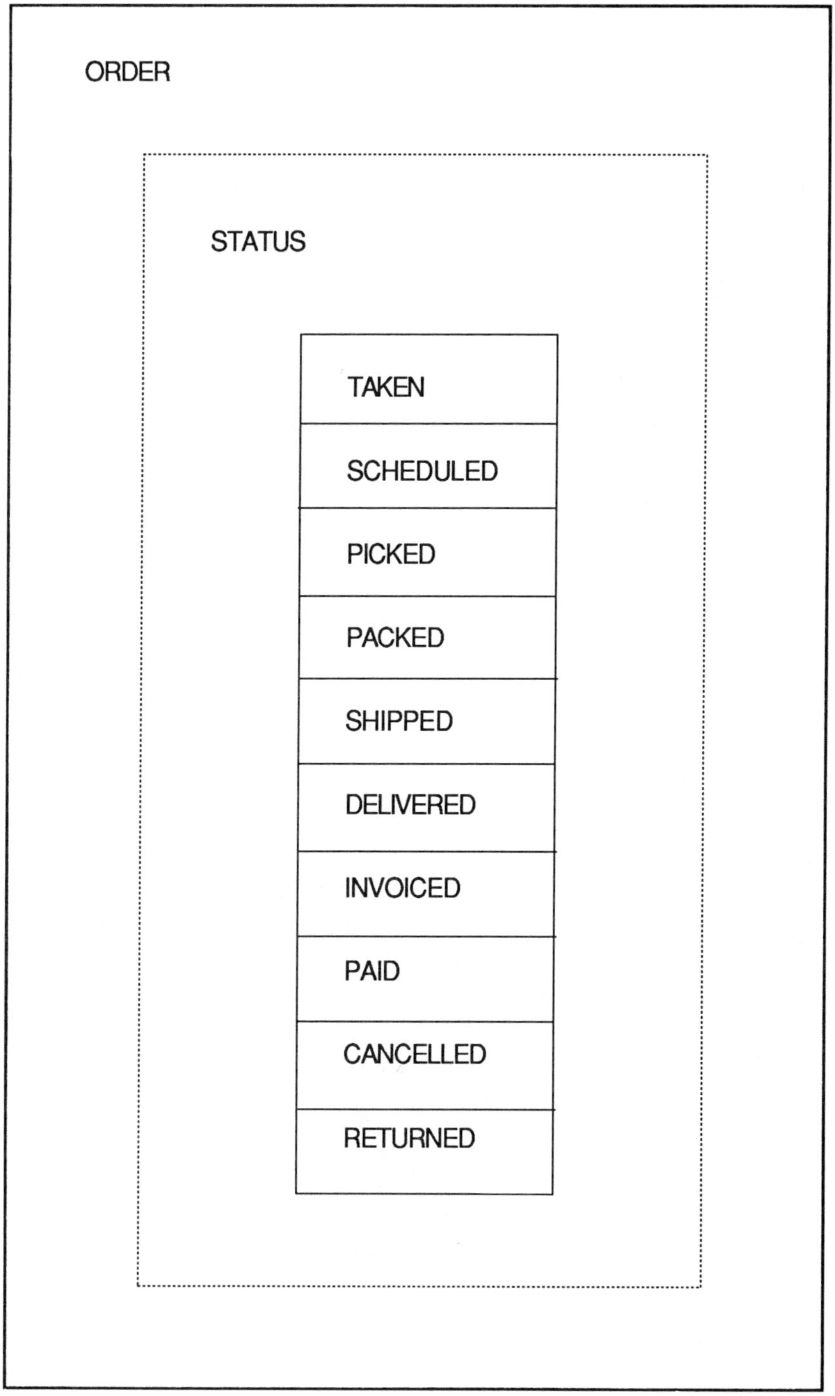

Figure 14-1. Life Cycle Partitioning of ORDER

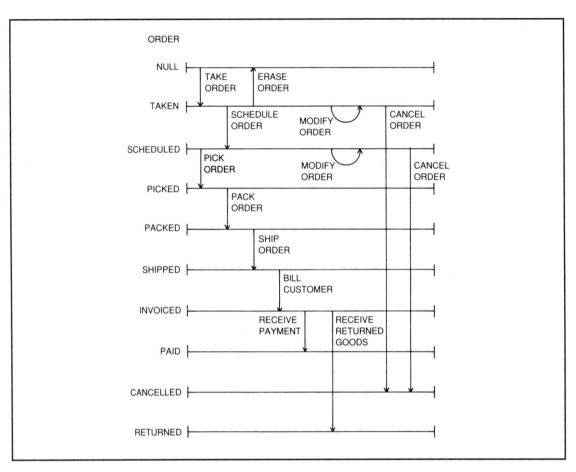

Figure 14-2. Entity Life Cycle Diagram for ORDER

well as change the state of an entity of type ORDER from SHIPPED to INVOICED. Since this diagram relates only to ORDER, INVOICE is not shown.

• The null state *does* appear on the Entity Life Cycle Diagram, although it is omitted from the life cycle partitioning on the Entity Relationship Diagram.

Figure 14-3 illustrates an Entity Life Cycle Diagram for CUSTOMER, an entity type with a trivial life cycle. A CUSTOMER either exists or it does not. Thus, its creation state is simply EXISTS and its termination state is the null state. CUSTOMER does not have a life cycle partitioning.

As mentioned previously, it is not usually necessary to construct an Entity Life Cycle Diagram for such a trivial case.

Entity State Change Matrix

The same level of information shown on the Entity Life Cycle Diagram can appear on a manually prepared Entity State Change Matrix as well. One prepares an Entity State Change Matrix for entity types with very complex life cycles, in order to clarify which processes can reference entities in which states.

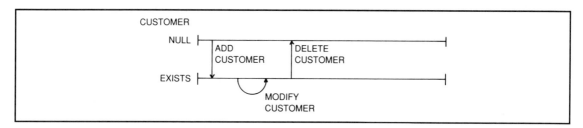

Figure 14-3. Entity Life Cycle Diagram for CUSTOMER

The horizontal axis of this matrix shows all possible entity states for the entity type under consideration. The vertical axis contains all the elementary processes that reference the entity type. Each cell indicates the state to which the process in the cell's row may change an entity in the cell's column. An example of such a matrix corresponding to the Entity Life Cycle Diagram in Figure 14-2 appears in Figure 14-4.

	NULL A	TAKEN B	SCHEDULED C	PICKED D	PACKED E	SHIPPED F	INVOICED G	PAID H	CANCELLED I	RETURNED J
TAKE ORDER	B									
ERASE ORDER		A								
SCHEDULE ORDER		C								
MODIFY ORDER		B	C							
PICK ORDER			D							
PACK ORDER				E						
SHIP ORDER					F					
BILL CUSTOMER						G				
RECEIVE PAYMENT							H			
RECEIVE RETURNED GOODS							J			
CANCEL ORDER		I	I							

Figure 14-4. Entity State Change Matrix

Any column with no cell entries represents a termination state. Any row with no cell entries represents an error: the analyst either omitted cell entries erroneously or included processes that did not reference the entity type under consideration.

INTRODUCTION TO PROCESS LOGIC ANALYSIS

During entity life cycle analysis, the analyst focuses on one entity type at a time, describing the effects of various processes on entities of that type. During process logic analysis, the analyst changes his or her frame of reference to elementary processes. The analyst focuses on one elementary process at a time, describing its effects on various entity types. Figure 14-5 illustrates these two different perspectives on the interaction between data and activity models.

Figure 14-5 shows neither all the processes that affect ORDER nor all the entity types affected by Take Order (hence the dashed lines). Still, the illustration makes it clear that during entity life cycle analysis, the process Take Order is but a single component affecting the life cycle of the entity type ORDER. Similarly, during

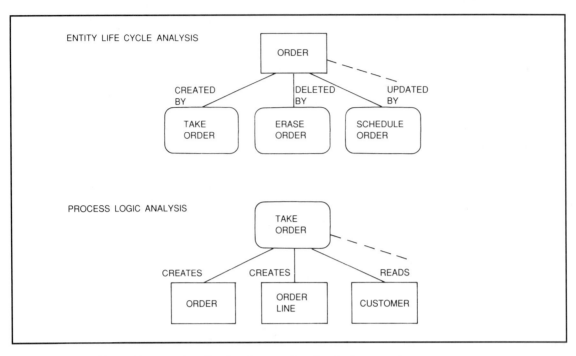

Figure 14-5. Different Perspectives During Interaction Analysis

process logic analysis, the entity type ORDER is but a single component with which the process Take Order must deal. One can use a comparison of these two different viewpoints on a single interaction model to confirm the correctness of the business model, since both viewpoints must be compatible. Likewise, as with any subject approachable from different angles, the use of different perspectives on the interaction model improves both the analyst's and user's understanding of the business model.

The IEF currently supports only one viewpoint for interaction analysis, process logic analysis, and just one tool for its accomplishment, the Process Action Diagram. Although additional techniques in interaction analysis will be supported in the future, the Process Action Diagram allows the analyst to completely specify a detailed interaction analysis, albeit from a single perspective. For this reason, most of this chapter is devoted to process logic analysis in general, and the Process Action Diagram in particular.

One final, important point: analysts only perform process logic analysis on elementary processes, not on their parent processes. In the remainder of this chapter, the term **process** denotes elementary processes only, unless the text makes an explicit distinction.

INFORMATION VIEWS

Basic Concepts

The means by which a process *sees* information about entities is called an **information view.** An information view is a collection of entity type attributes of interest to the process in some context or other. As shall be demonstrated later, different kinds of information views serve different purposes. Before launching into these details, however, one must understand the subtle difference between an entity and information about an entity.

An entity is a real thing. For example, an entity of the type CUSTOMER might be a real flesh and blood human being named "Fred Frelb." Information about an entity is merely that: some collection of data associated with the entity and of interest to the business. For example, Fred Frelb's Name, Address, and Credit Rating are probably of interest to the business, while other of his characteristics (like I.Q., Height, and Favorite Cola) may not be. Thus, the definition of an entity type developed during data modeling describes the characteristics of entities of that type *about which the business may wish to store information.*

This distinction is important because the analyst specifies the details of an elementary process in terms of information about entities, not entities themselves. For example, in process logic and Process Action Diagram terminology, an entity is said to be "created" once the business learns of it. Obviously, Fred Frelb is not actually created once the business learns of his existence. The term **create** refers to the recording of information about Fred Frelb (an entity of the type CUSTOMER).

In the IEF (and throughout Information Engineering in general), the term **entity** is used to represent information about entities as well as entities themselves. This convention is used throughout the following discussion, with distinctions made where necessary.

View Sets and Subsets

Imagine that Take Order is a manual process which works as follows:

1. A CUSTOMER contacts the store and provides the clerk with his or her Name, a list of PRODUCTS, and the Quantity of each he or she wishes to order.

2. The clerk walks back to a file cabinet containing records on all CUSTOMERS with which the store deals, and checks to make certain that the CUSTOMER is on file.

   If the CUSTOMER is not on file, the ORDER cannot be taken until certain information about the CUSTOMER is recorded in the file.

3. The clerk then types up an ORDER for all the items the CUSTOMER wishes to purchase, and places it in a basket containing open ORDERS. (Assume that the ORDER Number is a pre-printed unique number on the ORDER form.)

4. For each PRODUCT requested, the clerk looks up its price in the PRODUCT book and records it on the appropriate ORDER LINE. Additionally, the clerk calculates the value of the ORDER LINE by multiplying the PRODUCT Price by the Quantity Ordered.

5. The clerk sums the Value of each ORDER LINE to determine the Total Value of the ORDER.

6. Finally, the clerk contacts the CUSTOMER and tells him or her the ORDER Number and the Total Value of the ORDER.

This situation is depicted in Figure 14-6. The circled numbers correspond to the numbered steps listed above. The large box encompassing the clerk and all the circled letters represents the boundaries of the elementary process Take Order.

A quick analysis reveals four entity types with which the process Take Order deals:

- CUSTOMER
- ORDER
- PRODUCT
- ORDER LINE

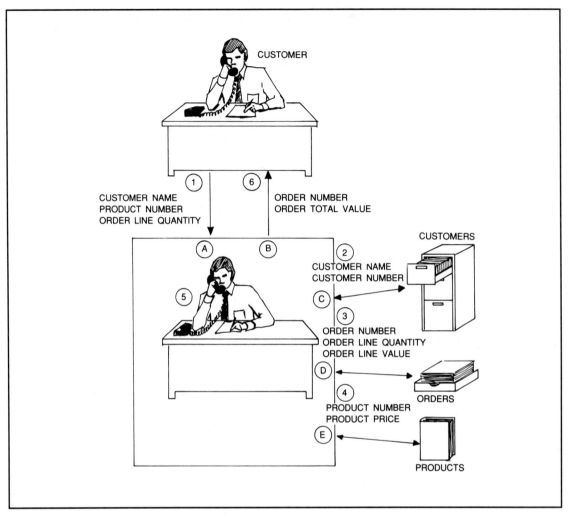

Figure 14-6. A Manual TAKE ORDER Process

The data model fragment presented in Figure 14-7 shows how these four entity types interact. The figure is annotated with the names of attributes.

One can think of Take Order in Figure 14-6 as relating to entities in three different ways, as follows:

- It receives information about a CUSTOMER entity and several PRODUCT entities from a real, live CUSTOMER. Since one can think of these views as being "imported" by Take Order, they are called **import views.**

  The circled letter A in Figure 14-6 indicates the import views of Take Order.

- It produces information about an ORDER that is returned to the real, live CUSTOMER entity at its conclusion. Since one can think of this view as being "exported" by Take Order, it is called an **export view.**

  The circled letter B in Figure 14-6 indicates the export view of Take Order.

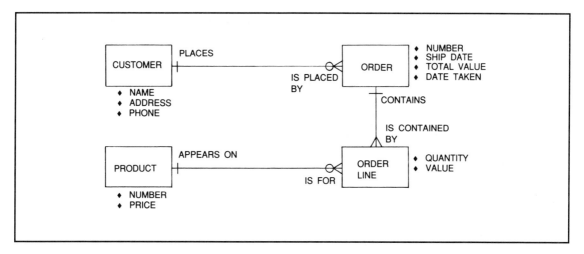

Figure 14-7. A Data Model Fragment for the Manual TAKE ORDER Process

- It manipulates stored information about entities. In the case of CUSTOMER (circled letter C) and PRODUCT (circled letter E), information is referenced. In the case of ORDER (circled letter D), information is created or newly stored.

  A view of stored information about an entity is called an **entity action view.**

Note the views that Take Order has of CUSTOMER: an import view and an entity action view. Both are views of the same CUSTOMER entity; they are simply used for different purposes.

As a point of interest, the real, live CUSTOMER (the one shown holding a telephone in Figure 14-6) is an external object. It is a real entity that both provides information to and receives information from Take Order, but it is "external" to the stored information about the business.

The term **view set** refers to the collection of views used by a single process. Thus, all of the views appearing in Figure 14-6 (A, B, C, D, and E) are part of Take Order's view set. The term **view subset** refers to the collection of views belonging to the classifications described above. Thus, Take Order has three view subsets: an import subset (containing the import view A), an export subset (containing the export view B) and an entity action subset (containing the entity action views C, D and E.) Each process may have four view subsets; the fourth is called the **local subset** (not illustrated in Figure 14-6). This subset, which contains local views, is used infrequently during BAA.

The following definitions summarize the information just presented:

View   A window through which a process can communicate information about entities.

View Set   The collection of views used by a process.

View Subset   One of four possible groupings of views in a view set. The four kinds of grouping are import, export, entity action and local.

Import View   A view through which a process may receive information when it begins execution.

Export View   A view through which a process may provide information when it ends execution.

Entity Action View   A view through which a process may inspect or manipulate stored information about entities during its execution.

Local View   A view in which a process may temporarily save information during its execution. Such views are used infrequently during BAA.

Entity Views

An **entity view** (not to be confused with an entity action view) is a view of a single entity. An entity view can belong to any view subset for a process. Figure 14-8 lists the entity types for which views are required for the Take Order process depicted in Figure 14-6.

Import Views
CUSTOMER
PRODUCT
ORDER LINE
Export Views
ORDER
Entity Action Views
CUSTOMER
ORDER
ORDER LINE
PRODUCT

Figure 14-8. Entity Types for Which Views Are Required by Process TAKE ORDER

Attribute Views

Each entity view contains one or more **attribute views**. These attribute views are selected from the attributes of an entity type based on the needs of the process. For example, Figure 14-7 shows that the entity type CUSTOMER contains three attributes: Name, Address and Phone. Based on the illustration in Figure 14-6, the entity view of CUSTOMER in the import view subset of Take Order only includes an attribute view for Name. Thus, the only information required for a CUSTOMER is the value of its Name.

Entity View Names

In Figure 14-8, two views of entity type CUSTOMER appear. When defining the detailed process logic for Take Order, one will need to refer to elements of each of these two views separately. However, as yet there is no way to tell them apart. At first glance, it might appear that one can use the view subset to differentiate between them, but this is not always the case. Consider, for example, the situation where one requires information from two separate CUSTOMERS in the same execution of a process. In such a case, the process will require two import views of the same entity type, thus making the combination of entity type (CUSTOMER) and view subset (import) insufficient to distinguish between the two views.

It appears, then, that entity views require distinct names in certain cases. The IEF provides for these cases by allowing each entity view to have a name.

Whenever a reference to an entity view appears in the detailed process logic, the name takes the form:

entity-view-name entity-type-name

Thus, if the import view of CUSTOMER in Figure 14-8 were named Requesting, the entity view would be referred to as Requesting CUSTOMER in the detailed process logic. Entity view names, then, should always act as modifiers of the entity type name. The combination of entity view name and entity type name must be unique within a process.

For each entity type for which a view is required in a single process, one view may be unnamed. As long as only one is unnamed, it is still distinguishable from other views of the same entity type. By convention, entity views in the entity action view subset are normally left unnamed (unless there are multiple entity action views of the same entity type). As will become evident later, this convention improves the readability of the detailed process logic which appears in the Process Action Diagram.

Figure 14-9 is a more complete list of the views of Take Order originally shown in Figure 14-8. It includes both entity view names and attribute views. The notation along the left side of the list is the same as used in the IEF:

> *view of* precedes an entity view name
>
> *entity* precedes an entity type name
>
> *attr* precedes an attribute name

Import Views		
view of	REQUESTING	
entity	CUSTOMER	
attr	NAME	
view of	REQUESTED	
entity	PRODUCT	
attr	NUMBER	
view of	REQUESTED	
entity	ORDER LINE	
attr	QUANTITY	
Export Views		
view of	ACCEPTED	
entity	ORDER	
attr	NUMBER	
attr	TOTAL VALUE	
Entity Action Views		
view of	(unnamed)	
entity	CUSTOMER	
attr	NAME	
attr	NUMBER	
view of	(unnamed)	
entity	ORDER	
attr	NUMBER	
view of	(unnamed)	
entity	ORDER LINE	
attr	QUANTITY	
attr	VALUE	
view of	(unnamed)	
entity	PRODUCT	
attr	NUMBER	
attr	PRICE	

Figure 14-9. More Complete View Set for TAKE ORDER

Group Views and Their Detail

Despite our best efforts so far, the view set presented in Figure 14-9 is deficient. In the original description of the Take Order process, it was clear that multiple PRODUCTS could be ordered on a single ORDER. Thus, the import view must allow for multiple occurrences of PRODUCT (for its Number) and ORDER LINE (for Quantity). This is accomplished by means of a **repeating group view.**

A **group view** is strictly defined as a collection of one or more entity views. A group view is the only kind of view that may be designated as **repeating**. Thus, any time a process imports or exports a list of entities, the list is included as a repeating group view.

To complete the view set for Take Order, one must add a group view to which the entity views Requested PRODUCT and Requested ORDER LINE will belong. Figure 14-10 shows the finished view set for Take Order. Notice that the symbol (r) precedes the group view Repeating Product Information.

Import Views	
view of	REQUESTING
entity	CUSTOMER
attr	NAME
group (r)	REPEATING PRODUCT INFORMATION
view of	REQUESTED
entity	PRODUCT
attr	NUMBER
view of	REQUESTED
entity	ORDER LINE
attr	QUANTITY
Export Views	
view of	ACCEPTED
entity	ORDER
attr	NUMBER
attr	TOTAL VALUE
Entity Action Views	
view of	(unnamed)
entity	CUSTOMER
attr	NAME
attr	NUMBER
view of	(unnamed)
entity	ORDER
attr	NUMBER
view of	(unnamed)
entity	ORDER LINE
attr	QUANTITY
attr	VALUE
view of	(unnamed)
entity	PRODUCT
attr	NUMBER
attr	PRICE

Figure 14-10. Complete View Set for TAKE ORDER

As hinted at previously, a group view can be composed of other group views. Since group views can repeat, one can use this feature to build a structure of nested repeating views (called, in computer science parlance, a **multi-dimensional array**).

For example, consider the case where a process called Analyze Market Share produces a list of PRODUCTS and, for each PRODUCT, a list of market share percentages by SALES REGION. This process must build a list within a list, as in Figure 14-11.

PROD NO.1234556	HAIR TRIMMER	
WESTERN U.S.	8%	
EASTERN U.S.	27%	
EUROPE	14%	
FAR EAST	29%	
PROD NO.6222990	DOOR HANDLE	
WESTERN U.S.	15%	
EASTERN U.S.	37%	
CANADA	5%	
AFRICA	1%	
PROD NO.3245627	LEFT HANDED BROOM CLOSET	
WESTERN U.S.	6%	
EASTERN U.S.	45%	
CANADA	18%	
EUROPE	2%	
FAR EAST	1%	

Figure 14-11. Example of a List within a List

Figure 14-12 shows the export view subset required to represent this nested repeating group view. Note how indentation is used to indicate that Repeating Sales Region Information is a component of Repeating Product Information.

Export Views	
group (r)	REPEATING PRODUCT INFORMATION
view of	ANALYZED
entity	PRODUCT
attr	NUMBER
attr	SHORT DESCRIPTION
group (r)	REPEATING SALES REGION
view of	CALCULATED
entity	SALES REGION
attr	NAME
attr	PERCENTAGE

Figure 14-12. Nested Repeating Group Views

Given the foregoing discussion, one can now consider the detailed information available for group views. The IEF can capture the following details about group views:

- Name

- Description

- Cardinality

- Minimum cardinality

- Maximum cardinality

- Average cardinality

- Optionality (import view subset only)

- Method of Subscripting

Group views may not appear in the entity action view subset for a process.

Name

Each group view **name** should accurately reflect its contents. Unlike entity view names, group view names always stand alone in the detailed process logic and so should carry the full weight of meaning of their components. This explains the name Repeating Product Information in Figure 14-10 rather than simply Repeating.

Description

The **description** for a view of any kind is optional. It is necessary only when the view's content is ambiguous.

Cardinality

The value of **cardinality** indicates whether the group view repeats. The value of cardinality may be *one* (non-repeating) or *one or more* (repeating).

In practice, there is little reason for building a non-repeating group view. As clarified later under the heading "Process Action Statements," the detailed process logic never references non-repeating group views. Instead it references their component entity views.

For each repeating group view, one must also specify the following information:

- Minimum cardinality (the least number of occurrences it can contain)

- Maximum cardinality (the greatest number of occurrences it can contain)

- Average cardinality (the average number of occurrences it can contain)

For minimum and maximum cardinality, the analyst may indicate whether the value specified is an estimate (such as "there will probably never be more than ten") or an absolute limit (such as "there must never be more than ten").

Optionality

One may specify **optionality** for import views only. If the analyst specifies an import group view as *mandatory*, each component specified as *mandatory* must have a value when the process to which it belongs begins execution.

For example, if Group View 1 is mandatory and consists of Group View 2 and Entity View 3, as follows:

group	GROUP VIEW 1
group	GROUP VIEW 2
entity	ENTITY VIEW 3

then all mandatory components of Group View 2 and Entity View 3 must have values when the process to which Group View 1 belongs begins.

One may specify the optionality condition for an optional group view in the same way as the optionality conditions for attributes or relationship memberships. This condition can be stored as part of the group view description.

Method of Subscripting

Each repeating group view (that is, a group view with a cardinality of *one or more*) must be defined as either **implicitly** or **explicitly** subscripted. *Subscripting* is the means by which a particular occurrence of a repeating group view (say, one CUSTOMER in a list of CUSTOMERs) is identified by an action diagram.

In most cases, repeating group views should be handled using implicit subscripting; only in very complex process logic is there a need for explicit subscripting.

The implications of using implicit versus explicit subscripting are discussed in detail in the "Advanced Topics" section in this chapter.

Entity Views and Their Detail

The IEF can capture the following details for each entity view:

- Name
- Description
- Optionality (import view subset only)

Name

As mentioned previously, the entity view **name** should be a modifier of the entity type name. The combination of entity view name and entity type name must be unique within a process's view set.

Description

The **description** for a view of any kind is optional. It is necessary only when the view's content is ambiguous.

Optionality

One may only specify **optionality** for import views. If the analyst specifies an import entity view as *mandatory*, each component attribute view specified as *mandatory* must have a value when the process to which it belongs begins execution.

One may specify the optionality condition for an optional entity view in the same way as the optionality conditions for attributes or relationship memberships. This condition can be stored as part of the entity view description.

Attribute Views and Their Detail

The only property available for an attribute view is its **optionality** within an import view subset. If an import attribute view is specified as *mandatory*, it must have a value when process execution begins.

FORMULATING PROCESS LOGIC

The formulation of detailed process logic is generally regarded as the most difficult part of Business Area Analysis. Because of its extremely detailed nature and the precise language used to record it in the Process Action Diagram, process logic analysis is much less intuitive than other activities discussed earlier.

To help make the transition from the high level of detail at which activity analysis stops to the low level of detail required in the Process Action Diagram, this section presents a 10-step approach to detailing the logic of an elementary process. This approach employs a technique called **Data Navigation Diagramming** or

Process Logic Diagramming to describe aspects of process behavior. Beginning with a very general definition, the analyst adds detail at each step. In the final step, the analyst combines all these details to form a Process Action Diagram.

The ten steps used in this approach are as follows:

1. Select an elementary process to analyze.
2. Identify the primary entity types used in the process.
3. Examine the neighborhoods of the primary entity types to determine whether the process uses them.
4. Determine the kind of action to be performed on the entities of each type.
5. Determine which attributes of the affected entity types are used and how they are used.
6. Determine which relationship memberships of the affected entity types are used and how they are used.
7. Determine the required sequence of actions.
8. Determine the selection criteria for entities.
9. Build the entity action views.
10. Construct the action diagram.

In cases where the process logic is reasonably straightforward, it may be possible to shortcut these steps by using the IEF's automatic action diagram generator (**stereotyping**). This feature allows one to build an action diagram to either create, update, delete, read or list entities of the type selected (typically a primary entity type, as in Step 2, below). It leads the analyst through a dialog in which actions on relationships and related entities are selected.

In other cases, when the process logic is more complex, this feature can be used to establish a starting point for the construction of entity action views (Step 9, below) and action diagrams (Step 10, below) after the initial formulation of process logic is complete.

This feature is described in detail in the *IEF Analysis Toolset Guide*.

Step 1 — Select an Elementary Process to Analyze

The analyst should specify process logic for each elementary process in the business area. The sample process selected for use throughout this discussion is the familiar Take Order process. The ERD fragment presented in Figure 14-13, an expansion of the one shown earlier in Figure 14-7, applies to the business area in which Take Order exists.

At this point, the analyst must have defined the following details for the process being analyzed:

- Its name.
- A definition.
- Import and export views.
- Its identification as an elementary process.

No other views or expected effects are required before beginning this analysis.

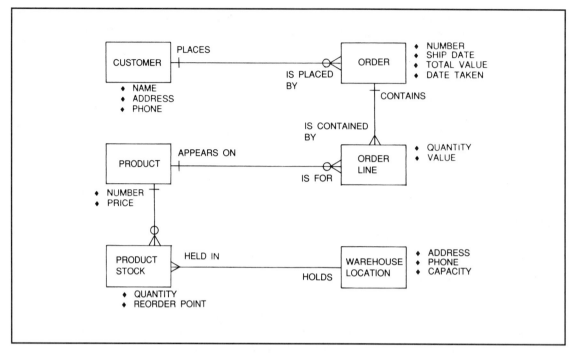

Figure 14-13. Expanded ERD Fragment for TAKE ORDER's Business Area

Step 2 — Identify Primary Entity Types

This is the first step in creating the Process Logic Diagram or, as it is sometimes called, the Data Navigation Diagram. Analysts can use this diagram to sketch out process logic before specifying it precisely in the action diagram.

The general principle behind the Process Logic Diagram is to superimpose actions to be performed in the process on a subset of the Entity Relationship Diagram showing entity types to be affected. The purpose of this step and the following one is to scope this Entity Relationship Diagram fragment.

The **primary entity types** are simply those entity types that immediately spring to the analyst's mind when visualizing the process. In the case of Take Order, for example, obviously the entity type ORDER is required. (Assume, for the moment, that the requirement for PRODUCT, ORDER LINE and CUSTOMER does not occur to the analyst, despite the work done on Take Order's information views in the previous section.)

At this point, the analyst notes the fact that Take Order uses the entity type ORDER.

Step 3 — Examine the Primary Entity Types' Neighborhoods

To finish constructing the Entity Relationship Diagram subset, the analyst must inspect the **neighborhood** of the primary entity types. The neighborhood of an entity type is the set of all entity types directly related to the subject entity type.

The analyst examines the neighborhood in an effort to find additional entity types required by the process. For each such entity type discovered, the analyst also examines that entity type's neighborhood. The analyst repeats this activity until he or she has considered the neighborhoods of all affected entity types.

In Step 2, the analyst identified ORDER as the only primary entity type for this process. Based on Figure 14-13, the analyst would proceed as follows:

1. Examine the neighborhood of ORDER. The neighborhood of ORDER contains two entity types, ORDER LINE and CUSTOMER.

   a. As stated in the section on information views, a CUSTOMER *places* an ORDER and is, thus, of interest to Take Order.

      The analyst records the fact that CUSTOMER is important.

   b. ORDERS consist of ORDER LINES. Since the relationship between ORDER and ORDER LINE is fully mandatory, they must both be created in the same process. ORDER LINE, thus, is of interest to Take Order.

      The analyst records the fact that ORDER LINE is important.

2. Examine the neighborhood of CUSTOMER. CUSTOMER, according to Figure 14-13, has only one entity type in its neighborhood: the original primary entity type ORDER. Since the analyst has already identified ORDER as important and since CUSTOMER has no more relationships, that set of neighborhoods is exhausted.

3. Examine the neighborhood of ORDER LINE. Besides ORDER, ORDER LINE has one entity type in its neighborhood: PRODUCT. Since one can only identify the kind of PRODUCT ordered on an ORDER LINE by the ORDER LINE's pairing with a PRODUCT, it is clear that PRODUCT, too, is important to Take Order. (Additionally, the relationship membership ORDER LINE *is for* PRODUCT is mandatory. This indicates that the analyst must establish the pairing between ORDER LINE and PRODUCT in the same elementary process in which the ORDER LINE is created.)

   The analyst records the fact that PRODUCT is important.

4. Examine the neighborhood of PRODUCT. Besides ORDER LINE, the only entity type in the neighborhood of PRODUCT is PRODUCT STOCK. After careful consideration, the analyst determines that ORDER taking does not affect PRODUCT STOCK levels. Thus PRODUCT STOCK is not important to the Take Order process.

   Since none of the elements of PRODUCT's neighborhood is important to Take Order, the analyst has exhausted all potential neighborhood entity types.

The list of entity types discovered during this step is:

- ORDER
- CUSTOMER
- ORDER LINE
- PRODUCT

The final activity in this step is to create an Entity Relationship Diagram showing the entity types required for the process. Usually, the set of entity types with which a single process deals is small enough to be contained in a page print or plot from the IEF Entity Relationship Diagram.

In the Take Order example, the Entity Relationship Diagram fragment in Figure 14-7 happens to show the exact required subset of the ERD in Figure 14-13.

This set of entity types should resemble the composite list of import and export views of the process. The analyst must resolve any anomalies, such as an entity type missing from this diagram but listed as an export view.

Step 4 — Determine the Entity Actions Required

In this step, the analyst annotates the Entity Relationship Diagram with the actions to be performed on the identified entity types. The four actions that may be performed on an entity are:

- CREATE (which stores information about an entity)
- READ (which makes stored information about an entity available)
- UPDATE (which modifies stored information about an entity)
- DELETE (which erases stored information about an entity)

These actions are called **entity actions.** The entity actions required in the Take Order process are:

- ORDER must be CREATED.
- CUSTOMER must be READ.
- ORDER LINE must be CREATED.
- PRODUCT must be READ.

Note that this list of actions on entity types contains exactly the same information as the expected effects of the process. If expected effects have already been recorded, the analyst should compare them against this list as a verification measure.

Figure 14-14 shows the annotated Entity Relationship Diagram fragment (hereafter called a **Data Navigation Diagram**) for the Take Order process.

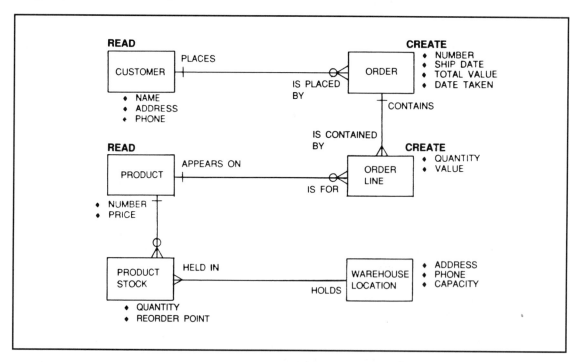

Figure 14-14. Data Navigation Diagram for TAKE ORDER after Step 4

Step 5 — Determine Actions on Attributes

The entity actions CREATE and UPDATE may have attribute actions subordinate to them. In this step, the analyst identifies these attribute actions and updates the Data Navigation Diagram to show them.

A CREATE action can contain subordinate SET actions that assign values to attributes. A CREATE action must SET each mandatory attribute of the affected entity type. In addition, it may SET any optional attributes as required by the process.

An UPDATE action can contain both SET actions and REMOVE actions. SET assigns a value to an attribute, while REMOVE removes the value from an attribute. An UPDATE action can modify any attribute of the affected entity type.

In the Take Order process, CREATE actions operate on two entity types: ORDER and ORDER LINE. Assume that the attributes of those entity types have the following optionality:

```
ORDER
     NUMBER            (mandatory)
     SHIP DATE         (optional)
     TOTAL VALUE       (mandatory)
     DATE TAKEN        (mandatory)

ORDER LINE
     QUANTITY          (mandatory)
     VALUE             (mandatory)
```

The only optional attribute of either ORDER or ORDER LINE is Ship Date. The analyst must SET all mandatory attributes of both ORDER and ORDER LINE in the statements that CREATE them. As for Ship Date, it will probably not be SET until the ORDER is filled and shipped, so it is not SET in the Take Order process.

Figure 14-15 shows the Data Navigation Diagram for Take Order annotated with subordinate attribute actions to the CREATE actions for ORDER and ORDER LINE.

Step 6 — Determine Actions on Relationships

In this step, the analyst identifies actions on relationships of the affected entity types and records them on the Data Navigation Diagram.

Relationship actions, like attribute actions, are subordinate to the entity actions CREATE and UPDATE. A CREATE action may establish (ASSOCIATE) pairings. An UPDATE action may establish (ASSOCIATE) or eliminate (DISASSOCIATE) pairings.

As with attribute actions, a CREATE action normally contains ASSOCIATES for all mandatory relationship memberships. However, in the case of fully mandatory relationships, this is not possible.

For example, based on Figure 14-7, the relationship between ORDER and ORDER LINE is fully mandatory. Assuming that one creates an order before its order lines, the CREATE for ORDER cannot include an ASSOCIATE to ORDER LINE; the order line does not yet exist. One must establish the relationship between ORDER and ORDER LINE when each ORDER LINE is CREATED.

The rule to remember, then, is that all mandatory relationships must be established by the time the elementary process finishes executing. An individual entity action might leave things inconsistent for a moment, but the total collection of actions that form a process must leave the business in a completely consistent state.

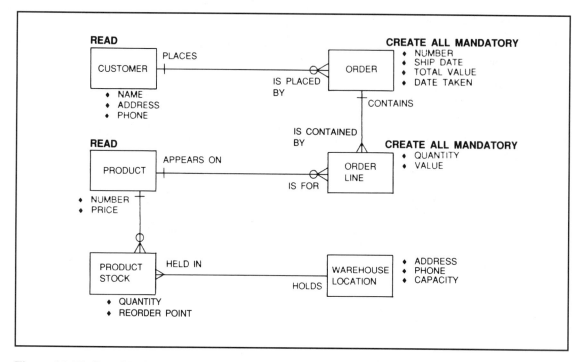

Figure 14-15. Data Navigation Diagram for TAKE ORDER after Step 5

For the Take Order process, one must consider the relationships of ORDER and ORDER LINE. As it turns out, each relationship membership of ORDER and ORDER LINE is mandatory so they must all be established. Figure 14-16 shows the Data Navigation Diagram for Take Order, annotated to include relationship actions.

Step 7 — Determine Sequence of Actions

After identifying all actions on entity types, attributes and relationships, the analyst can determine the sequence in which those actions should be performed during process execution. The analyst records this sequence on the Data Navigation Diagram by numbering each of the entity and relationship actions to be specified.

The analyst should bear the following points in mind when determining the sequence of actions to be performed:

- Before pairing two entities, one must make them both available through a READ or a CREATE. In general, one should READ existing entities, then CREATE entities with which they will be paired.

- In some cases, the sequence of actions is irrelevant. This situation typically occurs when sets of actions can either be performed in parallel or exclusive of one another. In such cases, the analyst must assign an arbitrary sequence to the actions in question.

- The Data Navigation Diagram is very good at showing a linear sequence of entity actions. It is not particularly good at showing the details of conditional and repetitive processing. Thus, while one might naturally wish to add such details at this point, the analyst should defer this task until Step 10.

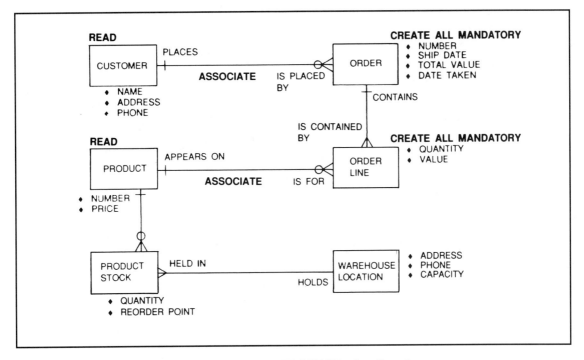

Figure 14-16. Data Navigation Diagram for TAKE ORDER after Step 6

Step 8 — Determine Entity Selection Criteria

Before entities can be READ, one must establish a set of criteria for selecting them from among other entities of the same type. In this step, the analyst identifies these criteria and uses them to annotate the Data Navigation Diagram.

Selection criteria can include three primary components:

- An attribute value of the entity being READ
- An attribute value of an entity directly or indirectly related to the entity being READ
- The existence of a relationship

The analyst constructs selection criteria by combining these components using a series of ANDs and ORs to fully identify the entity to be retrieved. More information about constructing selection criteria can be found in the discussion of the READ action statement later in this chapter.

In the Take Order example, entities of two types will be READ: CUSTOMER and PRODUCT. The selection criteria in each case is based on the import view of Take Order. The CUSTOMER to be retrieved is the one whose Name is the same as the Requesting CUSTOMER Name; the PRODUCTS to be retrieved are those with Numbers equal to the list of PRODUCT Numbers in Requested PRODUCT and Requested ORDER LINE (see Figure 14-10).

Figure 14-17 shows the Data Navigation Diagram for Take Order annotated with entity selection criteria.

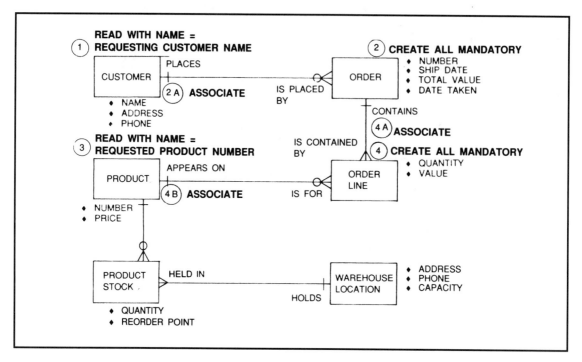

Figure 14-17. Data Navigation Diagram for TAKE ORDER after Step 8

Step 9 — Define the Entity Action Views

After completing the previous eight steps, the analyst may define entity action views. One entity action view is required for each entity type participating in an entity action. Entity action views were discussed earlier in this chapter in the section on information views.

The phrase "participating in an entity action" in the preceding paragraph is precise. Sometimes an entity type is only mentioned as part of the selection criteria for an entity of some other type. Regardless, an entity action view is required for it.

For example, a READ which finds any CUSTOMER who placed an ORDER for a certain PRODUCT might look like this:

```
READ customer
    WHERE DESIRED customer places SOME order
    AND THAT order contains SOME order_line
    AND THAT order_line is for SOME product
    AND THAT product_number IS EQUAL TO requested_product_number
```

This example requires an entity action view for all four entity types (CUSTOMER, ORDER, ORDER LINE, and PRODUCT), even though attributes are only retrieved for CUSTOMER.

Step 10 — Build the Process Action Diagram

When the analyst reaches this step, some important process logic questions remain to be answered. These include:

- How to handle conditions? For example, how does one specify that the process should only READ a certain entity under certain circumstances?

- How to handle repetition? For example, a list of PRODUCT Numbers and ORDER LINE Quantities serve as input to the Take Order process. How can one specify that actions on PRODUCT and ORDER LINE should occur repeatedly?

- How to handle exception conditions? For example, what happens if, during TAKE ORDER, there is no CUSTOMER associated with the CUSTOMER Number requested?

These questions are best addressed when building the Process Action Diagram. The building blocks of this diagram are the process action statements. Remaining sections of this chapter discuss each kind of action statement. After each discussion, a sample completed action diagram for Take Order appears.

ACTION DIAGRAM NOMENCLATURE

Before learning about the action statements that describe the detailed process logic, one should become familiar with some terms used in action diagramming. This section describes the following terms:

- Process Action Diagram
- Process Action Block
- Common Action Block
- Business Algorithm
- Action Group

Process Action Diagram

The term **Process Action Diagram** refers to a collection of action statements that directly support an elementary process.

Process Action Block

A **Process Action Block** (or simply **action block**) is a named collection of action statements that do not directly support an elementary process. An action block is either:

- The definition of a derivation algorithm for a derived attribute.
- The definition of a default algorithm for a basic or designed attribute.
- The definition of a business algorithm used to calculate an attribute value in a SET...USING action.
- The definition of a business algorithm invoked through a USE action.

Common Action Block

A **Common Action Block** is an action block that is invoked by more than one process. Only business algorithms can be Common Action Blocks.

Business Algorithm

A **business algorithm** is an action block that is invoked through a SET...USING action or through a USE action.

Action Group

An **action group** is any bracketed collection of actions in a Process Action Diagram or Process Action Block. All statements appearing within a bracket participate in the action group enclosed by the bracket.

PROCESS ACTION STATEMENTS

This section explains the detailed actions that can be performed by processes. All action statement descriptions and examples appear as they would in a Process Action Diagram. An abbreviated reference for these action statements is found in Appendix D, "Action Diagram Syntax." Although the syntax is complex, one need not memorize it, since the IEF leads the analyst through the creation of each action statement. This automated feature is discussed in more detail under the heading "Considerations for Process Action Diagramming."

Process actions include the following kinds of actions:

- **Entity Actions**, used to retrieve and manipulate stored information about entities.
- **Relationship Actions,** used to manipulate pairings of stored entities.
- **Assignment Actions,** used to assign values to attribute views.
- **Conditional Actions,** used to change the flow of a process based on some condition.
- **Repeating Actions,** used to manipulate components of a repeating group view.
- **Control Actions,** used to change the flow of the process unconditionally.
- **Miscellaneous Actions.**

Unless otherwise noted, all examples in this section refer to the Entity Relationship Diagram presented in Figure 14-7 and the view set of Take Order presented in Figure 14-10.

Descriptions of action diagram statements employ the following conventions:

- UPPER CASE LETTERS are used for keywords.
- [Options] are enclosed in brackets.
- Alternatives are presented within a large bracket. For example:

SET entity-view-1 attribute-view-1
    TO expression
    USING process-action-block

- Lower-case-letters joined by hyphens represent a variable, user-supplied value.
- Ellipses (...) following any clause in an action statement indicate that the clause can occur multiple times within the action statement.

Entity Actions

There are five types of entity action statements:

- READ
- READ EACH
- CREATE
- UPDATE
- DELETE

READ

READ action statements retrieve information about previously stored entities. The format of the READ action statement is:

```
─── READ entity-view-list

        [WHERE selection-condition]

───     [WHEN SUCCESSFUL
                action-statement-list-1]
───     [WHEN NOT FOUND
                action-statement-list-2]
```

Notes:

1. Every view being read in *entity-view-list* must be an entity action view.

2. The READ action only affects the attribute views of entity views specified in *entity-view-list*.

3. The WHERE conditions (optionally combined and joined by ANDs, ORs, and parentheses) qualify the READ action. They test attribute values and test for the existence of a pairing. The collection of these conditions is called the **selection criteria** for the READ. A *selection-condition* is any expression that can be judged either true or false.

4. Each view being read should be qualified by at least one selection criterion somewhere in the statement. Otherwise, an arbitrary occurrence will be read.

5. The optional WHEN SUCCESSFUL clause may be followed by a list of actions to be performed if the selection criteria were satisfied.

6. The WHEN NOT FOUND clause may be followed by a list of actions to be performed if the selection criteria were not satisfied.

Selection Conditions for READ/READ EACH

The selection conditions for READ and READ EACH may be very simple or very complex. In either case, the sentences are easy to build since the IEF presents only valid choices during the READ/READ EACH statement comstruction.

A *selection-condition* takes the form:

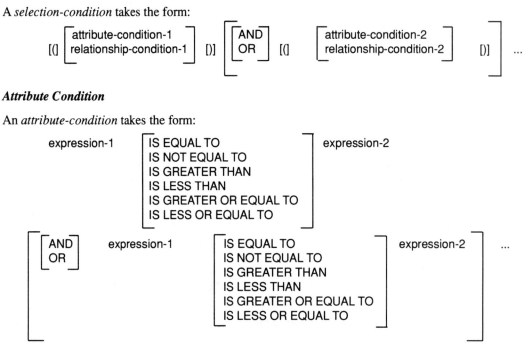

Attribute Condition

An *attribute-condition* takes the form:

Notes:

1. An *attribute-condition* must include an attribute of an entity action view on at least one side of each relational operator (for example, IS EQUAL TO, IS NOT EQUAL TO).

2. Comparisons must involve combinations of operands of the same domain (character, number, date, or time).

3. Each reference to an attribute of an entity action view is preceded by a view qualifier (DESIRED, SOME, CURRENT, or THAT). DESIRED refers to one of the views being read. SOME refers to any other entity action view, while THAT refers to a view previously referenced by SOME. CURRENT refers to any entity action view previously populated by a READ or CREATE action.

4. For details on formulating expressions, see the section entitled "Advanced Topics."

Examples:

Discover whether the business knows about the CUSTOMER who is attempting to place an ORDER (in the process Take Order).

```
READ  customer
      WHERE DESIRED customer name IS EQUAL TO requesting customer name
```

Read all CUSTOMERS whose name begins with Q.

```
┌─  READ  customer
│       WHERE SUBSTR(DESIRED customer name,1,1) IS EQUAL TO "Q"
└
```

Relationship Condition

A *relationship-condition* takes the form:

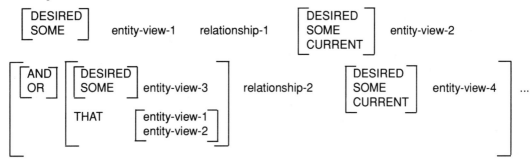

Notes:

1. Each relationship (*relationship-1*, *relationship-2*) must be a relationship that exists between two entity action views.

2. Each reference to an entity action view is preceded by a view qualifier (DESIRED, SOME, CURRENT, or THAT). DESIRED refers to one of the views being read (that is, in the *entity-view-list* of the READ action.) SOME refers to any other entity action view, while THAT refers to a view previously referenced by SOME. CURRENT refers to any entity action view previously populated by a READ or CREATE action.

3. CURRENT may only precede the second of the two entity action views joined by each relationship (that is, *entity-view-2* and *entity-view-4*.)

Example:

First, read the PRODUCT which has a PRODUCT Number of 1295. Then, read any CUSTOMER who placed an ORDER for the PRODUCT just read. Read any ORDER(s) placed for that PRODUCT as well.

```
┌─  READ product
│       WHERE DESIRED product number IS EQUAL TO 1295
└

┌─  READ  customer, order
│       WHERE DESIRED customer places DESIRED order
│       AND DESIRED order contains SOME order line
│       AND THAT order line is for CURRENT product
└
```

Combined Examples:

As explained previously, it is possible to combine *attribute conditions* and *relationship conditions* in a single READ action. For example, assume the existence of an entity type PERSON and another entity type, FOOD. Assume that the relationship *has as favorite/is favorite of* allows a pairing of a PERSON with his or her favorite FOOD (Figure 14-18).

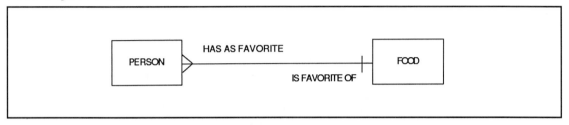

Figure 14-18. A Many-to-One Relationship Between PERSON and FOOD

The following READ action will retrieve information about the PERSON named "Fred Frelb" and subsequently discover his favorite FOOD.

```
  ┌─ READ person
  │      WHERE DESIRED person name IS EQUAL TO "Fred Frelb"
  ├─ WHEN SUCCESSFUL
  │        ┌─ READ food
  └─       └   WHERE DESIRED food is favorite of CURRENT person
```

The following READ action will find any person (if one exists) whose favorite food is liver:

```
  ┌─ READ person
  │      WHERE DESIRED person has as favorite SOME food
  └─         AND THAT food type IS EQUAL TO "liver"
```

Reading Multiple Entity Views

As indicated in the preceding discussion, it is possible to retrieve attributes of multiple entity views within a single READ or READ EACH action. If used judiciously, the use of this feature can result in action diagrams of fewer statements and greater clarity.

For example, based on Figure 14-7 it is possible to imagine that an analyst might, in some case, need to retrieve details of an ORDER and the CUSTOMER who placed it based on a value of ORDER Number. The following READ will accomplish this:

```
  ┌─ READ    order
  │          customer
  │       WHERE DESIRED order number IS EQUAL TO import order number
  └─          AND DESIRED customer places DESIRED order
```

This is an example of the judicious use of a multiple-view READ. Note the following:

- Since the relationship membership on the "one" side of the PLACES/IS PLACED BY relationship is mandatory (that is, each ORDER must be placed by one CUSTOMER), the meaning of the WHEN NOT FOUND clause is unambiguous. If the ORDER exists, the CUSTOMER must also, so NOT FOUND means that the ORDER was not found.

- There is no question about which occurrences of ORDER and CUSTOMER will be retrieved; there is only one ORDER with a particular ORDER Number, and there is only one placing CUSTOMER for each ORDER.

However, there are times when a multiple-view READ does not work well. For example, consider the following READ (still based on Figure 14-7):

```
READ    customer
        product
        WHERE DESIRED customer number IS EQUAL TO import customer number
        AND DESIRED product number IS EQUAL TO import product number
```

In this example, the meaning of the WHEN NOT FOUND condition is ambiguous. Remember that the *action-statement-list* following the WHEN NOT FOUND is processed if the selection criteria for the READ are not fully met or successfully applied. Thus, whether the desired CUSTOMER, the desired PRODUCT, or both cannot be located, the actions in the WHEN NOT FOUND clause will be processed; there is no way to tell exactly what caused the READ to fail.

Another example of the mis-use of the multiple-view READ is this:

```
READ    customer
        order
        WHERE DESIRED customer number IS EQUAL TO import customer number
        AND DESIRED order is placed by DESIRED customer
```

Since the relationship membership CUSTOMER PLACES ORDER is optional, the WHEN NOT FOUND is again ambiguous. Additionally, since the ORDER lies at the "many" end of the *places/is placed by* relationship, there is no way to know which occurrence of ORDER will be retrieved.

The best time to use multiple entity views on a READ, then, is when the following criteria are satisfied:

- The entity types of the specified views are related through a chain of 1:M relationships.
- The desired entity belonging to the type on the last "many" relationship is identified using attribute selection.
- The other entities are identified using relationship selection based on the "one" ends of their relationships.
- The relationship membership on the "one" end of each relationship is mandatory.

Given these rather complex criteria, the analyst may wish to pretend that multiple-view READs are not possible. However, they provide an additional, albeit completely hidden, advantage. By using the multiple-view form of READ, it becomes possible to take advantage of a special kind of database optimization during the Technical Design stage of Information Engineering called **transparent denormalization**. Although the analyst should not be concerned with performance considerations in general, the use of transparent denormalization provides a significant performance benefit without requiring changes to the business model. A discussion of transparent denormalization and its implications in the action diagram takes place in Appendix H.

READ EACH

READ EACH behaves both as an entity action and a repeating action. Because of this unique behavior, the discussion of the READ EACH action is deferred to the subsection on repeated actions.

CREATE

CREATE action statements record information about entities once they are of interest to the business. The format of the CREATE action statement is:

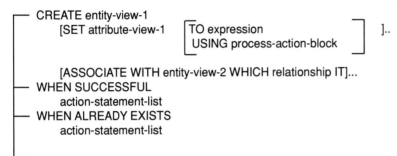

Notes:

1. *Entity-view-1* is an entity action view of the entity for which information is to be recorded.

2. A number of SET clauses may appear, one for each attribute to be assigned a value. All mandatory attributes must be assigned a value.

3. The expression following the TO in the SET clause must evaluate to the same primitive domain as *attribute-view-1*. In most cases, the expression is simply a different view of the same attribute.

4. The *process-action-block* after USING in the SET clause is the name of a business algorithm used to calculate the attribute's value.

5. The ASSOCIATE WITH clause allows pairings to be established between the entity referenced in *entity-view-1* and the entity referenced in *entity-view-2*. *Entity-view-2* must be an entity action view. During a CREATE, each identifying relationship membership must have a pairing established for it.

6. The WHEN SUCCESSFUL clause is optional. It specifies a set of actions to be performed if the CREATE completes successfully.

7. The WHEN ALREADY EXISTS clause is optional. It specifies a set of actions to be performed if there is already information stored about an entity with the same identifier as *entity-view-1* (remember, all identifiers of an entity must be unique).

Example:

In this sample action diagram fragment, an ORDER is CREATED after a READ action verifies the prior existence of a CUSTOMER.

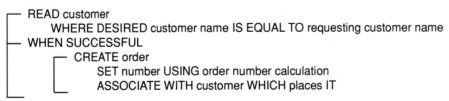

Comments:

1. The CREATE only happens if the READ of CUSTOMER was successful (that is, if a CUSTOMER with the correct value for its Name attribute already exists).

2. The business algorithm Order Number Calculation is assumed to return the value of the next available ORDER Number.

3. In the ASSOCIATE clause, Customer is the unnamed entity action view into which information about the Requesting CUSTOMER entity was placed as the result of the READ action.

4. In the ASSOCIATE clause, *places* is the name of the relationship membership between CUSTOMER and ORDER (see Figure 14-7).

UPDATE

UPDATE action statements modify the information stored about an entity. The format of an UPDATE action statement is:

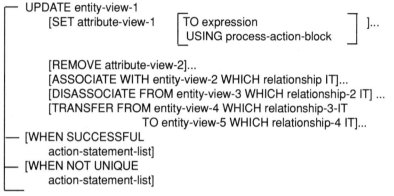

```
┌─ UPDATE entity-view-1
│      [SET attribute-view-1  ┌ TO expression                    ┐ ]...
│                             └ USING process-action-block       ┘
│
│      [REMOVE attribute-view-2]...
│      [ASSOCIATE WITH entity-view-2 WHICH relationship IT]...
│      [DISASSOCIATE FROM entity-view-3 WHICH relationship-2 IT] ...
│      [TRANSFER FROM entity-view-4 WHICH relationship-3-IT
│                         TO entity-view-5 WHICH relationship-4 IT]...
├─ [WHEN SUCCESSFUL
│      action-statement-list]
├─ [WHEN NOT UNIQUE
│      action-statement-list]
└─
```

Notes:

1. Before performing the UPDATE, the process logic must have CREATED or READ *entity-view-1*.

2. *Entity-view-1*, *2*, *3*, *4* and *5* must be entity action views.

3. The rules for the SET clause are the same as for the CREATE action.

4. Mandatory attributes may not be the subject of the REMOVE clause.

5. Identifying relationships may not be the subject of a DISASSOCIATE clause.

6. ASSOCIATE establishes a pairings while DISASSOCIATE eliminates a pairing.

7. TRANSFER moves a pairing from one entity to another, provided that the affected relationship membership has been marked as *transferable*.

8. The optional WHEN SUCCESSFUL clause is followed by a list of actions to be performed if the UPDATE succeeds.

9. The optional WHEN NOT UNIQUE clause is followed by a list of actions to be performed if the UPDATE causes an entity identifier to conflict with another entity identifier.

Example:

Since the Take Order process includes no UPDATE entity actions, the following UPDATE example relies on the entity types shown in Figure 14-18.

The activity to be performed by this UPDATE action is to:

1. Change the NAME of the PERSON "Fred Frelb" to "Mark Harmon."

2. Delete the PERSON's Address (assuming, of course, that the Address attribute of PERSON is optional).

3. Change the PERSON's favorite FOOD from whatever it currently is to "banana split" (assuming, of course, that the relationship membership from PERSON to FOOD is transferable).

Assume that Original Food, New Food and Person are entity action views.

```
1   ┌─ READ person
    │      WHERE DESIRED person name IS EQUAL TO "Fred Frelb"
    └─

2   ┌─ READ original food
    │      WHERE DESIRED original food is favorite of  CURRENT  person
    └─

3   ┌─ READ new food
    │      WHERE DESIRED new food kind_of_food IS EQUAL To "banana split"
    └─

4   ┌─ UPDATE person
5   │      SET name TO "Mark Harmon"
6   │      REMOVE address
7   │      TRANSFER FROM original food WHICH is favorite of IT
    │                TO     new food     WHICH is favorite of IT
    └─
```

Comments:

1. The READ action at (1) retrieves information about Fred Frelb and places it in the entity action view Person.

2. The READ action at (2) retrieves information about the favorite FOOD of the PERSON in the entity action view Person and places it in the entity action view Original Food. In this case, it finds Fred Frelb's favorite FOOD.

3. The READ action at (3) retrieves information about the FOOD whose Kind_Of_Food is "banana split" and places the information in the entity action view New Food. This retrieval is necessary in order for the TRANSFER to be performed.

4. The UPDATE action at (4) signals modifications to the information stored about the PERSON entity in the entity action view Person.

5. The SET clause at (5) causes the stored Name of the PERSON to be changed to "Mark Harmon."

6. The REMOVE clause at (6) causes the stored Address of the PERSON to be eliminated.

7. The TRANSFER clause at (7) causes the original pairing between the one-time "Fred Frelb" and his favorite FOOD to be replaced by a pairing between the former "Fred Frelb" (now "Mark Harmon") and his new favorite, "banana split."

DELETE

DELETE action statements eradicate all knowledge of an entity. The format of the DELETE action statement is:

```
DELETE entity-view-1
```

Notes:

1. Before performing the DELETE, the process logic must have CREATED or READ *entity-view-1*.

2. *Entity-view-1* must be an entity action view.

3. As a result of the DELETE, the IEF also deletes all entities that participate in mandatory pairings with *entity-view-1*. This effect is called **cascade deletion.**

Examples:

Given the ERD in Figure 14-7, assume that it becomes necessary to DELETE the ORDER with an ORDER Number of "111." The following action statements will satisfy the requirement:

```
┌─ READ order
│      WHERE DESIRED order number IS EQUAL TO 111
└─

   DELETE order
```

Since ORDER has a mandatory relationship to ORDER LINE, the IEF will also delete all ORDER LINES associated with the affected ORDER when the DELETE is executed. Additionally, had ORDER LINE been involved in any other mandatory relationship, the IEF would have deleted any entity paired with an ORDER LINE based on that relationship. The cascade delete continues until all pairings based on mandatory relationships have been eliminated.

Cascade deletion can also happen as a result of a DISASSOCIATE or TRANSFER. Any time an entity no longer participates in a mandatory relationship as a result of a DELETE, DISASSOCIATE, or TRANSFER, the entity will be cascade deleted.

Relationship Actions

There are three types of relationship actions:

- ASSOCIATE
- DISASSOCIATE
- TRANSFER

As shown earlier, ASSOCIATE can also appear as a clause in either CREATE or UPDATE action statements. Similarly, DISASSOCIATE and TRANSFER can also appear as clauses in UPDATE action statements. The stand alone relationship actions presented in this section operate exactly the same as the relationship clauses in the CREATE and UPDATE entity actions.

The examples in this section are based on the Entity Relationship Diagram appearing in Figure 14-18.

ASSOCIATE

An ASSOCIATE action statement records a pairing based on a relationship membership. The format of the ASSOCIATE action statement is:

```
ASSOCIATE entity-view-1 WITH entity-view-2 WHICH
         relationship-1 IT
```

Notes:

1. *Entity-view-1* and *entity-view-2* must both be entity action views and must have already been READ or CREATED before the ASSOCIATE action is performed.

2. In stand alone ASSOCIATE action statements, *relationship-1* cannot be an identifying relationship.

Example:

In Figure 14-18, the relationship between FOOD and PERSON is fully optional. Thus, FOODS can exist that are nobody's favorite and PERSONS can exist who are not willing to commit to a favorite FOOD. In this example, assume that there is a PERSON, Fred Frelb, who, up until this very moment, could not settle on a favorite FOOD. Now, however, he has decided that beef vindaloo, a spicy Indian dish, has captured the heart of his palate. This interesting fact can be recorded in the following action diagram fragment:

```
┌── READ person
│       WHERE DESIRED person name IS EQUAL TO "Fred Frelb"
└

┌── READ food
│       WHERE DESIRED food kind_of_food IS EQUAL TO "beef vindaloo"
└

    ASSOCIATE food WITH person WHICH favors IT
```

As an alternative, the ASSOCIATE statement could have read "ASSOCIATE person WITH food WHICH is favorite of IT." In either case, the meaning is clear though the English is slightly questionable.

DISASSOCIATE

The DISASSOCIATE action statement eliminates an existing pairing. The format of the DISASSOCIATE action statement is:

```
DISASSOCIATE entity-view-1 FROM entity-view-2 WHICH
        relationship-1 IT
```

Notes:

1. *Entity-view-1* and *entity-view-2* must both be entity action views and must have already been READ or CREATED before the DISASSOCIATE action is performed.

2. In stand alone DISASSOCIATE action statements, *relationship-1* cannot be an identifying relationship.

3. As mentioned in the DELETE action description, the DISASSOCIATE action can potentially cause cascade deletion of entities.

Example (based on Figure 14-18):

After a painful and sleepless night following a feast of beef vindaloo, Fred Frelb decides that the stomach of an occidental man is not equal to the strange and wonderful spices present in this Asian foodstuff, and reconsiders his decision that beef vindaloo is, indeed, his favorite food.

Assuming he has no other favorite in mind, the following action diagram fragment reflects his change of heart:

```
┌── READ person
│       WHERE DESIRED person name IS EQUAL TO "Fred Frelb"
└

┌── READ food
│       WHERE DESIRED food is favorite of  CURRENT person
└

    DISASSOCIATE food FROM person WHICH favors IT
```

TRANSFER

The TRANSFER action moves a pairing between the subject entity and object entity to a new object entity (of the same type as the original object entity). The format of the TRANSFER action statement is:

```
TRANSFER entity-view-1
          FROM entity-view-2 WHICH relationship-1 IT
          TO      entity-view-3 WHICH relationship-1 IT
```

Notes:

1. *Entity-view-1*, *entity-view-2* and *entity-view-3* must all be entity action views. They must all have been populated by a READ or CREATE before the TRANSFER action executes.

2. *Relationship-1* must be defined as transferable.

3. *Relationship-1* may not be an identifying relationship.

Example (based on Figure 14-18):

Assume that Fred Frelb's friend, Frank Freen (another PERSON), has enjoyed a fondness for a Turkish dish called donor kebab. However, after attending a major sporting event he becomes incurably addicted to Nachos drenched in imitation cheese food sprinkled with jalapeno peppers. This turn of events is reflected in the following action diagram fragment:

```
┌─ READ person
│     WHERE DESIRED person name IS EQUAL TO "Frank Freen"
└

┌─ READ old_favorite food
│     WHERE DESIRED old_favorite food  is favorite of  CURRENT  person
└

┌─ READ new_favorite food
│     WHERE DESIRED new_favorite food kind_of_food
│          IS EQUAL TO "ballpark Nachos"
└

┌─ TRANSFER person
│     FROM old_favorite food WHICH is favorite of IT
│     TO  new_favorite food WHICH is favorite of IT
└
```

Note that Old_Favorite and New_Favorite are two entity action views of the entity type FOOD.

Assignment Actions

There are four kinds of assignment actions:

- SET
- MOVE
- EXIT STATE IS
- PRINTER TERMINAL IS

They are used to assign values to attribute views.

SET

SET assigns a value to an individual attribute view. It operates like the SET clause of CREATE and UPDATE statements.

The format of the SET action statement is:

SET
```
┌ entity-view-1 attribute-view-1 ┐          ┌ TO expression         ┐
│ NEXTTRAN                       │ [ROUNDED] │ USING action-block    │
│ SUBSCRIPT                      │          └                       ┘
└ LAST                           ┘
```

Notes:

1. *Entity-view-1* may be either a local or an export view. Import views may not be modified within a process. Attribute views in entity action views may only be modified through the SET and REMOVE clauses of CREATE or UPDATE action statements.

2. The expression following the TO clause must return a value in the same primitive domain as the attribute viewed by *attribute-view-1*.

3. The *action-block* after the USING clause must return a value in the same domain as the attribute viewed by *attribute-view-1*.

4. See the section entitled "Advanced Topics" for a detailed discussion of expressions.

5. The NEXTTRAN option sets an IEF special attribute whose use is normally restricted to the Business System Design stage of Information Engineering. A discussion of its function appears in Chapter 23.

6. The SUBSCRIPT and LAST options are used only for explicitly subscripted repeating group views. A general discussion of repeating group views appears in the section entitled "Advanced Topics" in this chapter

7. The ROUNDED option is available only if *attribute-view-1* is of the primitive domain Number.

Example:

Based on the Take Order example (Figures 14-6, 14-7 and 14-10), prepare to export the newly calculated ORDER Number by setting the value of the export attribute view for ORDER Number to that calculated in the entity action view.

        SET accepted order number TO order number

MOVE

The MOVE action assigns the values of multiple attribute views at once. The format of the MOVE action statement is:

        MOVE entity-view-1 TO entity-view-2

Notes:

1. *Entity-view-1* and *entity-view-2* are views of the same entity type. Each attribute view in *entity-view-2* is assigned the value of the corresponding attribute view in *entity-view-1*.

    For example, consider an entity type X for which two views exist in a single process. One view has the name Source and one has the name Destination. Assume the following to be true:

    a. Entity type X has attributes A, B, C, D and E.

    b. Entity view Source X contains attribute views A, B, and C, each of which contain the following values:

Attribute	Value
A	Alpha
B	Beta
C	Gamma

c. Entity view Destination X contains attribute views B, C, and D which contain the following values:

Attribute	Value
B	Bravo
C	Charlie
D	Dog

d. If the action statement "MOVE source x TO destination x" is performed:

    (1)   The value of Destination X B becomes "Beta," the value of Source X B.

    (2)   The value of Destination X C becomes "Gamma," the value of Source X C.

    (3)   The value of Destination X D remains "Dog" because there was no attribute view for D in Source X.

    (4)   Since Destination X has no attribute view of A, the value "Alpha" in Source X A is ignored.

This activity is equivalent to the following SET statements:

SET destination x b TO source x b
SET destination x c TO source x c

2. *Entity-view-1* may be either an import, entity action or local view.

3. *Entity-view-2* may be either a local or export view.

Example:

Based on the Take Order process (Figures 14-6, 14-7 and 14-10), prepare to send the information about the ORDER back to the CUSTOMER. (This means that the values in the entity action view of ORDER must be assigned to the export view of ORDER.)

MOVE order TO accepted order

The entity action view Order has only one attribute view (Number). It corresponds to the attribute view Number in Accepted ORDER. Thus, this MOVE only assigns the value of Accepted ORDER Number.

EXIT STATE IS

The EXIT STATE IS action sets the value of the special attribute Exit State. Exit State is used to indicate the outcome of a process. During BAA, it is most often set as a result of the failure of an entity action. The format of the EXIT STATE IS action is:

EXIT STATE IS exit-state-value

Notes:

1. A more complete description of exception handling using exit states is found in the section entitled "Advanced Topics" later in this chapter.

Example:

Inform the person attempting to locate the CUSTOMER with Number of 123 that no such CUSTOMER exists.

```
┌─  READ customer
│        WHERE DESIRED customer number IS EQUAL TO 123
├─  WHEN NOT FOUND
│            EXIT STATE IS customer_not_found
└─
```

PRINTER TERMINAL IS

The PRINTER TERMINAL IS action should not be used during BAA. It is a construct useful during Business System Design, and is discussed in Chapter 23.

Conditional Actions

There are two kinds of conditional actions:

- IF
- CASE

They are used to evaluate a situation and direct the process flow based on the result.

IF

The IF action statement tests the truth of an assertion. The format of the IF action statement is:

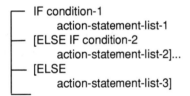

```
┌─  IF condition-1
│        action-statement-list-1
├─  [ELSE IF condition-2
│        action-statement-list-2]...
├─  [ELSE
│        action-statement-list-3]
└─
```

Notes:

1. *Condition-1* and *condition-2* are any expression that can be judged either true or false.
2. Any number of ELSE IF clauses may appear in a single IF statement.
3. Only the *action-statement-list* associated with the first condition evaluated as true is performed. If none of the conditions in the IF action prove true, *action-statement- list-3* following the ELSE is performed.

Instead of using the Take Order or favorite food example, a number of more abstract examples can better illustrate operation of the IF action.

Example 1:

Given the following action statement:

```
1   ┌─  IF a IS GREATER THAN b
2   │       SET a TO b
3   ├─  ELSE
4   │       SET b TO a
    └─
```

Case 1:

Assume that the value of A is 2 and the value of B is 1. Since A is greater than B, the condition specified in line 1 is true. As a result, the SET action at line 2 is performed and A is set to 1.

Case 2:

Assume that the value of A is 1 and the value of B is 2. Since A is not greater than B, the condition specified in line 1 is false. As a result, the SET action at line 4 is executed and B is set to 1.

Example 2:

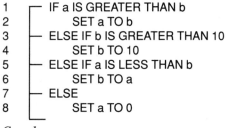

```
1   ┌─  IF a IS GREATER THAN b
2   │       SET a TO b
3   ├─  ELSE IF b IS GREATER THAN 10
4   │       SET b TO 10
5   ├─  ELSE IF a IS LESS THAN b
6   │       SET b TO a
7   ├─  ELSE
8   │       SET a TO 0
    └─
```

Case 1:

Assume that the value of A is 1 and the value of B is 2. Since A is not greater than B, the condition in line 1 is false. As a result, the SET at line 2 is ignored and the condition at line 3 is evaluated.

Since B is not greater than 10, the condition at line 3 is false. As a result, the SET at line 4 is ignored and the condition at line 5 is evaluated.

Since A is less than B, the condition at line 5 is true, so the SET action at line 6 is performed and the value of B becomes 1.

Case 2:

Assume that the value of A is 12 and the value of B is 11. Since A is greater than B, the condition at line 1 is true. As a result, the SET action at line 2 is performed and A takes on the value 11.

Case 3:

Assume that the value of A is 12 and the value of B is 13. Since A is not greater than B, the condition at line 1 is false. As a result, the next condition (line 3) is evaluated.

Since B is greater than 10, the condition at line 3 is true. As a result, the SET action at line 4 is executed and the value of B becomes 10.

Case 4:

Assume the value of A is 5 and the value of B is 5. Since A is not greater than B, the condition at line 1 is false. As a result, the next condition is evaluated.

Since B is not greater than 10, the condition at line 3 is false. As a result, the next condition is evaluated.

Since A is not less than B, the condition at line 5 is false. As a result, the next condition is evaluated...but there are no more conditions!

Since none of the conditions were true, the actions associated with the ELSE (line 7) are performed. In this case, the SET action at line 8 causes the value of A to be set to zero.

Example 3:

```
1  ┌─  IF a IS GREATER THAN b
2  │       SET a TO b
3  ├─  ELSE IF b IS GREATER THAN 10
4  │       SET b TO 10
5  ├─  ELSE IF a IS LESS THAN b
6  │       SET b TO a
```

Example 3 is the same as Example 2 except that there is no ELSE clause. Cases 1, 2 and 3 will act exactly the same for Example 3 as for Example 2. Case 4, however, behaves differently.

Case 4 revisited:

Assume, once again, that the value of A is 5 and the value of B is 5. Since A is not greater than B, the condition at line 1 is false. As a result, the next condition is evaluated.

Since B is not greater than 10, the condition at line 3 is false. As a result, the next condition is evaluated.

Since A is not less than B, the condition at line 5 is false. As a result, the next condition is evaluated...but there are no more conditions!

Since none of the conditions were true and there is no ELSE statement present, none of the SET statements is performed. Instead, the process continues with the next action past the IF statement (that is, at line 7 if there were one).

CASE

The CASE action statement is a special purpose condition used to perform actions based on the value of an expression. The format of the CASE action statement is:

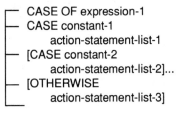

```
┌─  CASE OF expression-1
├─  CASE constant-1
│       action-statement-list-1
├─  [CASE constant-2
│       action-statement-list-2]...
├─  [OTHERWISE
└─      action-statement-list-3]
```

Notes:

1. *Expression-1* is most often a single attribute view whose value is to be evaluated, although it can be more complex.

2. *Constant-1* is a single possible value for *expression-1*. If the value of *expression-1* equals the value of *constant-1*, the actions in *action-statement-list-1* are performed. If the value of *expression-1* does not equal the value of *constant-1*, the constant associated with the next CASE clause is evaluated. This activity is repeated until either:

   a. The value of *expression-1* equals a constant in a CASE clause, in which case the actions in the associated *action-statement-list* are performed.

      or

b. The CASE clauses are exhausted and none of their constant values equal *expression-1*. If the OTHERWISE clause is present, the actions in its *action-statement-list* are performed. If not, process execution continues at the next action statement following the CASE action statement.

Example:

```
1  ┌─  CASE OF a
2  ├─  CASE 1
3  │       SET a TO 0
4  ├─  CASE 2
5  │       SET a TO b * 10
6  ├─  OTHERWISE
7  │       SET b TO a
   └─
```

Case 1:

Assume that A is an attribute view with a value of 2 and that B is an attribute view with a value of 8. CASE 1 (line 2) is false, so the next CASE clause is evaluated.

CASE 2 (line 4) is true (the value of A is 2), so the value of A becomes 80 as a result of the SET action at line 5.

Case 2:

Assume that the value of A is 10. CASE 1 (line 2) is false, so the next CASE clause is evaluated.

CASE 2 (line 4) is false, so the next CASE clause is evaluated...but there are no more CASE clauses.

Since the expression does not equal any of the possible constant values specified in the CASE clauses, the IEF performs the action statements associated with the OTHERWISE (line 6) and sets the value of B to 10 because of the SET statement at line 7.

Repeating Actions

Repeating actions support the repetition of a set of action statements under different conditions. There are five types of repeating action statements:

- READ EACH
- FOR EACH
- WHILE
- REPEAT UNTIL
- FOR

READ EACH

The READ EACH action statement retrieves information about multiple entities of a given type. The results of the READ EACH can be used to populate a repeating group view.

The format of the READ EACH action statement is as follows:

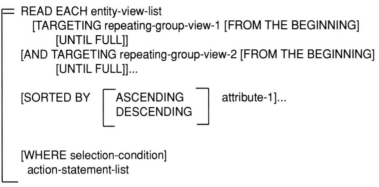

```
READ EACH entity-view-list
    [TARGETING repeating-group-view-1 [FROM THE BEGINNING]
        [UNTIL FULL]]
    [AND TARGETING repeating-group-view-2 [FROM THE BEGINNING]
        [UNTIL FULL]]...

    [SORTED BY    ASCENDING       attribute-1]...
                  DESCENDING

    [WHERE selection-condition]
       action-statement-list
```

Notes:

1. Every view being read in *entity-view-list* must be an entity action view.

2. The READ EACH action only affects the attribute views of entity views specified in *entity-view-list*.

3. The WHERE conditions (optionally combined and joined by ANDs, ORs, and parentheses) qualify the READ action. They test attribute values and test for the existence of a pairing. The collection of these conditions is called the **selection criteria** for the READ. A *selection-condition* is any expression that can be judged either true or false.

4. The READ EACH retrieves information about each entity that satisfies the criteria specified in the selection condition and places it in the appropriate view in *entity-view-list*. Each time the IEF retrieves a new set of occurrences, it performs the actions in the *action-statement-list*.

5. The TARGETING clauses are used to specify a repeating group view, which may be either a local or export view. This repeating group view is populated each time the READ EACH performs a repetition. After each repetition that MOVES to an entity view subordinate to the repeating group view, or SETS an attribute view subordinate to the repeating group view, the IEF primes the repeating group view to accept information in its next occurrence.

6. The FROM THE BEGINNING clause of the TARGETING clause is useful if multiple READ EACH or FOR EACH actions target the same repeating group view. Normally, a second READ EACH or FOR EACH will continue to populate the repeating group beginning immediately after the last occurrence populated. When the FROM THE BEGINNING clause is specified, however, the repeating group view is emptied and its population starts over (from the beginning).

7. The UNTIL FULL clause of the TARGETING clause causes the READ EACH to terminate if an attempt is made to add more occurrences to the repeating group view than were specified in its maximum cardinality.

8. Multiple TARGETING clauses are permitted, thus allowing the population of multiple repeating group views simultaneously.

9. The nesting of a READ EACH or FOR EACH action statement must coincide with the nesting of the repeating group views it targets. That is, if *rgroup1* is a repeating group view containing *rgroup2*, another repeating group view, they should be targeted in two nested READ/FOR EACH constructs as follows:

```
┌═  READ/FOR EACH entity-view-1
│        TARGETING rgroup1
│      ...selection criteria
│        ┌═  READ/FOR EACH entity-view-2
│        │        TARGETING rgroup2
│        └           action-statements
└
```

The IEF Action Diagramming Tool enforces this restriction, so that *rgroup2*, in this case, can only be manipulated in the context of a repeating action against *rgroup1*.

10. The SORTED BY clauses return entities in a particular sequence based on an attribute value. They can be returned in low-to-high (ASCENDING) sequence or high-to-low (DESCENDING) sequence.

11. The selection conditions operate in exactly the same fashion as in a READ entity action.

Example:

Imagine a process related to the Take Order process in Figure 14- 6. For a given ORDER, the process prepares a list of the ORDER LINES with a value over $100. This process, called List Expensive Line Items, has the following view set:

Import Views	
view of	REQUESTED
entity	ORDER
attr	NUMBER
Export Views	
group (r)	ORDER LINE LIST
view of	LISTED
entity	ORDER LINE
attr	QUANTITY
attr	VALUE
view of	LISTED
entity	PRODUCT
attr	NUMBER
attr	PRICE
Entity Action Views	
view of	(unnamed)
entity	ORDER
attr	NUMBER
view of	(unnamed)
entity	ORDER LINE
attr	QUANTITY
attr	VALUE
view of	(unnamed)
entity	PRODUCT
attr	NUMBER
attr	PRICE

The following action diagram fragment performs this function:

```
1    ┌─ READ order
            WHERE DESIRED order number IS EQUAL TO requested order number
2    └─
3    ┌═ READ EACH order line
4    │      TARGETING order line list UNTIL FULL
5    │      WHERE DESIRED order line  is contained in CURRENT order
6    │      AND DESIRED order line value IS GREATER THAN 100
7    │
8    │         ┌─ READ product
     │              WHERE DESIRED product appears on CURRENT order line
9    │         └─
10   │            MOVE order line TO listed order line
11   └─           MOVE product   TO listed product
```

The READ EACH (line 3) retrieves each ORDER LINE for the requested ORDER with a value for Value greater than $100. Each time the IEF retrieves an ORDER LINE, it performs the action statement list (lines 8 through 11). The MOVE actions set the values of the current entry in the repeating group view Order Line List, of which Listed ORDER LINE and Listed PRODUCT are components. When the action statement list concludes, the next entry in Order Line List becomes the current entry if (and only if) the MOVE actions are executed. In this way, each repetition of the READ EACH can create one element of the repeating group view.

FOR EACH

The FOR EACH action statement processes elements of a repeating group view. The format of the FOR EACH statement is:

```
┌═ FOR EACH repeating-group-view-1
│      [TARGETING repeating-group-view-2 [FROM THE BEGINNING]
│          [UNTIL FULL]]
│      [AND TARGETING repeating-group-view-3 [FROM THE BEGINNING]
│          [UNTIL FULL]]...
└─         action-statement-list-1
```

Notes:

1. *Repeating-group-view-1* must be either an import or a local view.

2. *Repeating-group-view-2* and *repeating-group-view-3* must be either a local view or export view.

3. The behavior of the TARGETING clause is exactly the same as for the READ EACH.

Example:

In the Take Order process of Figures 14-6, 14-7, and 14-10, a list of PRODUCTS and their Quantities must be accepted from a CUSTOMER and become ORDER LINES on an ORDER. Assuming the view set in Figure 14-10, the following action diagram fragment describes the creation of ORDER LINES based on an incoming list of PRODUCTS and Quantities.

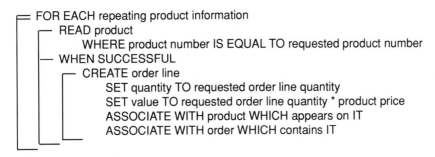

FOR EACH repeating product information
    READ product
        WHERE product number IS EQUAL TO requested product number
    WHEN SUCCESSFUL
        CREATE order line
            SET quantity TO requested order line quantity
            SET value TO requested order line quantity * product price
            ASSOCIATE WITH product WHICH appears on IT
            ASSOCIATE WITH order WHICH contains IT

WHILE

The WHILE action statement repeats a series of actions as long as a condition holds true. The format of the WHILE action statement is:

WHILE condition-1
    [TARGETING repeating-group-view-1 [FROM THE BEGINNING]
        [UNTIL FULL]]
    [AND TARGETING repeating-group-view-2 [FROM THE BEGINNING]
        [UNTIL FULL]] ...
          action-statement-list

Notes:

1. The WHILE action statement is primarily useful when dealing with explicitly subscripted repeating groups.

2. If *condition-1* is false when the WHILE is first encountered, the IEF never performs the *action-statement-list*.

3. The behavior of the TARGETING clause is exactly the same as for the READ EACH.

REPEAT...UNTIL

The REPEAT...UNTIL action statement repeats a series of actions until a condition is true. The format of the REPEAT...UNTIL action statement is:

REPEAT
    [TARGETING repeating-group-view-1 [FROM THE BEGINNING]
        [UNTIL FULL]]
    [AND TARGETING repeating-group-view-2 [FROM THE BEGINNING]
        [UNTIL FULL]] ...
          action-statement-list
UNTIL condition-1

Notes:

1. The REPEAT...UNTIL action statement is primarily useful when dealing with explicitly subscripted repeating groups.

2. The IEF does not test *condition-1* until the *action-statement-list* completes. Thus, when the IEF encounters the REPEAT, it always performs the actions in *action-statement-list* at least once.

3. The behavior of the TARGETING clause is exactly the same as for the READ EACH.

FOR

The FOR action repeats a series of statements until the value of a loop control variable reaches an established limit.

```
⊨ FOR attribute-view-1 FROM expression-1 TO expression-2
⌐        BY expression-3
|            action-statement-list
└
```

Notes:

1. *Attribute-view-1* is set to the value of *expression-1* before the first execution of *action-statement-list*.

2. Prior to each execution of *action-statement-list*, *attribute-view-1* is compared with *expression-2*. If *attribute-view-1* is equal to *expression-2*, or if *expression-3* is a positive number and *attribute-view-1* is greater than *expression-2*, or *expression-3* is a negative number and *attribute-view-1* is less than *expression-2*, the FOR loop is terminated and control is passed to the next action.

3. The value of *expression-3* is added to *attribute-view-1* after each execution.

4. *Attribute-view-1* is either a local attribute view or a subscript (subscripts are described in the section entitled "Advanced Topics" later in this chapter.)

5. *Expression-1, expression-2* and *expression-3* must be of the primitive domain Number.

Control Actions

There are three action statements classified as control actions:

- USE
- ESCAPE
- NEXT

USE

The USE action statement invokes a business algorithm (Common Action Block). Information can be passed to the import view of the business algorithm and retrieved from its export view.

The format of the USE statement is:

```
USE action-block
    [WHICH IMPORTS: view-1 [view-2]...]
    [WHICH EXPORTS: view-3 [view-4]...]
```

Notes:

1. The *action-block* may not be the Process Action Diagram of an elementary process.

2. The views in the WHICH IMPORTS list are sent to the import view of the *action-block* before it begins execution.

3. The views in the WHICH EXPORTS list are returned from the export view of the *action-block* after it completes execution.

4. The WHICH IMPORTS and WHICH EXPORTS lists are built using the IEF View Matching facility. This insures the compatibility of views that exchange data. Appendix E presents the rules for View Matching.

ESCAPE

An ESCAPE action statement terminates the execution of an action group. The format of the ESCAPE action statement is:

```
|← ESCAPE
 |
```

The arrow indicates the bracket of an action group. The action statement following the closure of that action group will be executed immediately after the ESCAPE.

Example:

In the Take Order process, terminate the process if the CUSTOMER cannot be found.

```
┌─── Process TAKE ORDER
│          .
│          .
│          .
│    ┌─ READ customer
│    │      WHERE DESIRED customer name IS EQUAL TO requesting customer name
│    │  WHEN NOT FOUND
│ ←──┴────────── ESCAPE
│    └
│    ┌═ FOR EACH ...
│    └
│          .
│          .
└─         .
```

Since there are no action statements following closure of the outer bracket, the process ceases after the ESCAPE is performed.

NEXT

The NEXT action statement bypasses action statements in a repeating action. The format of the NEXT action statement is:

```
|← NEXT
 |
```

The arrow must always point to a repeating action group (that is, a bracket enclosing a repeating action: READ EACH, FOR EACH, WHILE or REPEAT...UNTIL). NEXT causes the IEF to bypass subsequent actions and begin the next repetition of the repeating action.

Example:

In Take Order, while processing the list of PRODUCT Numbers and Quantities, avoid the CREATE of an ORDER LINE for which the PRODUCT Number is not found.

```
┌═ FOR EACH repeating product information
│  ┌─ READ product
│  │      WHERE DESIRED product number IS EQUAL TO requested product number
│  ├─ WHEN NOT FOUND
←──┼───────NEXT
│  └─
│  ┌─ CREATE order line
│  │      SET ...
└  └─     ...
```

The NEXT action following the WHEN NOT FOUND causes the FOR EACH to begin again with the next occurrence of Repeating Product Information. All statements between the NEXT and the conclusion of the FOR EACH are bypassed.

Miscellaneous Actions

There is only one miscellaneous action: NOTE. NOTE is not really an action; it is merely a means of adding a comment to the action diagram.

The format of the NOTE action statement is:

> NOTE text

Text is a free-form description up to 2000 characters in length.

Action Diagram Example

The set of action statements required to support the Take Order process appears in Figure 14-19 as an example of a complete Process Action Diagram.

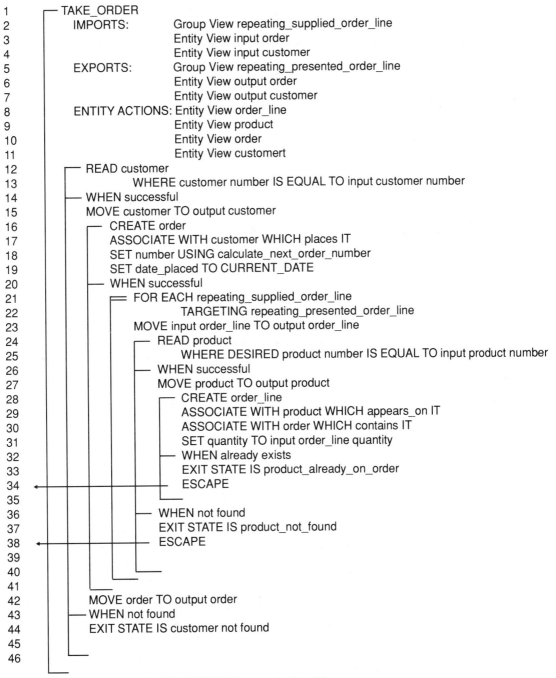

1	TAKE_ORDER
2	IMPORTS: Group View repeating_supplied_order_line
3	Entity View input order
4	Entity View input customer
5	EXPORTS: Group View repeating_presented_order_line
6	Entity View output order
7	Entity View output customer
8	ENTITY ACTIONS: Entity View order_line
9	Entity View product
10	Entity View order
11	Entity View customert
12	READ customer
13	WHERE customer number IS EQUAL TO input customer number
14	WHEN successful
15	MOVE customer TO output customer
16	CREATE order
17	ASSOCIATE WITH customer WHICH places IT
18	SET number USING calculate_next_order_number
19	SET date_placed TO CURRENT_DATE
20	WHEN successful
21	FOR EACH repeating_supplied_order_line
22	TARGETING repeating_presented_order_line
23	MOVE input order_line TO output order_line
24	READ product
25	WHERE DESIRED product number IS EQUAL TO input product number
26	WHEN successful
27	MOVE product TO output product
28	CREATE order_line
29	ASSOCIATE WITH product WHICH appears_on IT
30	ASSOCIATE WITH order WHICH contains IT
31	SET quantity TO input order_line quantity
32	WHEN already exists
33	EXIT STATE IS product_already_on_order
34	ESCAPE
35	
36	WHEN not found
37	EXIT STATE IS product_not_found
38	ESCAPE
39	
40	
41	
42	MOVE order TO output order
43	WHEN not found
44	EXIT STATE IS customer not found
45	
46	

Figure 14-19. Complete TAKE ORDER Process Action Diagram

The view definitions for the TAKE ORDER Process Action Diagram appear as Figure 14-20.

Import Views
Group View REPEATING_SUPPLIED_ORDER_LINE
Cardinality Min:1 Max: 100 Avg: 10
View INPUT of entity PRODUCT
Attributes:
NUMBER
View INPUT of entity ORDER_LINE
Attributes:
QUANTITY
View INPUT of entity CUSTOMER
Attributes:
NUMBER
Export Views
Group View REPEATING_PRESENTED_ORDER_LINE
Cardinality Min:1 Max: 100 Avg: 10
View OUTPUT of entity PRODUCT
Attributes:
NUMBER
View OUTPUT of entity ORDER_LINE
Attributes:
QUANTITY
View OUTPUT of entity CUSTOMER
Attributes:
NUMBER
Entity Action Views
View of entity ORDER_LINE
Attributes:
QUANTITY
View of entity PRODUCT
Attributes:
NUMBER
View of entity ORDER
Attributes:
NUMBER
DATE_PLACED
View of entity CUSTOMER
Attributes:
NUMBER

Figure 14-20. View Definitions for the TAKE ORDER Process Action Diagram

CONSIDERATIONS FOR PROCESS ACTION DIAGRAMMING

When building a Process Action Diagram or Process Action Block using the IEF, the analyst must consider a number of factors that go beyond the format of action statements. This section presents these additional factors for consideration.

Building Action Diagrams Using the IEF

Analysts can use the IEF Action Diagramming Tool to construct action diagrams and action blocks. This tool supports all the action statements described in the previous section. New users of the IEF Action Diagramming Tool will find the following points about its operation of interest:

- The IEF Action Diagramming Tool insures that the analyst makes no errors in syntax. As the analyst builds action statements, the IEF presents all valid options based on the context of the statement, and allows the analyst to choose from among them. As a result, the analyst never has to remember the exact format of an action statement.

- The IEF directly derives all names of variables in the action diagram from the underlying data model represented by the ERD. For example, each time the syntax of an action statement requires an entity view, the IEF produces a list of views of entity types defined for that process, based on the ERD. As a result, variable names are always consistent with the data model.

- The action diagram is a precise and unambiguous description of process logic. As a result, it can be used during the BSD, Technical Design, and Construction stages as a basis for generating computer programs to implement the process described.

- For elementary processes with expected effects defined, the IEF will interactively expand the expected effects to provide a basis for the process.

The action diagrams and action blocks built during BAA can be incorporated into Procedure Action Diagrams and Procedure Action Blocks used during BSD. The resulting action diagrams and action blocks can then be used to generate programs during the Construction stage.

Level of Detail

Although the action language is quite precise, analysts can specify logic at different levels of detail. The less detail supplied by the analyst, the more work required by designers to flesh out the detail in later stages. In any case, all details must be specified before starting the Construction stage.

One may carry process logic definitions to three easily identifiable levels of detail. Before building any action diagrams, analysts should agree on the amount of detail to be specified during interaction analysis. The decision depends largely on the technical skills of the analyst (some analysts find action diagrams very difficult to understand) and the quality of communication between analyst and designer. If the designer and analyst cannot communicate freely, the process logic specifications must be exact.

The three obvious levels of detail and the advantages of each are as follows:

- **Very little detail**. In this case, no action diagram is built for an elementary process. Instead, the analyst specifies only expected effects, import and export information views and provides a textual description of the process as part of the process definition.

  There are two main advantages to this approach:

  — The analyst can "think fuzzily" without worrying about the real details of process logic.

  — The analyst avoids the issue of coordinating BSD Procedure Action Diagrams and Action Blocks with BAA Process Action Diagrams and Action Blocks.

  The primary disadvantage, of course, is that process descriptions are ambiguous and imprecise. As a result, the designer is more likely to misinterpret the analyst's intent.

- **Mainline process logic only**. In this case, the analyst builds an action diagram, but specifies only the "bare bones" process logic and ignores exception conditions. The question "What if something goes wrong?" is left to the designer.

  For example, in the Take Order process, an analyst concerned only with mainline process logic will not address issues like:

  — What if the Requesting CUSTOMER is not found?

—— What if one of the PRODUCT Numbers is invalid?

The advantage to this approach is that the analyst avoids handling exception conditions, often a tedious exercise. In a few cases, the exception condition may have further implications on the process (for example, when a CUSTOMER entity must be CREATED if a Requesting CUSTOMER is not found). In most cases, however, the analyst can specify process logic unambiguously without exception conditions, so that the designer is likely to understand the analyst's intent.

The primary disadvantage to this approach is that the designer will have to specify the exception conditions during Business System Design, thereby changing the analyst-built Process Action Diagrams.

- **Complete process logic**. In this case, the analyst builds the complete definition of the actions required to support the process, including the exception conditions omitted above.

The advantage to this approach is that the process logic is even more precise and the designer must make fewer subsequent modifications. Readers wishing to implement complete process logic during BAA are encouraged to study the area of "Exception Conditions" in the "Advanced Topics" section of this chapter.

The disadvantage is that this level of detail requires more time and greater technical skill on the part of the analyst.

Pre and Post-Conditions and Integrity Constraints

Currently, the IEF does not directly enforce the maintenance of certain integrity contraints. Additionally, it does not directly enforce process pre- and post-conditions. As a result, the actions required to enforce these conditions must be explicitly included as part of the Process Action Diagram.

Previous sections of this guide have described these conditions and constraints, and suggested that they be recorded as comments in the textual descriptions of associated objects. The types of conditions and constraints that should be enforced in the action diagram are shown here as a reminder:

- Relationship optionality conditions
- Relationship cardinality conditions
- Attribute optionality conditions
- General integrity constraints (on entity types)
- Pre-conditions for process execution (based on the PDD)
- Post-conditions for process execution (based on the PDD)
- Group and entity view optionality conditions

ADVANCED TOPICS

This section deals with some of the more advanced concepts in action diagramming. The first three deal with topics that will help the analyst to more fully understand some of the action diagramming features frequently used during BAA. They are:

- Action Diagram Expressions
- Notes on SET...USING, Default and Derivation Algorithms
- Exit States

The next two deal with some action diagramming constructs which are less frequently used during BAA, but provide an additional level of flexibility for handling more complex detailed logic. They are:

- Action Diagram Functions
- Advanced Repeating Group Handling

The final topic in this section addresses the implications of using the same action blocks created during BAA in the subsequent BSD projects.

Action Diagram Expressions

Many times during the discussion of Process Action Statements, the term "expression" was used with little fanfare. Here it is discussed in a bit more detail.

Expressions are used in conditions of all sorts and in SET statements. Their purpose in life is to provide a value consistent with the primitive domain of the attribute view or special attribute to which they are being assigned (in SET statements and the FOR loop) or being compared to (in conditions). As a result, the construction of an expression is different depending on whether it is to return a Text, Number, Date or Time value.

Text Expressions

Expressions which evaluate to a text value may be one of the following components:

Character View	An attribute view on the primitive domain Text, like CUSTOMER NAME
Character String	A literal value enclosed in quotes, like "Davy Crockett"
Character Function	An Action Diagram Function which evaluates to a character value, like SUBSTR (CUSTOMER NAME,3,2)

Spaces

A text expression may also be one of the following IEF special attributes: Terminal ID, User ID, Printer Terminal ID, or Trancode. However, since these special attributes are not used during BAA they are not defined here.

Number Expressions

Expressions which evaluate to a number can include parentheses for grouping and the arithmetic operators –, +, /, * and **, as well as the following components:

Numeric View	An attribute view on the primitive domain Number, like ORDER_LINE QUANTITY
Number	A numeric constant, like 153
Numeric Function	An Action Diagram Function which evaluates to a number, like JULDATE (CURRENT_DATE)
Subscript	The current value of a subscript for an explicitly subscripted repeating group view

Last   The occurrence number of the last populated entry of an explicitly subscripted repeating group view

Max   The maximum cardinality of an explicitly subscripted repeating group view

Date Expressions

Expressions which evaluate to a date must begin with one of the following components:

Date View An attribute view on the primitive domain Date, like ORDER DATE_SHIPPED

Date Func- An Action Diagram Function which evaluates to a date, like
tion   DATEJUL(WORKING JULIAN_DATE)

Current Date The IEF special attribute which contains current date

However, they can then include a numeric modifier which adds to or subtracts from the initial date component a number of years, days or months. For example, the following expression will return the date exactly one week prior to the current date:

   current_date - 7 days

and the following expression returns the date three months after an order was placed:

   order date_placed + 3 months

Time Expressions

Expressions which evaluate to a time are similar to those which evaluate to a date. Like dates, a time expression must begin with one of the following time components:

Time View An attribute view on the primitive domain Time, like FLIGHT TIME_OF_ARRIVAL

Time Func- An Action Diagram Function which evaluates to a time, like
tion   TIMENUM(IMPORT APPOINTMENT NUMERIC_TIME)

Current Time The IEF special attribute which contains the current time

Like dates, they can then include a numeric modifier to adjust the time component by a number of hours, minutes or seconds.

Notes on SET...USING, Default and Derivation Algorithms

Action blocks used in SET...USING actions, default algorithms for attributes, and derivation algorithms have some special restrictions which do not apply to ordinary action blocks. They are mentioned here.

Action Blocks used in SET...USING Actions

The SET...USING action statement causes the invocation of an action block which establishes the value of the attribute view being SET. The USEd action block may have any number of import, local or entity action views, but it may only have one export attribute view, and it must be a view of the attribute being set in the USEing action block.

For example, if action block Create Customer includes the following SET...USING statement:

> SET customer number USING customer_number_calculation

the action block Customer Number Calculation must contain only a single export attribute view, and it must be a view of CUSTOMER Number.

Default Algorithms

Default algorithms are just another kind of SET...USING. During data modeling, it is possible to specify a default algorithm for an attribute which is to be executed whenever entities of the type to which the attribute belongs are CREATEd. However, the onus is on the analyst to insure that the default algorithm is mentioned in a SET...USING within the CREATE.

Derivation Algorithms

An attribute's derivation algorithm is executed whenever an entity of the type to which the attribute belongs is READ, provided the entity action view includes a view of that attribute.

A derivation algorithm has the same restriction as a default algorithm (that is, it must return a single export attribute view of the attribute being derived). However, it has an additional one: it can have only a single import view, and that is a view of the entity type to which the derived attribute belongs. When the derivation algorithm is invoked, all non-derived attributes for the entity occurrence for which the derived attribute is to be calculated will already have been populated.

The import view of a derivation algorithm has a special property: it can be referenced as the equivalent of a CURRENT view (a distinction normally reserved for entity action views) in READ statements appearing in the derivation algorithm.

The following derivation algorithm example will calculate a value for the attribute Total of the entity type ORDER, which is the sum of the value of all its ORDER LINEs.

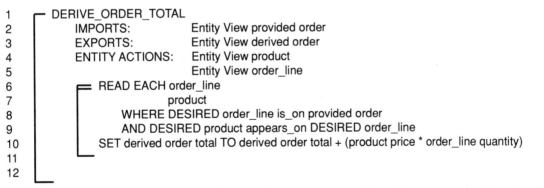

```
1     ┌─ DERIVE_ORDER_TOTAL
2     │      IMPORTS:          Entity View provided order
3     │      EXPORTS:          Entity View derived order
4     │      ENTITY ACTIONS:   Entity View product
5     │                        Entity View order_line
6     │   ┌═ READ EACH order_line
7     │   │         product
8     │   │      WHERE DESIRED order_line is_on provided order
9     │   │      AND DESIRED product appears_on DESIRED order_line
10    │   │   SET derived order total TO derived order total + (product price * order_line quantity)
11    │   └─
12    └─
```

As mentioned in Chapter 12, it is possible to simulate composite attributes by using a derivation algorithm which includes string functions. For example, assume that the analyst desires a composite attribute Phone Number to have elementary attributes Area Code, Exchange and Station (not a far-fetched example for a phone company.) To simulate the composite attribute, Phone Number can be defined as a derived attribute with the following derivation algorithm:

```
1  ┌── DERIVE_PHONE_NUMBER
2  │      IMPORTS:        Entity View provided customer
3  │      EXPORTS:        Entity View derived customer
4  │   SET derived customer phone_number TO CONCAT(provided customer area_code,
5  │          CONCAT(provided customer exchange, provided customer station))
6  └
```

Exit States

As mentioned earlier, exit states provide a means by which the analyst can specify that the user be informed of the outcome of a process. In general, during BAA, exit states are set only as a result of an exception condition (for example, in the WHEN NOT FOUND clause of a READ action).

Some analysts believe that the handling of exception conditions in general and exit states in particular is beyond the scope of process logic analysis and relegate the resolution of the associated issues to Business System Design. This is fine in the context of limiting the level of detail to which action diagrams are specified (see "Considerations for Action Diagramming" earlier in this chapter). However, there is nothing inherently wrong with specifying actions to be taken as a result of exceptions during BAA. In fact, it is unlikely that business rules can be specified completely without them. If, during an execution of the Take Order process, a PRODUCT requested cannot be found, the person initiating the process is likely interested. Likewise, if the Add Customer process fails because there was already a CUSTOMER on file with the same identifier, it is important that the person initiating the process be made aware of it.

Exit State is provided as a special attribute in order to support a common way for analysts to specify the outcome of a process to an end user. Each exit state has the following properties:

- Name
- Message
- Type

Name

The name of the exit state should reflect the condition which resulted in its being set. For example, if the process Take Order fails because the CUSTOMER placing the ORDER was not known to the business, appropriate names for the corresponding exit state might be:

```
CUSTOMER_NOT_FOUND
CUSTOMER_UNKNOWN
```

Message

The exit state message reflects the exact text the end user will see if, when the process finishes execution, the exit state has been set. The following are examples of exit state messages:

Exit State	Message
CUSTOMER_NOT_FOUND	The requested customer was not on file
DUPLICATE_ORDER_NUMBER	An order already exists with the requested order number

Type

Exit state type is used to specify special exception handling logic to be executed by the IEF if the exit state is set at the end of process execution. In general, exit state type is not specified during BAA. However, in some rare instances it may be useful so it is discussed here.

An exit state can be of one of three types:

* Normal

* Rollback

* Abort

Normal is the default type for any newly added exit state. If, when the process finishes executing, the special attribute Exit State is set to an exit state of type "normal," no special processing takes place.

Rollback, on the other hand, is used to undo any CREATE, UPDATE or DELETE actions which took place during the process. If, when the process finishes executing, the special attribute Exit State is set to an exit state of type "rollback," the effect of all CREATEs, UPDATEs and DELETEs are "backed out."

Abort is never specified as an exit state type during BAA. If Exit State is set to an exit state of type "abort," the process will abnormally terminate (ABEND). This is most definitely a Business System Design level concept.

Action Diagram Functions

Action diagram functions (not to be confused with the high-level business functions discovered during ISP) are special-purpose subroutines invoked as part of an expression. They always take the form:

        FUNCTION_NAME(parameter_list)

When the action diagram function executes, the value it returns is substituted for it in the expression.

A different set of functions is available depending on the primitive domain of the expression in which it is included; thus, there are text functions, numeric functions, date functions and time functions.

A detailed list of action diagram functions is available in the *IEF Analysis Toolset Guide*. However, most of the functions available fall into one of the following categories:

String manipulation	These functions are used to manipulate and inspect text attributes and portions of text attributes. For example, string manipulation functions might be used to extract an employee's last name from the attribute EMPLOYEE Name.
Domain conversion	These functions are used to convert a value from one primitive domain to another. For example, a domain conversion function might be used to convert a date value to a numeric value.
Date format conversion	These functions are used to convert date values from one form to another. For example, date format conversion might be used to convert a julian date to a gregorian date.
Date/Time extraction	These functions are used to extract a portion of a date or time value. For example, a function of this type might be used to extract the DAY portion of CURRENT_DATE.

Notes:

1. Functions can themselves be parameters of functions. See example below.

2. Some functions are not available in READ actions. These are clearly identified in the IEF Toolsets.

Example:

Assume that an employee's name is stored as three separate attributes: First Name, Middle Name, and Last Name. The following actions will set the value of EMPLOYEE Full Name to Last Name, followed by a comma and a space, First Name followed by a space, and the first character of Middle Name followed by a period.

```
SET employee full_name TO CONCAT(TRIM(employee last_name,   CONCAT(', ',employee first_name)
SET employee full_name TO CONCAT(TRIM(employee full_name),
CONCAT(' ',CONCAT(SUBSTR(employee middle_name,1,1),'.'))
```

CONCAT is an action diagram function which combines two character strings.

TRIM is an action diagram function which removes trailing blanks from a character string.

SUBSTR is an action diagram function which extracts a portion from a character string. It requires a starting position within the string and the length of the string to extract.

If the values of Employee First Name, Middle Name and Last Name are "Charles," "Taze," and "Russell," respectively, the value of Employee Full Name after the execution of the example statements would be "Russell, Charles T."

Advanced Repeating Group Handling

As was mentioned earlier, each repeating group view is defined as being either **implicitly** or **explicitly** subscripted. In this section the distinction is addressed in detail.

Implicit Subscripting

If a repeating group view is implicitly subscripted, the IEF keeps track of position within the group view and relieves the analyst of the task of doing so explicitly. For example, when the FOR EACH action is used, the IEF automatically bumps to the next occurrence of the subject repeating group view of the FOR EACH after each iteration. Likewise, when the TARGETING clause is used, the IEF automatically bumps to the next occurrence of the targeted repeating group view after each iteration (if the current occurrence has been modified).

The following constructs are used to support implicit subscripting and only apply to implicitly subscripted repeating group views:

- FOR EACH
- The TARGETING clause on FOR EACH, READ EACH, WHILE and REPEAT actions
- The conditions IS FULL, IS NOT FULL, IS EMPTY and IS NOT EMPTY

In most cases, implicit subscripting is sufficient for the handling of repeating group views, particularly during BAA. However, there are some cases where the processing requirement for repeating group views exceeds the capabilities of implicit subscripting. For example, it is impossible to iterate through two different repeating group views simultaneously using this technique. Likewise, there is no way to reverse direction or select arbitrary occurrences from the group. In cases where such processing is required, explicit subscripting can be helpful.

Explicit Subscripting

When explicit subscripting is used, the onus is on the analyst to insure that the proper occurrence of the repeating group view is being accessed at any given time. The current occurrence is identified by its **subscript.** The value of a repeating group view's subscript is a number which corresponds to its position in the repeating view.

For example, consider a circus application in which the names and relative sizes of the circus's elephants are stored in a repeating group view. It might look like this:

Elephant Name	Size
DUMBO	puny
HUMONGO	large
KING FORTINBRAS THE BRAVE	huge
LEON	medium

If the repeating group view's subscript is set to 1, the occurrence for DUMBO is current. If it is set to 4, the occurrence for LEON is active.

Subscript values are set using the SUBSCRIPT option of the SET action. Each explicitly indexed repeating group view has a single subscript called "SUBSCRIPT OF *repeating-group-view.*" Assuming, then, that the list presented above is stored in repeating group view Elephants, the following action will point to the occurrence for KING FORTINBRAS THE BRAVE:

> SET SUBSCRIPT OF elephants TO 3

When iterating through an explicitly subscripted repeating group view, the analyst must increment the subscript explicitly and must test for the end of the group explicitly. The following example causes the size of each elephant in the repeating group view to be set to "elephantine":

```
SET SUBSCRIPT OF elephants TO 1
WHILE
    SUBSCRIPT OF elephants IS LESS OR EQUAL TO LAST OF elephants
        SET elephant_size TO "elephantine"
        SET SUBSCRIPT OF elephants TO SUBSCRIPT OF elephants + 1
```

In contrast, had the repeating group view Elephants been defined as implicitly subscripted, the following example would have accomplished the same result:

```
FOR EACH elephants
    SET elephant_size TO "elephantine"
```

Note that using implicit subscripting relieves the analyst of the need to initialize, maintain, and test the subscript value.

Certain action diagram constructs apply only to explicitly indexed repeating group views. They are:

- The FOR action

- The SUBSCRIPT OF *repeating-group-view* special attribute

- The LAST OF *repeating-group-view* special attribute (which identifies the highest subscript value for which a repeating group view occurrence exists)

- The MAX OF *repeating-group-view* special attribute (which identifies the maximum cardinality of the repeating group view)

The special attributes SUBSCRIPT OF, LAST OF and MAX OF can be used in numeric expressions; SUBSCRIPT OF and LAST OF can be the target of a SET statement.

Sharing Action Blocks between BAA and BSD

The Process Action Diagrams and Action Blocks developed during BAA can be used directly during Business System Design. A discussion of exactly how this is done is deferred to Part III, but the fact that it happens is worthy of note here.

There are benefits and liabilities to using the same action block developed in BAA during Business System Design. The benefits are:

- The analysis-level specifications and the design-level specifications will always remain in sync: they are exactly the same specification.
- The size of the model is reduced.

The liabilities are:

- The designer may change the action block during the BSD project and (hopefully inadvertently) violate the intent of the analyst.
- In order to complete Business System Design, the designer must completely flesh out the process logic, including exception conditions. If the analyst constructed action diagrams at a high level of detail, avoiding such mundanities, he may be surprised to find that the fuzzy action block he defined has more statements in it after Business System Design than when he completed Process Logic Analysis.
- The designer may be required to add implementation-specific details to the action diagram (for example, the testing of a terminal operator's user-id). In this case, it will appear to the analyst that his Process Action Diagram has been corrupted with design-oriented statements.

In general, the primary benefit (keeping analysis and design in sync) outweighs the liabilities. However, it is possible to avoid using the same action blocks in both stages by creating a copy of the action block during BSD. This topic is addressed in Part III.

SUMMARY OF INTERACTION MODELING DELIVERABLES

Interaction analysis results in the following deliverables:

- A Process Action Diagram for each elementary process. (The Data Navigation Diagram discussed in this chapter is merely an intermediate result captured while constructing the Process Action Diagram.)
- An Entity Life Cycle Diagram for each selected entity type.

In total, these two diagrams constitute the interaction model of the business area being analyzed.

15
CURRENT SYSTEMS ANALYSIS

OVERVIEW

This chapter describes current systems analysis. During this major task of Business Area Analysis, analysts examine existing systems that support the business area, to insure the completeness of the data, activity, and interaction analyses. In particular, analysts examine current procedures and user views, and combine sets of user views to remove any inconsistencies.

When carrying out current systems analysis, analysts employ a bottom-up approach. By contrast, Information Engineering takes a top-down approach that begins with entity analysis or function analysis. Analysts should never begin with current systems analysis when building a business area model. However, before completing Business Area Analysis, one must have analyzed current systems for several reasons:

- To identify current problems to avoid
- To record data and procedures in a form usable during completeness checking in business model confirmation
- To prepare for the transition from existing systems to new systems

Current systems analysis includes three techniques, each of which is discussed in a major section of this chapter:

- Current systems procedure analysis
- User view analysis
- Canonical synthesis

SELECTING SYSTEMS TO ANALYZE

During current systems analysis, analysts examine existing systems that support processes in the business area model. Two matrices produced during Information Strategy Planning help analysts identify these systems:

- Business Function/Current Information System Matrix (Figure 15-1)
- Current Information System/Current Data Store Matrix (Figure 15-2)

The IEF Planning Toolset supports both of these matrices.

From the Business Function/Current Information System Matrix, the analyst should select all systems that support processes in the defined business area.

From the Current Information System/Current Data Store Matrix, the analyst can determine the data stores to be analyzed in the defined business area.

In general, analysts should examine the following existing systems:

- Systems that update files essential to the business area (whether batch or online)

KEY:
C = CURRENT SYSTEMS
U = MAJOR UPGRADE PLANNED
P = PLANNED

RESPONSIBILITY CODE:
E = EXCLUSIVE
J = JOINT
D = DEPENDENT

CURRENT INFORMATION SYSTEMS/ACRONYM		PRODUCT ENGINEERING	METHODS ENGINEERING	DESIGN AND PACKAGING	GENERAL ACCOUNTING	COS ACCOUNTING	REPAIR AND MAINTENANCE	ORDER PROCESSING	MANUFACTURING PLANNING	PRODUCTION SCHEDULING	PRODUCTION MONITORING AND CONTROL	QUALITY ASSURANCE	PURCHASING	RECEIVING	WAREHOUSING
LABORATORY MANAGEMENT	(LAB MGT)		C												
PRODUCT ENGINEERING FACILITY	(DESIGNAID)	C	P	P											
MARKETING	(MKT/2000)			P				C							C
SALES	(NTBS)					C	C								C
MATERIAL REQUIREMENTS PLANNING	(MRP IV)	C					C	C	C	C			C	C	C
CAPACITY PRODUCTION SCHEDULING	(CAPCSS--)					C		C	C	C				C	C
PURCHASING/RECEIVING	(PURCHASING)						C	C	C	C			C	C	C
STORES CONTROL	(INV/2000)						C	C	C	C			C	C	U
TRAFFIC MANAGEMENT	(TRAFFIC)						P	P					P	P	P
HUMAN RESOURCES	(PFM)					C		C	C	C					
GENERAL LEDGER	(G/L)				C	C									

Figure 15-1. Business Function/Current Information System Matrix

- Systems that produce specified output from these files (for any purpose except *ad hoc* inquiry)

- Application packages that access these files

- Manual procedures that operate on essential files independently or are otherwise associated with the above systems

In analyzing non-computerized systems or associated manual procedures, one should only examine procedures significant to the business. These do not include routine clerical tasks, unless they affect the content of data files or the form of information presented to or collected from end users.

CURRENT SYSTEMS PROCEDURE ANALYSIS

During **current systems procedure analysis**, the analyst builds a definition of current procedures and examines their structure and dependencies. The analyst also documents data flow between procedures. Procedure analysis within current systems analysis resembles function analysis within process dependency analysis.

To assist in this task, the analyst creates two kinds of diagrams to reflect his or her understanding of current systems: the Procedure Decomposition List and the Data Flow Diagram. The analyst prepares these diagrams manually or using some automated means other than the IEF. Both diagrams serve to check the completeness of the business area model.

CURRENT INFORMATION SYSTEMS/ACRONYM	CUSTOMER MASTER (CUSTOMER)	CUSTOMER ORDER (SALES & BILLINGS)	PRODUCT MASTER (POD)	PRODUCT STRUCTURE (BILL OF MATERIALS)	STORES (INVENTORY CONTROL)	SHOP ORDER (WIP)	PROCESS ROUTINGS (BOUNTY II)	INTRANSIT (WWIS)	CARRIER ROUTINGS (PTH A)	VENDOR MASTER (PTH C)	OPEN COMMITMENTS (PTH B)	HUMAN RESOURCES (HRN)	GENERAL LEDGER (G/L)	PAYROLL (PAYROLL)
LABORATORY MANAGEMENT (LAB MGT)			X	X	X					X	X	X		
PRODUCT ENGINEERING FACILITY (DESIGNAID)			X	X	X	X	X			X	X			
MARKETING (MKT/2000)	X	X	X		X				X	X		X		
SALES (NTBS)	X	X	X		X	X			X	X				
MATERIAL REQUIREMENTS PLANNING (MRP IV)			X	X	X	X	X	X		X	X			
CAPACITY PRODUCTION SCHEDULING (CAPCSS--)			X	X	X	X	X	X				X		
PURCHASING/RECEIVING (PURCHASING)			X	X	X	X	X	X	X	X	X			
STORES CONTROL (INV/2000)		X	X		X	X		X	X	X	X			
TRAFFIC MANAGEMENT (TRAFFIC)	X	X	X		X			X	X					
HUMAN RESOURCES (PFM)												X		X
GENERAL LEDGER (G/L)												X	X	X

Figure 15-2. Current Information System/Current Data Store Matrix

Basic Concepts

This subsection documents some key concepts related to procedures and data flow. It also introduces the concept of a data view.

Procedure

In current systems analysis, the word **procedure** includes both computer programs and manual processes. In procedure analysis, the analyst includes only meaningful packages of procedures or processes: programs referenced in procedure manuals and manual processes that users perceive as meaningful units. The formal definition of a procedure is:

Procedure   A method of carrying out one or more elementary processes.

Data View and Layout

A person or program normally requires only a subset of the data in a system. The subset is a limited view of the information and is known as a **data view**. The formal definition of a data view is:

Data View   An organized collection of fields that is meaningful to a procedure, business system, or organizational unit.

Data views appear within **layouts**; for example, within screens, files, manual and computerized forms, and reports. A layout can contain more than one data view. For example, a report may contain data about several things. A data view is the part of a layout required for a particular procedure. The formal definition of a layout is:

Layout   A grouping of fields used to present data to a module or user.

Data Flow

A **data flow** represents the passing of a data view between two procedures or between a procedure and a data store. A data flow represents *how* a dependency has been implemented. Its formal definition is:

Data Flow   A requirement for a data view to pass between two designed elements, each being a business system, procedure, data store, or external object.

Data Store

A **data store** is a repository of data used by the system. A data store can be permanent or temporary, depending on the system. In current systems procedure analysis, analysts identify the files, data bases, and clerical stores that the selected procedures use or update.

Although data stores are sometimes temporary, the analyst should not include transitory files, such as sort files, in the list of data stores. Current systems analysis techniques apply to business data repositories, longer-lived files.

The formal definition of a data store is:

Data Store   A repository of data, possibly temporary, of which users are aware and from which data can be read repeatedly and non-destructively.

Procedure Decomposition

Procedure decomposition techniques are similar to function decomposition techniques. Analysts identify systems and progressively break them down until procedures are distinguishable.

Procedure Decomposition List

The Procedure Decomposition List is a type of decomposition diagram. Using a tree structured list, the analyst documents the hierarchy of current procedures, as observed or described in documentation. In the list, indentation indicates subordination among procedures within the hierarchy (Figure 15-3). Creating a Procedure Decomposition List for each system defines the sequence and structure of procedures within that system.

Rules for Procedure Decomposition Lists

- List one procedure per line.
- Use equal indentation for procedures of the same rank.
- Follow the sequence of procedure manuals and other documentation.
- When possible, use the same names as current documentation.

Data Flow Diagram

Just as a Process Dependency Diagram represents successive levels in the process hierarchy, Data Flow Diagrams represent successive levels of detail for the current system. A Data Flow Diagram represents three types of data flow:

PROCEDURE LIST
Manufacturing Planning
Material Requirements Planning
Demand Modeling
Determine Gross Requirements
Model Firm Demand
Collect Sales Order Status
Collect Backorder Status
Model Anticipated Demand
Exponential Smoothing
Seasonal Adjustment
Build Demand Model
Determine Net Requirements
Determine Inventory Position
Build Net Model
Lot Sizing
Build Smoothed Release Forecast
Apply Lot-Sizing Rules
Calculate Release Plan
Test Load Release Forecast
Balance Forecast to Shop Load
Build Release Plan
Calculate Salability Models
Model Inventory Levels
Apply Obsolescence Rules
Calculate Raw Materials Requirements
Explode Release Plan
Net Inventory Balances
Apply Order Sizing Rules
Create Requests for Purchase
Create Purchase Order Change Notices

Figure 15-3. A Procedure Decomposition List

- From procedure to data store
- From data store to procedure
- From procedure to procedure

By showing the flow of data between data stores and procedures on the Procedure Decomposition List, the diagram shows how the procedures interact. By contrast, Process Dependency Diagrams show only the attributes input to a business process or output from it. Data Flow Diagrams not only show the basic information dependencies between processes, but also how the dependencies occur.

Data Flow Diagram Conventions

Figure 15-4 presents the conventions of Data Flow Diagrams.

The next three figures represent Data Flow Diagrams in increasingly greater detail.

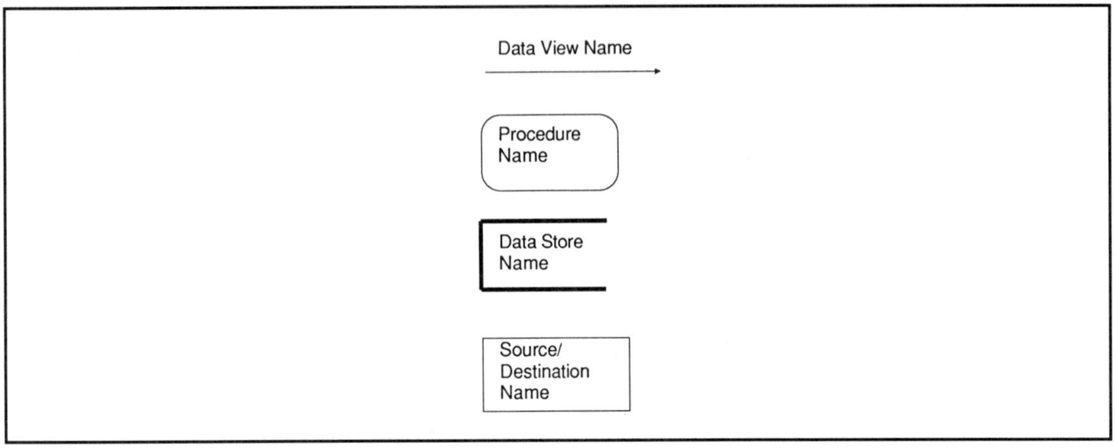

Data View Name

Procedure
Name

Data Store
Name

Source/
Destination
Name

Figure 15-4. Data Flow Diagram Conventions

In Figure 15-5, the Data Flow Diagram includes five systems, among them Demand Modeling and Lot Sizing. The diagram also includes four principal data stores: Marketing, Materials Management, Factory Monitoring and Control, and Purchasing.

Arrows on the lines represent flows into and from data stores. The direction of the arrows indicates the direction of the flow. For instance, the downward direction of the arrow head indicates the flow from Demand Modeling to Lot Sizing.

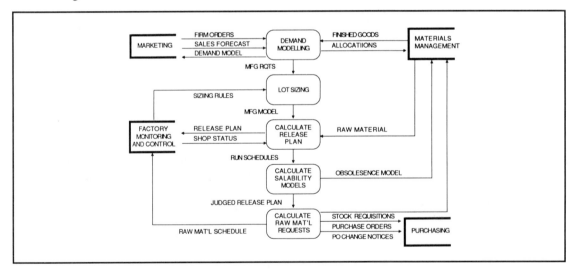

Figure 15-5. Example of a Data Flow Diagram (Top Level)

The diagram in Figure 15-6 shows more detail of the Demand Modeling System. The system contains five major modules. The high-level data stores in the previous Data Flow Diagram (Marketing and Materials Management) now appear as three, more detailed data stores.

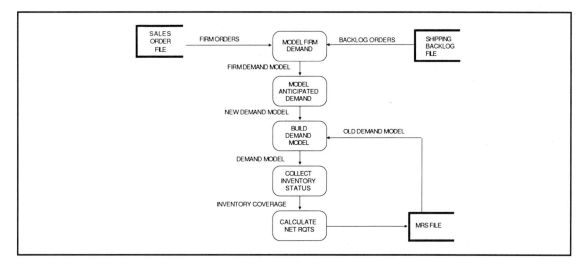

Figure 15-6. Example of a Data Flow Diagram (Second Level)

The diagram in Figure 15-7 shows a low-level Data Flow Diagram for Build Demand Model, one of the modules in the previous example. The MRS File data store in Figure 15-6 now appears as four, more detailed data stores.

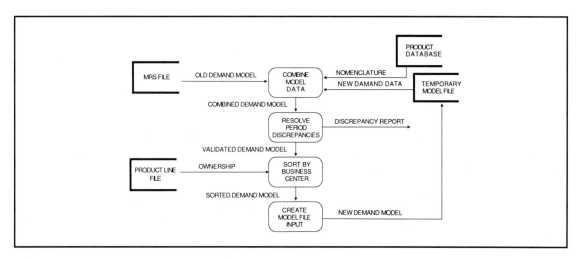

Figure 15-7. Example of a Data Flow Diagram (Third Level)

Rules for Data Flow Diagrams

- Do not include procedures that are system maintenance activities, such as Log Transaction or Reorganize Data Base.

- Complex systems may require more than one level of Data Flow Diagram. If so, construct a series of Data Flow Diagrams to include each appropriate level of detail.

- Keep the lower-level diagrams consistent with the higher-level ones. For example, a lower-level Data Flow Diagram cannot contain more inputs and outputs than a higher-level diagram. A data store that appears on a higher-level must also appear on each lower-level diagram.

- Label data flows.

- Label procedures.

- Represent only the normal, regular state, not start-up procedures.

- Ignore trivial error paths.

- Retain enough detail for transition analysis.

- Do not relate procedures to specific tools.

USER VIEW ANALYSIS

During **user view analysis**, the analyst collects a full representation of all data used in current systems and the associations between the data. In contrast to the top-down approach of entity analysis, user view analysis is essentially a bottom-up approach. As such, it provides a check against the conceptual business views that are confirmed during business model confirmation. (**Conceptual business views** are views that are theoretically independent of system details.)

One can analyze user views from the bottom-up because they differ from conceptual business views. With conceptual business views, the details of data fields and their associations are not apparent. With user views, however, such details are evident. Using canonical synthesis, one can group individual user views to construct the equivalent of an Entity Relationship Diagram.

Basic Concepts

This subsection documents some key concepts related to user views and the layout of fields within them.

User View and Layout

A **layout** represents a designed collection of data. Examples of layouts include reports, transaction screens, computer files, manual files, and other paper forms. In analyzing user views, analysts examine any layout that contains data relevant to the business area.

One can view layouts in different ways. For example, Figure 15-8 shows a layout of an employee's personnel record. The payroll office is interested in the employee's name and salary details. The employee's manager, on the other hand, is interested in the employee's experience. This one layout, then, contains two user views of the information.

A **user view** is a collection of data on a single layout. The layout reflects use of the view by some procedure. A single user view may include part or all of the data on the layout. The formal definition of a user view is:

User View   A collection of associated fields of interest to a user during procedure execution.

While a layout may contain several user views, each user view can reflect only one layout. If a view would otherwise include more than one layout, the view must be split into separate views for each layout.

During user view analysis, analysts examine the structure of every significant user view to determine its nature and content.

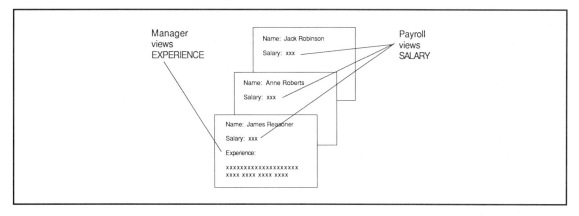

Figure 15-8. Example of a Layout

Field

Fields, or individual data items, are the most important element in defining user views. They correspond to attributes in entity analysis. The formal definition of a field is:

Field   A type of container for either data values or headings.

Associations Between Fields

Associations between fields are single or multiple, mandatory or optional. The associations are always directional. The field the association is from is called the **determinant**. The field the association is to is called the **dependent**. In each case, the determinant and/or the dependent may be a concatenated or compound field.

A **single association** between two fields indicates that, for each value of one field, the associated field has one and only one value. For example, for each value of Customer Number, Customer Name can be only one name.

If Customer Number and Customer Name have a single association, Customer Name is functionally dependent on Customer Number. Functional dependency figures largely in normalization, discussed later in this chapter.

A **multiple association** between two fields indicates that, for each value of one field, the associated field may have one or more values. For example, for each value of Customer Number, Customer Address can be one or more addresses. Such associations are typically inverses of single, functional dependencies.

For each association, one must identify the direction of the dependency. This specifies the dependency of one data item on another. For example, if one must know Customer Number in order to determine Customer Name, Customer Name is dependent on Customer Number.

An association between two fields can be mandatory or optional. A **mandatory association** is one that must always exist. For example, the association between Account Number and Customer Name is mandatory. In other words, for every account number there must be a customer's name.

An **optional association** is one that may or may not exist. For example, a user view may sometimes include an association between Customer Name and Customer Contact. The association is optional since every customer need not have an identified contact.

Key Field

User views contain fields with values that can uniquely identify values of an associated field. Such fields are known as **key fields**, or simply **keys**.

Any field with a single association leading from it is a key. Fields with multiple associations leading from them may also be keys. If so, they are **secondary keys**. One can follow a multiple association to find the values of associated fields, but one cannot identify field values uniquely.

A key field may include a single field or multiple fields. If a key field represents several values that identify associated field values, it is a **concatenated** key.

Transitive Association

A **transitive association** is like a redundant relationship. In such an association, one can always identify the values of the dependent field from other associations. Transitive associations occur when the determinant is not the full key of the view. In other words, the determinant is either not any portion of the key or is some proper subset of a concatenated key.

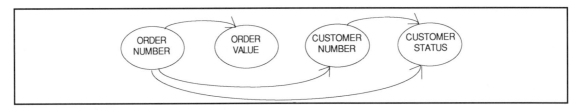

Figure 15-9. Example of a Transitive Association

Figure 15-9 shows four single associations:

- Order Number to Order Value
- Order Number to Customer Number
- Order Number to Customer Status
- Customer Number to Customer Status

Note that Customer Status is a dependent for single associations from both Order Number and Customer Number. Since every field in the view is a determinant of Order Number, Order Number is the key of the view. Customer Number acts as a determinant but is not the key of the view. Therefore, the association between Customer Number and Customer Status indicates that Customer Number is likely to be the key of some other view. Further, the association from Order Number to Customer Status is transitive, provided that the Customer Status value determined by a Customer Number value is the same as the Customer Status value determined by the corresponding Order Number value.

User View Diagram

A separate User View Diagram can represent each user view of a layout. The diagram represents the fields that compose the user view and the associations between the fields. User View Diagrams are sometimes called **bubble charts**. Figure 15-10 depicts user view analysis symbols.

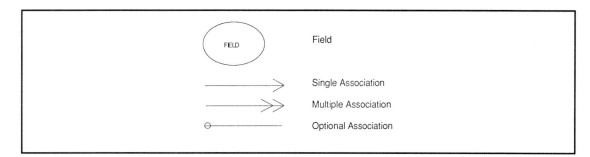

Figure 15-10. User View Analysis Symbols

Examples of User View Diagrams

Figure 15-11 represents a stock requisition tag. Figure 15-12 shows the corresponding User View Diagram.

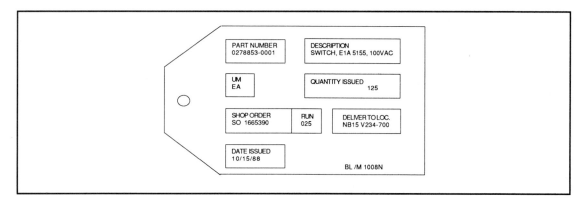

Figure 15-11. Stock Requisition Tag

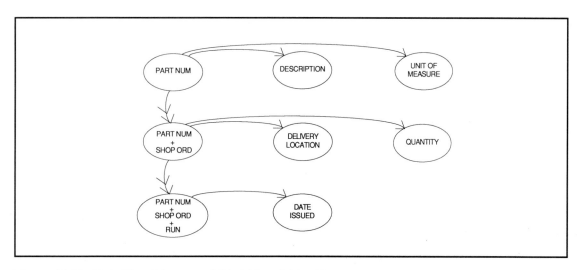

Figure 15-12. User View Diagram of Stock Requisition Tag

Figure 15-13 represents an online stock status inquiry. Figure 15-14 shows the corresponding User View Diagram.

```
INV22                    STOCK STATUS INQUIRY                    10/15/88
                                                                 10:55 AM


PART NUMBER:    0278553-0001                          COMM CODE : 15331

DESCRIPTION:  SWITCH, E1A 5155,  110VAC                          UM: EA.

...................... INVENTORY ACCOUNTS ......................
                      1209-1366    1210-6600    1610-9543

BALANCE ON HAND           0           132         1011
ALLOCATED                 0            10          820
AVAILABLE                 0           122          191
MIN ISSUE QTY             1            12           12
LOCATION BALANCES
    A/345/101             0           120          521
    A/345/215             0             0          490
    B/150/100             0            12            0
```

Figure 15-13. Online Stock Status Inquiry

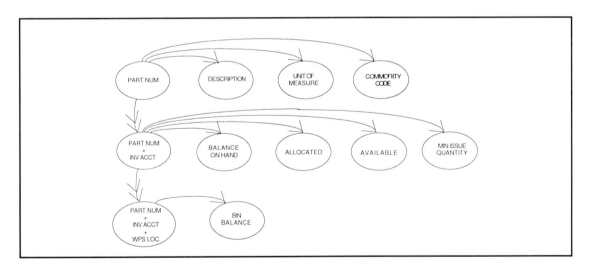

Figure 15-14. User View Diagram of Stock Status Inquiry

Rules For User View Diagrams

- Associations between fields have only one direction. When an association seems to point in both directions, split it. Specify two associations, each pointing in the appropriate direction.

- When more than one association is required between the same fields, name the associations to distinguish them.

- Eliminate transitive associations.

- A concatenated key (bubble) must contain all fields that compose the key.

CANONICAL SYNTHESIS

Canonical synthesis is a technique for combining sets of user views to remove inconsistencies. Its objective is to produce the equivalent of an Entity Relationship Model and an implied Entity Relationship Diagram. The implied diagram corresponds to the sum of all user views analyzed for current systems. During the confirmation stage of Business Area Analysis, the analyst checks the main diagram of the analysis against the implied diagram.

Basic Concepts

This subsection introduces some basic concepts related to canonical synthesis, including the use of key groups and indexes.

Key Group

Within user views, **key groups** occur. Key groups consist of a key and a set of fields that are functionally dependent on the key. A single arrow pointing to the dependent field represents functional dependency.

Figure 15-15. A Key Group

The three fields in Figure 15-15 represent a key group. Employee Name and Salary are functionally dependent on the key field Employee Number. The key field is an identifier, and each field is an implied attribute.

One may also accomplish functional dependency by creating two entity types, where the determinant is the identifier of one and the dependent is the identifier of the other, and creating a relationship with a cardinality of one from the determinant entity type to the dependent entity type. This alternative allows for the addition of new fields that will depend on the dependent field.

In Figure 15-16, the key group Employee Number, Employee Name, and Employee Salary imply an entity type, the key of which is Employee Number. This implied entity type might later be called simply EMPLOYEE.

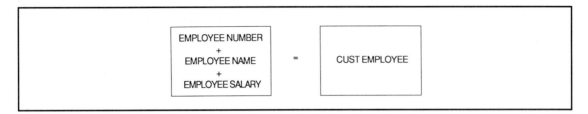

Figure 15-16. An Implied Entity Type

Key Index

A **key index** is an alphabetical list of all key fields, whether single or concatenated (Figure 15-17).

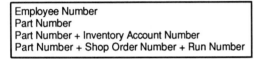

Employee Number
Part Number
Part Number + Inventory Account Number
Part Number + Shop Order Number + Run Number

Figure 15-17. Part of a Key Index

Key-Oriented List

A **Key-Oriented List** is a manual working document on which the analyst accumulates three items, as shown in Figure 15-18:

- Keys
- Non-key fields dependent on each key
- Associations between keys

CANONICAL SYNTHESIS FORM		
BUSINESS AREA: Personnel	**CURRENT SYSTEM:** Payroll	
ANALYST: J. Evers	**DATE:** 01/01/88	
KEY	**NON-KEY FIELDS**	**ASSOCIATIONS**
EMPLOYEE-#	EMPLOYEE-NAME EMPLOYEE-SALARY-RATE	1 : 1 with DEPT-NUMBER

Figure 15-18. A Key-Oriented List

Association

As recorded in canonical synthesis, an **association** is a link between two keys. A double arrow represents the link, or association. Unlike the associations in user data views, these associations are in both directions. One can derive the relationship memberships of the implied entity types from the associations between their keys on the Key-Oriented List. Every association becomes two relationship memberships, one for the main direction of association, and one for the reverse. When an association appears on more than one User View Diagram, it becomes a single relationship with two memberships.

Equivalent Entity Relationship Model

From the sum of the user views, the analyst constructs an Entity Relationship Diagram representing the Equivalent Entity Relationship Model. The analyst gathers these views on Key-Oriented Lists. The conventions used in this ERD are exactly the same as those introduced during entity analysis.

Rules for Equivalent Entity Relationship Diagrams

* Include each key group as an entity type.

  Within a concatenated key, each key identifies a separate key group. Each of the separate key groups will be related to the key group containing the concatenation.

* Construct relationships between all key groups.

* Include every relationship. (The implied Entity Relationship Diagram includes many relationships, most of which are not redundant. During comparison checking, determine which relationships to keep.)

* Do not name relationships unless they are parallel and between key groups.

* Resolve many-to-many relationships by creating associative entity types. To do this, use the composite identifier (the identifying attributes of the two entity types involved) and add the necessary relationships.

* Do not represent the optionality of relationships.

* Remove duplicate attributes that are not identifiers. To remove duplicates without losing information, it may be necessary to create relationship memberships between the duplicate attribute's entity type and the entity type that the attribute currently identifies. However, the required memberships may exist already in normal or transitive relationships.

The User View Diagrams in Figures 15-19, 15-20, and 15-21 depict three related user views.

Figure 15-23 shows an Entity Relationship Diagram that corresponds to the Key-Oriented List in Figure 15-22. This diagram contains two implied entity types, each consisting of a key group. The analyst must name each of these implied entity types. In this case, the first one (Course-Number and Presentation-Date) might be named PRESENTATION.

During the confirmation stage of Business Area Analysis, analysts add all of these implied entity types to the business model developed during top-down analysis.

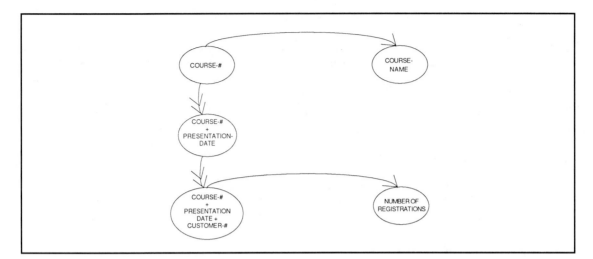

Figure 15-19. Example for Canonical Synthesis: First User View

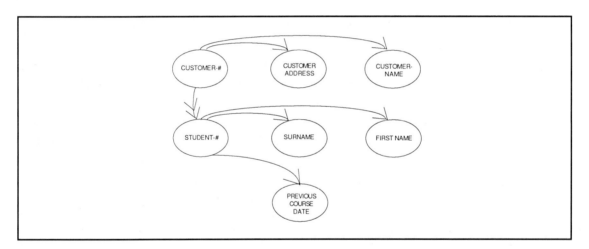

Figure 15-20. Example for Canonical Synthesis: Second User View

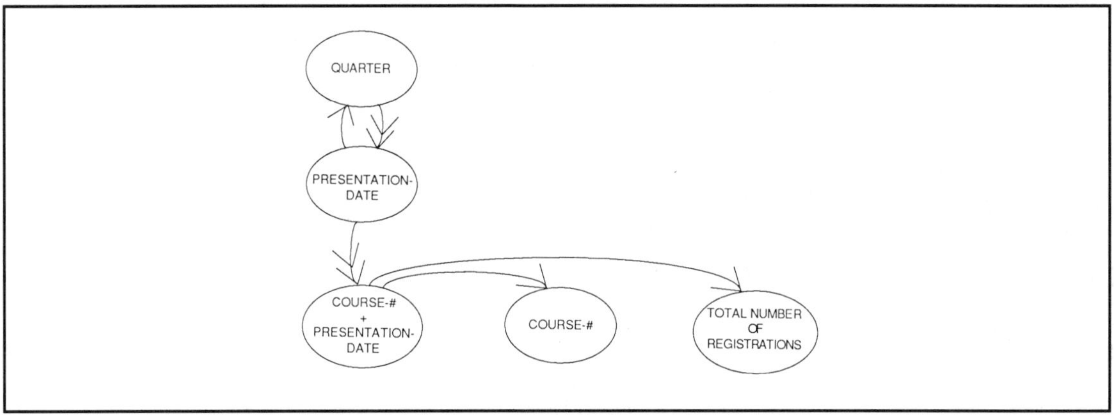

Figure 15-21. Example for Canonical Synthesis: Third User View

KEYS	ATTRIBUTES	ASSOCIATIONS
Course-#	Course-Name	1:m with Course-# + Presentation-Date
Course-# + Presentation- Date	Total Number of Registrations	1:1 with Course-# 1:1 with Presentation-Date 1:m with Course-# + Presentation_Date + Customer-#
Course-# + Presentation- Date + Customer-#	Number of Registrations	1:1 with Course-# + Presentation-Date 1:1 with Customer-#
Customer-#	Customer Name Custiomer Address	1:m with Customer-# + Presentation-Date + Customer 1:m with Student
Student-#	Surname First Name Previous Course Dates	1:1 with Customer-#
Presentation- Date	Quarter-ID (secondary key)	1:m with Course-# + Presentation_Date

Figure 15-22. Key-Oriented Lists from Canonical Synthesis

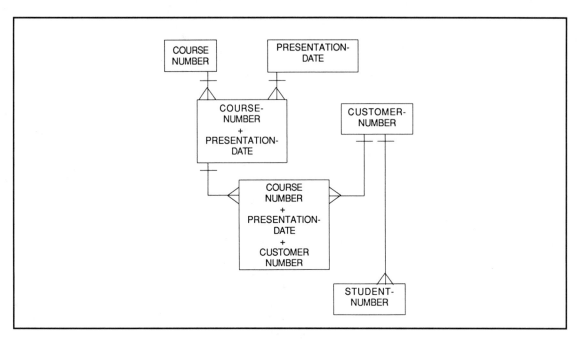

Figure 15-23. Entity Relationship Diagram from Figure 15-22

16
CONFIRMATION

OVERVIEW

During the confirmation step of Business Area Analysis, analysts verify that the business area model is correct and complete. By applying several confirmation techniques, analysts ensure that the model is ready for continued refinement during the next stage of Information Engineering, Business System Design.

The IEF Consistency Check facility performs much of this checking automatically. This facility is described in detail in the *IEF Design Toolset Guide*. Consistency Check can be run against a single object (such as an entity type or process), against process portions of the model, against the entire data or against the entire model. The IEF will not allow inconsistent objects to progress to the Business System Design stage.

While the automated Consistency Check facility verifies that the model conforms to the rules of Information Engineering in the strictest sense, the confirmation techniques described in this chapter help the analyst ensure that the model's *meaning* is correct as well.

There are three techniques used during confirmation:

- Completeness checking
- Correctness checking
- Stability analysis

Although the IEF does not provide full automated support for these techniques, it does provide some help along the way. The tasks during which IEF facilities can be useful are noted in the chapter.

COMPLETENESS CHECKING

Analysts perform **completeness checking** to confirm that the model for the business area under analysis is complete. In particular, they address these questions:

- Have all the processes, entity types, attributes, and relationships been found?
- Does the model include processes to create, delete, update, and reference each entity type, attribute, and relationship?

The result of completeness checking is a complete but unconfirmed business model. To ensure confirmation, one must also check the model for correctness and stability.

Completeness checking includes two main techniques:

- Comparison checking
- Matrix cross-checking

Comparison Checking

Comparison checking involves comparing the new business model against the current systems architecture. This activity helps the analyst find further analysis objects, particularly attributes and low-level processes.

The table in Figure 16-1 shows some likely objects for comparison.

Business Area Model	Current System Model
Subject Area	Subject Database
Entity Type	Record, Data Store, Key Group
Attribute	Field, Data Element, Implied Relationship
Relationship	Field, Implied Relationship
Function	System
Process	Procedure, Program
Information View	Data View, Data Store
Dependency	Data Flow

Figure 16-1. Objects in Comparison Checking

Matrix Cross-Checking

Involvement matrices show how business activities use entity analysis objects. They summarize the involvement of processes with entity types, attributes, or relationships. For example, an Elementary Process/Entity Type Matrix indicates whether every defined entity is fully used.

One may construct three involvement matrices:

- Elementary Process/Entity Type Matrix
- Elementary Process/Relationship Matrix
- Elementary Process/Attribute Matrix

Analysts use the three matrices to determine whether the new business model contains a process for each of the following purposes:

- To create, read, update, or delete each entity type
- To associate and disassociate each relationship
- To create values for attributes and to reference, change, or remove these values

The following paragraphs reference examples of each matrix.

Conventions Used in Elementary Process/Entity Type Matrix

The Elementary Process/Entity Type Matrix is available as part of the IEF BAA Matrix Processor. Upon entry, it is automatically populated with the list of elementary processes along one axis and entity types along the other, with cell values populated from the elementary process's expected effects. (Note that the cell values come from expected effects, NOT from the actual entity action statements from the Action Diagram.)

When the matrix is initially populated:

- Each row represents an elementary process.

- Each column represents an entity type.

- Letters in cells indicate action types:

  — **C** represents a CREATE action.

  — **D** represents a DELETE action.

  — **U** represents an UPDATE action.

  — **R** represents a READ action.

- A cell may contain only one letter and always contains the highest value if more than one action is involved, where:

  — CREATE and DELETE are the highest value.

  — UPDATE is the next highest value.

  — READ is the lowest value.

Figure 16-2 shows a Elementary Process/Entity Type Matrix that reveals several problems within the current model:

Process \ Entity Types	Course	Segment	Item	Version	Presentation	Session	Customer	Student	Registration	Attendance	Payment	Lecturer	Subject	Room
Agree course outline	C	C											R	
Prepare segment	U	R	C	C								R		
Produce segment		R	U									R		
Maintain segment		U	R	C								R		
Plan program	R	R			C	C						R	R	R
Advertise	R				R							R		
Direct mail shot	R	R			R		R	R				R		
Sell presentation	R	R			C	C	C					R		
Register attendance					R		C	C	C					
Present sesseion							R	R	C			R		R
Grade student							R	U	U					
Cancel presentation	R				D	D			D					
Prepare invoice														
Receive payment							R		R					
Hire lecturer												C	R	

Key: C - Create   U - Update   R - Read   D - Delete

Figure 16-2. Process/Entity Type Matrix

- The entity type VERSION is created in two places. Creation in two places is unlikely.

- The entity type PAYMENT is not used. Either it is not required or the processes that use it are incorrectly defined.

- The process Prepare Invoice uses no entity types. According to the matrix, the process does nothing.

Conventions Used in Elementary Process/Relationship Matrix

- Each row represents a process.
- Each column represents a relationship.
- Letters in cells indicate action types:
  - — **A** represents an ASSOCIATE action.
  - — **D** represents a DISASSOCIATE action.
  - — **T** represents a TRANSFER action.
- A cell may contain only one letter.

Figure 16-3 shows an example of a Elementary Process/Relationship Matrix. This matrix raises several questions about the current model:

Processes \ Relationships	Course consists of segment	Segment is about subject	Segment uses item	Item developed as version	Lecturer prepared version	Course presented as presentation	Presentation consists of session	Item is used for lecture	Lecture is presented by lecturer	Customer commissions presentation	Customer employs student	Student applies by registration	Presentation requested in registration	Registration permits attendance	Attendance is at session	Customer makes payment	Payment covers registration	Lecturer can teach subject
Agree course outline	A	A																
Prepare segment	T		A	A	A													
Produce segment			T	T	T													
Maintain segment			D	A	A													
Plan program		T				A	A	A	A	A								
Advertise	T	T				T												
Direct mail shot	T	T				T							T					
Sell presentation	T	T				A	A	A			A							
Register attendance													D	A	A			
Present sesseion								T	T				T			A		
Grade student													T	T	T	T		
Cancel presentation						T	T						D		A			
Prepare invoice											T	T	T	T				
Receive payment																A	A	
Hire lecturer																		A

Key: A - Associate   D - Disassociate   T - Transfer

Figure 16-3. Process/Relationship Matrix

- The relationships PRESENTATION *consists of* SESSION and COURSE *presented as* PRESENTATION are associated in two processes, Plan Program and Sell Presentation. The double association suggests potential duplication.

- The matrix shows transfers involved with many relationships in the model, whereas in fact, most relationships are fixed. The analyst must investigate this discrepancy.

Conventions Used in Elementary Process/Attribute Matrix

- Each row represents a process.

- Each column represents an attribute.

- Letters in cells indicate action types:

  — **S** represents a SET or CHANGE action.

  — **R** represents a REFERENCE action.

  — **X** represents a REMOVE action.

- A matrix includes attributes from one entity type only.

Figure 16-4 shows an example of a Elementary Process/Attribute Matrix that raises questions about the current model:

Process \ Attributes	Session Number	Session Name	Course Number	Course Presentation Sequence Number	Session Presentation Date/Time	Room	Lecturer Number	Lecturer's fee	Session Lecturer's Notes (Text)	Session Student Notes (Text)	Session Abstract For Publicity (Text)
Agree course outline											
Prepare segment	S	S	S								
Produce segment									S	S	
Maintain segment		S							S	S	
Plan program	R	R	S	S	S	S					
Advertise	R	R	R	R	R		R				S
Direct mail shot							R				R
Sell presentation	R	R	R	R	R		R				R
Register attendance			R	R	R						
Present session											
Grade student	R	R	R		R		R				
Cancel presentation				X	X	X	X	X			
Prepare invoice											
Receive payment											
Hire lecturer	R	R	R	R	R						

Key: S - Set or change a value   R - Reference   X - Remove a value

Figure 16-4. Process/Attribute Matrix

- The process Cancel Presentation removes the attribute Lecturer Number, but no value has been given to the attribute (it has not been set).

- The processes Agree Course Outline, Present Session, Prepare Invoice, and Receive Payment use no attributes. Is this consistent with the Elementary Process/Entity Type Matrix? If so, what do the processes do?

CORRECTNESS CHECKING

Analysts perform **correctness checking** to confirm that the business area model accurately represents the business area and conforms to the rules and conventions of Information Engineering.

In particular, analysts address these questions:

- Have attributes been grouped with correct entity types?
- Does the model exclude all unnecessary elements?
- Are the information views consistent across processes?
- Does the model look right to the end users?

Correctness checking includes five techniques:

- Normalization
- Process-dependency checking
- Redundancy checking
- Quantity cross-checking
- Structured walkthroughs

After performing correctness checking, one can assume that the business area model is correct in terms of Information Engineering rules. The analyst can then use this verified model in subsequent stages of Information Engineering.

Normalization

Normalization is a three-step process used to insure that the analyst has assigned each attribute to the proper entity type and defined a sufficient number of entity types. The process of normalization involves refining an entity type based on the interdependencies of its component attributes. Each step of the process results in the entity type's conforming to a **normal form.**

For the purposes of confirmation, it is sufficient to normalize to the **third normal form** (usually abbreviated 3NF). Figure 16-5 presents the three normal forms in tabular form along with the steps that cause an entity type to conform to them.

1st Normal Form (1NF)	Multi-valued attributes are removed to form a separate entity type. Thus, no entity type in 1NF can have repeating groups (multi-valued attributes).
2nd Normal Form (2NF)	Attributes that are not fully dependent on the identifiers of the group are removed to a separate entity type.
3rd Normal Form (3NF)	Attributes that are dependent on attributes other than the identifiers are removed to a separate entity type.

Figure 16-5. Three Normal Forms

Subsequent figures illustrate normalization based on the entity type ORDER FORM and its attributes:

Product Code	Customer Number
Product Description	Tax Number
Stock Quantity	Customer Priority
Order Number	Quantity Ordered
Export Status	

Figure 16-6 shows the entity type laid out as a table with attribute values. Separate line items within an order appear as lines in the table.

ORDER FORM

Product code	Product desc.	Stock quantity	Order number	Export status	Customer number	Tax number	Customer priority	Quantity ordered
142	Methanol	601	23G	X	4629	79482	1	144
			49G	X	3751	79482	8	200
830	Sulphuric Acid	95	27K	N	2007	11973	6	12
			23G	X	4629		1	10
			98Y	N	3751	79482	8	36
876	Cyanide	90	88M	X	8320		7	2

Figure 16-6. An Un-Normalized Attribute Group

The next three figures show the normalization of the attribute group in Figure 16-6. Normalization involves dividing the original entity type into implied entity types. In this case, ORDER FORM breaks down into four implied entity types:

- PRODUCT
- ORDER LINE
- ORDER
- CUSTOMER

In addition, normalization involves assigning attributes to the correct entity types. This is useful for subsequent data design.

Figure 16-7 shows the attribute group in Figure 16-6 in first normal form (1NF). Removing multi-valued attributes results in two 1NF attribute groups: PRODUCT and ORDER LINE. Product Code appears twice — as the identifier of PRODUCT and as the foreign identifier of ORDER LINE.

1NF: Multi-valued groups of attributes are removed to form a separate entity type.

PRODUCT

* = KEY

Product Code *	Product Description	Stock Quantity
142	Methanol	601
830	Sulphuric Acid	95
876	Cyanide	90

← Single-value attributes assigned to entity type Product.

Multi-value attributes are removed to entity type Order Line.

ORDER LINE

Product Code *	Order Number *	Export Status	Customer Number	Tax Number	Customer Priority	Quantity Ordered
142	23G	X	4629		1	144
142	49S	N	3751	79482	8	200
830	27K	N	2007	11973	6	12
830	23G	X	4629		1	10
830	98Y	N	3751	79482	8	36
876	88M	X	8320		7	2

Figure 16-7. First Normal Form

2NF: Attributes that are not fully dependent on the identifiers of the group are removed to a separate entity type.

PRODUCT

Product Code *	Product Description	Stock Quantity
142	Methanol	601
830	Sulphuric Acid	95
876	Cyanide	90

* = KEY

ORDER LINE

Product Code *	Order Number *	Quantity Ordered
142	23G	144
142	49S	200
830	27K	12
830	23G	10
830	98Y	36
876	88M	2

↑
Quantity Ordered is fully dependent on the identifiers Product Code and Order Number

ORDER

Order Number *	Export Status	Customer Number	Tax Number	Customer Priority
23G	X	4629		1
49S	N	3751	79482	8
27K	N	2007	11973	6
23G	X	4629		1
98Y	N	3751	79482	8
88M	X	8320		7

← These attributes are not dependent on Product Code, one of the previous group's identifiers.

Figure 16-8. Second Normal Form

Figure 16-8 shows the original attribute group in second normal form (2NF). PRODUCT is already in 2NF because its attributes are totally dependent on the identifier Product Code. However, if one examines ORDER LINE (Figure 16-7), one discovers that four of the attributes are dependent on Order Number but not on Product Code. Removing the four attributes to a third attribute group (ORDER) removes partial dependencies (attributes that are not dependent on the whole identifier).

Figure 16-9 shows the original attribute group in third normal form (3NF). For a group to be in 3NF, every attribute must be dependent on the whole identifier and nothing else. PRODUCT and ORDER LINE are already in 3NF. In ORDER, Customer Number is wholly dependent on the identifier Order Number, but the other attributes are not. To remedy this, one must split ORDER into two attribute groups: ORDER and CUSTOMER.

For a more complete treatment of conventional normalization techniques, refer to *An Introduction to Database Systems, Vol. I*, by C. J. Date.

3NF: Attributes dependent on attributes other than the identifiers are removed.

PRODUCT

Product Code *	Product Description	Stock Quantity
142	Methanol	601
830	Sulphuric Acid	95
876	Cyanide	90

* = KEY

ORDER LINE

Product Code *	Order Number *	Quantity Ordered
142	23G	144
142	49S	200
830	27K	12
830	23G	10
830	98Y	36
876	88M	2

ORDER

Order Number *	Customer Number
23G	4629
49S	3751
27K	2007
98Y	3751
88M	8320

CUSTOMER

Customer Number *	Export Status	Tax Number	Customer Priority
4629	X		1
3751	N	79482	8
2007	N	11973	6
8320	X		7

←

Export Status, Tax Number, and Customer Priority are dependent on Customer Number, not Order Number.

They are removed to entity type Customer.

Figure 16-9. Third Normal Form

Process Dependency Checking

During process dependency checking, the analyst verifies the activity portion of the business area model by confirming the following:

• Every elementary process appears in a Process Dependency Diagram.

• Process Dependency Diagrams are consistent with one another.

• Every elementary process is dependent upon an event and/or another process.

• Every elementary process has entity actions defined and at least one input and output. (An output may be an export view or an entity view associated with a CREATE, DELETE, or UPDATE action.)

Redundancy Checking

During redundancy checking, the analyst looks for unnecessary attributes and relationships. Attributes and relationships are unnecessary when they already appear in the model under some other guise or can be deduced from other objects in the model. The analyst also identifies overlapping entity types and duplicated processes.

Quantity Cross-Checking

During quantity cross-checking, the analyst checks the consistency of all quantitative information gathered about objects in the business area model. In particular, the analyst checks the following:

- Subtype volume
- Relationship cardinality

Subtype Volume

The number of entities of a given type cannot exceed the combined total of maximums for all subtypes in a partitioning. Each mandatory partitioning must have the same combined total.

Relationship Cardinality

When two entity types are associated, the entity volume figures must be consistent with the cardinality of the relationship associating them. For example, if CUSTOMER has 15 occurrences and ORDER has 150 occurrences, the cardinality of the relationship between CUSTOMER and ORDER should average 10 (150 divided by 15).

The cardinality of a relationship depends on the optionality of the entity types it associates. The table in Figure 16-10 indicates the cardinality of a relationship between entities A and B under three conditions.

CONDITION	AVERAGE CARDINALITY AT B-END OF A TO B
If both A and B are mandatory members	$= \dfrac{\text{Entity B volume}}{\text{Entity A volume}}$
If A is optional and B is mandatory	$< \dfrac{\text{Entity B volume}}{\text{Entity A volume}}$
If A is mandatory and B is optional	$> \dfrac{\text{Entity B volume}}{\text{Entity A volume}}$

Figure 16-10. Relationship Cardinality

Structured Walkthroughs

Structured walkthroughs are formal, step-by-step inspections of analysis deliverables. Analysts present the walkthroughs verbally to the business personnel most familiar with the business area under analysis.

One may use structured walkthroughs at any stage of Business Area Analysis. Within correctness checking, the walkthroughs help users verify the following:

- Entity Relationship Diagram
- Process Hierarchy Diagram
- Comparison Check Report
- Stability Analysis Report

During the walkthrough, those who constructed the model systematically explain the model's meaning and interpretation, the modeling decisions that have been made, and the impact of those decisions.

Participants check, discuss, and agree on each component of the model. The level of detail varies according to the audience.

Rules and Conventions

Normalization

- Every attribute is dependent upon the key (1NF), the whole key (2NF), and nothing but the key (3NF).
- Every 3NF collection of attributes is an entity type.
- Normalization is based on understanding the functional dependencies of attributes.

Process Dependency Checking

- Every elementary process must appear in a dependency diagram.
- Every elementary process must have an input and an output.

Redundancy Checking

- An attribute may describe only one entity type.
- An algorithm must be defined for each derived attribute.

STABILITY ANALYSIS

Stability analysis is the study of the impact of potential business changes on the analysis area, especially on the entity and process models.

During stability analysis, the analyst identifies modifications that will result in a resilient business area model — one that will not need to change, even when business requirements change. Although one cannot achieve total resilience, one can and must strive to make the model as resilient as possible.

Summary of Stability Analysis Steps

1. Identify likely changes to the business.
2. Study the impact of such changes on the business area model.
3. Modify the model to lessen the impact of possible changes.
4. Prepare Stability Analysis Report.
5. Review completeness and correctness checking.

Rules and Conventions

Stability analysis has no rules or conventions.

Deliverables

The deliverables of stability analysis are as follows:

- A resilient business area model
- A Stability Analysis Report (optional)

The Stability Analysis Report tabulates the changes postulated, outlines the impact of each change on the business area model, and describes the modifications made to cope with each change.

17
BUSINESS SYSTEM DEFINITION

OVERVIEW

Business system definition is the final activity performed during Business Area Analysis. It provides a springboard into the next stage of Information Engineering, Business System Design (BSD). During business system definition, analysts produce the following information:

- Groupings of elementary processes called **business systems**, each of which will form the basis for a Business System Design project

- A prioritized plan for the business area, identifying the projected implementation sequence for business systems

- A prioritized plan for each business system, identifying the projected implementation sequence for processes

To produce these results, analysts perform the following tasks:

- **Elementary Process Clustering**. Cluster analysis helps analysts determine which processes belong together in a single business system. Cluster analysis can be automatically performed by the IEF and produces a single deliverable: the Clustered Elementary Process/Entity Type Usage Matrix.

- **Cost/Benefit Analysis**. Cost/benefit analysis helps analysts assess the net benefit of each elementary process. Cost/benefit analysis yields three deliverables: the Process Net Benefit Matrix, the Business System Net Benefit Matrix, and the Weighted Process Benefit Matrix.

- **Implementation Plan Construction.** During implementation plan construction, analysts use the deliverables from cluster and cost/benefit analysis to identify business systems, the sequence in which they will be implemented, and the sequence in which their components will be implemented.

At the conclusion of these activities, Business System Design projects to support the business area may commence.

Cluster analysis is a technique for grouping objects together based on some set of common characteristics. In the case of business system definition, cluster analysis is used to group elementary processes together based on their use of data. The result of this grouping is represented in the Clustered Elementary Process/Entity Type Usage Matrix.

The IEF does provides automatic support for this matrix. However, the analyst should note that the cell values with which this matrix is populated derive from the elementary processes's expected effects definitions, NOT from entity action statements included in their Process Action Diagrams. If the expected effects do not correspond with the action diagram, the cell values in this matrix will not be valid.

The steps for performing Elementary Process Clustering are as follows:

1. Use the IEF to cluster the elementary processes based on their common usage of entity types.

2. Adjust the clusters if necessary.

3. Determine process/entity cluster boundaries.

The following paragraphs explain these steps in detail.

Step 1 — Cluster the Elementary Processes

This step simply involves executing the "cluster" command while accessing the Elementary Process/Entity Type Usage Matrix in the IEF. Figure 17-1 shows an Elementary Process/Entity Type Usage Matrix prior to the clustering operation.

ELEMENTARY PROCESSES	DELIVERY	LOCATION	SALE	CUSTOMER	BENEFIT	TRANSPORT	ORDER	SALARY	PERSON	SUPPLIER	PRODUCT
DISPOSE OF TRUCK											
PLACE ORDER							C			R	R
REVIEW SALARY								U	R		
PURCHASE TRUCK											
ADD SUPPLIER										C	R
MAKE SALE			C								R
DISPATCH ORDER		R				R					
REVIEW BENEFITS					U				R		
RECEIVE DELIVERY	C										U
HIRE EMPLOYEE					C			C	C		
TERMINATE EMPLOYEE					D			D	U		

Figure 17-1. Elementary Process/Entity Type Usage Matrix

Following the clustering operation, you should expect to see a matrix more like that in Figure 17-2.

ELEMENTARY PROCESSES	SUPPLIER	ORDER	DELIVERY	PRODUCT	SALE	PERSON	SALARY	BENEFIT	LOCATION	TRANSPORT	CUSTOMER
ADD SUPPLIER	C			R							
PLACE ORDER	R	C		R							
RECEIVE DELIVERY			C	U							
MAKE SALE				R	C						
HIRE EMPLOYEE						C	C	C			
REVIEW SALARY						R	U				
REVIEW BENEFITS						R		U			
TERMINATE EMPLOYEE						U	D	D			
DISPATCH ORDER									R	R	
PURCHASE TRUCK											

Figure 17-2. Elementary Process/Entity Type Usage Matrix after Clustering

Step 2 — Adjust the Clusters If Necessary

Sometimes the clusters automatically calculated by the IEF are not as tidy as those appearing in Figure 17-2. If this is the case, the facilities of the IEF Matrix Processor can be used to move rows and columns around until the analyst is pleased with the appearance of the clusters.

Step 3 — Determine Business System Boundaries

Finally, the analyst uses the results of clustering to identify business systems. Figure 17-3 shows an obvious grouping of the Elementary Process/Entity Type Usage Matrix into business systems. This final modification to the Elementary Process/Entity Type Usage Matrix yields the Clustered Elementary Process/Entity Type Usage Matrix, the final deliverable from cluster analysis.

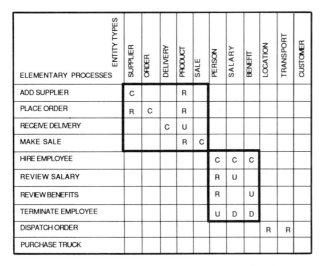

ELEMENTARY PROCESSES \ ENTITY TYPES	SUPPLIER	ORDER	DELIVERY	PRODUCT	SALE	PERSON	SALARY	BENEFIT	LOCATION	TRANSPORT	CUSTOMER
ADD SUPPLIER	C			R							
PLACE ORDER	R	C		R							
RECEIVE DELIVERY			C	U							
MAKE SALE				R	C						
HIRE EMPLOYEE						C	C	C			
REVIEW SALARY						R	U				
REVIEW BENEFITS						R		U			
TERMINATE EMPLOYEE						U	D	D			
DISPATCH ORDER									R	R	
PURCHASE TRUCK											

Figure 17-3. Clustered Elementary Process/Entity Type UsageMatrix

Before pronouncing the cluster analysis task complete, the analyst should consider the following items:

- One should compare the results of this analysis to the Business System Architecture developed during the ISP stage of Information Engineering. Although the business systems just derived are much more detailed than those predicted during ISP, their shapes should be roughly the same. If not, the analyst must reconcile the two views, either by revising the ISP Business System Architecture or by changing the grouping of processes.

- Since a business system is the basis for a Business System Design project, one must size it appropriately for that project. Depending on time and resource constraints, the number of elementary processes included in a business system may be too large or too small. In either case, the analyst must reestablish cluster boundaries by revising the affinity boundary used to derive the initial clusters, until this exercise produces the desired project boundary.

- In many cases, clusters do not fall out as neatly as in the example. If they do not, one must address the anomalies before completing cluster analysis. There are two kinds of anomalies, as illustrated in Figure 17-4.

ELEMENTARY PROCESSES	ENTITY TYPES	SUPPLIER	ORDER	DELIVERY	PRODUCT	SALE	PERSON	SALARY	BENEFIT	LOCATION	TRANSPORT	CUSTOMER
ADD SUPPLIER		C			R		U					
PLACE ORDER		R	C		R							
RECEIVE DELIVERY				C	U							
MAKE SALE					R	C						.
HIRE EMPLOYEE							C	C	C			
REVIEW SALARY		U					R	U				
REVIEW BENEFITS							R		U			
TERMINATE EMPLOYEE							U	D	D			
DISPATCH ORDER										R	R	
PURCHASE TRUCK												

Figure 17-4. Clustering Anomalies

— The first kind of anomaly, represented by the U at the intersection of Review Salary and ORDER, indicates an information flow between business systems. This sort of anomaly is potentially harmless, but indicates that the two business systems shown on the matrix share the entity type ORDER.

In this sort of situation, one must consider whether the elementary processes were clustered properly, particularly (as in the example) when one business system creates an entity and another updates or deletes it. The case in which one business system creates an entity and another reads it is not nearly as serious.

— The second kind of anomaly, evident in the PRODUCT column, may or may not reflect a problem. Any time a column does not have at least one of each of the four possible values (C, D, U, R) represented, the analyst should review it. In this case, there is no C indicating that PRODUCT was created. This suggests two possibilities: either another business area creates PRODUCT entities, an entirely acceptable situation, or the analyst has erroneously omitted the elementary process that creates PRODUCT entities. One must either explain or resolve this apparent inconsistency before proceeding.

COST/BENEFIT ANALYSIS

The object of **cost/benefit analysis** is to discover the net financial benefit each elementary process will yield when implemented. The analyst uses the results of this analysis to determine which of those elementary processes defined in the business area to actually implement. Additionally, these results provide insight into the best implementation sequence for business systems and elementary processes within business systems.

With regard to cost/benefit analysis, two points are critical:

• Some costs and benefits are intangible. Figure 17-5 shows examples of the differences between tangible and intangible costs and benefits. One must quantify both tangible and intangible costs and benefits in order to assess the net benefit of an elementary process. An unquantifiable cost or benefit is probably invalid.

• At this early stage, an accurate assessment of costs and benefits is probably not possible. One can predict neither with much precision until other components come into play during Business System Design.

CLASSIFICATION	COST	BENEFIT
Tangible	Training Employees Transition to Process	Increased Revenue Decreased Labor Cost Decreased Overhead Cost
Intangible	Disruption of Work Employee Comprehension	Better Information Improved Service

Figure 17-5. Examples of Tangible and Intangible Costs and Benefits

Therefore, the analyst must recognize estimates for what they are and waste no time agonizing over minutiae. As long as he or she determines the relative worth of one process over another with reasonable accuracy, the analyst will have fulfilled the objective of cost/benefit analysis.

The analyst should follow these steps to accomplish cost/benefit analysis:

1. Identify the information needs related to the business area and the total benefit realized by satisfying each one.

2. Analyze net benefits by evaluating how much each elementary process contributes to the satisfaction of each specific information need. This activity yields two deliverables: the Process Net Benefit Matrix and the Business System Net Benefit Matrix.

3. Weight the benefits to favor those elementary processes that participate in satisfying the greatest number of information needs. This activity yields one deliverable: the Weighted Process Benefit Matrix.

The following paragraphs explain these steps in detail.

Step 1 — Identify and Assess Information Needs

The concept of an **information need** is not as rigorously defined as most Information Engineering concepts. It refers to an item of information that provides some benefit to system users when exported from the system. One can assign a value to an information system, then, based on the total value of the information needs it satisfies.

This step consists of three sub-steps:

1. List the information needs satisfied by the business area.

2. Select a unit of time over which to measure benefits.

3. Assign a benefit value to each information need.

Step 1.1 — List Information Needs

Planners initially derive information needs during the first stage of Information Engineering, Information Strategy Planning (ISP). If an ISP was performed for the enterprise being analyzed, one should use the information needs listed in the ISP Report as a basis for the list used at this point. However, because Business Area Analysis achieves a greater level of detail than ISP, the list of information needs is likely to grow beyond those recognized during ISP.

In general, each information need corresponds to an export view or group of export views defined during Business Area Analysis. However, not all export views satisfy an information need. The analyst must judge whether an export view contributes information significant to the business before identifying it as an information need. For example, an export view that contains sales information for each product the business produces is probably of vital importance to the business. Thus, it is an information need. Other export views might be necessary operationally but not vital to the business. These include export views that verify proper completion of the update of an entity. These are not classified as information needs.

Figure 17-6 illustrates how one might derive information needs from a Process Dependency Diagram.

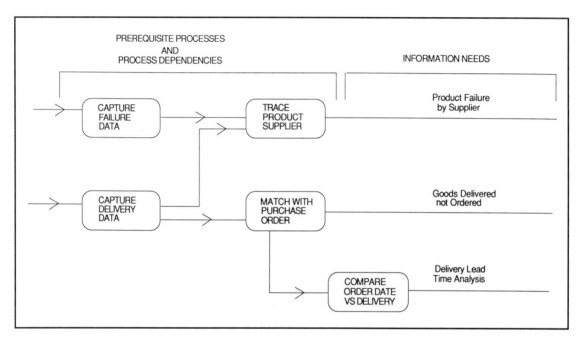

Figure 17-6. Deriving Information Needs

Step 1.2 — Select Time Period to Measure Benefit

To compare costs and benefits, one must consider them over some discrete unit of time. For instance, if one measures the benefit provided by an elementary process over the period of a year, one must also measure the operational cost of the elementary process over a year to achieve a valid comparison.

At this point, the analyst must select the appropriate time period. In most cases, one can calculate benefits on a yearly basis, but individual circumstances may dictate a different unit of time.

In considering which unit of time to use, bear in mind that the following assessments are made using the selected unit of time:

- The benefit yielded by satisfying an information need
- The portion of the initial cost of implementing an elementary process that is allocated to the selected time period (sometimes known as **development costs**)
- The cost of operating an implemented elementary process (sometimes known as **operating costs**)

Step 1.3 — Assign Benefit Values to Information Needs

Next, the analyst considers each information need in terms of its benefit to the business over the selected time period. Remember that one must quantify both tangible and intangible benefits and that rough estimates are acceptable.

The analyst lists the resulting benefit values beside the information needs discovered in step 1.1. Figure 17-7 shows the Information Needs Benefit List from which the analyst will derive the remaining matrices in cost/benefit analysis.

INFORMATION NEEDS	BENEFIT VALUE PER ANNUM (0000)
Product Failure by Supplier	9
Goods Delivered not Ordered	6
Delivery Lead Time Analysis	10

Figure 17-7. Information Needs Benefit List

Step 2 — Assess Net Benefits

In this step, the analyst estimates the net benefit associated with implementing each elementary process. One can divide this activity into several sub-steps to simplify its execution:

1. Allocate a benefit to each elementary process that contributes to satisfying each information need over the selected unit of time.

2. Estimate the development cost of implementing the elementary process over the selected unit of time.

3. Estimate the operating cost of executing the elementary process over the selected unit of time. At the conclusion of this sub-step, the Process Net Benefit Matrix will be complete.

4. Summarize the Process Net Benefit Matrix into the Business System Net Benefit Matrix.

Step 2.1 — Allocate Benefits to Elementary Processes

In this step, the analyst allocates the benefit of satisfying an information need, determined in step 1 (Identify and Assess Information Needs), to each elementary process that contributes to its satisfaction.

For example, return to the Process Dependency Diagram in Figure 17-6, which reveals that the execution of several elementary processes satisfies three information needs. In this example, the elementary process Trace Product Supplier directly satisfies the information need Product Failure by Supplier. However, the elementary process Capture Failure Data indirectly contributes to the satisfaction of the information need Product Failure by Supplier, since it is a prerequisite to Trace Product Supplier. Therefore, one must assign part of the benefit value of satisfying the information need Product Failure by Supplier to the elementary process Trace Product Supplier, while assigning the remainder to the elementary process Capture Failure Data.

The portion allocated to each elementary process should reflect the importance of the process's contribution to satisfying the information need, in the judgement of the analyst.

The analyst enters the result of this allocation into the Process Net Benefit Matrix. An example of a Process Net Benefit Matrix after benefit value allocation appears in Figure 17-8.

INFORMATION NEEDS	ELEMENTARY PROCESSES	CAPTURE_FAILURE_DATA	TRACE_PRODUCT_SUPPLIER	CAPTURE_DELIVERY_DATA	MATCH_WITH_PURCH_ORDR	COMPARE_ORDR/DLVRY_DT	TOTAL
PRODUCT FAILURE BY SUP		4	3	2			9
GOODS DLVRD NOT ORDERED				2	4		6
DLVRY LEAD TIME ANLYSIS				3	3	4	10
TOTAL BENEFIT		4	3	7	7	4	25

Figure 17-8. Initial Process Net Benefit Matrix

This matrix lists information needs along the vertical axis and elementary processes along the horizontal axis. Benefit values appear in individual cells in the body of the matrix. In the last column along the horizontal axis, marked Total, the benefit value of satisfying each information need appears. In the bottom row entitled Total Benefit, the total benefit produced by each elementary process appears. At the intersection of the Total column and the Total Benefit row, the grand total benefit associated with implementing all elementary processes in the business system appears.

Step 2.2 — Estimate Implementation Costs

Next, the analyst calculates the development cost associated with each elementary process. One must consider all components of development cost including personnel costs, the cost of any new hardware required, and the cost of machine time. Since a number of details about these components are still unknown at this point, all estimates reflect the best guess of the analyst.

Some costs may not be directly associated with a single elementary process. One should record these indirect costs for later inclusion in the Business System Net Benefit Matrix, but omit them when evaluating the net benefit of individual elementary processes. For example, if a major piece of hardware benefits an entire business system, one should consider its cost when assessing the worth of the business system as a whole. One should ignore this cost when judging the cost of individual elementary processes.

After estimating the total development cost of each elementary process, one must adjust the results to reflect the portion to be allocated to the selected time period, based on installation accounting standards.

For example, consider an elementary process whose implementation cost is estimated at $5,000. Further, assume that installation accounting standards dictate that the development cost of a system is to be allocated over a five-year period. Finally, assume that the analyst has selected two years as the time period for measuring costs and benefits. The following formula yields allocated development cost:

(DEV COST / ALLOCATION PERIOD) * ASSESSMENT PERIOD

In this example, the portion of the development cost allocated to the selected time period is:

($5000 / 5) * 2

or $2000.

The allocated development cost of each elementary process appears in a single row below the Total Benefit row, as illustrated in Figure 17-9. The cell at the intersection of the Development Cost row and the Total column reflects the total allocated cost of implementing the business area over the selected time period.

INFORMATION NEEDS / ELEMENTARY PROCESSES	CAPTURE_FAILURE_DATA	TRACE_PRODUCT_SUPPLIER	CAPTURE_DELIVERY_DATA	MATCH_WITH_PURCH_ORDR	COMPARE_ORDR/DLVRY_DT	TOTAL
PRODUCT FAILURE BY SUP	4	3	2			9
GOODS DLVRD NOT ORDRD			2	4		6
DLVRY LEAD TIME ANLYSI			3	3	4	10
TOTAL BENEFIT	4	3	7	7	4	25
LESS DEVELOPMENT COST	2	1	3	1	1	8

Figure 17-9. Process Net Benefits Matrix with Development Costs

Step 2.3 — Estimate Operating Costs

Finally, the analyst estimates the cost of operating each elementary process over the selected time period. As with other cost and benefit predictions, this estimate reflects the analyst's best guess of the costs involved, including both ongoing labor costs and machine time costs.

The operating costs for each elementary process over the specified time period appear in the row directly beneath development costs, as shown in Figure 17-10.

INFORMATION NEEDS / ELEMENTARY PROCESSES	CAPTURE_FAILURE_DATA	TRACE_PRODUCT_SUPPLIER	CAPTURE_DELIVERY_DATA	MATCH_WITH_PURCH_ORDR	COMPARE_ORDR/DLVRY_DT	TOTAL
PRODUCT FAILURE BY SUP	4	3	2			9
GOODS DLVRD NOT ORDRD			2	4		6
DLVRY LEAD TIME ANLYSIS			3	3	4	10
TOTAL BENEFIT	4	3	7	7	4	25
LESS DEVELOPMENT COST	2	1	3	1	1	8
LESS OPERATIONAL COST	2	1	2	1	1	8
NET BENEFIT	0	1	2	5	2	9

Figure 17-10. Completed Process Net Benefit Matrix

Below the Operating Costs row is a row entitled Net Benefit. The analyst calculates the values appearing in each cell in the Net Benefit row by subtracting the sum of the values in the Development Cost and Operating Cost columns from the value in the Total Benefit column. This row represents the net benefit of implementing each elementary process in the business area. The intersection of the Net Benefit row and the Total column is the total net benefit of implementing all elementary processes in the business area.

Step 2.4 — Summarize Business System Net Benefit Matrix

At this point, the analyst has calculated the estimated net benefit at two levels: the business area level and the elementary process level. In this step, the analyst calculates the estimated net benefit associated with each business system.

Synthesizing the Business System Net Benefit Matrix is quite simple and requires three steps:

1. Arrange the elementary processes on the Process Net Benefit Matrix into business system clusters (as shown in the Clustered Elementary Process/Entity Type Usage Matrix developed during cluster analysis).

2. Sum all elementary process columns in each business system cluster to form a single column per business system. The result is the Business System Net Benefit Matrix. An example appears in Figure 17-11.

3. Add any indirect costs to be incurred for the business system (most notably, hardware costs) to its development cost (for one-time costs) or operational cost (for costs continuing over the selected time period) as appropriate.

BUSINESS SYSTEMS INFORMATION NEEDS	PRODUCT_DEVELOPMENT	PRODUCT_PLANNING	MATERIAL_ACQUISITION	PRODUCTION_MONITORING	TOTAL
COMPONENT INVENTORY	15				15
POTENTIAL SUPPLIERS	15				15
PRODUCT INVENTORY	50				50
PRODUCT AVAILABILITY		50			50
PRODCTN COST ANALYSIS		40			40
MATERIAL VOLUME RQMTS		30			30
SUPPLIER LEAD TIME ANL			30		30
TARGET VS ACTUAL PROD				90	90
TOTAL	80	120	30	90	320
LESS DEVELOPMENT COST	25	40	20	50	135
LESS OPERATING COST	10	20	15	40	85
NET BENEFIT	45	60	5	0	100

Figure 17-11. Business System Net Benefit Matrix

Step 3 — Assess Weighted Process Benefits

In this step, the analyst weights the benefit realized by each elementary process according to the total value of all information needs to which it contributes. The resulting value helps determine the proper implementation sequence for elementary processes within a business system.

The results of this analysis appear in the Weighted Process Benefits Matrix. Its preparation is very simple, given the completion of cost/benefit analysis steps 1 and 2. The analyst uses the following sub-steps:

1. Starting with the Initial Process Net Benefit Matrix, place the total benefit value of satisfying each information need at its intersection with each elementary process, replacing the allocated benefit value that originally appeared.

2. Calculate the weighted benefit value of each elementary process by summing the columns.

3. Identify the suggested implementation sequence by ordering the elementary processes in descending sequence by value. In other words, elementary processes with a greater weighted benefit are scheduled before elementary processes with a lower weighted benefit.

This approach highlights elementary processes that are prerequisites for multiple information needs. These processes should be implemented first.

Figure 17-12 illustrates a Weighted Process Benefit Matrix based on the Process Net Benefit Matrix in Figure 17-8.

INFORMATION NEEDS	ELEMENTARY PROCESSES	CAPTURE_FAILURE_DATA	TRACE_PRODUCT_SUPPLIER	CAPTURE_DELIVERY_DATA	MATCH_WITH_PURCH_ORDR	COMPARE_ORDR/DLVRY_DT	TOTAL
PRODUCT FAILURE BY SUP		9	9	9			9
GOODS DLVRD NOT ORDRD				6	6		6
DLVRY LEAD TIME ANLYSI				10	10	10	10
TOTAL BENEFIT		9	9	25	16	10	25
SEQUENCE		4	4	1	2	3	■

Figure 17-12. Weighted Process Benefit Matrix

IMPLEMENTATION PLAN CONSTRUCTION

After performing cluster analysis and cost/benefit analysis, the analyst should have produced the following deliverables:

- The Clustered Elementary Process/Entity Type Usage Matrix
- The Process Net Benefit Matrix
- The Business System Net Benefit Matrix
- The Weighted Process Benefit Matrix

In this final task within business system definition, the analyst uses these deliverables to define business systems using the IEF, and build an implementation plan for the business area. To achieve these results, the analyst must follow these steps:

1. Select elementary processes to implement.

2. Verify elementary process clusters, finalize business system boundaries, and define business systems using the IEF.

3. Determine the business system implementation sequence.

4. Determine the elementary process implementation sequence within each business system.

Step 1 — Select Elementary Processes to Implement

In this step, the analyst identifies elementary processes of questionable benefit and, if their implementation cannot be justified, removes them from the implementation plan. The technique for identifying low benefit processes is straightforward and requires the following sub-steps:

1. Review the Process Net Benefit Matrix (see the example in Figure 17-10) and list processes that have a negative net benefit. In the absence of other considerations, this means that the elementary processes cost more than they are worth.

2. Take the list from sub-step 1 and check each elementary process against the Weighted Process Benefit Matrix to point out hidden benefits. An elementary process with a low net benefit and a high weighted benefit may be a prerequisite of many high-benefit processes. In such a case, it might be worthwhile to implement the process to realize its hidden benefits.

    Remove from the list (from sub-step 1) any elementary processes deemed worthy of implementation despite low net benefit.

3. For the remaining questionable elementary processes, review the Clustered Elementary Process/Entity Type Usage Matrix to determine whether failure to implement any of the processes will result in a logical inconsistency. For example, if a low-benefit process creates an entity later referenced by many high-benefit processes, the cost of *not* implementing the process may be greater than the cost of implementing it.

    Remove from the list (from sub-step 2) any elementary processes deemed worthy of implementation to avoid a logical inconsistency. In the absence of other non-technical considerations, one should not implement any remaining elementary processes on the list.

Step 2 — Specify Business Systems to the IEF

Review the Clustered Elementary Process/Entity Type Usage Matrix generated during cluster analysis (see Figure 17-3). Assuming that one has addressed all anomalies and firmly defined all clusters, one can now define business systems to the IEF.

This step requires two component tasks:

1. Give each business system a name. If names have not yet been specified for the business systems discovered during cluster analysis, they must be invented now. There are no firm rules governing the formulation of business system names. Simply choose some collection of words that express the nature of the cluster.

2. For each named business system, select the elementary processes it will implement. Use the Clustered Elementary Process/Entity Type Usage Matrix to identify the elementary processes belonging to each business system, bypassing any that were not selected for implementation. (See step 1 of Implementation Plan Construction.)

The details of specifying business systems to the IEF appear in the *IEF Design Toolset Guide*.

Step 3 — Determine Business System Implementation Sequence

Barring other considerations, one should implement business systems according to their position in the business life cycle. That is, if the procedures in business system B require information captured in business system A, it stands to reason that business system A should be implemented before business system B. One can deduce this ordering, sometimes called the **natural implementation sequence**, from the Clustered Elementary Process/Entity Type Usage Matrix. (See Figure 17-3 for an example.)

Sometimes deviation from this natural sequence becomes necessary. Many non-technical factors, including management and user pressures, the desire to implement higher benefit systems first, and a variety of resource constraints can render the natural sequence impractical. However, any time one deviates from the natural sequence, one runs the risk of introducing logical inconsistencies which, in turn, require additional resources to resolve. Analysts should consider this additional cost, the cost of implementing systems out of their natural order, whenever such a deviation is proposed.

Step 4 — Determine Process Implementation Sequence

Finally, the analyst establishes the sequence in which elementary processes are to be implemented within each business system. In general, one should use the natural implementation sequence (mentioned in step 3) as much as possible. One can determine this sequence from the order in which elementary processes are specified on the Process Dependency Diagram.

In many cases, the natural sequence will be ambiguous because of mutually exclusive and parallel dependencies within the Process Dependency Diagram. One can use the Weighted Process Benefit Matrix to sequence these ambiguous elementary processes by placing those with higher-weighted benefits first.

The implementation sequence of elementary processes within a business system is subject to the same non-technical pressure for deviation as the implementation sequence for business systems themselves. As with business systems, one must address and acknowledge the cost of introducing logical inconsistencies before finalizing the decision to deviate from the natural sequence.

CONCLUSION

This concludes the discussion of business system definition. At this point, the analyst has prepared the way for the next stage of Information Engineering, Business System Design. During this stage, designers detail each business system fully, using the results of Business Area Analysis to describe the business systems that will fulfill the business's needs. Techniques for designing business systems appear in Part III of this guide.

PART III
A GUIDE TO BUSINESS SYSTEM DESIGN USING THE INFORMATION ENGINEERING FACILITY™

18
BUSINESS SYSTEM DESIGN OVERVIEW

This is the first chapter of Part III, which describes the practice of the third stage of Information Engineering, **Business System Design (BSD)**, using the Information Engineering Facility (IEF) from Texas Instruments. During Business System Design, designers use the information discovered during a Business Area Analysis project as the basis for describing an information system that can satisfy the business's needs.

The remainder of this chapter provides an overview of the Business System Design stage of Information Engineering and the support provided by the Information Engineering Facility.

AN OVERVIEW OF BUSINESS SYSTEM DESIGN

Objectives of Business System Design

A **business system** is a collection of procedures, each of which may implement one or more elementary processes defined during Business Area Analysis. An **elementary process** is a detailed definition of *what* must be done to support business activities, while a **procedure** is a detailed definition of *how* it is done.

For example, during Business Area Analysis, the analyst may have discovered a business need to keep track of customers. He or she might have defined an elementary process to support this requirement called Add Customer, in which the analyst specified the rules for adding a new customer. During Business System Design, the designer must address detailed issues like these to implement the process:

- Should customers be added online, or in batch, or both?

- If online, should a terminal operator be allowed to add multiple customers in a single execution?

- What should the screen look like?

- Can Add Customer be combined with other elementary processes (such as Change Customer and Delete Customer) into a single procedure?

The objective of Business System Design, then, is to define the human-to-computer interactions required to perform the business activities identified during Business Area Analysis.

Note that the designer does not consider the details of the operating environment at this point. The operating system, teleprocessing monitor, and data base management system are not relevant until the next stage of Information Engineering, Technical Design.

Tasks Performed During Business System Design

Designers perform the following major tasks to accomplish Business System Design:

1. **Prepare for Business System Design**. During this task, designers assemble the design team, review the results of Business Area Analysis, and establish system standards.

2. **Procedure Definition**. During this task, designers determine what kinds of procedures are required to implement the elementary processes discovered during Business Area Analysis, and use the IEF to transform the processes into procedures.

3. **Dialog Design**. During this task, designers specify the manner in which users will navigate among the various procedures.

4. **Layout Design**. During this task, designers build the external user interface (screens and reports).

5. **Procedure Logic Design**. During this task, designers specify the details of each procedure using the Action Diagramming Tool.

6. **Confirmation**. During this task, designers verify the consistency and completeness of the design.

7. **Technical Design Planning**. During this task, designers consider the approach to the next stage of Information Engineering, Technical Design.

A summarized list of the detailed tasks and subtasks performed during Business System Design is presented in Appendix C.

Automated Tools Available for a BSD Project

The Information Engineering Facility (IEF) from Texas Instruments provides several tools that are useful throughout a BSD project:

- The **Dialog Flow Diagramming Tool** in the IEF Design Toolset is used for procedure definition and dialog design.

- The **Screen Design Tool** in the IEF Design Toolset is used for layout design.

- The **Action Diagramming Tool** in the IEF Design Toolset is used for procedure logic design.

Part III of this guide deals primarily with the Business System Design portion of the Information Engineering methodology, not with a detailed description of the use of the IEF tools. Detailed instructions for using these appear in the *IEF Design Toolset Guide*.

At installations that use operating systems, data base management systems, and teleprocessing monitors supported by the IEF Construction Toolset, designers can use the results of Business System Design directly in the Technical Design and Construction stages. In other cases, designers can collect the plots and reports available from the IEF Design Toolset into a Business System Specification for use in implementing the systems manually.

Some users may experience limited tool usage based on the IEF software version being used. Users should read and thoroughly understand the Release Notes that accompany each version before using the software. These notes clearly document all restrictions applicable to the current version.

19
PREPARING FOR BUSINESS SYSTEM DESIGN

OVERVIEW

This chapter discusses preparations for beginning a Business System Design project. Some preparations are technical while others are not. Regardless, designers should consider all the issues in this chapter before actually beginning design work. These include the following:

- Project team characteristics
- Designer familiarity with Business Area Analysis
- Verifying business system definition
- Setting system standards
- Designing for the Transition stage
- Online help requirements
- Design data requirements

PROJECT TEAM CHARACTERISTICS

The project team for Business System Design should be drawn from two quarters:

- From the systems area, one should choose experienced systems designers. They should be familiar with Information Engineering in general and Business System Design techniques in particular.
- From the user community, one should select representatives who can clearly determine end user needs and help the designers translate those needs into aspects of the design.

In addition, some or all of the users should have participated in the Business Area Analysis project that led to this Business System Design project.

DESIGNER FAMILIARITY WITH BUSINESS AREA

If the members of the design team also participated in the Business Area Analysis project, they will be well acquainted with the characteristics of the business area. However, if the designers are new to the project, one must allocate time for them to review and familiarize themselves with the results of Business Area Analysis. By taking the time to understand the data with which the business deals, the activities the business performs, and the interaction between the two, the designer will develop a clear picture of both the underlying Information Architecture and the user's work environment. A detailed understanding of these two components is essential for all designers on any Business System Design project.

For a review of the concepts, tools, and techniques used during Business Area Analysis, see Part II of this guide.

VERIFYING BUSINESS SYSTEM DEFINITION

During the last major task in BAA, business system definition, analysts identify which elementary processes will be implemented by which business systems during Business System Design. Consequently, when the Business System Design project begins, designers should already know the answers to the following questions:

- What business systems will be created to support the business area?

- For each business system defined, which elementary processes will be implemented?

- What is the recommended implementation sequence for those elementary processes?

At this point, the IEF should provide direct answers to questions 1 and 2. To verify this, one can review the business system definition results using the IEF Analysis Toolset. (See the *IEF Analysis Toolset Guide* for a complete description of this toolset.) The Implementation Plan developed during business system definition should answer the last question.

If this information is not available, the business system definition task in Business Area Analysis was not properly completed. If this is the case, one must address the situation before beginning any work in Business System Design. Part II of this guide describes the task of establishing business system boundaries based on the results of Business Area Analysis.

SETTING SYSTEM STANDARDS

One aim of Business System Design is to create a consistent user interface to the system being constructed. This is especially important in an online environment where ambiguity can lead a user to make serious mistakes.

Before a Business System Design project begins, the IEF allows the designer to specify a number of system standards through System Defaults panels, available in the IEF Design Toolset. One can establish other standards using individual tools in the toolsets. These standards relate to the following:

- **Commands**. A command provides a way for a user to direct the execution of an implemented procedure. Commands should be consistent across the system so that users are comfortable in their choice of commands, regardless of the procedure being executed.

  For example, one designer might choose the command D to mean DISPLAY while another chooses D to mean DELETE. Such ambiguity can have serious consequences. For this reason, it is wise to maintain a list of standard commands from which designers may choose.

  One may also specify standard synonyms for commands. For example, the primary command MODIFY can be assigned the synonym M to reduce the number of keystrokes required to invoke it. Whether the user enters M or MODIFY, the logic associated with the command MODIFY will execute.

  More about commands appears in Chapter 20, "Procedure Definition. "

- **Function Keys**. Function keys (sometimes referred to as PF keys) are available on many types of video display terminals. Designers use them to provide a shorthand way for users to communicate commands to procedures in an online environment. For example, a designer can specify that pressing function key 1 will have the same effect as entering the command ADD.

  If a function key represents a particular command, it should represent that same command in all procedures that use it. For example, if function key 1 invokes the command CHANGE in one procedure and function key 10 invokes it in another, this will result in user confusion and error.

  In some cases, one may wish to identify a function key as a **standard** throughout the system. (For example, no matter which procedure is being executed, function key 1 means HELP.) A designer *cannot* override a standard function key. In other cases, one may wish to identify a function key as a **default**, which allows a designer to override it. (For example, procedures that support a DISPLAY command must all use function key 4 for DISPLAY, but a procedure with no DISPLAY capability can use function key 4 to represent some other command.)

The IEF supports the maintenance of both standard and default function keys across the system.

- **Display Properties**. Standards for the use of highlighting and onscreen color are important. All data entry fields should be one color or intensity, prompts and literals another, and fields in error yet another.

- **Edit Patterns**. Edit patterns dictate the output format of a field on a screen or report. The use of consistent edit patterns for fields containing the same information is usually desirable. In a system with part numbers, for example, one designer might cause a part number to be displayed as "123456789, " while another might format it as "12-34567/89. " Such inconsistency could lead to user confusion.

  The IEF supports the maintenance of standard edit patterns to help enforce consistency throughout a system.

- **Screen Formats**. The general format of screens should remain consistent throughout a system. For example, error messages should appear at the same place on each screen, and users should enter commands at the same place on each screen.

  The IEF accomplishes this standardization by establishing screen design templates. Chapter 22, "Layout Design, " describes templates in detail.

- **Field Prompts**. A prompt is a label for a variable field appearing on a screen or report. Where possible, the use of common prompts for fields implementing the same attribute is desirable. For example, if the attribute Customer Number appears on two screens, a user will have a better chance of recognizing it as the same value on both screens if a consistent label is used (such as "CUSTOMER NUMBER:") rather than two different ones (such as "CLIENT NUM:" on one and "CUST NO:" on the other).

  The IEF supports the standardization of prompts by reminding the designer of all previous prompts used to describe a particular attribute. This assistance takes place whenever the designer places a field using the Screen Design tool.

- **Common Exit State Definitions**. Exit State is an IEF special attribute used to describe the outcome of a process or procedure. During Business System Design it can be associated with a message that appears on the screen. It is generally wise to establish standard exit state definitions for outcomes common to many procedures, most notably successful outcomes (for example, REQUESTED OPERATION COMPLETE) and outcomes reflecting an invalid value entered for the Command special attribute (for example, INVALID COMMAND).

  It is interesting to note that exit state definitions are shared across all of the business systems and business areas defined in a single model.

- **Clear Screen Input Delimiters**. Permissible parameter and string delimiters for clear screen input to a procedure must be established if any of the procedures in the business system are to use clear screen input. Clear screen input is discussed in Chapter 22.

DESIGNING FOR TRANSITION

In Information Engineering, designers move a newly constructed system into production during the Transition stage. Although Transition is still three stages away at this point, one should consider the strategy for making the transition during Business System Design.

When considering transition, the following issues are critical:

- **Loading new data bases**. How will the newly implemented entities be initially populated? Manually, or through a conversion program? All at once, or portions at a time?

- **Replacing old systems with new**. What technique will be used to phase in the newly implemented system while the old ones phase out? Will the new system cut over overnight or will the old and new systems run in parallel? Will the new system be implemented all at once or a portion at a time? Will duplicate maintenance be required to synchronize the old and new data bases? Will such duplicate maintenance be handled dynamically, or will synchronization transactions be batched?

The answers to these questions are largely installation- dependent, but the intent here is to fire the imagination to consider Transition-stage issues. This consideration may yield a requirement for some special procedures to be designed for Transition, or may point out some special Transition-stage logic to be addressed during BSD procedure logic design. In any event, identifying and addressing Transition stage issues at this point helps the designer avoid unpleasant surprises downstream.

ONLINE HELP REQUIREMENTS

The term **help,** when used in the context of an online system, refers to system documentation directly accessible from the terminal. An online help system is useful to both infrequent users who need constant assistance in performing normal operations, and frequent users who attempt unusual operations. One should consider the inclusion of online help before starting Business System Design.

At installations with an online help system already in place, one should investigate whether the business system can be designed to interface to it. If such a facility is unavailable, one should consider the possibility of constructing procedures that display help information as part of the Business System Design project.

Regardless of the decision, designers should address the issue of online help requirements before designing their procedures.

DESIGN DATA REQUIREMENTS

Designers perform no refinement to the data model during Business System Design. In the IEF implementation of Information Engineering, the IEF automatically transforms the conceptual data model, expressed as an Entity Relationship Diagram during Business Area Analysis, into a Data Base Definition in the Technical Design stage.

However, when addressing implementation issues, the designer may need to use the conceptual model in different ways than the analyst foresaw or, in some cases, to invent data needed in a particular implementation. The IEF provides four techniques for the designer to satisfy data requirements identified during Business System Design:

- **Special Attributes**. These IEF system-supplied variables can be used to communicate with the execution environment. Examples include Current Date, Error Message, and Transaction Code. The appendix "Special Attributes" lists the special attributes available to the designer. Individual special attributes are explained as needed in the text of later chapters.

- **Local Views**. The concept of local views is not new in Business System Design. Local information views are available during Business Area Analysis, but tend to be used very infrequently.

  A local data view is a view of an entity type, and some or all of its attributes, in which one can temporarily store and check attribute values. Unlike import and export data views, a local view can neither receive data from nor present data to screens or calling Procedure Action Blocks (except in the context of a USE statement). A local view cannot be used to communicate with the underlying data model as can entity action views. The sole purpose of a local data view is to temporarily store attribute values.

For example, consider the task of locating, among all products known to the business, the product with the highest price under $100. A local view of PRODUCT can be used to this end. As each PRODUCT is read (into an entity action view), its price is compared with that in the local view. If the price in the entity action view is higher, it replaces the price in the local view. Of course, neither import nor export views could have been used in this instance: import views cannot be modified and export views cannot be tested.

As in Business Area Analysis, local data views tend to be used infrequently during Business System Design. However, they are useful on occasion and, thus, worth mentioning here.

- **Work Attribute Set**. Often, one cannot satisfy an implementation-specific data requirement by creating a new view of an item already known in the data model. In these instances, one must define a new data item. These data items are not entity types because they do not reflect the reality of the business. However, they can be thought of as "pseudo-entity types" because they are composed of attribute definitions. These pseudo-entity types are called **work attribute sets**.

Designers generally use work attribute sets to keep track of execution time information like totals and counts. Work attribute sets work like entity types in many ways. They can appear in import, export, and local views. They can be placed on screens. They can be passed by a USE action in an action diagram. However, no entity actions (CREATE, READ, UPDATE, and DELETE) are available for work attributes, so they can never find their way to a data base.

- **Design Entity Types**. In some cases, there is a real requirement to store implementation-specific data discovered during Business System Design. When this happens, and the requirement is clearly not related to the business itself, one may define a design entity type.

The IEF does not support the creation of design entity types as distinct from analysis entity types. Thus, any design entity type must be added to the Entity Relationship Diagram built in Business Area Analysis.

The designer might require design entity types in the following instances:

— To maintain security information for the business system (such as user IDs and passwords)

— To maintain quality and productivity statistics for users of the business system (such as error rates of high volume procedures and keystrokes per hour)

— To maintain information specific to a particular implementation technique (such as job accounting information and printer IDs by user)

20
PROCEDURE DEFINITION

OVERVIEW

This chapter describes how procedures are defined during Business System Design. It includes the following major sections:

- **Categories of Procedure**. This section distinguishes between process-implementing and designer-added procedures and between online procedures and batch procedures.

- **The Purpose of Commands**. This section defines the special attribute Command and explains its relationship to procedures.

- **Building Process-Implementing Procedures**. This section describes process to procedure transformation.

- **Building Designer-Added Procedures**. This section presents the rationale and techniques for creating non-process-oriented procedures.

- **Procedures and Procedure Steps**. This section defines procedure steps and gives detailed guidelines for implementing a procedure in multiple steps.

CATEGORIES OF PROCEDURE

In Business Area Analysis, one describes business requirements in terms of *processes*. During Business System Design, one describes the method by which each elementary process is carried out in terms of *procedures*.

Part II of this guide describes elementary processes in detail. In Business System Design, the important point to recall is that elementary processes are the objects for which Process Action Diagrams are built.

During Business System Design, one describes all activities in terms of procedures and components of procedures. A **procedure**, then, is a precise set of instructions that facilitates completion of one or more specific processes.

Although all procedures support the execution of elementary processes in some way, one may consider them in two broad categories based on their level of support:

- **Process-implementing procedures** directly implement elementary processes defined during Business Area Analysis. For example, one may directly implement an elementary process that describes the adding of an order using the online procedure Take Order.

  Process-implementing procedures generally USE action blocks built to support elementary processes during Business Area Analysis.

- **Designer-added procedures** are implementation-specific activities that improve or simplify some characteristics of the overall implementation. For example, the designer might add a Menu procedure to allow users to select between multiple process-implementing procedures.

  Designer-added procedures are specified during Business System Design.

The majority of procedures defined during Business System Design are process-implementing procedures.

Another way to categorize procedures is based on whether they will be executed **online** or in **batch**.

- **Online procedures** execute under the control of a teleprocessing monitor (for example, IMS/DC, CICS or TSO in an IBM/MVS environment) and interact with the user by means of screens presented on a display terminal.

- **Batch procedures,** on the other hand, execute with no interaction with the user under the control of the operating system (for example, as a batch job under JES in an IBM/MVS environment).

  Although the IEF provides full support for most batch processing needs, it does **not** support sequential file processing or report creation. Sequential file access must be accomplished through external action blocks, and the reports are generated either through a user-written program or a purchased reporting package.

THE PURPOSE OF COMMANDS

Command is a special attribute in the IEF implementation of Information Engineering. It allows the designer to specify a means for users to influence procedure execution. This special attribute is defined here because the concept of a command is important to the discussion of procedure definition, which follows.

In an online environment, the designer can place a command field on a screen. At execution time, a user can enter a value into this command field to cause a procedure to behave differently. For example, consider a procedure called Maintain Customer that implements three elementary processes: Add Customer, Change Customer, and Delete Customer. If the procedure is specified properly, the user can select among the three elementary processes at execution time by placing the appropriate value in the command field.

The special attribute Command is used in several places during Business System Design. The designer can place it on a screen, set or interrogate it in a Procedure Action Diagram, and send it along a dialog flow on the Dialog Flow Diagram. One can define synonyms for a Command and associate it with a function key.

Possible values for Command should be standardized across the system (see Chapter 19).

It is important to note that the IEF Dialog Manager (the execution-time component that governs procedure execution) reserves several commands for its own use. The user should be aware of these and use them appropriately.

The following command values receive special attention from the Dialog Manager:

HELP   Causes the Dialog Manager to invoke its HELP exit. See the *IEF Construction Toolset Guide* for details.

RESET   Causes the Dialog Manager to go back to the initial screen for the business system.

RESTART   Causes the Dialog Manager to redisplay the last screen the user displayed for the business system.

NEXT   For a procedure step using the automatic scrolling feature (see Chapter 22), causes the Dialog Manager to scroll forward based on the value of the Scroll Amt special attribute. If, however, NEXT is requested after the last occurrence of a repeating group has been displayed, the NEXT action is passed to the Procedure Action Diagram (see Chapter 23). For a procedure step not using the automatic scrolling feature, NEXT has no special meaning.

PREV	For a procedure step using the automatic scrolling feature (see Chapter 22), causes the Dialog Manager to scroll backward based on the value of the Scroll Amt special attribute. If, however, PREV is requested after the last occurrence of a repeating group has been displayed, the PREV action is passed to the Procedure Action Diagram (see Chapter 23). For a procedure step not using the automatic scrolling feature, PREV has no special meaning.
TOP	For a procedure step using the automatic scrolling feature (see Chapter 22), causes the Dialog Manager to scroll to the first item of the repeating group. For a procedure step not using the automatic scrolling feature, TOP has no special meaning.
BOTTOM	For a procedure step using the automatic scrolling feature (see Chapter 22), causes the Dialog Manager to scroll to the last item of the repeating group. For a procedure step not using the automatic scrolling feature, BOTTOM has no special meaning.

BUILDING PROCESS-IMPLEMENTING PROCEDURES

The purpose of a process-implementing procedure is to implement directly one or more elementary processes specified during Business Area Analysis. The technique for converting the analysis-stage objects into design-stage objects is called **transformation**. Any elementary process that has been fully defined can be transformed into a procedure.

The IEF software automatically performs transformation. This section describes the principles, techniques, and results of transformation.

Important Terms

The following discussion relies on a precise understanding of several terms, some from Business Area Analysis and some new to Business System Design. The terms are:

Elementary Process	The smallest unit of activity of meaning to a user which, when complete, leaves the business in a self-consistent state. The elementary process is the object for which Process Action Diagrams are defined.
Process Action Diagram	An ordered collection of actions that defines an elementary process.
Procedure	A method by which one or more elementary processes is carried out using a specific implementation technique. In a batch environment, a procedure is implemented as a single batch job.
Procedure Step	A useful subdivision of a procedure that performs a discrete and definable amount of processing necessary to complete a procedure. Each procedure contains at least one procedure step. Many procedures have only one step; these are called single-step procedures. Although it is not immediately apparent when looking at the Dialog Flow Diagram, the procedure step (*not* the procedure) is the object for which a Procedure Action Diagram and a screen are defined.
	In an online procedure, a procedure step is roughly equivalent to a single online transaction definition with a single screen. In a batch procedure, a procedure step is implemented as a single job step.

Procedure   An ordered collection of actions that defines a procedure step.
Action
Diagram

Action Block   Any named, ordered collection of actions. Process and Procedure Action Diagrams are special cases of action blocks. During Business System Design, all process action diagrams and other action blocks built using the Action Diagramming Tool during Business Area Analysis are available to the designer as action blocks.

The relationship between processes and procedures is many-to-many (see Figure 20-1). This means that each elementary process can be implemented by more than one procedure and each procedure can implement more than one elementary process.

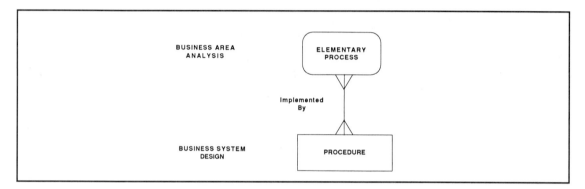

Figure 20-1. Relationship Between Processes and Procedures

Typically, one procedure implements one elementary process, as in Figure 20-2. This case, the one-to-one case, is the easiest to implement because it requires less complex logic and is simpler to maintain.

Figure 20-2. One-to-One Process Implementation

In some cases, however, other arrangements are necessary. For example, consider the case in which a single elementary process named Take Order is executed by two groups of users. One group, the *expert* group, takes orders day in and day out. To satisfy their needs, a single procedure must be able to take many orders. The other group, a *casual* group, takes orders only occasionally and so needs more reference material on the screen. To satisfy their needs, a single procedure must take only one order.

In both cases, the elementary process Take Order is being implemented. Only the details of *how* Take Order is implemented vary. In this instance, one elementary process is implemented in multiple procedures (see Figure 20-3). This is known as the one-to-many case.

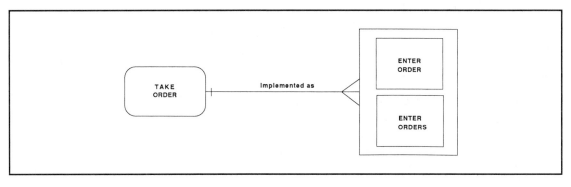

Figure 20-3. One-to-Many Process Implementation

In other cases, a single procedure implements several elementary processes, as in Figure 20-4. In this example, three separate elementary processes have been implemented by the same procedure. This is possible if two conditions are met:

- The information required by the elementary processes is very similar. (In Figure 20-4, all three elementary processes probably require Customer Details.)

- The same set of users performs all of the elementary processes under consideration. In other words, if one person is responsible for all phases of Customer Maintenance, the arrangement depicted in Figure 20-4 is acceptable. However, if different people are responsible for adding, changing, and deleting customers, the three processes should be implemented separately.

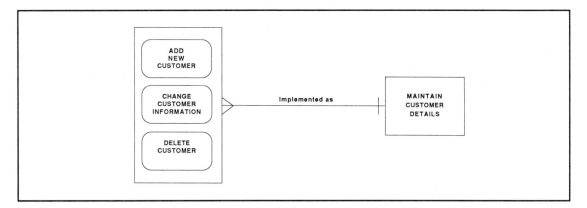

Figure 20-4. Many-to-One Process Implementation

One can summarize the criteria for determining process-to-procedure relationships as follows:

- **One-to-one** is easiest to implement. It is the typical situation.

- **One-to-many** is used for alternative implementations of the same elementary process.

- **Many-to-one** is used when multiple elementary processes have similar information views and are required by a common set of users.

- **Many-to-many** is a combination of the one-to-many and many-to-one cases.

Transformation Overview

Given this background information, one can now consider the steps that take place during the transformation process. The designer initiates this process and the IEF completes it. The designer initiates transformation for a procedure by following these steps:

1. Add a procedure using the IEF Dialog Flow Diagram.
2. Select the elementary processes to be implemented by the procedure from the list of processes available for implementation in the Business System. This list is the result of the business system definition task, which took place at the conclusion of Business Area Analysis.

The details of performing these steps are described in the *IEF Design Toolset Guide*.

When the designer finishes selecting the processes to be implemented, the IEF completes transformation by performing the following functions:

1. Ensures that all of the elementary processes selected are consistent.
2. Asks the designer to select commands from the command list, each of which will invoke one of the processes implemented in the procedure.
3. Synthesizes a Procedure Action Diagram that USEs the process action diagrams being implemented in the procedure. Logic is included to switch between the processes based on the value of the command associated with each process in step 2.
4. Synthesizes a set of data views for the Procedure Action Diagram based on the combined views of all elementary processes implemented.

Figure 20-5 illustrates these functions. The lower portion of the diagram shows Business Area Analysis objects, where EP1 and EP2 are elementary processes, IV1 and IV2 are information views being imported by those elementary processes, and EV1 and EV2 are information views exported from those elementary processes.

The upper portion of the figure shows Business System Design objects. PROCEDURE STEP 1 is automatically generated and includes USE actions for EP1 and EP2 as well as logic to select between them based on the value of the Command special attribute. IV1+IV2 is a composite import data view synthesized by merging IV1 and IV2, and EV1+EV2 is a composite export data view synthesized by merging EV1 and EV2.

Note that even in the case of a one-to-one process to procedure relationship, the IEF creates a Procedure Action Diagram, even though the diagram implements only one process.

The Products of Transformation

The next few figures represent an actual transformation example performed by the IEF. Familiarity with the concepts and syntax of action diagramming is helpful in understanding these figures. This information is available in Part II and Appendix D.

Figures 20-6 and 20-7 represent the Process Action Diagram and information views for the elementary process Add New Customer. Figures 20-8 and 20-9 represent the Process Action Diagram and information views for the elementary process Delete Customer. Although both elementary processes use views of the entity type CUSTOMER exclusively, note some of the differences between the import and export information views:

•   The import view to Add New Customer (Figure 20-7), called Candidate Customer, has no attribute view for the attribute Number. This is because the process must calculate the Number automatically whenever it creates a new customer. (See the SET ... USING action in Figure 20-6.)

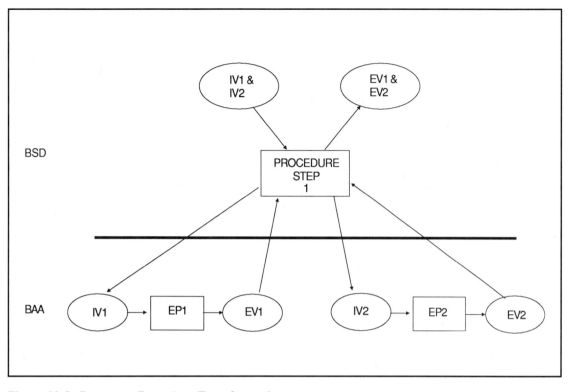

Figure 20-5. Process to Procedure Transformation

The import view to Delete Customer (Figure 20-9), also called Candidate Customer, has as its only attribute view a view of Number.

- Likewise, the export view from Add New Customer, called Newly Added Customer, contains only Number, while the export view from Delete Customer, called Deleted Customer, contains only a view of Name.

Given these two elementary processes, assume that the designer wishes to implement them in a single procedure called Maintain Customer. The designer must:

1. Add a procedure called Maintain Customer to the Dialog Flow Diagram.
2. Select the elementary processes Add New Customer and Delete Customer for implementation by the procedure Maintain Customer.

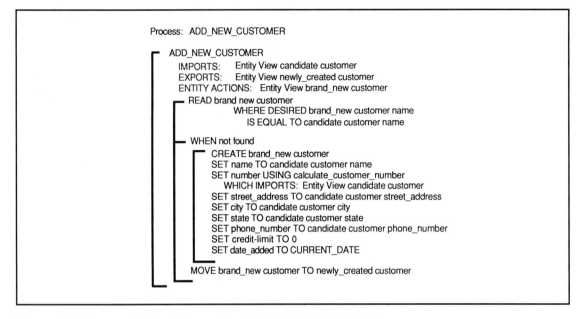

Figure 20-6. Process Action Diagram for ADD NEW CUSTOMER

Process   ADD_NEW_CUSTOMER

Import Views
      View CANDIDATE of entity CUSTOMER
            Attributes:
                        NAME
                        STREET_ADDRESS
                        CITY
                        STATE
                        PHONE_NUMBER
                        CREDIT_LIMIT
                        DATE_ADDED

Export Views
      View NEWLY_CREATED of entity CUSTOMER
            Attributes:
                        NUMBER

Local Views

Entity Action Views
      View BRAND_NEW of entity CUSTOMER
            Attributes:
                        NAME
                        NUMBER
                        STREET_ADDRESS
                        CITY
                        STATE
                        PHONE_NUMBER
                        CREDIT_LIMIT
                        DATE_ADDED

Figure 20-7. Information Views for ADD NEW CUSTOMER

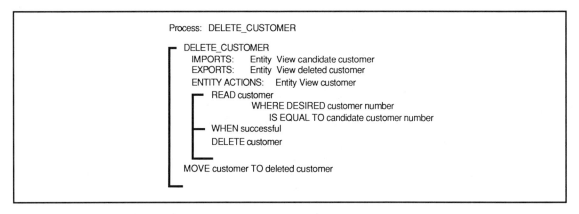

Figure 20-8. Process Action Diagram for DELETE CUSTOMER

Process: DELETE_CUSTOMER

Import Views
    View CANDIDATE of entity CUSTOMER
        Attributes:
            NUMBER

Export Views
    View DELETED of entity CUSTOMER
        Attributes:
            NAME

Local Views

Entity Action Views
    View of entity CUSTOMER
        Attributes:
            NAME
            NUMBER

Figure 20-9. Information Views for DELETE CUSTOMER

When this task is complete, the IEF will perform the remainder of transformation as follows:

1. Checks Add New Customer and Delete Customer for consistency.

2. Requests the designer to choose command values to select between Add New Customer and Delete Customer when the procedure executes. Assume that the designer selects the command value "add" to invoke Add New Customer and "delete" to invoke Delete Customer.

3. Synthesizes a Procedure Action Diagram which USEs the processes selected for implementation.

    Figure 20-10 is the IEF-generated Procedure Action Diagram that supports the procedure Maintain Customer. Note that a CASE construct has been created to allow switching between the Process Action Diagrams Delete Customer and Add New Customer based on the values of the special attribute Command chosen by the designer during step 2.

4. Synthesizes a set of data views by combining the views of Add Customer and Delete Customer.

    Figure 20-11 is the IEF-generated data view set for the Maintain Customer procedure. Note that the import view, called Import Customer, contains the combined list of attributes from the import views of Add New Customer and Delete Customer. Likewise, the export view, called Export Customer, contains the combined list of attributes from the export views of Add New Customer and Delete Customer.

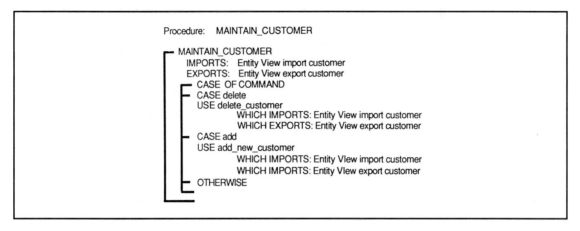

Figure 20-10. Synthesized Procedure Action Diagram for Procedure MAINTAIN CUSTOMER

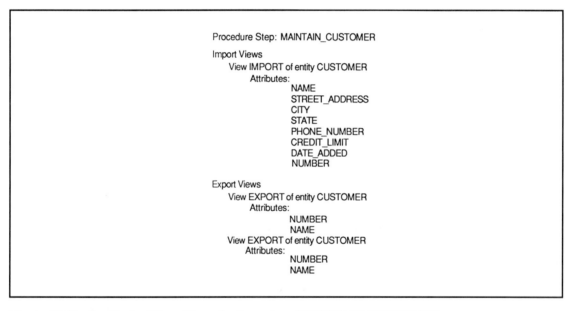

Figure 20-11. Synthesized Data Views for Procedure MAINTAIN CUSTOMER

The USE statements in the Procedure Action Diagram (Figure 20-10) will cause the appropriate subset of the total information view for the procedure to be transmitted from Maintain Customer to either Add New Customer or Delete Customer, depending on the value in the special attribute Command, when the procedure executes.

BUILDING DESIGNER-ADDED PROCEDURES

Designer-added procedures are implementation-specific procedures that improve or simplify some characteristics of the overall implementation. The designer must take care when creating a designer-added procedure to avoid altering the results of Business Area Analysis.

The classic example of a designer-added procedure is a Menu procedure in an online environment. A Menu procedure typically gives the user a way to navigate among the process-implementing procedures in the business system. For example, the Menu screen in Figure 20-12 allows selection among three procedures, each of which implements an elementary process. The Menu procedure that supports the screen has no direct relevance to the business, so a business area analyst would not have identified it. In this case, however, the designer has added the procedure simply to improve the system flow.

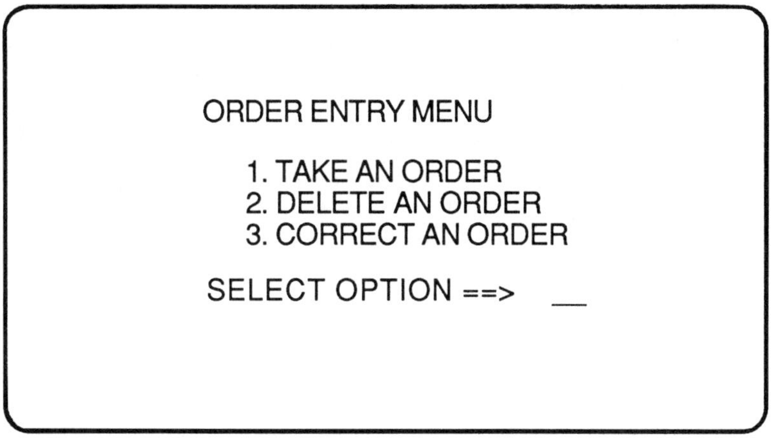

```
ORDER ENTRY MENU

    1. TAKE AN ORDER
    2. DELETE AN ORDER
    3. CORRECT AN ORDER

SELECT OPTION ==>    __
```

Figure 20-12. A Screen Supported by a MENU Procedure

Many times, a designer is tempted to add a procedure that does not implement an elementary process, but is still relevant to the business rather than to the system. One must resist this temptation. The urge to create such a designer-added procedure indicates that the results of Business Area Analysis are incomplete, and the fault must be remedied there. In particular, a designer-added procedure should never perform CREATE, UPDATE or DELETE actions on entity types identified during Business Area Analysis.

PROCEDURES AND PROCEDURE STEPS

A definition of procedure step appeared earlier in this chapter along with the following comment:

> Note that each procedure contains at least one procedure step. Many procedures have only one step; these are called single-step procedures. Although it is not immediately apparent when looking at the Dialog Flow Diagram, the procedure step (*not* the procedure) is the object for which a Procedure Action Diagram and a screen are defined.

This comment requires clarification. Since most procedures are single-step procedures, the existence of procedure steps is sometimes not obvious to the designer. On the Dialog Flow Diagram, where procedures and procedure steps both appear, procedure steps are not actually drawn on the diagram unless more than one is required to support the parent procedure.

The meaning of the terms "procedure" and "procedure step" differ slightly based on whether the procedure is defined as online or batch.

Online Procedures and Procedure Steps

Each online process-implementing procedure is responsible for implementing complete elementary processes. An online procedure step is the portion of a procedure associated with one screen and one procedure Action Diagram. It follows that any procedure that requires multiple screens to support the elementary processes it implements requires a procedure step for each screen.

Consider the example in Figure 20-13. It shows a single procedure called Enter Order Details. Assume that this procedure implements an elementary process called Take Order. The designer determines that the user should visit two screens when taking an order: one to enter the base order information and another to enter order line items. As a result, two procedure steps (Enter Order Header Details and Enter Order Line Details) are created to support the Enter Order Details procedure.

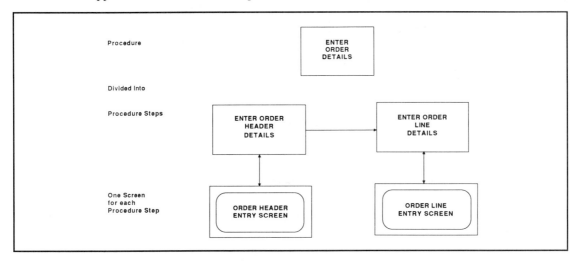

Figure 20-13. A Procedure with Two Procedure Steps

Whenever possible, designers should implement online procedures in a single procedure step. As described in Chapter 23, multi-step procedures are much more difficult to develop and maintain than single-step ones. Since the result of process-to-procedure transformation is always a single-step procedure, splitting the results into multiple steps is largely a manual process.

However, multi-step procedures are difficult to avoid when one of the following conditions occurs:

• The contents of the procedure's data views are too large to fit on a single screen.

• Implementing the procedure in one procedure step is awkward and might lead to user confusion.

In either case, one must manipulate the action blocks developed during Business Area Analysis carefully to ensure that the business requirement for the elementary process being implemented is not compromised. The IEF does not automatically maintain the integrity of the elementary process once a procedure is divided into procedure steps.

To ensure the integrity of the business across multiple procedure steps, **it is strongly recommended that all entity actions that will cause data base modifications (that is, CREATE, UPDATE, and DELETE) be executed in the final procedure step.** In this way, interruption of a procedure between procedure steps will not leave the business in an inconsistent state. An example of a procedure implemented in this way appears in Chapter 23.

Batch Procedures and Procedure Steps

As mentioned earlier, batch procedures are implemented as **jobs** while batch procedure steps are implemented as **job steps.** As a result, the issues associated with parceling a procedure into multiple procedure steps are somewhat different.

Since batch procedure steps have no screens, the case where the procedure's data views are too large to fit on a single screen does not apply. Likewise, since there is no interaction with a user, the notion that a procedure be split into steps to reduce confusion does not hold.

As a result, most batch procedure steps which deal with elementary processes at all implement at least an entire elementary process (and maybe multiple ones). The only reason, then, for defining multi-step batch procedures is to arbitrarily combine different process-implementing procedure steps together so that they execute as a single batch job for the sake of convenience.

21
DIALOG DESIGN

OVERVIEW

The term **dialog** refers to the movement, or flow, between procedures and procedure steps. In an online environment in particular, successful implementation often depends on allowing the user quick and easy access to relevant information. The essence of good dialog design is to define paths between procedures that support flexible navigation but are simple enough not to intimidate the user community.

This chapter includes the following major sections:

- **Online Dialog Design.** This section describes the techniques for designing an online dialog and representing it using the Dialog Flow Diagram.

- **Batch Dialog Design.** This section describes the use of the Dialog Flow Diagram in specifying batch procedures.

ONLINE DIALOG DESIGN

The section includes the following subsections:

- **Principles of Online Dialog Design.** This subsection introduces the terms used in dialog design and presents general guidelines for online conversations.

- **Flow Definition Using the Dialog Flow Diagram**. This subsection describes the details of defining a dialog flow. It explains the symbols used in the Dialog Flow Diagram, types of dialog flow, the conditions for initiating flows, types of flow actions, the use of commands to initiate flows, the properties of flows, and the techniques for passing data between procedures through a dialog flow.

Principles of Online Dialog Design

A dialog describes the movement, or flow, between procedures and procedure steps within a business system. In an online environment, a dialog defines the possible series of interactions between a user and the procedures in the business system through screens.

Dialog Interactions

An **interaction** in a dialog refers to a single instance in which a user requests an action of the system and the system responds. Figure 21-1 illustrates a very simple interaction that begins with a terminal operator entering data on the starting screen. When the operator indicates that data entry is complete, the system responds by processing the data according to the procedure definition. When processing is complete, the result screen is returned to the terminal operator.

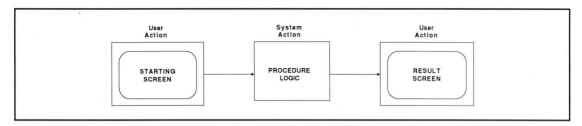

Figure 21-1. A View of a Simple Interaction

Figure 21-2 is a view of a slightly more complex interaction. In this interaction, the processing of data by the procedure definition results in either the return of the result screen to the operator (Result Screen 1) or the invocation of a second procedure (Procedure 2) that produces a different result screen (Result Screen 2).

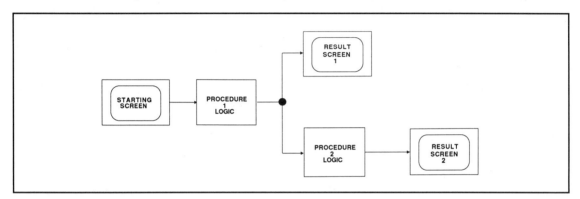

Figure 21-2. A View of a Slightly Complex Dialog

Although neither of these examples is very difficult in itself, both point out two important characteristics of the interactions that comprise dialogs:

- From the user's perspective, an interaction involves two components:

  — The user enters data on a screen.

  — The system acts and responds with another screen. The screen may be in the same format as the one on which data was entered, or it may be in a completely different format.

  After the system responds, the user may be motivated by the response to begin the cycle anew by entering more data.

- From the designer's perspective, an interaction involves an indeterminate number of components. Remember that the procedure step is the unit at which a screen is defined (see Chapter 20). Thus, the designer must add a flow to a separate procedure step whenever the system response must appear on a differently formatted screen from the one used to enter data. Viewed from the designer's perspective:

  — The user enters data.

  — The system acts by initiating a procedure step to process the data. If the user's request is satisfied, the system responds with a result screen in the same format as that on which the user originally entered data.

Otherwise:

— Another procedure step is initiated to process the results of the preceding procedure step's execution. If the user's request is satisfied, the system responds with a result screen in a different format from that on which the user originally entered data.

Otherwise:

— Repeat the previous step until the user's request is satisfied.

The slightly complex interaction in Figure 21-2 brings to light a whole class of more complex interactions that may be useful in a dialog.

Factors Influencing Dialog Design

Given that the design of an online dialog must comprehend all possible interactions the user community might have with the business system, one must consider certain characteristics of the intended users. In particular, the following factors will greatly influence the final appearance of the dialog:

- The degree of volatility in the work environment
- The user's role in the business
- The frequency of the dialog's use

Volatility of the Work Environment

Work environments fall into two broad categories based on their degree of volatility:

- **Constant**, in which deviation from a predictable, established pattern of work is unlikely.
- **Dynamic**, in which the work pattern is so variable that a sequence of operations is unlikely to be repeated frequently.

For example, a job that involves tabulating the results of questionnaires day in and day out tends to be constant. A customer service job, in which the work flow can be dramatically affected by a phone call, is dynamic.

The dialogs designed to support a particular work environment must reflect its degree of volatility. A constant work environment requires a highly structured dialog in which the system guides the user through the work pattern. A dynamic work environment requires a loosely structured dialog in which the user directs the system based on shifting priorities.

A highly structured dialog tends to exhibit the following characteristics:

- It allows the user limited control because the system determines the sequence of actions.
- It uses few menus.

A loosely structured dialog, on the other hand, has the following attributes:

- It allows the user great flexibility in switching between procedures because the sequence of actions is largely unpredictable.
- It may use a number of menus to simplify navigation among procedures.
- It may use function keys and short command synonyms (usually single characters) to provide quick access to many procedures.

User Roles

One must also consider the position and responsibilities of individuals using dialogs. The dialog design may vary based on a user's job function, level of authority, or frequency of use of a particular procedure.

Figure 21-3 illustrates how a difference in job function can result in different dialogs. The menu used by a data entry clerk (left) identifies the type of work the clerk performs. Since supervisors in the data entry department have broader responsibilities, their menu (right) supports additional functions as well as access to the same data entry functions as the clerks they supervise.

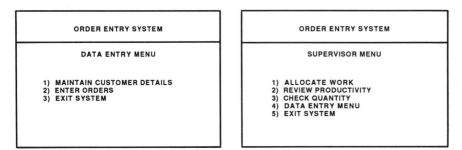

Figure 21-3. Dialog Variation Based on Job Function

Figure 21-4 shows how two users with different levels of authority might require different responses based on a common request. In this example, the response to a request for employee details by an employee's peer is less revealing than the response to the same request made by his supervisor.

Frequency of Use

Finally, a difference in frequency of use can affect a dialog. The frequent user of a system, after becoming familiar with the system's operation, wants to complete each task with the fewest interactions possible. This results in fewer screens, more data packed onto those screens, and less help offered by the system. The infrequent user, however, needs a great deal more assistance from the system to complete the same task as the frequent user. As a result, the infrequent user will not object to a greater number of interactions.

Figure 21-5 illustrates two separate sets of interactions that implement the same elementary process (Take Order) using a different dialog design and different procedures to accommodate frequent and infrequent users.

Command and Function Key Considerations

In addition to the factors mentioned above, two other noteworthy guidelines have a bearing on dialog design:

• The use of commands to initiate dialog flows, and

• The appropriate use of function keys.

When designing dialogs, particularly loosely structured ones, a number of cases arise in which a command is required merely to initiate a dialog flow. In these cases, the designer should adopt some standard so that users can easily distinguish between commands that cause real work to be done (such as adding a customer, cancelling an order, or displaying a report) and those that merely invoke another procedure.

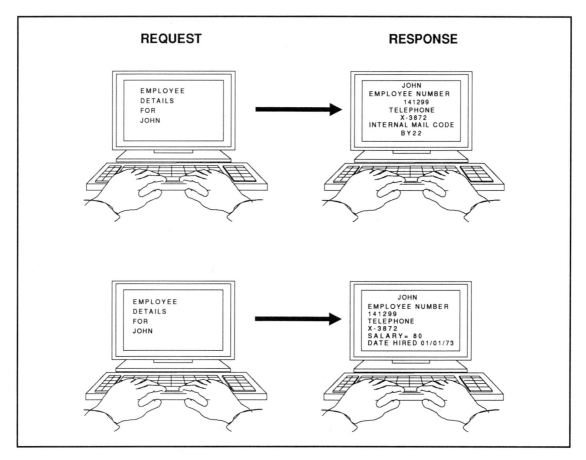

Figure 21-4. Dialog Variation Based on Level of Authority

One example of such a standard is the prefixing of all flow-oriented commands with an X. For example, ADD, CANCEL, and DISPLAY are appropriate for adding customers, cancelling orders, and displaying reports. The commands XADD, XCANCEL, and XMENU can mean "transfer to the Add Customer procedure," "transfer to the Cancel Order procedure," and "transfer to the MENU procedure," respectively. This distinction minimizes user confusion.

Chapter 19 discussed the use of standard function keys. All commands for a procedure step should be accessible by function key, provided that the standard function keys are not violated. The use of function keys to navigate an online system is more convenient for the frequent user than entering commands.

Procedure Step Execution Concepts

To understand the intricacies of building dialog flows between procedures, one must understand how procedure steps, Procedure Action Diagrams, screens, and dialog flows are related. Each makes a different contribution to the implementation of a business system. This subsection discusses those contributions in detail.

The procedure step is the anchor for screens and Procedure Action Diagrams. Dialog flows provide the means by which one procedure step, based on the results of its execution, can pass control and data to another procedure step.

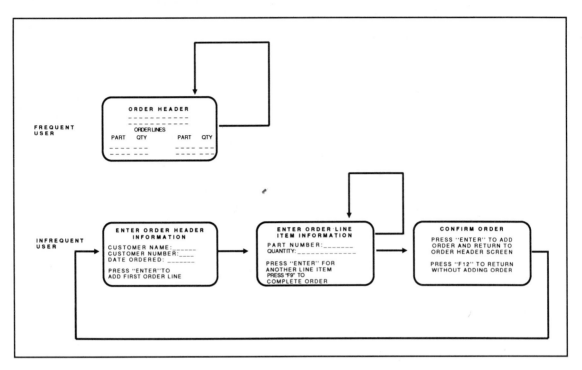

Figure 21-5. Dialog Variation Based on Frequency of Use

Figure 21-6 illustrates how a screen, Procedure Action Diagram, and dialog flow work together during the execution of a procedure step in the IEF environment. The circled numbers in the figure refer to the following text:

1. Procedure step execution usually begins when a terminal operator enters data on a screen and presses either the Enter key or a function key.

2. The data captured on the screen is mapped into the import data view for the procedure step. (Chapter 22 discusses the connection between fields on the screen and a procedure step's data views.)

3. The import data view, whether from a screen (2) or another procedure step (7), is processed by the Procedure Action Diagram that supports the procedure step being executed. At its conclusion, the procedure step populates its export data view. (Chapter 23 discusses Procedure Action Diagramming.)

4. Based on a condition set by the Procedure Action Diagram, the procedure step either displays a screen or flows to another procedure step. Such a condition, called an **exit state**, is described later in this chapter.

5. If the decision in (4) is to display a screen, the data from the procedure step's export data view is mapped into the associated screen and the screen is redisplayed.

6. If the decision in (4) is to flow to another procedure step, the export view from the current procedure step is matched to the import view of the procedure step to which the flow will take place. Data view matching is discussed later in this chapter.

7. If the dialog flow has the **Execute First** property, the import data view for the new procedure is passed to its Procedure Action Diagram. Otherwise, the contents of the import data view are placed on the screen.

   The Execute First property is described in the subsection entitled "Flow Actions."

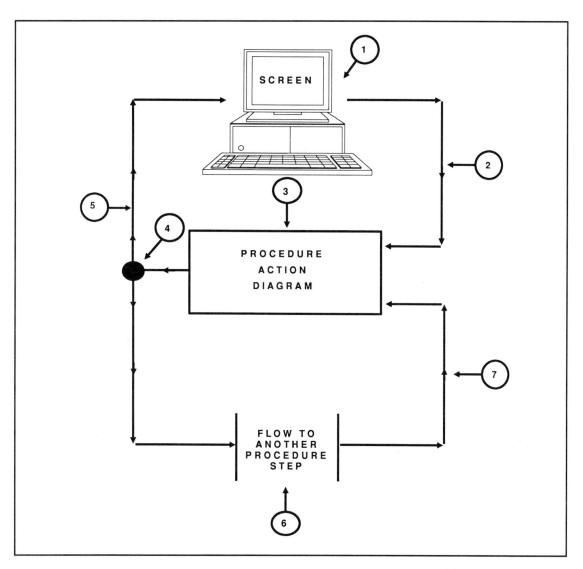

Figure 21-6. Procedure Step Execution Concepts

In one special case, it is possible to shortcut this cycle by avoiding the execution of the Procedure Action Diagram (Step 3). This case is discussed in the next section under the heading "Autoflows."

This description of procedure step execution reveals that the Procedure Action Diagram is essentially independent of the screen and dialog flow. No explicit actions are required to accept and display screens. No explicit actions are required to initiate dialog flows. No special logic is required to detect whether the Procedure Action Diagram was initiated from a screen or a dialog flow, or whether the result of its execution is to display a screen or initiate a dialog flow.

Flow Definition using the Dialog Flow Diagram

This subsection presents the symbols used in the Dialog Flow Diagram and explains in detail the techniques for building flows between procedures and procedure steps.

Diagramming Conventions

The Dialog Flow Diagram uses four primary symbols. These are illustrated in Figure 21-7.

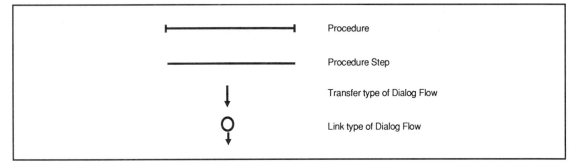

Figure 21-7. Dialog Flow Diagram Symbols

Notes:

1. The bars representing procedures and procedure steps are always accompanied by the name of the procedure or step. This name appears to the left of the bar.

2. The symbol for procedure step only appears if a procedure has more than one step.

3. If multiple procedure steps support a procedure, they may be contracted into a single procedure bar annotated with the contraction symbol (three dots).

4. Transfers and links (discussed in the next subsection) represent flows between procedures and steps. The arrowhead indicates the direction of the flow.

5. A dialog flow (that is, a transfer or link) to a multi-step procedure must always flow to the first step in that procedure.

A Dialog Flow Diagram drawn using the IEF appears in Figure 21-8.

Figure 21-8 is interpreted as follows:

- Menu is a single-step procedure, since no procedure steps appear directly beneath it and the contraction symbol (three dots) does not appear.

- At execution time, when certain conditions are met (explained in the subsection entitled "Flow Conditions"), the Menu procedure can initiate transfers to the procedures Take Order, Cancel Order and Maintain Cust.

- Take Order is a procedure with two procedure steps, Add Header and Add Lines.

- Under certain conditions, the Add Header procedure step can initiate a transfer to its companion procedure step, Add Lines. Under other conditions, it can initiate a link to a different procedure, Maintain Cust.

- Under certain conditions, the Add Lines procedure step can initiate a transfer to Add Header. Note that no flows enter Add Lines from outside the Take Order procedure, in accordance with Note 5 above.

- Cancel Order is a single-step procedure.

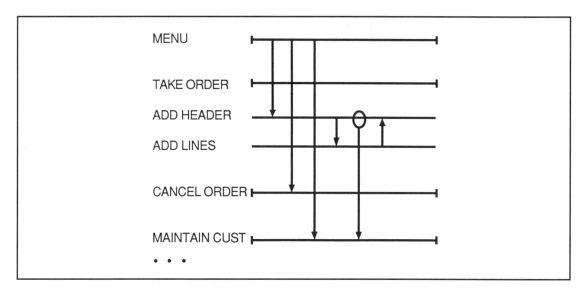

Figure 21-8. Sample Dialog Flow Diagram

- Maintain Cust is a multi-step procedure with its procedure steps and the flows between them contracted (note the contraction symbol beneath the procedure label). Two flows enter Maintain Cust. If Maintain Cust were expanded to show its included procedure steps, the flows would be shown as entering the first procedure step of Maintain Cust, just as the flows in Take Order are shown as entering Add Header.

Types of Dialog Flow

The designer can describe two kinds of flows with the Dialog Flow Diagram: transfers and links.

A **transfer** type of dialog flow indicates that the source procedure step passes control and, optionally, data to the target procedure step if appropriate conditions are met. In Figure 21-8, for example, the transfer from Add Header to Add Lines shows that after Add Header completes, Add Lines is initiated. Thus, Add Header can send data to Add Lines via the dialog flow.

A **link** type of dialog flow is more complex. As with a transfer, a link indicates that the source procedure step passes control and, optionally, data to the target procedure step. However, the link also allows the target procedure step to return control and data to the source procedure step. In addition, all export data known to the source procedure step when it completes its original execution will be saved and made available after the target procedure step returns.

For example, Figure 21-8 shows a link between the procedure steps Add Header and Maintain Cust. Assume that this link only takes place when the user takes an order from a customer not yet known to the system. By linking to Maintain Cust, the system allows the user to add the customer without losing any of the information already entered into the Add Header screen. After the user adds the customer, the Add Header procedure step begins again with all the information from its original export view available in its import view, augmented by data returned by Maintain Cust.

In other words, a link allows an operator to acquire additional information from another procedure step when it is needed by the initial procedure step. After the information is acquired, the initial procedure step reexecutes from the beginning with all the information from its initial execution intact.

If multiple links execute consecutively, all information from each linked procedure step is saved in anticipation of its restart. Suppose, for example, that Maintain Customer flows to another procedure step called Check Credit Bureau under certain circumstances. If Take Order links to Maintain Customer, all information required for Take Order is saved. If Maintain Customer then links to Check Credit Bureau, all information required by Maintain Customer is saved. When Check Credit Bureau ends, the data saved for Maintain Customer is restored and Maintain Customer reexecutes. When Maintain Customer ends, the data saved for Take Order is restored and Take Order reexecutes. If a transfer flow took place at any time during this sequence, however, all of the information saved during the links would be discarded.

Flow Conditions

For a dialog flow to take place, certain conditions, called **exit states,** must be met. Exit states were introduced in Chapter 12. This subsection explains how exit states can be used to trigger dialog flows.

Remember that each exit state is made up of three components: its **name**, a **message**, and a **type** (Normal, Rollback or Abort). Some examples of meaningful exit state names might include:

> Customer Was Not Found
> Order Taken Successfully
> Duplicate Item Number

The designer causes the exit state value to be placed in the Exit State special attribute by using the EXIT STATE IS action statement, explained in Chapter 14, or by using the Autoflow feature, described later in this subsection.

Each transfer on a Dialog Flow Diagram must be associated with one or more exit state definitions that will trigger the transfer. These are called **Flows On** exit states.

Likewise, each link on a Dialog Flow Diagram must have at least one Flows On exit state. Each link must also have at least one **Returns On** exit state. After the target procedure step finishes executing, the Returns On exit state causes control to be returned to the source procedure step.

The use of exit states in the Dialog Flow Diagram can be summarized as follows:

- When the logic of a procedure step concludes, the value of Exit State is evaluated.

- If this value matches that associated with any dialog flow from the procedure step (whether it be a transfer, link, or return from a link), the dialog flow is executed.

- If this value does *not* match any exit state values associated with any dialog flows, **the screen associated with the procedure step is redisplayed with the exit state message appearing in the IEF-supplied Error Message field.**

For example, consider Figures 21-9 through 21-11. Figure 21-9 shows the same Dialog Flow Diagram as Figure 21-8, annotated with exit state values for each dialog flow from the Menu procedure. Figure 21-10 is the Procedure Action Diagram for the Menu procedure. (Procedure Action Diagrams are discussed in Chapter 23.) Figure 21-11 shows the exit state value and exit state message for each exit state definition required by Menu.

Based on these figures, there are four possibilities at the conclusion of the execution of the Menu procedure:

- The value of Exit State is Take Order Requested. In this case, the Take Order procedure (actually, the Add Header procedure step) will be initiated.

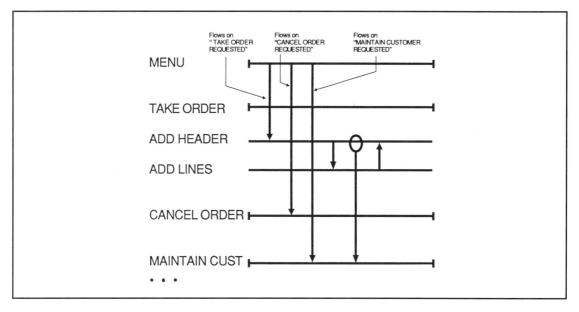

Figure 21-9. Annotated Dialog Flow Diagram

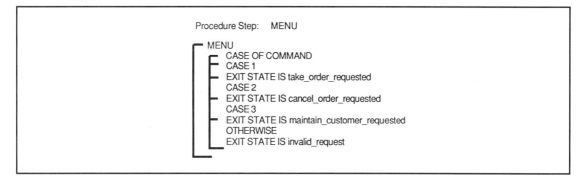

Procedure Step: MENU

```
MENU
     CASE OF COMMAND
     CASE 1
     EXIT STATE IS take_order_requested
     CASE 2
     EXIT STATE IS cancel_order_requested
     CASE 3
     EXIT STATE IS maintain_customer_requested
     OTHERWISE
     EXIT STATE IS invalid_request
```

Figure 21-10. Procedure Action Diagram for MENU Procedure

Exit State Value	Exit State Message	Exit State Type
TAKE ORDER REQUESTED	- - - -	Normal
CANCEL ORDER REQUESTED	- - - -	Normal
MAINTAIN CUSTOMER REQUESTED	- - - -	Normal
INVALID REQUEST	You have made an invalid request. Please make another selection.	Normal

Figure 21-11. Exit State Definitions Used in MENU Procedure

- The value of Exit State is Cancel Order Requested. In this case, the Cancel Order procedure will be initiated.

- The value of Exit State is Maintain Customer Requested. In this case, the Maintain Cust procedure will be initiated.

- The value of Exit State is Invalid Request. In this case, the Menu screen is redisplayed along with the message "You have made an invalid request. Please make another selection."

When an exit state is set during a procedure step execution, the results must be unambiguous. Consequently, the following rules govern the assignment of exit state definitions to dialog flows:

- An exit state value may appear on the Flows On exit state list of only one dialog flow from a given procedure step.

- No exit state value that appears on the Returns On exit state list of a link to a given procedure step may appear on a Flows On exit state list of dialog flows from the same procedure step.

Figure 21-12 shows violations of both rules using an annotated Dialog Flow Diagram. It shows three procedures (P1, P2 and P3) and six dialog flows, each of which has been assigned a number. The Flows On and Returns On exit states associated with each flow are also listed.

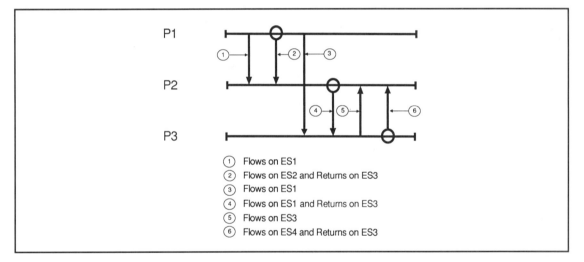

Figure 21-12. Exit State Rule Violations

Despite the confused use of exit states in this diagram, there are actually only two violations:

- For procedure P1, flows 1 and 3 violate rule 1 because they both use ES1 as a Flows On exit state.

- For procedure P3, flows 5 and 6 violate rule 2 because flow 5 uses ES3 as a Flows On exit state and flow 6 uses ES3 as a Returns On exit state.

This discussion reveals an interesting property of Returns On exit states: they depend entirely on the context of a particular link. In Figure 21-13, for example, both Take Order and Change Order can link to Maintain Cust. Assume that the Returns On exit state for both links is Request Successful. If Maintain Customer sets Request Successful during its execution, there are three possible results based on this diagram, depending on how Maintain Customer was initiated:

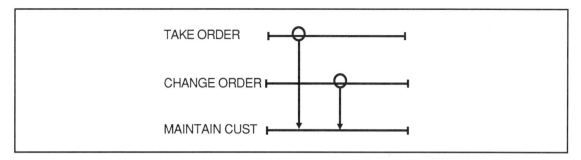

Figure 21-13. Context Sensitivity of RETURNS ON Exit States

- If Maintain Customer was linked to from Take Order, control is returned to Take Order.

- If Maintain Customer was linked to from Change Order, control is returned to Change Order.

- If Maintain Customer was not the target of a link, the Maintain Customer screen is redisplayed along with the exit state message associated with the exit state value Request Successful.

Flow Actions

Whenever a flow takes place in either direction, the procedure step to be initiated can begin in one of two ways:

- It can display the screen associated with the target procedure step and wait for operator input to begin the logic of the procedure step.

- It can execute the logic of the procedure step, which will result in either the procedure step's screen being displayed or a dialog flow being executed.

This distinction relies on the definition of a **flow action** associated with each procedure step.

The guideline for determining flow action is quite simple: if the target procedure step requires information from the user before it can execute, the **Display First** option is used. If the originating procedure step provides all of the information required by the target procedure step, the **Execute First** option is used.

Figure 21-14 shows three examples that call for a Display First flow action. Display First is most often used in flows from menus (1), flows in loosely structured dialogs between dissimilar procedure steps that exist purely for operator convenience (2), and occasions when the target procedure step is required to create entities (3). Note that in example (3), the Command field and Customer Number field are pre-populated with pertinent information, even though Display First was specified. The interactions between commands, data views, and dialog flows are discussed shortly.

Figure 21-15 shows two examples of dialogs using Execute First flow actions. Execute First is most often used when the target procedure step is to present data identified in the originating procedure step (1) or in menus that allow the capture of key information relevant to the target procedure step (2).

For dialog flows that are transfers, a flow action is specified for the target procedure step. For dialog flows that are links, two flow actions are specified: one for the target procedure step and another for the originating procedure step on return.

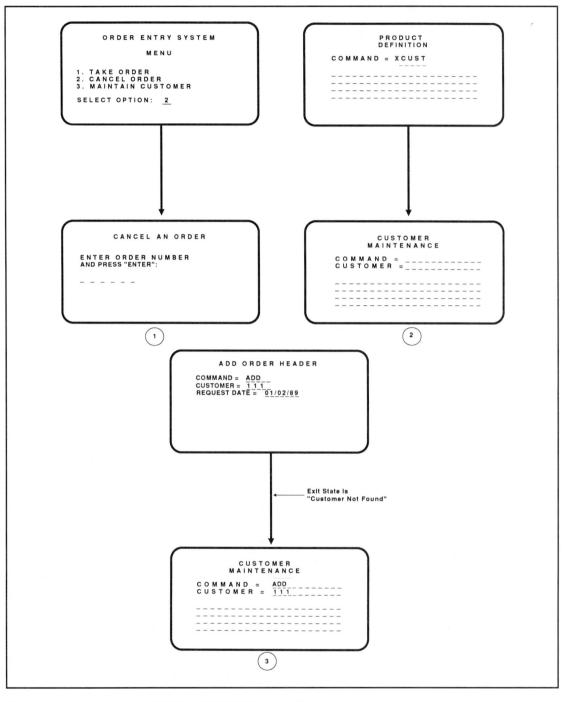

Figure 21-14. Examples of DISPLAY FIRST Flow Actions

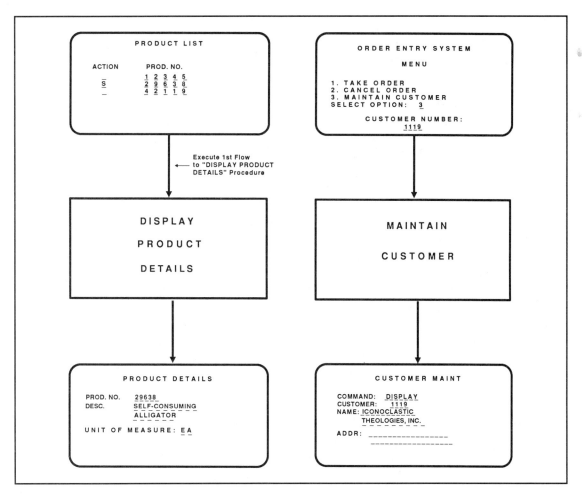

Figure 21-15. Examples of EXECUTE FIRST Flow Actions

One interesting aspect of the Execute First flow is that its execution, when followed by any other flow, can cause user interaction with procedure steps to be bypassed. Consider Figure 21-16. Assume that the link between procedures P1 and P2 specifies Execute First in both directions (that is, for P2 when the link originates and P1 when the link completes). Further, assume that the link flows on ES1 and returns on ES2. The following situation is then possible:

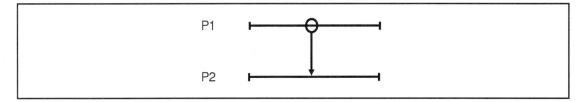

Figure 21-16. Hidden Procedure Step Execution

1. The operator fills in the screen for P1 and presses Enter.
2. P1 executes and, at its conclusion, sets Exit State to ES1.
3. Based on the value of Exit State, P1 links to P2.
4. Since the flow action is Execute First, P2 executes. At its conclusion it sets Exit State to ES2.
5. Based on the value of Exit State, P2 returns to P1.
6. Since the flow action for return is Execute First, P1 executes. At its conclusion it sets Exit State to ES3.
7. There is no dialog flow associated with exit state value ES3, so the screen for P1 is displayed.

From the operator's perspective, the execution of procedure P2 was completely hidden. The screen for P1 was used for input and subsequently redisplayed, just as if P2 had never been invoked, although one must assume that P2 contributed to the successful execution of the procedure.

Autoflows

There are many cases in which the only processing associated with a value of Command is the setting of Exit State with a particular value. For example, review figures 21-9 through 21-11. The MENU procedure does nothing but inspect the incoming command and set a value in exit state based on its value in anticipation of flowing to a different procedure step.

In cases like this, it is possible to associate a particular value of Command with a particular value of Exit State. A command associated with an exit state value for a procedure step is called an **autoflow** because it can be used to cause a dialog flow to take place without any action diagram logic to support it.

This is how autoflows are processed at execution time:

1. The IEF Dialog Manager evaluates the Command special attribute. If the value it contains is an **autoflow**, the execution of the procedure's action diagram is bypassed. (Otherwise, the value of Command is passed along to the action diagram as usual.)
2. Exit State is set to the exit state value associated with the autoflow.
3. If the value of Exit State is associated with a dialog flow, the flow happens *just as if Exit State had been set with the EXIT STATE IS action in an action diagram.*

In the MENU example, then, it would have been possible to simplify the construction of the Procedure Action Diagram shown in Figure 21-10 even further by specifying the following autoflows:

Autoflow Command	Exit State Value
1	TAKE ORDER REQUESTED
2	CANCEL ORDER REQUESTED
3	MAINTAIN CUSTOMER REQUESTED

Since all valid exit states are handled by autoflows, the MENU Procedure Action Diagram has only to set the INVALID REQUEST condition as shown in Figure 21-17; if it ever executes it means that an invalid value was placed in Command.

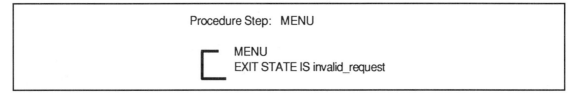

Procedure Step: MENU

   MENU
   EXIT STATE IS invalid_request

Figure 21-17. Revised MENU Procedure Action Diagram

Note that the combination of the autoflow definitions listed above, the Dialog Flow Diagram from Figure 21-9 and the action diagram shown in Figure 21-17 will give the same execution time result as the original MENU procedure example (Figures 21-9 through 21-11).

Autoflows are also a key component of workstation prototyping using the IEF. See Appendix G for a discussion of prototyping.

Setting Command via a Flow

Most online procedure steps rely on the value in the Command special attribute to direct their processing. When a procedure step is initiated from a screen, a terminal operator must enter a value in the Command field or press a function key to influence procedure step execution. The same kind of value is required when a procedure step is initiated by a dialog flow from another procedure step.

For this reason, one may specify a command value for each direction of a dialog flow. When the target procedure step of the flow executes, its underlying Procedure Action Diagram treats the value exactly as if it were entered on a screen. The designer can choose to send a specific command value, the **current** value of Command (that is, its value at the conclusion of the source procedure step's execution) or, in the case of a return from a link, the **previous** value of Command (that is, the value in the Command field when the procedure step initiating the link finished executing).

For a transfer, one can specify the command value that triggers the target procedure step. For a link, one can specify both the command value that triggers the target procedure step and the command value that triggers the source procedure step.

When commands are passed along a dialog flow using a Display First action, the value of Command specified on the flow will appear on the screen of the target procedure step. (See Figure 21-14, example (3).)

Data Passing

It is often useful to send data between procedure steps along a dialog flow. For example, consider the Take Order procedure in Figure 21-8. It is composed of two procedure steps, Add Header and Add Lines. Assuming that the Order Number is assigned in the Add Header procedure step, the ability to pass its value from Add Header to Add Lines eliminates the need for the user to retype (and possibly mistype) it when Add Lines starts.

The Dialog Flow Diagram in Figure 21-18 represents a slightly more complex example. It shows a fragment of an airline reservation system. The Check Reservation procedure is intended to show the flights on which a particular passenger is booked. The Locate Passenger procedure, given a passenger name (like Smith) will attempt to find and list all names that might be confused with it (like Smiff, Smithe, or Smythe). If Check Reservation fails because it cannot find the passenger's name, Locate Passenger is invoked to resolve a possible misspelling.

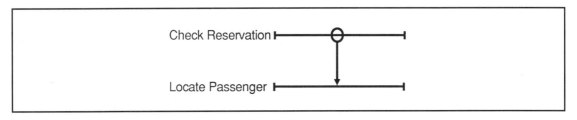

Figure 21-18. Airline Reservation System Fragment

In this case, sending the passenger's name along the dialog flow from Check Reservation to Locate Passenger frees the user from having to retype the name when Locate Passenger is invoked. Likewise, after Locate Passenger identifies the correct passenger name, sending it back to Check Reservation over the link's return allows Check Reservation to reexecute without additional user intervention.

These examples demonstrate that passing data between procedure steps can improve system flow, simplify dialog interactions, and reduce the chance for error.

One can send data over both transfers and links from the originator of the flow to its target. Any data in the originator's export data view can be passed to the target's import data view, as long as the views are compatible. (The appendix entitled "View Matching Rules" presents rules for view compatibility.)

Over links, one can also return data from the target of the link to its originator. Any data in the target's export data view can be passed to the originator's import data view, as long as the views are compatible. Remember that during a return from a link, the originator's import view is populated from the export view of its previous execution. However, any data returned from the target to the originator will overlay the corresponding elements of the originator's import view.

For example, consider Figure 21-18 once again. Assume that the import data view for Check Reservation has two components: Passenger Name and Reservation Date. Assume that the export data view for Check Reservation includes Passenger Name and a list of flights. Further assume that Check Reservation is unable to locate a passenger by the name of John Doe. When Check Reservation links to Locate Passenger, the following takes place (assuming an Execute First dialog flow):

1. The export view from Check Reservation is saved (including the name John Doe).
2. The appropriate elements of the export view (in this case, the passenger's name, John Doe) are placed in the import view of Locate Passenger.
3. Locate Passenger begins execution, looking for names that are similar to John Doe. In its export view it returns Shawn Toe, Jon Deaux, and John Dough.

The user may now select from among these alternatives to identify the correct passenger. If John Dough is the correct choice, the following takes place when Locate Passenger returns to Check Reservation (assuming that the return has a flow action of Execute First):

1. The import view of Check Reservation is populated from its saved export view (so John Doe appears as the passenger name).
2. The appropriate elements of the export view of Locate Passenger are then used to overlay the import view of Check Reservation (so John Dough replaces John Doe as the passenger name).
3. Check Reservation executes. This time, the procedure finds the passenger John Dough, and displays the list of flights reserved for him.

Flows between IEF and non-IEF Transactions

It is sometimes desirable to flow between online procedures generated by the IEF and transactions built using some other method. Although these kinds of flows cannot be represented on the Dialog Flow Diagram, they *can* be implemented using some other IEF features: clear screen input and the special attribute NEXTTRAN.

To flow **from** an IEF generated transaction **to** a non-IEF generated transaction, the appropriate input message must be set in the NEXTTRAN special attribute. NEXTTRAN can either be placed directly on the screen (see Chapter 22) or SET in an action diagram (see Chapter 23). In either case, whenever the IEF Dialog

Manager spots a value in NEXTTRAN, it "flows" to the transaction in question using the native facilities of the teleprocessing monitor (for example, IMS/DC and CICS).

To flow **to** an IEF generated transaction **from** a non-IEF generated transaction, the non-IEF generated transaction is responsible for creating a message to invoke the IEF generated transaction. It then uses the facilities of the teleprocessing monitor to transfer control to the IEF generated transaction. The message it creates must be in the same format used for clear screen input (see Chapter 22).

Online Flow Definition Summary

There are two types of dialog flows: transfers and links. Links support a return to the originating procedure step without loss of data, while transfers do not.

Transfers have the following properties:

- Flows On exit states
- Flow actions (Execute First, Display First) for target procedure step
- Command triggers execution of the target procedure step
- Data sent from the originating to the target procedure step

Links have the following properties:

- Flows On exit states
- Flow actions (Execute First, Display First) for the target procedure step
- Command triggers execution of the target procedure step
- Data sent from the originating to the target procedure step
- Returns On exit states
- Flow actions (Execute First, Display First) for the originating procedure step on return
- Command triggers execution of the originating procedure step on return
- Data returned from the target to the originating procedure step

BATCH DIALOG DESIGN

The design of batch dialogs is also accomplished using the Dialog Flow Diagram. However, a number of features available for online dialog design are inapplicable in a batch dialog, so the options available to the designer are more limited.

Batch procedures can be identified on the Dialog Flow Diagram by the parenthetical designation "BATCH" beneath the procedure's label (see Figure 21-19). Aside from that, the diagramming symbols used are the same as those for online procedures.

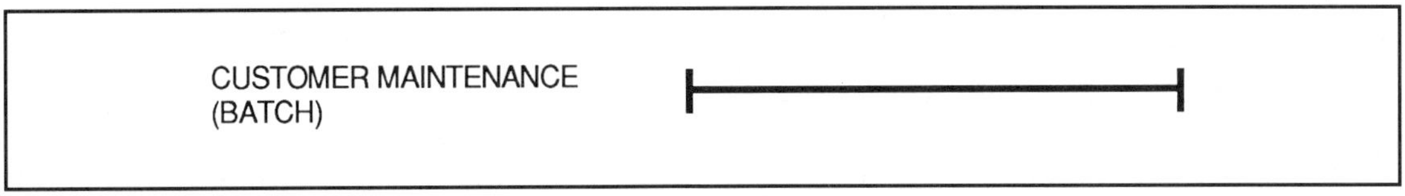

CUSTOMER MAINTENANCE
(BATCH)

Figure 21-19. A Batch Procedure

Flow Restrictions for Batch Dialogs

The following restrictions apply to dialogs involving batch procedures:

- Flows between procedure steps in other procedures are not permitted. That is, it is only possible to create flows between procedure steps in the same procedure. (Remember that a batch procedure is analogous to a batch job and a batch procedure step is analogous to a batch job step in the IBM MVS world.)

- Only **transfer** type dialog flows are permitted; no **links** may be specified.

- Only flows **forward** (that is, arrows pointing downward on the Dialog Flow Diagram) are permitted. There is one exception to this rule, the **involuted transfer**, explained in the next section.

- The designation "display first" has no meaning in a batch procedure; all flows are processed as **execute first.**

Designing for Restartability

One consideration unique to batch procedures is **restartability**. A procedure step is restartable when, if it abnormally terminates midway through its execution, it can be restarted from the point at which it terminated.

For example, consider a banking application in which checking accounts are updated in a nightly batch procedure. The step which applies the updates based on incoming checks is likely to run for several hours. Imagine that after five hours of processing, the procedure abnormally terminates due to a hardware failure (a bad record on a tape, maybe), a DBMS error (database full, perhaps), an error in the job control language (like a timeout because the TIME= parameter was incorrectly specified) or, heaven forbid, a program bug. If the procedure were not designed to be restartable, it would have to be started over *from the beginning*! Five hours of processing time are lost, countless computing cycles are wasted, the bank opens late the next morning, and several new openings are created in the IS department.

If, on the other hand, the procedure *were* designed to be restartable, it can be restarted from where it left off after the condition which abbreviated its execution is corrected.

There are two aspects to restartability: **establishing checkpoints**, which is analogous to leaving a trail of bread crumbs in one's path through the forest, and **restarting from the last checkpoint**, which is something like following the trail of bread crumbs back into the forest after being mysteriously teleported back to your initial starting point.

An example of the procedure logic required to establish checkpoints and restart from the last checkpoint is presented in Chapter 23.

Establishing Checkpoints

A "checkpoint" is a point during processing at which it is certain that everything in the processing environment is synchronized and at which the procedure can be restarted. In order to establish a checkpoint, it is necessary to **commit all outstanding database updates** and to take a **process snapshot**.

Database Commit

With most DBMS's, any requests for update are saved in some kind of temporary storage and the physical database is not actually updated until a "commit point" is reached. In the absence of an explicit request for a database commit, the updates are not committed until the end of a procedure step's execution.

In a typical restartable procedure step, a commit is explicitly requested by the procedure step every so often during processing, usually after a certain number of operations have taken place. This means that in the event of a restart, *only updates made since the last commit are lost.*

For instance, in the banking example cited above the procedure step may explicitly request a database commit after every hundred checks are processed. If, after a failure of some kind, the procedure has to be restarted, at most one hundred checks will require reprocessing.

In the IEF, a database commit is requested by using an **involuted transfer** type of flow on the Dialog Flow Diagram. An involuted transfer causes the Dialog Manager to commit all outstanding database requests and re-invoke the Procedure Action Diagram logic for the procedure step.

For example, Figure 21-20 shows a single step batch procedure called Account Update. Whenever the execution of the Account Update Procedure Action Diagram concludes and the value of exit state is PROCESS_COMMIT, the IEF Dialog Manager will commit all outstanding updates and return to the beginning of the Account Update procedure.

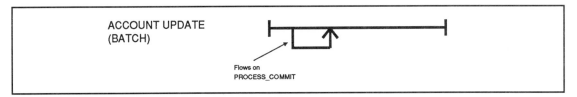

Figure 21-20. A Batch Procedure with Involuted Transfer

Process Snapshots

The term **process snapshot** refers to any information that might be required to return the procedure step to its state at the last commit point in the event of a restart. Otherwise, duplicate database updates may result.

For instance, in the checking account update example, assume that the checks are presented to the procedure step from a sequential file. In the event of a restart, it is critical that the procedure step be able to relocate the position in the sequential file that corresponds to the last commit point. Otherwise, the checks already processed would be re-processed causing their associated accounts to be debited twice for the same checks, a situation that quickly draws the attention of depositors.

Enough information to allow the procedure step to return to a commit point must therefore be saved each time a commit is issued. In the checking account update example, the designer might count the number of checks processed in the Procedure Action Diagram and write that number to a file each time a commit takes place. Then, in the event of a restart, the file containing that number can be read and the sequential file containing the incoming checks can be advanced by that number of checks before the update is continued.

Restarting at the Last Checkpoint

In order to take advantage of the checkpoints established by conscientiously issuing database commits and taking process snapshots, the designer must include logic in the procedure step which can interpret the snapshot and restore things to the state in which they were at the last checkpoint. This usually involves repositioning sequential files and, possibly, resetting the values of some local views.

22
LAYOUT DESIGN

OVERVIEW

This chapter discusses the visual layouts of data views imported to and exported from procedure steps. In an online environment, the primary visual layouts are screens, while in a batch environment they are reports.

The IEF currently provides no direct support for the creation of reports. Thus, the principles described in this chapter apply primarily to screen design, although many of the comments about export views pertain to reports as well.

PRINCIPLES OF SCREEN DESIGN

By the time screen design takes place, the designer has already defined the import and export data views of the procedure steps involved. During screen design, then, the designer arranges the fields that implement those data views and specifies explanatory text to support them.

The object of screen design is to maximize the performance of those who will use the resulting screens. To this end, the designer should adhere to the following guidelines:

*   Design screens to fit the intended user. As discussed in Chapter 21, different individuals have different requirements.

    For example, the frequent user of a system tends to want the greatest amount of information possible on the screen, commands and function keys to streamline navigation, minimal descriptive and help text, and minimal interruption. The infrequent user of a system tends to want descriptive headings and labels, longer messages, a low volume of data per screen, and comprehensive help facilities.

*   Arrange fields on data entry screens to closely resemble the source document if one is used.

*   In the absence of a source document, arrange fields on a screen in priority sequence, top-to-bottom, left-to-right.

*   Set standards for colors, highlighting, and general format (see "Setting System Standards" in Chapter 19) so that the look and feel of all components of the system is the same.

An understanding of the user's environment and meaningful standards generally result in good screen designs.

SCREEN DEFINITION DETAILS

This section describes the components of screens in detail. There are two major types of objects defined during screen design:

*   **Screens**, which are the user's view of the system. Each online procedure step is associated with a screen.

*   **Templates**, which are definitions of portions of a screen. A template may be incorporated into many screens, thus giving them all a common look and feel.

These two major objects contain the following fundamental components:

- **Fields**, which implement import and export data views

- **Literals**, for constant information

- **Prompts**, labels for fields and special fields

- **Special fields**, which reflect the set of special attributes that are appropriate for placement on a screen

A screen can contain fields, special fields, prompts and literals. It can also include one or more templates. A template can contain only literals, special fields, and prompts. Fields, which implement import and export data views, are specific to a particular procedure step. Because templates can be shared by many screens and, thus, many procedure steps, they cannot support fields.

The following subsections describe characteristics of each of these objects.

Screen Details

In addition to providing anchor points for fields, prompts, literals, and special fields, screens have a few properties of their own. Since each screen describes exactly one online procedure step, some screen characteristics are borrowed from the procedure step definition. For example, screens do not have names of their own. They are identified by the name of the procedure step they support. Nor do they have their own descriptions: they assume the same description as the procedure step.

As a result, only these properties are unique to the screen as a whole:

- **Scrolling**. This property, which may have either the value "yes" or "no," indicates whether the user can scroll back and forth through a repeating group appearing on the screen using the IEF's Automatic Scrolling feature. Repeating groups and scrolling are discussed in detail later in this chapter.

- **Help Identifier**. Online systems should be supported by help data as suggested in Chapter 19. Many installations have systems in place that support the capture and display of help text. The Help ID is used to tell the installation help system where to locate the help text for the screen.

- **Protection of Unused Occurrences**. For screens that support repeating groups, this property is used to specify whether occurrences of the repeating group appearing on the screen that were not populated in the procedure step's export view should be automatically protected.

- **Positioning on a Dialog Flow RETURN**. For screens that support repeating groups, this property is used to specify which occurrence of the repeating group will be displayed at the top of the group after a return from a link type of dialog flow. There are two options:

  — Restore the position of the group to its position when the link was requested. For example, if the tenth occurrence of the repeating group was displayed on the top of the screen when the link was requested, it will still be on the top of the screen after the corresponding return.

  — Reset the position of the group so that the first repeating group occurrence is displayed on the first line of the repeating group on the screen. For example, if the tenth occurrence of the repeating group was displayed on the top of the screen when the link was requested, the **first** occurrence will be displayed on the top of the screen after the corresponding return.

  In practice, the second option is rarely used.

Template Details

Templates are simply named collections of special fields and literals. They have only two properties:

- **Name**, used to reference the template when it is included on a screen.

- **Description**, where the designer can record in detail the intended use of the template.

Field Details

Throughout Information Engineering, the term **field** refers to the implementation of an attribute. In the case of screen design, a field implements an attribute for which an import data view, an export data view, or both have been defined for the procedure step. One must understand the relationship between screen fields and import and export data views before addressing the properties of fields on screens.

The single screen associated with each procedure step is responsible for providing data to its import view and displaying data from its export view. Thus, one can use each field on the screen to implement both an import and an export view of an attribute. Figure 22-1 illustrates this point. In this example, the procedure step Get Customer Address requires an import view of Customer Name and produces an export view composed of Customer Name, Customer Address Line 1, Customer Address Line 2 and Customer Address Line 3.

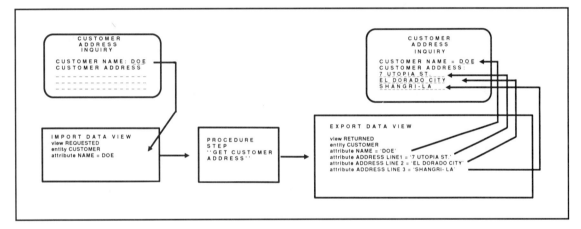

Figure 22-1. Relating Screen Fields to Import and Export Views

Figure 22-1 shows the screen for Get Customer Address in two states: once after the terminal operator has specified the data required in the import view and once after the system has formatted the export view in response. The field labeled "CUSTOMER NAME:" provides input to the import view Requested Customer Name before procedure step initiation, and displays the contents of the export view Returned Customer Name at the procedure step's conclusion. The fields identified as "CUSTOMER ADDRESS:" only display the contents of the export view's Returned Customer Address Lines 1, 2, and 3.

As a general rule, all fields for which an import view is defined should have a corresponding export view.

Each field has the following properties:

- **Import Data View**. This view receives data input to the field, if any, as described above.

- **Export Data View**. This view provides data to the field, if any, as described above.

- **Display Length**. This indicates the number of character positions required to display the field on the screen. Many times a field's display length will be the same as that of the attribute it implements, but in some cases it will not. The most frequent reason for a difference in display length and attribute length is the use of an **edit pattern**.

  For example, consider an attribute of EMPLOYEE called Date Hired that contains a four-digit year, a two-digit month and a two-digit day, eight digits in all. The designer, when placing a field representing Date Hired on a screen, determines that it should be displayed in the format YYYY-MM-DD. The insertion of two additional characters (the dashes) requires a display length of ten characters. Thus, the attribute length is eight while the display length is ten.

  In some cases, the designer may choose to truncate a field value to make it fit on a screen. For example, an 80-character description may not fit on a densely packed screen. The designer can squeeze it in by reducing the display length. However, designers should avoid this approach wherever possible because of the potential loss of meaning resulting from the partial display.

- **Number of Decimals**. For numeric views, this property indicates the number of decimal places to be displayed or accepted in the field.

- **Hidden Field Indicator**. In an online system, one sometimes needs to save information between procedure step executions. Of course, every field that both comes from an export data view and goes to an import data view can be considered "saved" because it passes between procedure steps without an operator retyping it (see the upper portion of Figure 22-2). However, in some cases one may need to save information without displaying it on the screen. This is typically done using the **hidden field** concept.

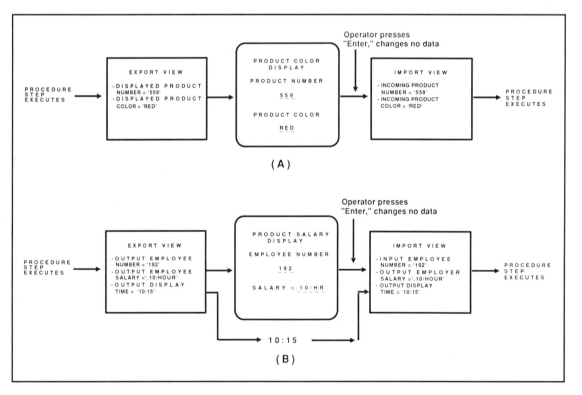

Figure 22-2. The Use of Hidden Fields

The hidden field property provides a way to hide a field from display on the screen, but still pass it from export to import view between transaction executions. The lower portion of Figure 22-2 shows an example of a procedure step using a hidden field to pass data between executions. In this example, a secure procedure step has been designed to require a user password. Whenever the screen is displayed, the Output Display Time is saved as a hidden field. When the operator presses Enter to start the next procedure step execution, the value of Output Display Time saved in the hidden field is compared with the current time. If too much time has elapsed, the operator can be prompted to reenter the password.

Traditionally, one implements hidden fields as dark, protected fields (see video properties, below) and actually places them on the screen. However, the IEF automatically saves hidden fields and restores them at execution time without requiring space on the screen.

The IEF imposes two requirements:

— Any field identified as a hidden field must be associated with both an import and an export data view. Otherwise, it cannot pass data between procedure step executions.

— Each component of a procedure step's import and export data views must either be implemented by a field placed on the screen or as a hidden field.

- **Edit Pattern**. Edit patterns are used to make the values in views more readable when they appear on a screen. For example, a U.S. Social Security number is nine digits long. If the contents of an export view of Social Security Number were displayed, it might appear as:

  888888888

  However, by applying the edit pattern XXX-XX-XXXX before displaying it, the result is:

  888-88-8888

  which is the format in which Social Security numbers commonly appear.

  There are two categories of edit patterns: **standard** and **local**. Chapter 19 mentions standard edit patterns in connection with the System Defaults panel in the section entitled "Setting System Standards." The designer should name them for the domain of the data they represent. For example, to ensure that all currency values are displayed consistently on every screen that uses them, one might establish a standard edit pattern called Currency.

  One striking advantage of using standard edit patterns is the ease with which one can change the appearance of fields across the system. For example, imagine that a standard edit pattern called Date has the value "MM/DD/YY." Assume that all fields implementing attributes of type Date have been assigned the edit pattern Date. If, later, one wishes to change the format to "DD.MM.YY," one can change every field in the system that uses the Date edit pattern simply by changing the edit pattern definition. There is no need to modify every screen in the system.

  Local edit patterns are specific to a particular field. One should avoid them in favor of standard edit patterns wherever possible, but they are available when required.

  The characteristics of edit patterns vary by the attribute type of the view implemented by the field. For example, "YYYY-MM-DD" is valid for a field implementing a date attribute but not for one implementing a time attribute. A complete definition of the edit patterns supported by the IEF appears in the *IEF Design Toolset Guide*.

- **Field Video Properties**. Video properties control a number of terminal-dependent aspects of field display. In general, designers should standardize them across the system as suggested in Chapter 19. However, in certain cases one may need to deviate from the standard by specifying local video properties.

  The following video properties (either standard or local) can be defined for a field:

— **Cursor Position,** which indicates whether the cursor is to be placed in the field when the screen is displayed. The **cursor** identifies where the next character entered will appear on the screen. The possible values of this property are "yes" and "no." If no fields on a particular screen have a value of "yes" specified for this property, the cursor will appear in the first field on the screen. If multiple fields have a value of "yes" specified, the cursor will appear in the first one on the screen (beginning in the upper left corner and working left-to-right through each row on the screen).

— **Protection**, which indicates whether data can be entered into a field.

— **Intensity**, which, on a terminal that supports different intensities, allows fields to appear at different levels of brightness (high intensity, normal intensity, or dark, which does not appear at all).

— **Color**, which allows fields to appear in any of the colors supported by the terminal.

— **Highlight**, which allows fields to be displayed with any highlighting characteristics supported by the terminal (such as reverse video or blink).

— **Justification**, which controls the alignment of data at either the right or the left of the field. Normally, text is left-justified and numbers are right-justified.

— **Blank when zero**, which causes a numeric field to be displayed as blank, regardless of its edit pattern, if its value is zero.

— **Fill character**, which is inserted in remaining character positions after justification. For example, a value of "999" right-justified in a field five digits long with a fill character of "0" would appear as 00999

The above list is the same for both standard and local video properties of fields. Designers should avoid using local video properties to specify intensity, color or highlighting unless absolutely necessary, since it represents a deviation from the system standard.

• **Error Video Properties**. Error video properties are similar to field video properties except that they are used to highlight a field in error. For example, on a data entry screen, data that does not conform to an attribute's permitted value list can be redisplayed to the operator in reverse video to highlight the error.

The designer can specify that a field be displayed using its error video properties by using the MAKE...ERROR action statement explained in Chapter 23.

The list of error video properties is a subset of the list of field video properties which includes **cursor position, protection, intensity, color** and **highlight**. As with field video properties, it is always best to default to the system standard. Use of a local error video property is likely to confuse an operator accustomed to reacting to the standard error video property.

• **Prompt**. A prompt is a label for either a field or a special field. It is placed on the screen near the field itself. For example, consider the screen in Figure 22-3. "CUSTOMER NAME:" and "HAIR COLOR:" are labels, or prompts, for the fields with which they are associated.

Literals, described shortly, can be used to create the same effect as prompts. However, the IEF keeps a list of each prompt used with fields to implement each attribute across the system, and allows the designer to choose among them. This improves the opportunity to standardize field labels across the system.

For example, in Figure 22-3, assume the field preceded by the "CUSTOMER NAME:" prompt implements an attribute called Customer Name. Suppose another designer builds a screen that requires a field implementing Customer Name. When the designer is positioning the field, the IEF will issue a reminder that "CUSTOMER NAME:" was previously used as a prompt for the attribute and will encourage the designer to use it again rather than inventing a new one like "NAME OF CUST IS " or "CLIENT MONICKER IS ===>. "

```
┌─────────────────────────────────────────────────────────┐
│                                                         │
│            C U S T O M E R   H A I R   C O L O R        │
│                     I N Q U I R Y                       │
│                                                         │
│      CUSTOMER NAME = JOHN DOE _ _                        │
│                                                         │
│      HAIR COLOR        = BROWN _ _ _ _                   │
│                                                         │
│                                                         │
│                                                         │
└─────────────────────────────────────────────────────────┘
```

Figure 22-3. Example of Field Prompts

- **Prompt Video Properties.** These properties allow the designer to specify terminal-dependent characteristics of the prompt display. As with field properties, designers should establish a standard for prompt properties and override it only in extreme situations.

  Since prompts contain no variable data, few video properties are available for them. They are: **intensity**, **color**, and **highlight**.

- **Help Identifier**. The value of this property can be communicated to an installation's Help Facility if it supports field-level help.

Designers experienced in building screens using other techniques may notice an apparent omission. No mention is made here of the Modified Data Tag (MDT), used on IBM Model 3270 and compatible terminals to indicate that a field on the screen has been changed. The IEF makes all Modified Data Tag handling invisible to the designer and, thus, provides no way for a designer to manipulate it. As a result, one can assume that all data exported from the procedure step that is not modified will be available in the import view of the next execution, just as though all Modified Data Tags had been set on.

Literal Details

Literals contain only constant data. As a result, literals have only two components: the constant data to be displayed and its video property. Where possible, one should use the system standard video properties and avoid literal-specific local video properties.

The designer may specify the following video properties for a literal: **intensity**, **color,** and **highlight**. These properties were described under "Field Details."

Prompt Details

Although prompts appear separately on the screen, each is intimately connected with a field. The characteristics of prompts were described under "Field Details."

Special Field Details

Special fields implement special attributes that are appropriate for placement on a screen. The following list enumerates the special fields available during IEF Screen Design:

- **Current Date**, the system date at the time a screen is displayed.

- **Current Time**, the system time at which the screen is displayed.

- **Transaction Code**. This field is required by transaction-oriented teleprocessing monitors (like IMS and CICS) to identify the programs required to execute the procedure step. IEF screen generation, a Construction Stage facility, requires that Transaction Code appear as the first item (that is, in the upper-left) on each screen.

- **Command Area**, in which a terminal operator may specify a value for the Command special attribute.

- **System Error Message**, where messages associated with Exit States are displayed.

- **Program Function Keys**, where a list of the function keys available for the procedure step can be displayed on a single line as a reminder to the operator.

- **Terminal ID** displays the system terminal identification of the terminal on which the screen is displayed.

- **User ID** displays the User ID by which the terminal operator is known to the teleprocessing monitor.

- **Printer Terminal ID** allows an operator to specify the system terminal identification of a printer on which the screen will print, should the operator request it.

- **Local System ID** displays the kind of teleprocessing monitor under which the procedure step is executing (for example, IMS, CICS and TSO).

- **Panel ID** displays the **mapname** associated with the screen. Mapnames are assigned during the construction stage; see the *IEF Construction Toolset Guide* for more details.

- **Scroll Indicator Message** is used for automatically scrolled repeating groups. If there are more items in the repeating group than appear on the screen, it displays as "MORE:" followed by a minus sign ("–") to indicate there are items preceding the first occurrence displayed, a plus sign ("+") to indicate that there are items following the last occurrence displayed, or both.

- **Scroll Amount Message** prompts the user to specify the scrolling interval desired. Options are: CURS (for cursor, or single line scrolling), HALF, and PAGE.

- **Scroll Location Message** is used for automatically scrolled repeating groups. It displays a message in the form:

    LINES *aaa* TO *bbb* OF *ccc*

    where *aaa* is the occurrence number, within the repeating group view, of the first occurrence displayed on the screen, *bbb* is the occurrence number of the last occurrence displayed on the screen, and *ccc* is the occurrence number of the last populated occurrence in the repeating group view.

- **Next Transaction**, in which the terminal operator can specify a transaction code and unformatted input to use to invoke a transaction (usually one not generated by the IEF). The information placed in this field is processed as though the operator had cleared the screen and entered clear screen input to invoke the transaction.

The properties of special fields are the same as for previously-listed fields, with the following exceptions:

- Special fields do not require import or export data views.

- Special fields may not be implemented as hidden fields.

- Special fields may not have edit patterns.

Screen Definition Summary

- **Screens** can contain fields, literals, prompts, special fields, and templates. Each screen has the following properties:

  — Scroll Indicator

  — Help Identifier

  — Protection of Unused Occurrences Indicator

  — Positioning on Dialog Flow RETURN Indicator

- **Templates** can contain literals, prompts, and special fields. Each template has the following properties:

  — Name

  — Description

- **Fields** are implementations of attributes appearing in the import and export data view of a procedure step. Each field has the following properties:

  — Import Data View

  — Export Data View

  — Display Length

  — Number of Decimal Places

  — Cursor Indicator

  — Hidden Field Indicator

  — Edit Pattern

  — Field Video Properties

  — Error Video Properties

  — Prompt

  — Prompt Video Properties

  — Help Identifier

- **Literals** are for constant information appearing on the screen. Each literal has the following properties:

  — Literal Value

  — Field Video Properties

- **Prompts** are for constant information used as labels of fields and special fields. They are defined as part of the definition of the field or special field with which they are associated. Each prompt has the following properties:

  — Prompt Value (same as Prompt in the list of field properties)

  — Prompt Video Properties (same as Prompt Video Properties in the list of field properties)

- **Special fields** are implementations of special attributes. Each special field has the following properties:

— Display Length

— Cursor Indicator

— Field Video Properties

— Error Video Properties

— Prompt

— Prompt Video Properties

— Help Identifier

CONSIDERATIONS FOR REPEATING GROUPS

Repeating Groups and Automatic Scrolling

Some procedure steps deal with repeating import or export data views. For example, consider a procedure step called List Customers, which provides a list of customer names and phone numbers beginning with a certain value. Such a procedure step might have import and export views that look like those in Figure 22-4.

```
          Procedure Step    LIST_CUSTOMERS

          Import  Views
               View STARTING of entity CUSTOMER
                    Attributes:
                              NAME

          Export Views
               Group View LISTED
                    Cardinality  Min: 0  Max: 100  Avg: 50
               View RETURNED of entity CUSTOMER
                    Attributes:
                              NAME
                              PHONE_NUMBER
```

Figure 22-4. Repeating Export Data View

```
                          LIST  CUSTOMERS


     STARTING CUSTOMER NAME = = = >   X X X X X X X X X X X X X X X X X X X X X X X X X X X


            CUSTOMER NAME                      PHONE NUMBER

         X X X X X X X X X X X X X X X X X X X X X X      ( X X X )  X X X - X X X X
         X X X X X X X X X X X X X X X X X X X X X X      ( X X X )  X X X - X X X X
         X X X X X X X X X X X X X X X X X X X X X X      ( X X X )  X X X - X X X X
         X X X X X X X X X X X X X X X X X X X X X X      ( X X X )  X X X - X X X X
         X X X X X X X X X X X X X X X X X X X X X X      ( X X X )  X X X - X X X X
         X X X X X X X X X X X X X X X X X X X X X X      ( X X X )  X X X - X X X X
         X X X X X X X X X X X X X X X X X X X X X X      ( X X X )  X X X - X X X X
         X X X X X X X X X X X X X X X X X X X X X X      ( X X X )  X X X - X X X X
         X X X X X X X X X X X X X X X X X X X X X X      ( X X X )  X X X - X X X X
         X X X X X X X X X X X X X X X X X X X X X X      ( X X X )  X X X - X X X X
```

Figure 22-5. Screen Containing a Repeating Group

Note that the group view Listed is a repeating group view, as indicated by its cardinality. The maximum cardinality, shown as 100, indicates that at most 100 values for CUSTOMER Name and Phone_Number will be returned as the result of executing procedure step List Customers.

The implementation of such a procedure step in an online environment will require a screen looking something like Figure 22-5.

The multiple occurrences of CUSTOMER Name and Phone_Number shown on this screen are referred to collectively as a **repeating group**. Notice that only ten occurrences of the repeating group appear on the screen, yet the maximum cardinality of the group view is 100. In a case like this, one can use scrolling to provide a *window* on the repeating group. Through this window, a user can see ten values for CUSTOMER Name and Phone_Number at a time.

A designer implements the scrolling feature via the Scroll Indicator property of a screen. When the IEF-generated procedure step executes, it automatically includes support for moving backward and forward ten occurrences at a time through the 100 occurrences of CUSTOMER Name and Phone_Number.

Automatic scrolling can only be used on one repeating group per screen. In the case of nested repeating groups, only the highest level repeating group is scrolled. For example, the view definitions in Figure 22-6 reflect a modified version of List Customers, called List Customers 2, in which each customer can have six phone numbers. Figure 22-7 shows one way to represent this data on a screen. In this case, the screen shows ten out of a possible 100 customers, and for each customer, three out of a possible six phone numbers. Automatic scrolling cannot be used both to scroll through the values of CUSTOMER Name and the values of CUSTOMER Phone_Number. It becomes the designer's responsibility to provide the scrolling capability with procedure action logic.

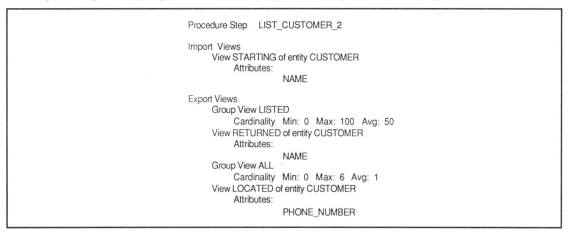

Figure 22-6. Nested Repeating Group Views

Automatic Scrolling Command Values

If the Scroll Indicator property for a screen is set to "Yes," the following values have special meaning to the Dialog Manager when placed in the Command field at execution time: NEXT, PREV, TOP and BOTTOM.

The meanings of these values are explained in Chapter 20.

Special Fields for Automatic Scrolling

The special fields Scroll Location Message, Scroll Indicator Message and Scroll Amount Message, explained earlier in this chapter, are automatically maintained at execution for screens with a Scroll Indicator property value of "yes."

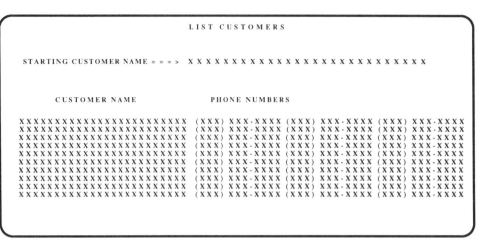

Figure 22-7. Screen with a Nested Partial Repeating View

When to Use Automatic Scrolling

Depending on the specific circumstances under which scrolling is to take place, automatic scrolling might not be the best approach. In some cases it is more straightforward, both for user and designer, to handle scrolling explicitly in the procedure logic.

Automatic scrolling is most effective when the following conditions are met:

* A single, non-nested repeating group is to be scrolled, and

* The number of occurrences which satisfy the user's selection criteria is likely to be small enough that all occurrences will fit in the repeating group view.

For example, consider a procedure step in which an ORDER and the ORDER LINES it contains are displayed. If the designer is confident that there will never be over one hundred ORDER_LINES per ORDER, automatic scrolling is an excellent alternative (although the designer should include logic to handle the case where there *are* more than one hundred ORDER_LINES for a particular ORDER).

On the other hand, consider a procedure step in which a list of employees is displayed in alphabetical order starting with a particular employee name. The number of occurrences to be returned is indeterminate; depending on the starting employee name and the size of the company, the number of occurrences satisfying the selection criteria might range anywhere from zero to tens of thousands. In such cases, explicit scrolling logic yields a more efficient and effective design.

The logic required for designer-specified explicit scrolling is discussed in Chapter 23.

Line Item Actions

If a repeating group implements both an import and an export repeating data view, one often needs to allow the user to specify the activity to be performed on each occurrence of the group. The designer can accomplish this by specifying a line item action using a work attribute set (described in Chapter 19).

For example, consider a procedure step similar to List Customers that allows a user to change or delete a customer's phone number. Figure 22-8 lists the import and export views for this procedure step, named Maintain Customer Phone Numbers. Note the appearance of the work attribute Action Code in the repeating

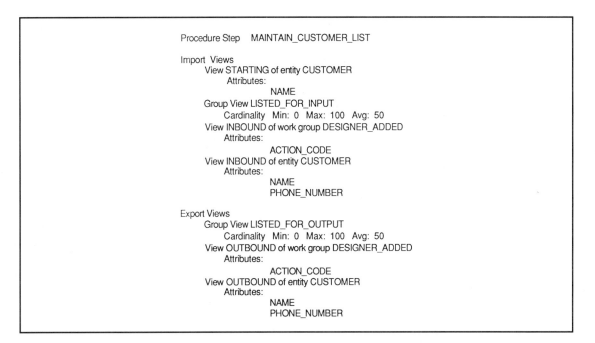

Figure 22-8. Data Views for MAINTAIN CUSTOMER PHONE NUMBERS

group view Listed. The designer can easily add logic in the Procedure Action Diagram to respond to the value of this work attribute. Figure 22-9 shows a screen that can be used to represent the data views from Figure 22-8.

Figure 22-9. Screen for MAINTAIN CUSTOMER PHONE NUMBERS

CLEAR SCREEN INPUT

In general, import views of online procedure steps are populated from screens. However, in many cases it is desirable to provide a shortcut initial entry into a procedure via clear screen input.

To illustrate, consider Figure 22-5. Ordinarily, in order for a terminal operator to invoke the List Customers procedure the following steps would be required at execution time:

1. The transaction code (assigned during the Construction stage) is entered on the screen and the operator presses ENTER.

2. The screen associated with List Customers is displayed with no values in its fields.

3. The operator keys in a value in the STARTING CUSTOMER NAME field and presses ENTER.

4. The screen associated with List Customers is displayed again, this time filled in with customer names and phone numbers.

However, it would be more convenient for frequent users of List Customers to be able to:

1. Enter the trancode, followed by a value for STARTING CUSTOMER NAME on a clear screen.

2. The screen associated with List Customers is displayed filled in with customer names and phone numbers.

The second alternative is made available through use of the **clear screen input** feature of the IEF.

The clear screen input feature also allows the population of a procedure's import views if it is "flowed to" from a non-IEF generated transaction. That is, by using the native facilities of the teleprocessing monitor, a non-IEF-generated transaction can send a message invoking an IEF generated transaction with parameters which map to the procedure step's import views.

Clear screen input can only be specified for the first procedure step in a procedure.

A complete description of the specification of the clear screen input feature is available in the *IEF Design Toolset Guide*.

23
PROCEDURE LOGIC DESIGN

OVERVIEW

This chapter addresses the design of detailed procedure logic using the Action Diagramming Tool. As mentioned in Chapter 18, the reader is assumed to have a working knowledge of Business Area Analysis. This working knowledge should include an understanding of action diagramming concepts. Chapter 14 of Part II, which introduces action diagramming and process logic analysis, is appropriate review material for the following discussion. In addition, the appendix entitled "Action Diagram Syntax" defines each action in the procedure action language. This appendix will prove useful as reference material for the reader who understands the basics of action diagramming.

The primary objective of this chapter is to present the tools and techniques available to the designer when defining the details of procedures. It describes in detail those action diagram features whose use is unique to the Business System Design stage and discusses when and how the designer uses them when dealing with BAA-specified action blocks, synthesized Procedure Action Diagrams, and designer-added procedures. The final section of this chapter examines the implications of dividing a single-step procedure into multiple procedure steps.

PROCEDURE ACTION DIAGRAM EXTENSIONS

The syntax of the Procedure Action Diagram is an extension of the Process Action Diagramming syntax used during Business Area Analysis. The discussion in this section is limited to those extensions unique to the Procedure Action Diagram. Consult Appendix D, "Action Diagram Syntax," for a brief review of the entire syntax.

The extensions explained in this section are:

- New action statements
- The use of special attributes
- The specification of External Action Blocks

New Action Statements

In addition to those available during Business Area Analysis, four new action diagramming statements are available during Business System Design. These language constructs relate to the use of special attributes and the setting of video properties.

The COMMAND IS Action Statement

The COMMAND IS action statement sets the value of the special attribute Command. For descriptions of the function and use of the Command special attribute, see the sections entitled "The Purpose of Commands" in Chapter 20 and "Commands and Flows" in Chapter 21.

The format of the COMMAND IS action statement is:

COMMAND IS command_value

The designer chooses the value of Command from a list of defined command values for the business system.

Since there is only one occurrence of the Command special attribute, the execution of a COMMAND IS action destroys its previous contents.

The PRINTER TERMINAL IS Action Statement

The PRINTER TERMINAL IS action statement sets the value of the special attribute Printer Terminal ID. If a value for this special attribute is present when a procedure step finishes executing, the procedure step prints a copy of its associated screen on the identified terminal. This statement has meaning only in online procedures.

The format of the PRINTER TERMINAL IS action statement is:

PRINTER TERMINAL IS literal_value

The literal_value is any eight-character text constant that represents a valid terminal ID.

Since there is only one occurrence of the Printer Terminal ID special attribute, the execution of a PRINTER TERMINAL IS action destroys its previous contents.

The PRINTER TERMINAL IS action statement is actually available when building action diagrams during Business Area Analysis, but it should not be used there.

The MAKE Action Statement

The MAKE action statement dynamically sets the video properties of onscreen fields and special fields from within an action diagram. Chapter 22 discusses video attributes in detail.

The MAKE action statement is valid only in a Procedure Action Diagram that represents a procedure step. It cannot appear in subordinate action blocks. MAKE has meaning only in online procedures.

The format of the MAKE action statement is:

MAKE export-attribute-view | ERROR
video-attribute-list |

The ERROR option causes the field associated with the export attribute view to be set to the Error Video Properties specified for that field. The *video attribute list* option allows the designer to explicitly specify video attribute properties within the action diagram.

In general, the use of the ERROR option is preferred over the *video attribute list* option because it provides a degree of standardization.

The following action diagram fragments feature the MAKE action statement:

```
┌─  IF employee_salary IS GREATER THAN 500000
│       MAKE output employee_number ERROR
│       MAKE output employee_salary Unprotected High Intensity Red Blinking
└─
```

Action Diagram Use of Special Attributes

In Chapter 14, the use of special attributes in the action diagram was mentioned only briefly. Here the use of specific special attributes of use during Business System Design is addressed in more detail.

- **Command**. The data type of the Command special attribute is Text. The designer can modify it with the COMMAND IS statement or compare it with any possible value of Command or text value.

  Examples:

  COMMAND IS add

```
┌─  IF COMMAND IS EQUAL TO 'add'
│       EXIT STATE IS command-ok
└─
```

- **Exit State**. The data type of Exit State is Text. The designer can modify it with the EXIT STATE IS statement and compare it to possible exit state values.

  Examples:

  EXIT STATE IS customer_not_found

```
┌─  IF EXIT STATE IS EQUAL TO customer_not_found
│       MAKE customer number Unprotected High Intensity Red Blinking
└─
```

- **Current Date**. The data type of Current Date is Date. The designer cannot modify it, but can compare it with any view of a date attribute and use it as the source for a SET statement whose target is the view of a date attribute.

  Examples:

```
┌─  IF CURRENT DATE IS EQUAL TO client_checkup_date
│       EXIT STATE IS send_client_reminder
└─
```

  SET customer date_added TO CURRENT DATE

- **Current Time**. The data type of Current Time is Time. The designer cannot modify it, but can compare it with any view of a time attribute and use it as the source for a SET statement whose target is the view of a time attribute.

  The examples shown for Current Date also apply to Current Time, with appropriate substitutions.

- **Terminal ID**. The data type of Terminal ID is Text. The designer cannot modify it, but can compare it with any view of a text attribute or literal, and use it as the source for a SET statement whose target is the view of a text attribute.

Examples:

```
┌─  IF TERMINAL ID IS NOT EQUAL TO user usual_terminal_ID
│        EXIT STATE IS security_violation
└─

    SET user last_terminal_used TO TERMINAL ID
```

- **User ID**. The data type of the User ID special attribute is Text. The designer cannot modify it, but can compare it with any view of a text attribute or literal, and use it as the source of a SET statement whose target is the view of a text attribute.

Example:

```
┌─  IF USER_ID IS EQUAL TO "DAACJCN"
│        EXIT STATE IS call_the_fbi
└─
```

- **Printer Terminal ID**. The data type of the Printer Terminal ID special attribute is Text. The designer can modify it with the PRINTER TERMINAL IS statement, compare it with any view of a text attribute or literal, and use it as the source for a SET statement whose target is the view of a text attribute.

Examples:

```
    PRINTER TERMINAL IS 'LYP7P2'

┌─  IF PRINTER TERMINAL ID IS EQUAL TO 'LYP7P2'
│        EXIT STATE IS all_is_well
└─

    SET work save_pterm TO PRINTER TERMINAL ID
```

- **Trancode**. The data type of the Trancode special attribute is Text. The designer cannot modify it, but can compare it with any view of a text attribute or literal, and use it as the source for a SET statement whose target is the view of a text attribute.

Example:

```
┌─  IF TRANCODE IS EQUAL TO "DX01"
│      AND TERMINAL_ID IS NOT EQUAL TO valid_dx01_terminal
│        EXIT STATE IS security_violation
└─
```

- **Next Transaction ID.** The data type of the Next Transaction ID special attribute is Text. The designer can modify it with the SET NEXTTRAN statement, but cannot inspect its contents.

If, at the conclusion of procedure step execution, the Next Transaction ID special attribute contains a non-blank value, the Dialog Manager will attempt to cause the transaction specified to be invoked using the facilities of the teleprocessing monitor (for example, IMS, CICS and TSO). This feature is used to implement dialog flows to non-IEF-generated transactions.

Example:

```
SET NEXTTRAN TO
    CONCAT("DM01",CONCAT(" ",customer_name))
```

- **Subscript of...** There is one subscript available for each explicitly subscripted repeating group view (see Chapter 14) named "Subscript of <explicitly_subscripted_repeating_group_view>." Each one's data type is numeric. The designer can modify it with the SET SUBSCRIPT action statement, can compare it with any view of a numeric attribute, and can use it as the source of a SET statement for which the target is a numeric special attribute or the view of a numeric attribute.

  The value of Subscript OF determines the current occurrence within a repeating group view.

  Example:

  ```
  SET SUBSCRIPT OF repeating_product TO
      SUBSCRIPT OF repeating product + 1
  ```

- **Last of...** There is one "last of" special attribute available for each explicitly subscripted repeating group view (see Chapter 14) named "Last of <explicitly_subscripted_repeating_group_view>." Each one's data type is numeric. The designer can modify it with the SET LAST action statement, can compare it with any view of a numeric attribute, and can use it as the source of a SET statement for which the target is a numeric special attribute or the view of a numeric attribute.

  The value of Last Of for a repeating group view determines the highest used occurrence number.

  Examples:

  ```
  SET LAST OF repeating product TO
      SUBSCRIPT OF repeating product

  ┌─ IF LAST OF repeating_product IS GREATER THAN 100
  │      SET SUBSCRIPT OF repeating product TO 1
  └─
  ```

- **Max of...** There is one "max of" special attribute available for each explicitly subscripted repeating group view (see Chapter 14) named "Max of <explicitly_subscripted_repeating_group_view>." Each one's data type is numeric. The designer cannot modify it, but can compare it with any view of a numeric attribute, and can use it as the source of a SET statement for which the target is a numeric special attribute or the view of a numeric attribute.

  The value of Max Of for a repeating group view is its maximum cardinality.

  Example:

  ```
  ┌─ IF SUBSCRIPT OF repeating_product IS EQUAL TO
  │      MAX OF repeating_product
  ←├──────── ESCAPE
  └─
  ```

External Action Blocks

A procedure must sometimes make use of logic that is not defined using the IEF. For example, the designer may wish to use an installation standard date manipulation routine that takes into account its own holidays and work schedules. In another case, the designer may need to access data bases and files that are not yet supported by the IEF. Accessing logic not originally specified using the IEF is possible through the use of External Action Blocks.

An **External Action Block** is an action block that has only three components:

- Import Views

- Export Views

- The designation that it is external

An External Action Block contains no action statements of its own. The designation **external** on the action block definition indicates that a non-IEF-generated program will be used to obtain the data for the action block's export view. Action blocks of this sort can be the object of a USE statement in normal Procedure Action Diagrams or Blocks. During the Construction stage, the IEF ensures that the program referenced by the External Action Block is properly referenced by IEF-generated programs.

Figure 23-1 illustrates an IEF-defined Procedure Action Diagram that references an external date manipulation routine called Date Services. Figure 23-2 shows the External Action Block definition of the Date Services routine.

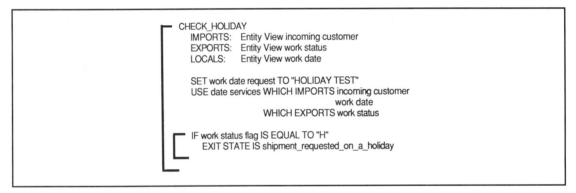

Figure 23-1. Procedure Action Block Referencing an External Action

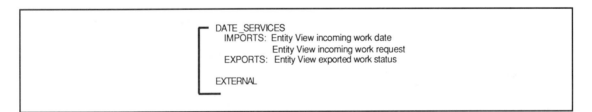

Figure 23-2. External Action Block

The *IEF Construction Toolset Guide* presents conventions for writing and interfacing to External Action Blocks.

DESIGNING PROCEDURE LOGIC

This section describes the detailed refinement of procedure logic for three separate cases:

- The refinement of action blocks developed during Business Area Analysis

- The refinement of synthesized Procedure Action Diagrams

• The construction of designer-added procedures

Refining Action Blocks Developed during Business Area Analysis

Action blocks developed during Business Area Analysis to support elementary processes or as business algorithms are available for implementation during BSD. In general, the designer should strive to avoid modifying these action diagrams. However, if a case arises in which, for implementation purposes, the BAA-developed action diagram must be changed, the following should be borne in mind:

• All changes made by the designer are visible to the analyst. The designer is actually modifying the *same specification* originally created by the analyst.

• The intent of the analyst must not be violated. The designer must limit himself to the specification of implementation-oriented modifications. Any modifications which reflect a change in the business model should be made by (or at least approved by) the analyst.

• Usually, if the analyst has specified complete process logic during Business Area Analysis, few changes to the resulting action blocks are necessary during Business System Design.

Refining Synthesized Procedure Action Diagrams

Synthesized Procedure Action Diagrams are created automatically by the IEF during process to procedure transformation (see Chapter 20). These action blocks can be considered a starting point for designing the detailed logic of the procedure.

Designers generally make changes to the Procedure Action Diagram to address the following kinds of processing:

• Handling termination conditions

• Dynamically modifying video properties

• Providing restartability

• Smoothing the implementation

Handling Termination Conditions

The designer must address all possible termination conditions for the procedure step's synthesized Procedure Action Diagram.

Figure 23-3 is a duplicate of the synthesized Procedure Action Diagram for the Maintain Customer procedure used to discuss transformation in Chapter 20. It shows how a procedure step's action diagram looks immediately after transformation. Note that Exit State is never set, even for the obvious condition that an invalid command is requested.

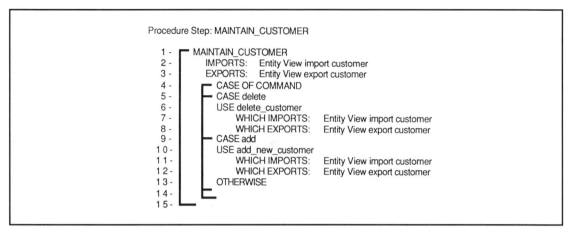

Figure 23-3. Procedure Action Diagram for MAINTAIN CUSTOMER

Figure 23-4 shows the same Procedure Action Diagram after the designer has addressed termination conditions.

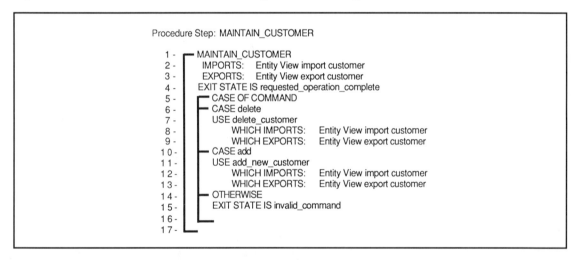

Figure 23-4. MAINTAIN CUSTOMER Supplemented with EXIT STATE IS Actions

This example raises two issues:

• Exit State is set to "Requested Operation Complete" before any other logic is executed (line 4). By initializing Exit State to the positive condition here, the designer need only consider exception conditions throughout the remainder of the procedure step logic. If Exit State is never set to a different value as the result of an exception, the positive condition will remain set.

Using this technique, positive conditions need never be addressed in the USEd action blocks.

• Exit State is not set after the USEd action blocks are invoked (lines 7 and 11). This is because one assumes that exception conditions are addressed in the action blocks themselves, as described above.

The EXIT STATE IS action added at line 15 is a typical case of setting Exit State for an exception.

Dynamically Modifying Video Properties

These comments apply only to online procedures.

As previously mentioned under the MAKE action statement description, the MAKE action statement is restricted to Procedure Action Diagrams that directly support procedure steps. Thus, any special handling of video attributes in a process-implementing procedure must take place in the synthesized Procedure Action Diagram.

The procedure logic can inspect the setting of Exit State on a return from a transformed Procedure Action Block to determine whether video properties should be dynamically modified. An example of this technique appears in Figure 23-5 where the designer has added a condition followed by a MAKE action to highlight the name of a duplicate customer (lines 14 through 16).

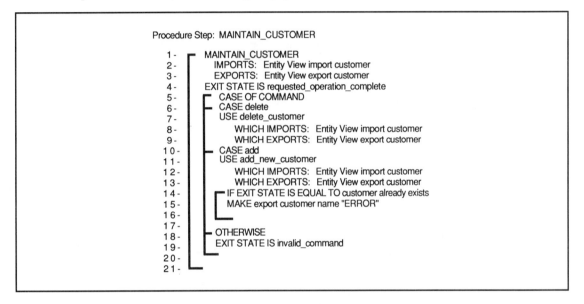

Figure 23-5. MAINTAIN CUSTOMER Including a MAKE Action

Providing Restartability

These comments apply only to batch procedures.

In chapter 21, the issues surrounding the restartability of batch procedures were discussed. Figure 23-7 is an example of a fully commented Procedure Action Diagram for the batch process-implementing procedure named Batch Maintenance. It handles checkpointing and restart at last checkpoint, based on the Dialog Flow Diagram in figure 23-6. The views used by Batch Maintenance are presented in figure 23-8. Note that the technique for using external action blocks for sequential file processing is also illustrated in these figures.

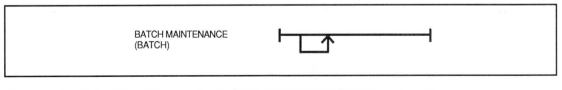

Figure 23-6. Dialog Flow Diagram for BATCH MAINTENANCE Procedure Step

Procedure Step: BATCH_MAINTENANCE

```
 1-  ┌─  BATCH_MAINTENANCE
 2- │       IMPORTS:            Work View   returned_from_transfer work
 3- │       EXPORTS:            Work View   sent_through_transfer work
 4- │       LOCALS:             Work View   restart work
 5- │                           Work View   target work
 6- │                           Work View   returned work
 7- │                           Entity View returned customer
 8- │                           Work View   commit ief_supplied
 9- │                           Work View   message work
10- │
11- │    EXIT STATE IS requested_operation_complete
12- │
13- │    NOTE ...FIRST, check to see if this is a RESTARTED
14- │           procedure. If the number written to the restart file by
15- │           WRITE RESTART RECORD in a previous execution is greater
16- │           than zero, it means that BATCH MAINTENANCE previously
17- │           failed in mid-execution.
18- │
19- │  ┌─ IF returned_from_transfer work restart_count IS EQUAL TO 0
20- │  │   USE get_restart_number
21- │  │      WHICH EXPORTS: Work View   target work
22- │  │   NOTE
23- │  │       GET RESTART NUMBER is an external action block which
24- │  │       reads the restart file (written by WRITE RESTART
25- │  │       NUMBER at the end of the action block.) It passes
26- │  │       back a value of zero if the restart file is empty
27- │  │
28- │  │   NOTE
29- │  │       GET TRANSACTION is an external action block that reads
30- │  │       a sequential file of CUSTOMERS. It returns CUSTOMER
31- │  │       details (in RETURNED CUSTOMER) and a request code (in
32- │  │       RETURNED WORK). Possible values of REQUEST TYPE are:
33- │  │       - A = Add (CREATE) this customer
34- │  │       - C = Change (UPDATE) this customer
35- │  │       - D = Delete this customer
36- │  │       - E = End of input file reached
37- │  │
38- │  │   USE get_transaction
39- │  │      WHICH EXPORTS: Entity View  returned customer
40- │  │                          Work View  returned work
41- │  │   NOTE
42- │  │       ...NEXT, if we're restarting, spin through the
43- │  │       transaction file until you get to the first one that
44- │  │       wasn't processed properly the first time
```

Figure 23-7. BATCH MAINTENANCE Procedure Action Diagram (Part 1)

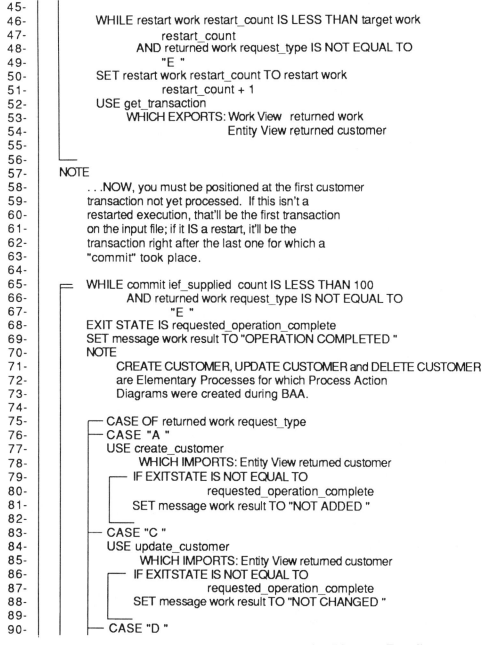

```
45-
46-         WHILE restart work restart_count IS LESS THAN target work
47-             restart_count
48-             AND returned work request_type IS NOT EQUAL TO
49-                 "E "
50-     SET restart work restart_count TO restart work
51-             restart_count + 1
52-     USE get_transaction
53-         WHICH EXPORTS: Work View  returned work
54-                        Entity View returned customer
55-
56-
57-  NOTE
58-      . . .NOW, you must be positioned at the first customer
59-      transaction not yet processed.  If this isn't a
60-      restarted execution, that'll be the first transaction
61-      on the input file; if it IS a restart, it'll be the
62-      transaction right after the last one for which a
63-      "commit" took place.
64-
65-      WHILE commit ief_supplied  count IS LESS THAN 100
66-             AND returned work request_type IS NOT EQUAL TO
67-                 "E "
68-     EXIT STATE IS requested_operation_complete
69-     SET message work result TO "OPERATION COMPLETED "
70-     NOTE
71-         CREATE CUSTOMER, UPDATE CUSTOMER and DELETE CUSTOMER
72-         are Elementary Processes for which Process Action
73-         Diagrams were created during BAA.
74-
75-      CASE OF returned work request_type
76-      CASE "A "
77-      USE create_customer
78-          WHICH IMPORTS: Entity View returned customer
79-          IF EXITSTATE IS NOT EQUAL TO
80-                     requested_operation_complete
81-          SET message work result TO "NOT ADDED "
82-
83-      CASE "C "
84-      USE update_customer
85-          WHICH IMPORTS: Entity View returned customer
86-          IF EXITSTATE IS NOT EQUAL TO
87-                     requested_operation_complete
88-          SET message work result TO "NOT CHANGED "
89-
90-      CASE "D "
```

Figure 23-7. BATCH MAINTENANCE Procedure Action Diagram (Part 2)

```
 91-          USE delete_customer
 92-              WHICH IMPORTS: Entity View returned customer
 93-          ┌─ IF EXITSTATE IS NOT EQUAL TO
 94-          │            requested_operation_complete
 95-          │  SET message work result TO "NOT DELETED "
 96-          │
 97-          └
 98-      NOTE
 99-          WRITE MESSAGE is an external action block that writes
100-          a result message to a message file.  It forms the
101-          message based on REQUEST_TYPE (in RETURNED WORK), the
102-          details in RETURNED CUSTOMER and RESULT (in MESSAGE
103-          WORK).
104-
105-      USE write_message
106-          WHICH IMPORTS: Entity View returned customer
107-                         Work View message work
108-                         Work View returned work
109-
110-      SET commit ief_supplied count TO commit ief_supplied
111-                  count + 1
112-      USE get_transaction
113-          WHICH EXPORTs: Entity View returned customer
114-                         Work View returned work
115- ┘
116- ┌─ IF returned work request_type IS EQUAL TO "E "
117-    SET sent_through_transfer work restart_count TO 0
118- ┌─ ELSE
119-    SET sent_through_transfer work restart_count TO
120-                returned_from_transfer work restart_count +
121-                commit ief_supplied count + restart work
122-                restart_count
123-    EXIT STATE IS process_commit
124- ┘
125- SET target work restart_count TO sent_through_transfer
126-              work restart_count
127- NOTE
128-       WRITE RESTART NUMBER is an external action block that
129-       records the number of input transactions for which
130-       database updates have been committed.
131-
132- USE write_restart_number
133-     WHICH IMPORTS: Work View  target work
134- ┘
```

Figure 23-7. BATCH MAINTENANCE Procedure Action Diagram (Part 3)

Import Views
View RETURNED_FROM_TRANSFER of work group WORK
Attributes:
RESTART_COUNT
Export Views
View SENT_THROUGH_TRANSFER of work group WORK
Attributes:
RESTART_COUNT
Local Views
View RESTART of work group WORK
Attributes:
RESTART_COUNT
View TARGET of work group WORK
Attributes:
RESTART_COUNT
View RETURNED of work group WORK
Attributes:
REQUEST_TYPE
View RETURNED of entity CUSTOMER
Attributes:
NUMBER
NAME
STATUS
CREDIT_RATING
BILL_TO_ADDRESS_LINE_1
BILL_TO_ADDRESS_LINE_2
BILL_TO_ADDRESS_LINE_3
BILL_TO_CITY
BILL_TO_STATE
BILL_TO_ZIP
View COMMIT of work group IEF_SUPPLIED
Attributes:
COUNT
View MESSAGE of work group WORK
Attributes:
RESULT

Figure 23-8. View Definitions for the BATCH MAINTENANCE Procedure Step

Smoothing the Implementation

Depending on the characteristics of the implementation, the designer may supplement the action diagram significantly, as in the restartability example above. In general, any logic required to provide a reasonable implementation of elementary processes is permissible. Suppose, for example, that while considering the implementation of Maintain Customer and the requirements of the user community, the designer reached the following conclusions:

- A user should never be allowed to delete a customer without first displaying it.

- If a delete fails, the Command special field should contain the value "Display" in anticipation of the user's next request.

- A user may delete the customer he just added.

Figure 23-9 presents one possible solution to these requirements in the Procedure Step Action Diagram called Maintain Customer Version 2.

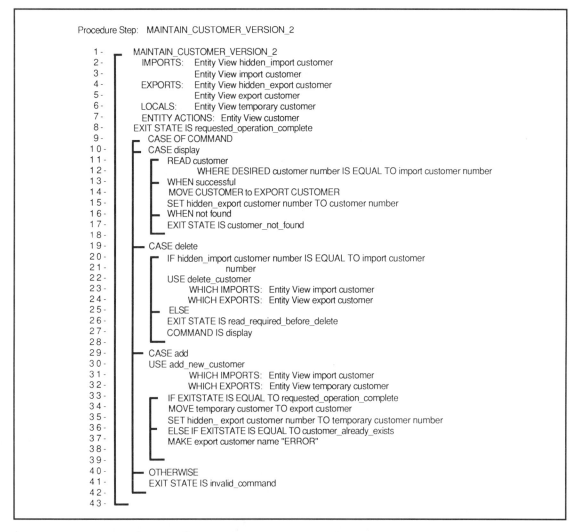

```
Procedure Step:   MAINTAIN_CUSTOMER_VERSION_2

 1-        MAINTAIN_CUSTOMER_VERSION_2
 2-          IMPORTS:    Entity View hidden_import customer
 3-                      Entity View import customer
 4-          EXPORTS:    Entity View hidden_export customer
 5-                      Entity View export customer
 6-          LOCALS:     Entity View temporary customer
 7-          ENTITY ACTIONS:  Entity View customer
 8-        EXIT STATE IS requested_operation_complete
 9-          CASE OF COMMAND
10-          CASE display
11-              READ customer
12-                  WHERE DESIRED customer number IS EQUAL TO import customer number
13-              WHEN successful
14-               MOVE CUSTOMER to EXPORT CUSTOMER
15-               SET hidden_export customer number TO customer number
16-              WHEN not found
17-               EXIT STATE IS customer_not_found
18-
19-          CASE delete
20-              IF hidden_import customer number IS EQUAL TO import customer
21-                          number
22-              USE delete_customer
23-                  WHICH IMPORTS:   Entity View import customer
24-                  WHICH EXPORTS:   Entity View export customer
25-               ELSE
26-              EXIT STATE IS read_required_before_delete
27-              COMMAND IS display
28-
29-          CASE add
30-          USE add_new_customer
31-                  WHICH IMPORTS:   Entity View import customer
32-                  WHICH EXPORTS:   Entity View temporary customer
33-              IF EXITSTATE IS EQUAL TO requested_operation_complete
34-              MOVE temporary customer TO export customer
35-              SET hidden_ export customer number TO temporary customer number
36-              ELSE IF EXITSTATE IS EQUAL TO customer_already_exists
37-              MAKE export customer name "ERROR"
38-
39-
40-          OTHERWISE
41-          EXIT STATE IS invalid_command
42-
43-
```

Figure 23-9. Procedure Action Diagram for MAINTAIN CUSTOMERVERSION 2

Note the following:

- This procedure step includes several new data views:
    - The requirement for a Display action implies the need for a READ statement, which requires a new entity action view of CUSTOMER (line 7).
    - The requirement that a Delete be preceded by a Display or an Add implies the need to save data after a Display or an Add. One can test the saved data before a Delete to verify that the correct occurrence was selected for deletion. A simple way to save data between procedure step executions without displaying it onscreen is to use the hidden field technique described in Chapter 22.
    - In this case, the Customer Number field is exported as a hidden field through the view Hidden Export Customer (line 4) and imported as a hidden field through the view Hidden Import Customer (line 2).
    - The local view of CUSTOMER (line 6) is explained later.
- This procedure step includes a new CASE option to the CASE OF COMMAND action. If the command is Display, the requested customer is read and displayed (lines 10 through 18). Notice that a MOVE action is required to populate the export view from the entity action view (line 14). Note also that if the READ statement is successful, the Customer Number is saved in the hidden field Hidden Export Customer Number.
- In the Add case (lines 30 through 39), since the user may delete the customer he just added, one must save the newly added customer's number as a hidden field just as in the Display case (see line 15).

Building Designer-Added Procedures

As described in Chapter 20, designer-added procedures are implementation-specific procedures that improve or simplify some characteristic of the overall implementation. They must not alter the results of Business Area Analysis.

To avoid compromising the results of analysis, designer-added procedures should never modify business information. In other words, designer-added procedures must never use the entity actions CREATE, UPDATE, or DELETE (except for design entity types, mentioned in Chapter 19). Such a requirement identified during Business System Design generally points out a deficiency in analysis that must be corrected by adding or modifying a process.

The sample Menu procedures shown in Chapter 21 (Figures 21-10 and 21-17) exemplify the typical use of a designer-added procedure. The action diagram appearing in that example is complete.

Another example of a designer-added procedure is shown in Figures 23-10 through 23-12. This procedure produces a list of CUSTOMERS and, based on the value of an action code next to each, flows to a process-implementing procedure, as illustrated in the Dialog Flow Diagram shown in Figure 23-13.

Procedure Step: LIST_CUSTOMERS

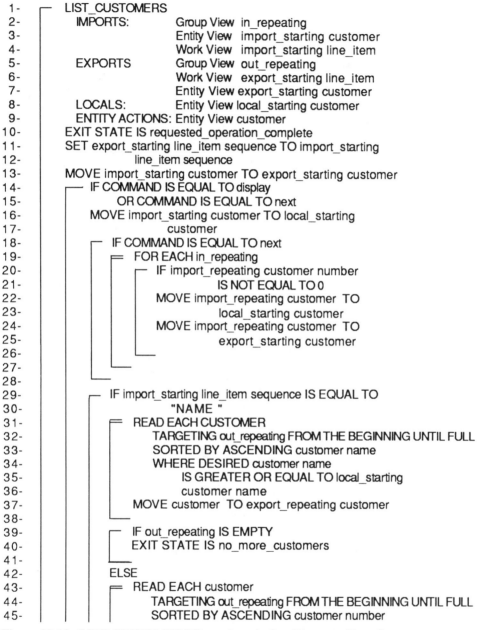

```
1-    ┌─  LIST_CUSTOMERS
2-    │      IMPORTS:          Group View  in_repeating
3-    │                        Entity View  import_starting customer
4-    │                        Work View  import_starting line_item
5-    │      EXPORTS           Group View  out_repeating
6-    │                        Work View  export_starting line_item
7-    │                        Entity View export_starting customer
8-    │      LOCALS:           Entity View local_starting customer
9-    │      ENTITY ACTIONS: Entity View customer
10-   │   EXIT STATE IS requested_operation_complete
11-   │   SET export_starting line_item sequence TO import_starting
12-   │              line_item sequence
13-   │   MOVE import_starting customer TO export_starting customer
14-   │   ┌─ IF COMMAND IS EQUAL TO display
15-   │   │        OR COMMAND IS EQUAL TO next
16-   │   │    MOVE import_starting customer TO local_starting
17-   │   │            customer
18-   │   │   ┌─ IF COMMAND IS EQUAL TO next
19-   │   │   │═  FOR EACH in_repeating
20-   │   │   │    ┌─ IF import_repeating customer number
21-   │   │   │    │        IS NOT EQUAL TO 0
22-   │   │   │    │   MOVE import_repeating customer  TO
23-   │   │   │    │           local_starting customer
24-   │   │   │    │   MOVE import_repeating customer  TO
25-   │   │   │    │           export_starting customer
26-   │   │   │    └─
27-   │   │   └─
28-   │   │
29-   │   │   ┌─ IF import_starting line_item sequence IS EQUAL TO
30-   │   │   │        "NAME "
31-   │   │   │═  READ EACH CUSTOMER
32-   │   │   │        TARGETING out_repeating FROM THE BEGINNING UNTIL FULL
33-   │   │   │        SORTED BY ASCENDING customer name
34-   │   │   │        WHERE DESIRED customer name
35-   │   │   │            IS GREATER OR EQUAL TO local_starting
36-   │   │   │            customer name
37-   │   │   │    MOVE customer  TO export_repeating customer
38-   │   │   └─
39-   │   │   ┌─ IF out_repeating IS EMPTY
40-   │   │   │    EXIT STATE IS no_more_customers
41-   │   │   └─
42-   │   │   ELSE
43-   │   │   │═  READ EACH customer
44-   │   │   │        TARGETING out_repeating FROM THE BEGINNING UNTIL FULL
45-   │   │   │        SORTED BY ASCENDING customer number
```

Figure 23-10. LIST CUSTOMERS Procedure Action Diagram (Part 1)

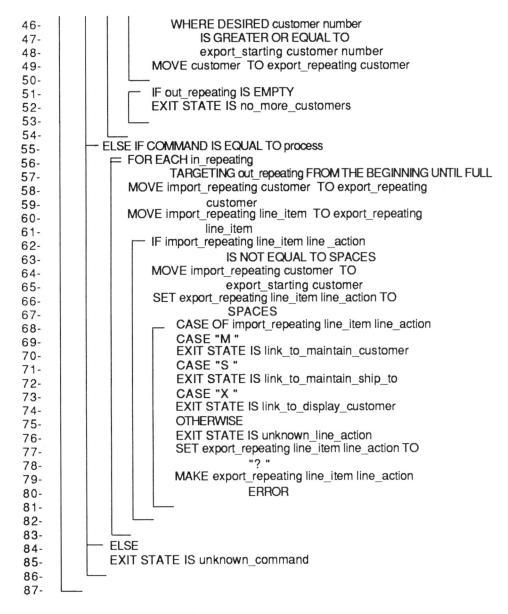

```
46-                        WHERE DESIRED customer number
47-                              IS GREATER OR EQUAL TO
48-                              export_starting customer number
49-                  MOVE customer  TO export_repeating customer
50-
51-          ┌─  IF out_repeating IS EMPTY
52-              EXIT STATE IS no_more_customers
53-          └─
54-
55-  ┌─ ELSE IF COMMAND IS EQUAL TO process
56-     ┌  FOR EACH in_repeating
57-              TARGETING out_repeating FROM THE BEGINNING UNTIL FULL
58-        MOVE import_repeating customer  TO export_repeating
59-                      customer
60-        MOVE import_repeating line_item  TO export_repeating
61-                      line_item
62-          ┌─  IF import_repeating line_item line _action
63-                          IS NOT EQUAL TO SPACES
64-              MOVE import_repeating customer  TO
65-                      export_starting customer
66-              SET export_repeating line_item line_action TO
67-                      SPACES
68-               ┌─  CASE OF import_repeating line_item line_action
69-                   CASE "M "
70-                   EXIT STATE IS link_to_maintain_customer
71-                   CASE "S "
72-                   EXIT STATE IS link_to_maintain_ship_to
73-                   CASE "X "
74-                   EXIT STATE IS link_to_display_customer
75-                   OTHERWISE
76-                   EXIT STATE IS unknown_line_action
77-                   SET export_repeating line_item line_action TO
78-                          "? "
79-                   MAKE export_repeating line_item line_action
80-                              ERROR
81-               └─
82-          └─
83-     └
84-  ┌─ ELSE
85-     EXIT STATE IS unknown_command
86-  └─
87-
```

Figure 23-10. LIST CUSTOMERS Procedure Action Diagram (Part 2)

Import Views

Group View IN_REPEATING
    Cardinality Min: 1 Max: 10 Avg: 10
    Optional Import
View IMPORT_REPEATING of entity CUSTOMER
    Optional Import
    Attributes:
        NUMBER
        NAME
        STATUS
        CREDIT_RATING
View IMPORT_REPEATING of work group LINE_ITEM
    Attributes:
        LINE_ACTION
View IMPORT_STARTING of entity CUSTOMER
    Attributes:
      opt   NUMBER
      opt   NAME
View IMPORT_STARTING of work group LINE_ITEM
    Attributes:
      opt   SEQUENCE

Export Views

Group View OUT_REPEATING
    Cardinality Min: 1 Max: 10 Avg: 10
View EXPORT_REPEATING of work group LINE_ITEM
    Attributes:
        LINE_ACTION
View EXPORT_REPEATING of entity CUSTOMER
    Attributes:
        NUMBER
        NAME
        STATUS
        CREDIT_RATING
View EXPORT_STARTING of work group LINE_ITEM
    Attributes:
        SEQUENCE
View EXPORT_STARTING of entity CUSTOMER
    Attributes:
        NUMBER
        NAME

Local Views

View LOCAL_STARTING of entity CUSTOMER
    Attributes:
        NUMBER
        NAME

Entity Action Views

View of entity CUSTOMER
    Attributes:
        NUMBER
        NAME
        STATUS
        CREDIT_RATING

Figure 23-11. View Definitions for the LIST CUSTOMERS Procedure Step

TRANCODE   FREENBLATT-TRUESPRECHER CONSOLIDATED LTD   MM-DD-YY
                             CUSTOMER LIST   HH:MM:SS
                                                            <USERID>

STARTING CUSTOMER NUMBER: 9999999999 LIST SEQUENCE (NAME or NUMBER): XXXXXXXX
STARTING CUSTOMER NAME: XXXXXXXXXXXXXXXXXXXXXXXXXXXXXX

```
        ACT Number      Name                                  Status     Credit Rating
        XX 9999999999   XXXXXXXXXXXXXXXXXXXXXXXXXXXXXX         XX         9
        XX 9999999999   XXXXXXXXXXXXXXXXXXXXXXXXXXXXXX         XX         9
        XX 9999999999   XXXXXXXXXXXXXXXXXXXXXXXXXXXXXX         XX         9
        XX 9999999999   XXXXXXXXXXXXXXXXXXXXXXXXXXXXXX         XX         9
        XX 9999999999   XXXXXXXXXXXXXXXXXXXXXXXXXXXXXX         XX         9
        XX 9999999999   XXXXXXXXXXXXXXXXXXXXXXXXXXXXXX         XX         9
        XX 9999999999   XXXXXXXXXXXXXXXXXXXXXXXXXXXXXX         XX         9
        XX 9999999999   XXXXXXXXXXXXXXXXXXXXXXXXXXXXXX         XX         9
        XX 9999999999   XXXXXXXXXXXXXXXXXXXXXXXXXXXXXX         XX         9
        XX 9999999999   XXXXXXXXXXXXXXXXXXXXXXXXXXXXXX         XX         9
```

ACT: X-Full Screen Display,   M-Maintain Customer Details,   S-Maintain Ship-To Info
Command ==>

Figure 23-12. Screen Layout for the LIST CUSTOMERS Procedure Step

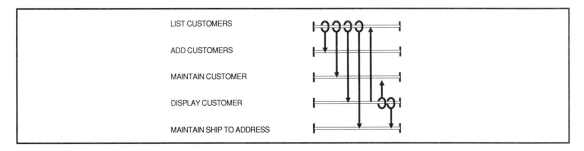

LIST CUSTOMERS

ADD CUSTOMERS

MAINTAIN CUSTOMER

DISPLAY CUSTOMER

MAINTAIN SHIP TO ADDRESS

Figure 23-13. Dialog Flow Diagram for the LIST CUSTOMERS Procedure Step

Note the following:

- The terminal operator can choose between displaying the customers in NAME or NUMBER sequence.

- If the operator requests a DISPLAY (by entering DISPLAY in the Command field or by pressing the function key associated with the command value "display"), LIST CUSTOMERS builds a list starting with the customer specified in the STARTING CUSTOMER fields.

- If the operator requests a NEXT operation, the last populated item in the incoming repeating group view is used as the starting point of the list. Assuming that the example screen does not use the automatic scrolling feature, this will result in the last entry on the screen before the NEXT operation appearing at the top of the list after the NEXT operation.

  It is interesting to note that the NEXT action in this example works whether or not the automatic scrolling feature is used. If automatic scrolling were specified for the screen, the IEF Dialog Manager would handle all NEXT operations until the operator displayed the final item of the repeating group; if the operator were to enter NEXT again, the Dialog Manager would pass the NEXT command to the Procedure Action Diagram for processing.

- If the operator requests a PROCESS operation, the first item in the list that has a valid line item action is used to trigger a process-implementing procedure (based on the setting of EXIT STATE in the action diagram in Figure 23-10 and the flows shown in Figure 23-13).

- Assuming that EXPORT_STARTING_CUSTOMER is specified as Data Sent on each of the flows from List Customers, each of the flowed-to procedures will have their import views populated with the number of the selected customer when they begin execution (if the flow action is execute first) or have their screens displayed (if the flow action is display first).

- Notice that all flows are implemented as links (Figure 23-13). Notice also that the logic in the Procedure Action Diagram sets the EXPORT LINE ITEM ACTION of the selected line item to spaces. Assuming that the flow action for the return of each link is execute first, List Customers will be re-executed whenever one of the process-implementing procedures returns to it. If List Customers finds another valid line item action, it will trigger another flow.

  If the terminal operator enters multiple valid line actions, then it will appear to him that all of those actions are processed in sequence without any intervening displays of the screen for List Customers.

There is another class of designer-added procedure that is less frequently used. This class of designer-added procedure is responsible for displaying and maintaining design entity types.

Imagine, for example, that the designer must determine the failure rate of each operator who adds customers using the Maintain Customer procedure step. This would involve the following actions:

- Add a design entity type that has attributes of Terminal ID (to identify the operator), number of executions of Add Customer, and number of failures of Add Customer.

- Modify the Maintain Customer action diagram to add to the number of executions each time Add Customer is invoked and to add to the number of failures each time it fails.

The mechanism for displaying this information on a terminal is a designer-added procedure. Figure 23-14 is a designer-added procedure that supports this example.

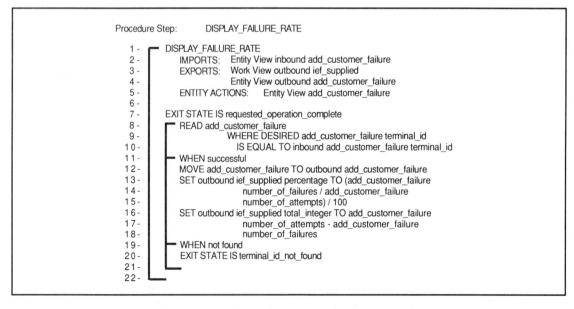

Figure 23-14. Procedure Action Diagram for Designer-Added Procedure

This example references two views of the IEF-supplied work attribute set: IEF Supplied Percentage is used to show the percentage of failures to attempts and IEF Supplied Total Integer shows the operator's total number of successes (calculated as number of attempts less number of failures).

DIVIDING PROCEDURES INTO MULTIPLE STEPS

This section explains the recommended technique for dividing a procedure into multiple procedure steps. The section entitled "Procedures and Procedure Steps" in Chapter 20 describes the reasons for and hazards of splitting the implementation of an elementary process. Performing such surgery on a procedure is difficult to avoid when a procedure processes more information than can fit on a single screen. In such a case, one must define multiple procedure steps, one for each screen required.

For example, consider the elementary process Add New Customer, which has been used in numerous examples in this guide. Rather than combining Add New Customer and Delete Customer into a single Maintain Customer procedure, as was done earlier, suppose that the designer opts to define Add New Customer in its own procedure. In reality, the list of attributes with which Add New Customer deals is small enough for all views to fit on a single screen. For the purpose of illustration, however, assume that the designer must divide Add New Customer into two procedure steps as follows:

- Add First Part is responsible for collecting the following attributes:
  - Name
  - Street Address
  - City
  - State
- Add Last Part is responsible for collecting the following attributes:
  - Phone Number
  - Credit Limit

In implementing the elementary process Add New Customer in two procedure steps, the designer should implement all update type entity actions (CREATE, UPDATE, and DELETE) in the final procedure step to avoid violating the integrity of the data base. By observing this guideline, the designer guarantees that the view of the business represented on the data base remains in a consistent state if the system fails between procedure steps.

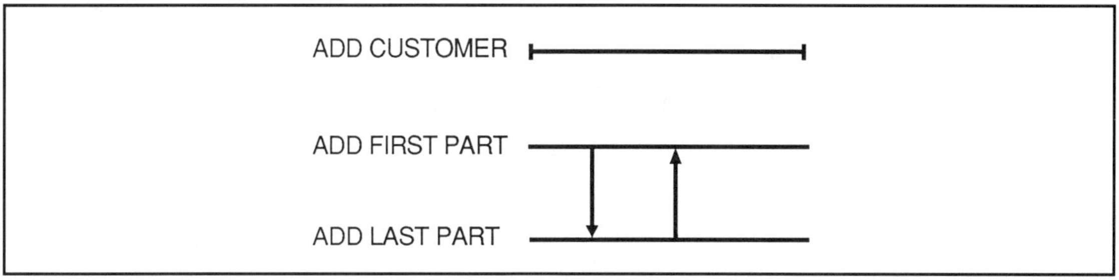

Figure 23-15. Dialog Flow Diagram with Two Procedure Steps

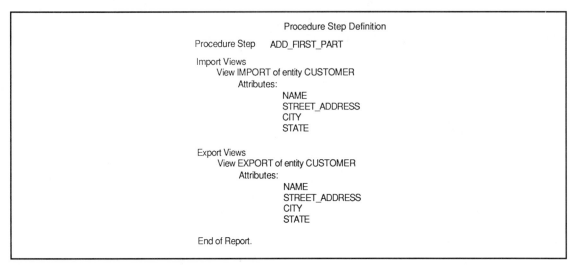

Figure 23-16. Data Views for Procedure Step ADD FIRST PART

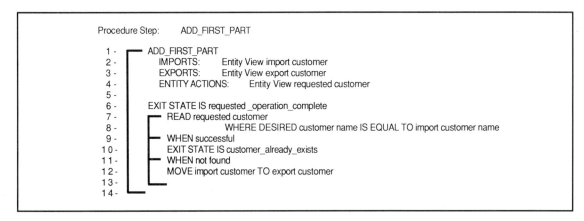

Figure 23-17. Action Diagram for Procedure Step ADD FIRST PART

Given this constraint, one can implement the sample Add Customer procedure shown in the Dialog Flow Diagram in Figure 23-15, with the Procedure Step Action Diagrams appearing in Figures 23-17 and 23-19. These use the data views appearing in Figures 23-16 and 23-18, respectively.

Assume the following details of the dialog flows shown in Figure 23-15:

- Add First Part transfers to Add Last Part when Exit State is "Requested Operation Complete."

- All data in the export view of Add First Part is sent to the import view of Add Last Part during the transfer.

- Add Last Part transfers back to Add First Part when Exit State is "Requested Operation Complete. "

- Both transfers have flow actions of Display First.

This division of procedures into steps requires no change to the original Add Customer Process Action Diagram (Figure 23-20).

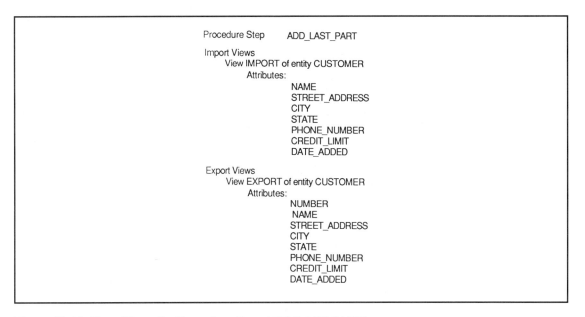

Figure 23-18. Data Views for Procedure Step ADD LAST PART

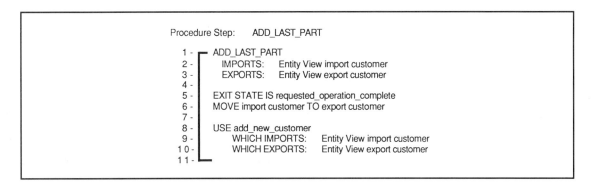

Figure 23-19. Action Diagram for Procedure Step ADD LAST PART

The following notes will help clarify the example:

• Add First Part (Figure 23-17) should validate all data for which it is responsible, even though the update is deferred until the final procedure step. Otherwise, the user may fill in several screens of data only to learn on the final screen that an item has failed validation.

In this case, the READ action (line 7) that tests for duplicate customer name appears in the Procedure Step Action Diagram for Add First Part. Note that this is the same logic specified in the transformed action block, Add New Customer.

An experienced designer of online procedures may notice a flaw in this portion of the example, should two operators concurrently attempt to add the same customer. The first procedure step may succeed where the second fails, if between the execution of the first and second, another operator adds the same customer. In this example, such a possibility is assumed to be remote. Even if it should occur, the worst that would

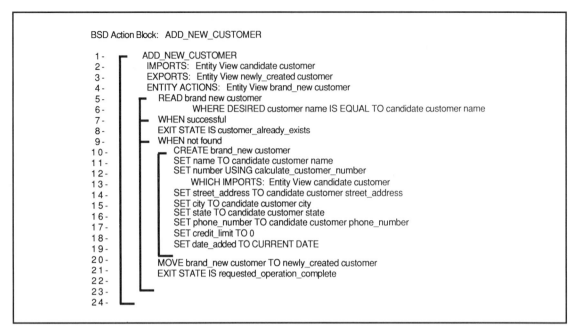

```
BSD Action Block:  ADD_NEW_CUSTOMER

 1-        ADD_NEW_CUSTOMER
 2-          IMPORTS:  Entity View candidate customer
 3-          EXPORTS:  Entity View newly_created customer
 4-          ENTITY ACTIONS:  Entity View brand_new customer
 5-          READ brand new customer
 6-                  WHERE DESIRED customer name IS EQUAL TO candidate customer name
 7-          WHEN successful
 8-          EXIT STATE IS customer_already_exists
 9-          WHEN not found
10-            CREATE brand_new customer
11-            SET name TO candidate customer name
12-            SET number USING calculate_customer_number
13-                WHICH IMPORTS:  Entity View candidate customer
14-            SET street_address TO candidate customer street_address
15-            SET city TO candidate customer city
16-            SET state TO candidate customer state
17-            SET phone_number TO candidate customer phone_number
18-            SET credit_limit TO 0
19-            SET date_added TO CURRENT DATE
20-          MOVE brand_new customer TO newly_created customer
21-          EXIT STATE IS requested_operation_complete
22-
23-
24-
```

Figure 23-20. ADD CUSTOMER Process Action Diagram

happen is operator inconvenience. There is no loss of system integrity because no real update takes place until Add Last Part completes.

- Those components of the import and export views of Add Last Part (Figure 23-18) that are not displayed on the screen (everything but Phone Number and Credit Limit) are implemented as hidden fields (see Chapter 21). This way, all information captured in Add First Part is available through multiple executions of Add Last Part.

- All attributes of the import view of Add Last Part appear in its export view, as well (Figure 23-13), even though some are not returned by the Add New Customer action block. By moving the contents of the import view to the export view (Figure 23-19, line 6), all information placed on the initial screen for Add Last Part is available through multiple executions.

This example satisfies the guidelines mentioned previously. The update takes place in Add Last Part using an unmodified Process Action Diagram, Add New Customer.

If, for any reason, one fails to follow these guidelines, one must ensure that the business requirement is satisfied and the integrity of the data is not compromised.

24
COMPLETING BUSINESS SYSTEM DESIGN

OVERVIEW

After finishing the design of a system, the designer must accomplish two tasks before considering the Business System Design stage complete and moving on to the next stage of Information Engineering, Technical Design:

- Confirm the results of design by verifying its completeness and correctness.
- Plan the activities required during Technical Design

DESIGN CONFIRMATION

The task of design confirmation involves inspecting the deliverables produced during Business System Design for completeness and correctness. In the IEF implementation of Information Engineering, design confirmation assures that each elementary process has been faithfully implemented by a procedure.

The IEF Consistency Check facility, described in detail in the *IEF Design Toolset Guide*, handles a great deal of the required checking automatically. The following paragraphs discuss the general guidelines for determining completeness and correctness and present some techniques the designer may use to augment the results of IEF Consistency Checking.

Completeness Checking

The object of completeness checking is to ensure that no major components have been overlooked during the Business System Design project. Business System Design completeness checking ensures that:

- Each elementary process has been implemented by a procedure.
- Each procedure has been fully defined.

Ensure that Each Elementary Process Has Been Implemented

To ensure that each elementary process has been implemented by at least one procedure, an Elementary Process to Procedure Matrix like the one in Figure 24-1 is useful. The elementary processes are listed along the vertical axis, the procedures are listed along the horizontal axis, and an X placed at an intersection indicates an elementary process's implementation by a procedure. Figure 24-1 illustrates a case where the elementary process Define Product has been overlooked during Business System Design. For the design to be complete, Define Product must be implemented by a procedure.

Ensure that Each Procedure is Fully Defined

Each online procedure must be detailed by a Procedure Action Diagram and a screen. The IEF Consistency Check facility automatically checks this rule.

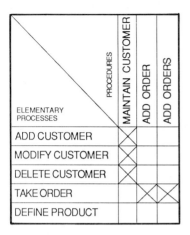

Figure 24-1. Elementary Process to Procedure Matrix

Correctness Checking

Correctness checking is performed to ensure that:

• Each process-implementing procedure accurately reflects the requirements of each of its client processes.

• Each object specified during Business System Design (such as screens, action diagrams, and dialog flows) is properly formed.

Accurate Process Implementation

To ensure that procedures faithfully reflect the processes they implement, one must compare the Process and Procedure Action Diagrams. This comparison should be performed by someone other than the designer who built the procedure.

Proper Formation of Design Objects

The IEF Consistency Check facility is used to verify the proper formation of most design objects. For example, the IEF checks to make sure that:

• Each dialog flow is initiated by an exit state.

• Each import and export view of an online procedure step is placed on a screen or defined as hidden.

• Each Procedure Action Diagram has at least one action statement.

No Business System Design project should be considered complete if any consistency checking errors are discovered by the IEF.

Confirmation Summary

As a final test of the correctness of the design, a series of structured walkthroughs is recommended. A **structured walkthrough** is a formal, step-by-step inspection of design deliverables. Two levels of walkthrough are recommended. At the first level, designers present the detailed design results to the analysts who built the business model on which it is based. At the second level, a subset of those deliverables is presented to the most knowledgeable intended users of the system. Such walkthroughs not only confirm the completeness and correctness of the design, but serve to point out potential problems in usability as well.

Designers must address the problems identified during design confirmation before considering Business System Design complete. They can then use the verified design in the following stages of Information Engineering.

PLANNING FOR TECHNICAL DESIGN

In the Technical Design stage of Information Engineering, designers address all environmental considerations of the target operating environment. During Business System Design, it was enough to identify a particular procedure as being an online procedure. During Technical Design, one must consider the implications of implementing that procedure using a particular teleprocessing monitor (such as IMS or CICS). During Business Area Analysis, it was enough to identify the business requirement for a particular entity type. During Technical Design, one must deal with implementing that entity type as a record in a particular Data Base Management System.

The IEF implementation of Information Engineering requires little designer involvement in the Technical Design stage. The IEF itself, by drawing inferences from the information captured in previous stages, automatically creates most of the objects required in the Technical Design stage. The only two tasks left for the designer are:

- Specifying which procedure steps will be bound together in a single execution unit. This task is called **load module packaging**. By applying a set of heuristics, the designer can identify packaging arrangements that optimize performance.

- Augmenting the results of automatic data base transformation. To achieve optimal performance, the designer can use the Data Structure Diagram to modify the data base design automatically created by the IEF to support the Entity Relationship Diagram built during Business Area Analysis.

In the IEF implementation, the boundary for procedure implementation is the business system, while the boundary for data base implementation is the business area. Thus, no scoping requirement (akin to business system definition at the end of Business Area Analysis) must precede Technical Design.

The plan for Technical Design, then, must include components for specifying load module packaging and modifying the IEF-created data base definition.

APPENDIX A
ISP SUMMARY TASK LIST

The following pages summarize the Information Strategy Planning tasks and subtasks identified in Part I of this guide along with the inputs and deliverables from each. Steps supported by the IEF Planning and Analysis Toolsets are annotated with an asterisk (*).

1. PLAN THE PROJECT

    1.1   Set the Project Scope

    1.2   Establish the Project Organization

    1.3   Build the Project Plan

    1.4   Review the Project Plan

    1.5   Deliverables

        1.5.1   Project Schedule

        1.5.2   Schedule of Interviews

2. MAKE THE INITIAL ASSESSMENT

    2.1   Identify and Record the Organization Structure

        2.1.1   Inputs

            2.1.1.1   Organization Charts

            2.1.1.2   Organization Handbooks or Manuals

            2.1.1.3   Policy and Procedure Manuals

            2.1.1.4   Reports from Organization Files or Data Bases

        2.1.2   Steps

            2.1.2.1   Document Organization Structure(*)

            2.1.2.2   Record Additional Information

        2.1.3   Deliverables

            2.1.3.1   Organizational Hierarchy Diagram

            2.1.3.2   Supportive Text

    2.2   Identify and Prioritize Business Objectives

        2.2.1   Inputs

            2.2.1.1   Written Documentation

            2.2.1.2   Organizational Hierarchy Diagram

        2.2.2   Steps

            2.2.2.1   List Mission, Objectives, Strategies, and CSFs

            2.2.2.2   Write a Mission Statement

            2.2.2.3   Relate Objectives of Enterprise to its Organizational Units

            2.2.2.4   Rank Objectives

        2.2.3   Deliverables

            2.2.3.1   Mission Statement

            2.2.3.2   List of Objectives, Strategies, and CSFs by Organizational Unit

            2.2.3.3   Enterprise/Organizational Unit Objectives Matrix

            2.2.3.4   Preliminary Ranked List of Objectives for the Enterprise and each Major Business Unit

2.3 Formulate Information Needs/Performance Measures

    2.3.1 Inputs

        2.3.1.1 Written Documentation

        2.3.1.2 Mission Statement

        2.3.1.3 List of Objectives, Strategies, and CSFs by Organizational Unit

        2.3.1.4 Enterprise/Organizational Unit Objectives Matrix

        2.3.1.5 Preliminary Ranked Lists of Objectives

        2.3.1.6 Organizational Hierarchy Diagram

    2.3.2 Steps

        2.3.2.1 Identify and Record Information Needs

        2.3.2.2 Build Information Need/Organizational Unit Matrix(*)

        2.3.2.3 Build Performance Measure/Organization Unit Matrix(*)

    2.3.3 Deliverables

        2.3.3.1 Information Needs List

        2.3.3.2 Information Need/Organizational Unit Matrix

        2.3.3.3 Performance Measure/Organizational Unit Matrix

2.4 Determine Potential Impact of Information Technology

    2.4.1 Inputs

        2.4.1.1 Publications

        2.4.1.2 Business Documentation

        2.4.1.3 Business Strategies Reliant on Information Technology

    2.4.2 Steps

        2.4.2.1 Assess Extent of Information Technology Usage

        2.4.2.2 Identify New Technologies

    2.4.3 Deliverable

        2.4.3.1 Statement of Potential Information Technology Impact

2.5 Define a Preliminary Information Architecture

    2.5.1 Inputs

        2.5.1.1 Annual Reports

        2.5.1.2 Any Models of the Enterprise Previously Developed

        2.5.1.3 Organizational Hierarchy Diagram

    2.5.2 Steps

        2.5.2.1 Identify Subject Areas (*)

        2.5.2.2 Associate Subject Areas (*)

        2.5.2.3 Identify Highest-level Business Functions(*)

        2.5.2.4 Decompose Business Functions into Lower-level Functions(*)

3.1.2   Steps

    3.1.2.1   Repetitively Decompose Functions into Component Functions/Processes(*)

3.1.3   Deliverables

    3.1.3.1   Completed Function Hierarchy Diagram

3.2   Analyze Function Dependencies

    3.2.1   Inputs

        3.2.1.1   Function Hierarchy Diagram

        3.2.1.2   Written Documentation

    3.2.2   Steps

        3.2.2.1   Identify the Functions for which Dependency Analysis is to be Performed

        3.2.2.2   Construct a Function Dependency Diagram for each Selected Function(*)

    3.2.3   Deliverables

        3.2.3.1   Function Dependency Diagrams

        3.2.3.2   Revised Function Hierarchy Diagram

3.3   Map Functions to Organizations

    3.3.1   Inputs

        3.3.1.1   Function Hierarchy Diagram

        3.3.1.2   Organizational Hierarchy Diagram

    3.3.2   Steps

        3.3.2.1   Build Business Function/Organizational Unit Matrix(*)

    3.3.3   Deliverables

        3.3.3.1   Business Function/Organizational Unit Matrix

3.4   Build Entity Relationship Diagram

    3.4.1   Inputs

        3.4.1.1   Subject Area Diagram

        3.4.1.2   Interview Results

        3.4.1.3   Written Documentation

    3.4.2   Steps

        3.4.2.1   Record Entity Types in an Entity Relationship Diagram(*)

        3.4.2.2   Define Relationships between Entity Types(*)

    3.4.3   Deliverables

        3.4.3.1   Entity Relationship Diagram

3.5   Map Entity Types to Information Needs

    3.5.1   Inputs

        3.5.1.1   Information Needs List

        3.5.1.2   Entity Relationship Diagram

        3.5.1.3   Written Documentation

        3.5.1.4   Interview Results

5.   DEFINE THE BUSINESS SYSTEM ARCHITECTURE

   5.1   Identify and Record Natural Data Stores

      5.1.1   Inputs

         5.1.1.1   Business Function/Entity Type Usage Matrix

      5.1.2   Steps

         5.1.2.1   Identify Clusters using the Business Function/Entity Type Usage Matrix(*)

         5.1.2.2   Identify Entity Type Clusters using the Entity Type/Entity Type Affinity Matrix(*)

         5.1.2.3   Identify Natural Data Stores(*)

         5.1.2.4   Build Data Cluster/Entity Type Matrix(*)

      5.1.3   Deliverables

         5.1.3.1   Clustered Business Function/Entity Type Matrix

         5.1.3.2   Data Cluster/Entity Type Matrix

   5.2   Identify and Record Natural Business Systems

      5.2.1   Inputs

         5.2.1.1   Business Function/Entity Type Usage Matrix

      5.2.2   Steps

         5.2.2.1   Identify Business Function Clusters using the Business Function/Business Function Affinity Matrix(*)

         5.2.2.2   Identify Natural Business Systems(*).

         5.2.2.3   Build Activity Cluster or Business System/Business Function Matrix (*)

      5.2.3   Deliverables

         5.2.3.1   Activity Cluster or Business System/Business Function Matrix

   5.3   Build the Business System Architecture Diagram

      5.3.1   Inputs

         5.3.1.1   Business Function/Entity Type Usage Matrix

         5.3.1.2   Activity Cluster or Business System/Business Function Matrix

      5.3.2   Steps

         5.3.2.1   Categorize Systems (*)

         5.3.2.2   Identify Information Flows (*)

         5.3.2.3   Draw the Business System Architecture Diagram

         5.3.2.4   Resolve/Explain Anomalies

      5.3.3   Deliverables

         5.3.3.1   Business System Architecture Diagram

   5.4   Record and Validate Business Areas

      5.4.1   Inputs

         5.4.1.1   Data Cluster/Entity Type Matrix

         5.4.1.2   Activity Cluster or Business System/Business Function Matrix

         5.4.1.3   Business Function/Entity Type Usage Matrix

5.4.2   Steps

    5.4.2.1   Identify Business Areas

    5.4.2.2   Record the Business Areas on the Business Area/Activity Cluster or Business System Matrix(*)

    5.4.2.3   Relate Business Areas to Natural Business Systems using the Business Area/Activity Cluster or Business System Matrix(*)

    5.4.2.4   Relate Business Areas to Natural Data Stores using the Business Area/Data Cluster Matrix(*)

    5.4.2.5   Relate Business Areas to Business Functions using the Business Area/Business Function Matrix(*)

    5.4.2.6   Relate Business Areas to Entity Types using Business Area/Entity Type Matrix(*)

5.5   Record Impact on Performance Measures

  5.5.1   Inputs

    5.5.1.1   Written Documentation

    5.5.1.2   Performance Measures Previously Recorded

    5.5.1.3   Business Functions Previously Recorded

  5.5.2   Steps

    5.5.2.1   Build Performance Measure/Business Function Matrix(*)

  5.5.3   Deliverables

    5.5.3.1   Performance Measure/Business Function Matrix

5.6   Rank Business Area Analysis Projects

  5.6.1   Inputs

    5.6.1.1   Information Needs List

    5.6.1.2   Performance Measure/Business Function Matrix

    5.6.1.3   Business Area/Business Function Matrix

    5.6.1.4   Business Area/Entity Type Matrix

    5.6.1.5   Entity Type/Information Need Matrix

  5.6.2   Steps

    5.6.2.1   Assess which Business Areas will have the Greatest Impact on Performance Measures

    5.6.2.2   Assess which Business Areas will Provide for the Greatest Increase in the Satisfaction of Information Needs

    5.6.2.3   Hold a Ranking Session

  5.6.3   Deliverables

    5.6.3.1   Ranked List of Business Area Analysis Projects

5.7   Review the Implementation Plan

6. DEFINE THE TECHNICAL ARCHITECTURE

   6.1   Perform Business Area Distribution Analysis

      6.1.1   Inputs

         6.1.1.1   Organizational Hierarchy Diagram and Supportive Text

         6.1.1.2   Business Function/Organizational Unit Matrix

         6.1.1.3   Activity Cluster or Business System/Business Function Matrix

         6.1.1.4   Data Cluster/Entity Type Matrix

         6.1.1.5   Business Area/Activity Cluster or Business System Matrix

         6.1.1.6   Business Area/Data Cluster Matrix

      6.1.2   Steps

         6.1.2.1   Determine Requirement for Support of each Predicted Business System by Location

         6.1.2.2   Determine Requirement for Support of each Natural Data Store by Location (*)

      6.1.3   Deliverables

         6.1.3.1   Activity Cluster or Business System/Location Matrix

         6.1.3.2   Data Cluster/Location Matrix

   6.2   Analyze Performance Requirements

      6.2.1   Inputs

         6.2.1.1   Assessment of Current Systems

         6.2.1.2   Technology Inventory

         6.2.1.3   Business Function/Current Information System Matrix

         6.2.1.4   Entity Type/Current Data Store Matrix

         6.2.1.5   Activity Cluster or Business System/Business Function Matrix

         6.2.1.6   Written Documentation

      6.2.2   Steps

         6.2.2.1   Identify Performance Criteria

         6.2.2.2   Build a Statement of Technical Requirement

      6.2.3   Deliverables

         6.2.3.1   Statement of Technical Requirement

   6.3   Analyze Technical Distribution Requirements

      6.3.1   Inputs

         6.3.1.1   Statement of Technical Requirement

         6.3.1.2   Activity Cluster or Business System/Location Matrix

         6.3.1.3   Data Cluster/Location Matrix

         6.3.1.4   Written Documentation

         6.3.1.5   Statement of Non-Technical Constraint

APPENDIX B
BAA SUMMARY TASK LIST

The following pages summarize the Business Area Analysis tasks and subtasks identified in Part II in simple outline form along with the inputs and deliverables from each. Steps supported by the IEF Analysis Toolset are annotated with an asterisk (*).

1. PREPARE FOR THE BAA PROJECT

   1.1   Inputs

       1.1.1   Business Area Analysis Models or Subsets (if Project is based on an Information Strategy Plan) from ISP Task 7

   1.2   Steps

       1.2.1   Set the Project Boundaries

       1.2.2   Perform Mini-ISP (if Project is not based on an Information Strategy Plan)

       1.2.3   Establish the Project Team

       1.2.4   Build the Project Plan

   1.3   Deliverables

       1.3.1   Project Plan

2. BUILD DATA MODEL

   2.1   Inputs

       2.1.1   ISP Data Model (if Project is based on an Information Strategy Plan)

       2.1.2   Business Knowledge Gathered through a Review of Written Documentation and Interviews with Business People

   2.2   Steps

       2.2.1   Build the Entity Relationship Diagram (*)

             2.2.1.1   Define Entity Types and their Properties

             2.2.1.2   Define Relationships and their Properties

             2.2.1.3   Define Attributes and their Properties

             2.2.1.4   Define Entity Type Life Cycles

             2.2.1.5   Define Entity Subtypes

             2.2.1.6   Define Entity Subtype Properties

       2.2.2   Revise the Graphics for Presentation (*)

       2.2.3   Verify the Resulting Entity Relationship Diagram with Users

   2.3   Deliverables

       2.3.1   Entity Relationship Diagram

       2.3.2   Supporting Documentation, including Entity, Relationship and Attribute Properties and Descriptions

3. BUILD ACTIVITY MODEL

   3.1   Inputs

       3.1.1   ISP Activity Model (if Project is based on an Information Strategy Plan)

       3.1.2   Business Knowledge Gathered through a Review of Written Documentation and Interviews with Business People

3.2   Steps

    3.2.1   Build Process Hierarchy Diagram (*)

        3.2.1.1   Decompose Processes

        3.2.1.2   Specify Properties for each Process

    3.2.2   Build Process Dependency Diagrams (*)

        3.2.2.1   Select Processes on Which to Perform Dependency Analysis

        3.2.2.2   Identify Dependencies between Sibling Processes

        3.2.2.3   Specify External Objects

        3.2.2.4   Identify Information Flows between Elementary Processes and External Objects

        3.2.2.5   Specify Events for Event-triggered Processes

        3.2.2.6   Refine Process Hierarchy Diagram based on the Results of Dependency Analysis

    3.2.3   Review Process Hierarchy Diagram and Process Dependency Diagrams with Users

3.3   Deliverables

    3.3.1   Process Hierarchy Diagram

    3.3.2   Process Dependency Diagrams for Selected Processes

    3.3.3   Supporting Documentation, including Properties and Descriptions for all Processes, Dependencies, External Objects and Events

4.   BUILD INTERACTION MODEL

4.1   Inputs

    4.1.1   Entity Relationship Diagram

    4.1.2   Process Decomposition Diagram

    4.1.3   Process Dependency Diagrams

4.2   Steps

    4.2.1   Perform Entity Life Cycle Analysis

    4.2.1.1 Select Entity Types to Analyze

        4.2.1.2   Build Entity Life Cycle Diagram for each Entity Type

        4.2.1.3   Build Entity State Change Matrix for each Entity Type

    4.2.2   Perform Process Logic Analysis

        4.2.2.1   Define Expected Import and Export Information Views for each Elementary Process

        4.2.2.2   Define Detailed Process Logic as a Process Action Diagram for each Elementary Process (*)

        4.2.2.3   Ensure that all Integrity Constraints Identified in the Data Modeling Activity are Handled in the Process Action Diagrams (*)

        4.2.2.4   Ensure that all Pre- and Post-conditions based on Dependency Analysis are Handled in the Process Action Diagrams (*)

        4.2.2.5   Define Action Blocks for each Default Algorithm Identifed during Data Modeling (*)

4.2.2.6   Define Action Blocks for each Derivation Algorithm Identified during Data Modeling (*)

4.2.2.7   Define Action Blocks for each Business Algorithm (Common Action Block) Identified during Process Logic Analysis (*)

4.2.3   Refine Data and Activity Models as Appropriate

4.3   Deliverables

4.3.1   Process Action Diagrams for Every Elementary Process

4.3.2   Action Blocks to Support All Business, Default and Derivation Algorithms

4.3.3   Entity Life Cycle Diagrams for Selected Entity Types

5. ANALYZE CURRENT SYSTEMS

5.1   Input

5.1.1   Current System Documentation

5.1.1.1   Programs and System Flow Documentation

5.1.1.2   Database Definitions and File Layouts

5.1.2   Business Function/Current Information System Matrix (if the Project is based on an Information Strategy Plan)

5.1.3   Entity Type/Current Data Store Matrix (if the Project is based on an Information Strategy Plan)

5.2   Steps

5.2.1   Select Systems to Analyze (*, assuming the use of the ISP Toolset matrices)

5.2.2   Perform Current System Procedure Analysis

5.2.2.1   Build Procedure Decomposition List

5.2.2.2   Build Data Flow Diagrams for Current Procedures

5.2.3   Analyze User Views of Current Database and File Layouts

5.2.4   Build the Equivalent Entity Relationship Model using Canonical Synthesis

5.3   Deliverables

5.3.1   Procedure Decomposition List

5.3.2   Data Flow Diagrams

5.3.3   Equivalent Entity Relationship Model

6. CONFIRM THE BUSINESS MODEL

6.1   Inputs

6.1.1   Entity Relationship Model

6.1.2   Process Hierarchy Diagram

6.1.3   Process Dependency Diagram

6.1.4   Process Action Diagrams

6.2   Steps

6.2.1   Perform Automated Consistency Check (*)

6.2.2   Perform Completeness Checking

       6.2.2.1   Compare Top-down Data and Activity Models against the Results of Current Systems Analysis

       6.2.2.2   Perform Matrix Cross Checking using:

          6.2.2.2.1   Elementary Process/Entity Type Usage Matrix (*)

          6.2.2.2.2   Elementary Process/Relationship Usage Matrix

          6.2.2.2.3   Elementary Process/Attribute Usage Matrix

   6.2.3   Perform Correctness Checking

       6.2.3.1   Verify Normalization of Data Model

       6.2.3.2   Verify Accuracy of Process Dependencies

       6.2.3.3   Eliminate Redundant Entity Types, Attributes, Relationships and Processes

       6.2.3.4   Verify Quantitative Information (Subtype Volume and Relationship Cardinality)

       6.2.3.5   Conduct Structured Walkthroughs

   6.2.4   Perform Stability Analysis

6.3   Deliverables

   6.3.1   Complete, Correct and Resilient Business Model

7. DEFINE BUSINESS SYSTEMS

7.1   Inputs

   7.1.1   Complete, Correct and Resilient Business Model

   7.1.2   Information Needs List

7.2   Steps

   7.2.1   Cluster Elementary Processes to Determine Business System Boundaries (*)

   7.2.2   Perform Cost Benefit Analysis for each Elementary Process

   7.2.3   Construct Implementation Plan

   7.2.4   Perform Business System Scoping (*)

7.3   Deliverables

   7.3.1   Business Systems Defined to IEF

   7.3.2   Implementation Plan

APPENDIX C
BSD SUMMARY TASK LIST

The following pages summarize the Business System Design tasks and subtasks described in Part III in simple outline form along with the inputs of and deliverables from each. Steps supported by the IEF Design Toolset are annotated with an asterisk (*).

1. PREPARE FOR BUSINESS SYSTEM DESIGN

   1.1 Inputs

      1.1.1 Business Model Constructed during Business Area Analysis

      1.1.2 Organization System Standards

   1.2 Steps

      1.2.1 Establish the Project Team (if Different from BAA Team)

      1.2.2 Review Results of Business Area Analysis (*)

      1.2.3 Verify the Results of Business System Definition (*)

      1.2.4 Set System Standards (*)

         1.2.4.1 Commands

         1.2.4.2 Function Keys

         1.2.4.3 Video Display Properties

         1.2.4.4 Edit Patterns

         1.2.4.5 Screen Templates

         1.2.4.6 Field Prompts

         1.2.4.7 Exit State Values

         1.2.4.8 Clear Screen Input Delimiters

      1.2.5 Identify Transition Requirements

      1.2.6 Determine Level of Online HELP Support

      1.2.7 Define Design Data Required (*)

   1.3 Deliverables

      1.3.1 Verified Business System Definition

      1.3.2 Entity Relationship Diagram augmented with Design Data

2. DEFINE AUTOMATED PROCEDURES

   2.1 Inputs

      2.1.1 Elementary Process Definitions

      2.1.2 System Standards

   2.2 Steps

      2.2.1 Design Process-implementing Procedures (*)

         2.2.1.1 Specify Whether Procedure is to Execute Online or in Batch

         2.2.1.2 Transform Elementary Processes (causing the Synthesis of Procedure Action Diagrams and Procedure Views)

         2.2.1.3 Identify Initial Requirements for Multi-step Batch and Online Procedures

2.2.2   Design Designer-added Procedures (*)

    2.2.2.1   Identify Procedures Required to Help Navigate through Online Conversations (e.g., MENUs)

    2.2.2.2   Identify Procedures Required to Display or List Business Information (this only applies to displays and lists which are not already specified in elementary processes)

    2.2.2.3   Define Procedures including Import and Export Views Required

2.3   Deliverables

    2.3.1   An Initial Dialog Flow Diagram showing only Procedure and Procedure Step Bars

    2.3.2   Synthesized Procedure Action Diagrams for the First Procedure Step of each Process-implementing Procedure

    2.3.3   A List of Elementary Processes Implemented for each Process-implementing Procedure

3.   DESIGN DIALOGS

3.1   Inputs

    3.1.1   Process Dependency Diagrams

    3.1.2   Initial Dialog Flow Diagram

3.2   Steps

    3.2.1   Define Online Dialogs

        3.2.1.1   Analyze User's Work Environment

        3.2.1.2   Analyze Process Dependencies

        3.2.1.3   Specify Function Key/Command Requirements (*)

        3.2.1.4   Define Online Dialog Flows (*)

            3.2.1.4.1   Source/Destination Procedure Step

            3.2.1.4.2   Type of Flow

            3.2.1.4.3   Flow Conditions

            3.2.1.4.4   Flow Actions

            3.2.1.4.5   Flow Command Setting

            3.2.1.4.6   Autoflows

            3.2.1.4.7   Data Passing

    3.2.2   Define Batch Dialogs

        3.2.2.1   Determine Restartability Requirements

        3.2.2.2   Define Batch Dialog Flows (*)

            3.2.2.2.1   Source/Destination Procedure Step

            3.2.2.2.2   Flow Conditions

            3.2.2.2.3   Flow Command Setting

            3.2.2.2.4   Data Passing

3.3 Deliverables

    3.3.1 Dialog Flow Diagram for the Business System showing all Procedures, Procedure Steps and Flows

    3.3.2 Details for each Flow

4. DESIGN LAYOUTS

4.1 Inputs

    4.1.1 Dialog Flow Diagram

    4.1.2 Import and Export Views for each Procedure

4.2 Steps

    4.2.1 Design Screen for each Online Procedure (*)

    4.2.2 Design Clear Screen Input Requirements for Selected Online Procedures (*)

    4.2.3 Design Reporting Requirements for Batch Procedures

4.3 Deliverables

    4.3.1 Screen Layouts

    4.3.2 Report Layouts

5. PROTOTYPE ONLINE CONVERSATIONS

5.1 Inputs

    5.1.1 Dialog Flow Diagram

    5.1.2 Screen Designs

5.2 Steps

    5.2.1 Review Online Conversation Behavior with Intended User using Workstation Prototyping (*)

    5.2.2 Revise Dialog Flow Diagram and Screen Design until User Accepts Design (*)

5.3 Deliverables

    5.3.1 Verified Dialog Flow Diagram

    5.3.2 Verified Screen Designs

6. DESIGN PROCEDURE LOGIC

6.1 Input

    6.1.1 Dialog Flow Diagram

    6.1.2 View Definitions for each Procedure

    6.1.3 Synthesized Procedure Action Diaqram for each Process-implementing Procedure

    6.1.4 Screen Design for each Online Procedure Step

6.2 Steps

    6.2.1 Refine Process Action Diagrams as Required (*)

    6.2.2 Refine Synthesized Procedure Action Diagrams as Required (*)

    6.2.3 Build Procedure Action Diagrams for Designer-added Procedures (*)

6.3   Deliverables

    6.3.1   Complete Set of Action Blocks for each Procedure Step in the Business System

7.   COMPLETE THE BUSINESS SYSTEM DESIGN PROJECT

    7.1   Inputs

        7.1.1   Design Model

            7.1.1.1   Dialog Flow Diagram

            7.1.1.2   Screen Designs

            7.1.1.3   Action Blocks

            7.1.1.4   Revised Entity Relationship Diagram

    7.2   Steps

        7.2.1   Confirm the Design

            7.2.1.1   Perform Automated Consistency Checking

            7.2.1.2   Perform Completeness Checking

            7.2.1.3   Perform Correctness Checking

            7.2.1.4   Plan for Technical Design

    7.3   Deliverables

        7.3.1   Confirmed Design Model

        7.3.2   Technical Design Plan

APPENDIX D
ACTION DIAGRAM SYNTAX

This appendix provides a brief description of the action statement types included in the Process Action Diagram and Procedure Action Diagram syntax.

The following conventions are used:

- UPPER-CASE LETTERS are used for keywords.

- [Options] are enclosed in brackets.

- Alternatives are presented within a large bracket, as in the following example:

    SET attribute-view
    $$\begin{bmatrix} \text{USING action-block} \\ \text{TO expression} \end{bmatrix}$$

- Lower-case letters joined by hyphens represent a variable value. Most of the variable types appearing in the syntax are self-explanatory. Where they are not, a note of explanation accompanies the definition.

- Ellipses (...) following any clause within an action indicate that it can occur many times within the action.

The action statement description is divided into seven sections as follows:

Entity Actions	
	CREATE
	UPDATE
	DELETE
	READ
	READ EACH
Relationship Actions	
	ASSOCIATE
	DISASSOCIATE
	TRANSFER
Assignment Actions	
	SET
	MOVE
*	COMMAND IS
*	PRINTER TERMINAL IS
	EXIT STATE IS
Conditional Actions	
	IF
	CASE
Repeated Actions	
	READ EACH
	FOR EACH
	WHILE
	REPEAT...UNTIL
	FOR
Control Actions	
	USE
	ESCAPE
	NEXT
Miscellaneous Actions	
*	MAKE
	NOTE

Those actions marked with an asterisk (*) should appear only in Procedure Action Diagrams, not Process Action Diagrams.

ENTITY ACTIONS

CREATE records information about entities once they are of interest to the business. The format of the CREATE action statement is:

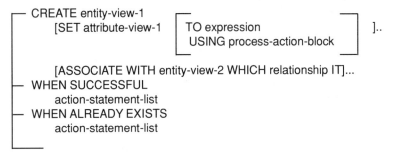

Notes:

1. *Entity-view-1* is an entity action view of the entity for which information is to be recorded.

2. A number of SET clauses may appear, one for each attribute to be assigned a value. All mandatory attributes must be assigned a value.

3. The expression following the TO in the SET clause must evaluate to the same primitive domain as *attribute-view-1*. In most cases, the expression is simply a different view of the same attribute.

4. The *process-action-block* after USING in the SET clause is the name of a business algorithm used to calculate the attribute's value.

5. The ASSOCIATE WITH clause allows pairings to be established between the entity referenced in *entity-view-1* and the entity referenced in *entity-view-2*. *Entity-view-2* must be an entity action view. During a CREATE, each identifying relationship membership must have a pairing established for it.

6. The WHEN SUCCESSFUL clause is optional. It specifies a set of actions to be performed if the CREATE completes successfully.

7. The WHEN ALREADY EXISTS clause is optional. It specifies a set of actions to be performed if there is already information stored about an entity with the same identifier as *entity-view-1*.

UPDATE modifies the information stored about an entity. The format of an UPDATE action statement is:

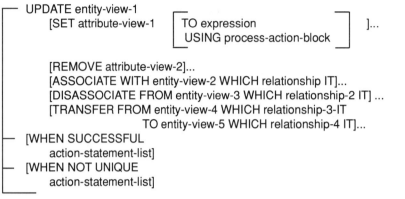

UPDATE entity-view-1
    [SET attribute-view-1   TO expression   ]...
                            USING process-action-block

    [REMOVE attribute-view-2]...
    [ASSOCIATE WITH entity-view-2 WHICH relationship IT]...
    [DISASSOCIATE FROM entity-view-3 WHICH relationship-2 IT] ...
    [TRANSFER FROM entity-view-4 WHICH relationship-3-IT
                   TO entity-view-5 WHICH relationship-4 IT]...
[WHEN SUCCESSFUL
    action-statement-list]
[WHEN NOT UNIQUE
    action-statement-list]

Notes:

1. Before performing the UPDATE, the process logic must have CREATED or READ *entity-view-1*.

2. *Entity-view-1, 2, 3, 4* and *5* must be entity action views.

3. The rules for the SET clause are the same as for the CREATE action.

4. Mandatory attributes may not be the subject of the REMOVE clause.

5. Identifying relationships may not be the subject of a DISASSOCIATE clause.

6. ASSOCIATE establishes a pairings while DISASSOCIATE eliminates a pairing.

7. TRANSFER moves a pairing from one entity to another, provided that the affected relationship membership has been marked as *transferable*.

8. The optional WHEN SUCCESSFUL clause is followed by a list of actions to be performed if the UPDATE succeeds.

9. The optional WHEN NOT UNIQUE clause is followed by a list of actions to be performed if the UPDATE causes an entity identifier to conflict with another entity identifier.

DELETE eradicates all knowledge of an entity. The format of the DELETE action statement is:

DELETE entity-view-1

Notes:

1. Before performing the DELETE, the process logic must have CREATED or READ *entity-view-1*.

2. *Entity-view-1* must be an entity action view.

3. As a result of the DELETE, the IEF also deletes all entities that participate in mandatory pairings with *entity-view-1*. This effect is called **cascade deletion.**

READ retrieves information about previously stored entities. The format of the READ action statement is:

```
READ entity-view-list

    [WHERE selection-condition]

    [WHEN SUCCESSFUL
         action-statement-list-1]
    [WHEN NOT FOUND
         action-statement-list-2]
```

Notes:

1. Every view being read in *entity-view-list* must be an entity action view.

2. The READ action only affects the attribute views of entity views specified in *entity-view-list.*

3. The WHERE conditions (optionally combined and joined by ANDs, ORs, and parentheses) qualify the READ action. They test attribute values and test for the existence of a pairing. The collection of these conditions is called the **selection criteria** for the READ. A *selection-condition* is any expression that can be judged either true or false.

4. Each view being read should be qualified by at least one selection criterion somewhere in the statement. Otherwise, an arbitrary occurrence will be read.

5. The optional WHEN SUCCESSFUL clause may be followed by a list of actions to be performed if the selection criteria were satisfied.

6. The WHEN NOT FOUND clause may be followed by a list of actions to be performed if the selection criteria were not satisfied.

READ EACH retrieves information about multiple entities of a given type. The results of the READ EACH can be used to populate a repeating group view. The format of the READ EACH action statement is as follows:

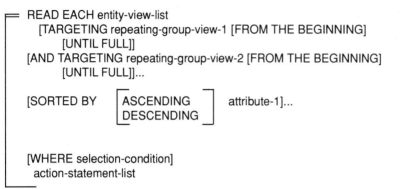

```
READ EACH entity-view-list
    [TARGETING repeating-group-view-1 [FROM THE BEGINNING]
        [UNTIL FULL]]
    [AND TARGETING repeating-group-view-2 [FROM THE BEGINNING]
        [UNTIL FULL]]...

[SORTED BY    ASCENDING      attribute-1]...
              DESCENDING


[WHERE selection-condition]
    action-statement-list
```

Notes:

1. Every view being read in *entity-view-list* must be an entity action view.

2. The READ EACH action only affects the attribute views of entity views specified in *entity-view-list*.

3. The WHERE conditions (optionally combined and joined by ANDs, ORs, and parentheses) qualify the READ action. They test attribute values and test for the existence of a pairing. The collection of these conditions is called the **selection criteria** for the READ. A *selection-condition* is any expression that can be judged either true or false.

4. The READ EACH retrieves information about each entity that satisfies the criteria specified in the selection condition and places it in the appropriate view in *entity-view-list*. Each time the IEF retrieves a new set of occurrences, it performs the actions in the *action-statement-list*.

5. The TARGETING clauses are used to specify a repeating group view, which may be either a local or export view. This repeating group view is populated each time the READ EACH performs a repetition. After each repetition that MOVES to an entity view subordinate to the repeating group view, or SETS an attribute view subordinate to the repeating group view, the IEF primes the repeating group view to accept information in its next occurrence.

6. The FROM THE BEGINNING clause of the TARGETING clause is useful if multiple READ EACH or FOR EACH actions target the same repeating group view. Normally, a second READ EACH or FOR EACH will continue to populate the repeating group beginning immediately after the last occurrence populated. When the FROM THE BEGINNING clause is specified, however, the repeating group view is emptied and its population starts over (from the beginning).

7. The UNTIL FULL clause of the TARGETING clause causes the READ EACH to terminate if an attempt is made to add more occurrences to the repeating group view than were specified in its maximum cardinality.

8. Multiple TARGETING clauses are permitted, thus allowing the population of multiple repeating group views simultaneously.

9. The nesting of a READ EACH or FOR EACH action statement must coincide with the nesting of the repeating group views it targets.

10. The SORTED BY clauses return entities in a particular sequence based on an attribute value. They can be returned in low-to-high (ASCENDING) sequence or high-to-low (DESCENDING) sequence.

11. The selection conditions operate in exactly the same fashion as in a READ entity action.

The *selection-condition* for READ and READ EACH takes the form:

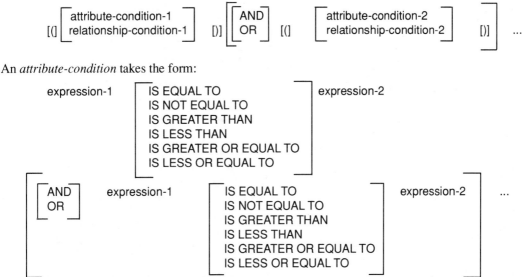

An *attribute-condition* takes the form:

Notes:

1. An *attribute-condition* must include an attribute of an entity action view on at least one side of each relational operator (for example, IS EQUAL TO, IS NOT EQUAL TO).

2. Comparisons must involve combinations of operands of the same domain (character, number, date, or time).

3. Each reference to an attribute of an entity action view is preceded by a view qualifier (DESIRED, SOME, CURRENT, or THAT). DESIRED refers to one of the views being read. SOME refers to any other entity action view, while THAT refers to a view previously referenced by SOME. CURRENT refers to any entity action view previously populated by a READ or CREATE action.

4. For details on formulating expressions, see the "Advanced Topics" section in Chapter 14.

A *relationship-condition* takes the form:

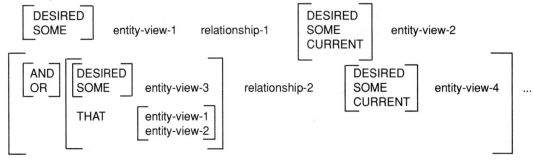

Notes:

1. Each relationship (*relationship-1*, *relationship-2*) must be a relationship that exists between two entity action views.

2. Each reference to an entity action view is preceded by a view qualifier (DESIRED, SOME, CURRENT, or THAT). DESIRED refers to one of the views being read (that is, in the *entity-view-list* of the READ action). SOME refers to any other entity action view, while THAT refers to a view previously referenced by SOME. CURRENT refers to any entity action view previously populated by a READ or CREATE action.

3. CURRENT may only precede the second of the two entity action views joined by each relationship (that is, *entity-view-2* and *entity-view-4*).

RELATIONSHIP ACTIONS

ASSOCIATE records a pairing based on a relationship membership. The format of the ASSOCIATE action statement is:

```
ASSOCIATE entity-view-1 WITH entity-view-2 WHICH
          relationship-1 IT
```

Notes:

1. *Entity-view-1* and *entity-view-2* must both be entity action views and must have already been READ or CREATED before the ASSOCIATE action is performed.

2. In stand alone ASSOCIATE action statements, *relationship-1* cannot be an identifying relationship.

DISASSOCIATE eliminates an existing pairing. The format of the DISASSOCIATE action statement is:

```
DISASSOCIATE entity-view-1 FROM entity-view-2 WHICH
             relationship-1 IT
```

Notes:

1. *Entity-view-1* and *entity-view-2* must both be entity action views and must have already been READ or CREATED before the DISASSOCIATE action is performed.

2. In stand alone DISASSOCIATE action statements, *relationship-1* cannot be an identifying relationship.

3. As mentioned in the DELETE action description, the DISASSOCIATE action can potentially cause cascade deletion of entities.

TRANSFER moves a pairing between the subject entity and object entity to a new object entity (of the same type as the original object entity). The format of the TRANSFER action statement is:

```
TRANSFER entity-view-1
         FROM entity-view-2 WHICH relationship-1 IT
         TO   entity-view-3 WHICH relationship-1 IT
```

Notes:

1. *Entity-view-1*, *entity-view-2* and *entity-view-3* must all be entity action views. They must all have been populated by a READ or CREATE before the TRANSFER action executes.

2. *Relationship-1* must be defined as transferable.

3. *Relationship-1* may not be an identifying relationship.

ASSIGNMENT ACTIONS

SET assigns a value to an individual attribute view. It operates like the SET clause of CREATE and UPDATE statements. The format of the SET action statement is:

SET ⎡ entity-view-1 attribute-view-1 ⎤   [ROUNDED]   ⎡ TO expression ⎤
     | NEXTTRAN | | USING action-block |
     | SUBSCRIPT OF repeating-group-view | ⎣   ⎦
     ⎣ LAST OF repeating-group-view   ⎦

Notes:

1. *Entity-view-1* may be either a local or an export view. Import views may not be modified within a process. Attribute views in entity action views may only be modified through the SET and REMOVE clauses of CREATE or UPDATE action statements.

2. The expression following the TO clause must return a value in the same primitive domain as the attribute viewed by *attribute-view-1*.

3. The *action-block* after the USING clause must return a value in the same domain as the attribute viewed by *attribute-view-1*.

4. See the "Advanced Topics" section in Chapter 14 for a detailed discussion of expressions.

5. The NEXTTRAN option sets an IEF special attribute whose use is normally restricted to the Business System Design stage of Information Engineering.

6. The SUBSCRIPT OF and LAST OF options are used only for explicitly subscripted repeating group views.

7. The ROUNDED option is available only if *attribute-view-1* is of the primitive domain Number.

MOVE assigns the values of multiple attribute views at once. The format of the MOVE action statement is:

MOVE entity-view-1 TO entity-view-2

Notes:

1. *Entity-view-1* and *entity-view-2* are views of the same entity type. Each attribute view in *entity-view-2* is assigned the value of the corresponding attribute view in *entity-view-1*.

2. *Entity-view-1* may be either an import, entity action or local view.

3. *Entity-view-2* may be either a local or export view.

COMMAND IS sets the value of the special attribute Command. The format of the COMMAND IS action statement is:

COMMAND IS command_value

Notes:

1. The designer chooses the value of Command from a list of defined command values for the business system. Since there is only one occurrence of the Command special attribute, the execution of a COMMAND IS action destroys its previous contents.

2. This action can only appear in Procedure Action Diagrams, not Process Action Diagrams.

PRINTER TERMINAL IS sets the value of the special attribute Printer Terminal ID.   The format of the PRINTER TERMINAL IS action statement is:

PRINTER TERMINAL IS literal_value

Notes:

1.   If a value for this special attribute is present when a procedure step finishes executing, the procedure step prints a copy of its associated screen on the identified terminal. This statement has meaning only in online procedures.

2.   The literal_value is any eight-character text constant that represents a valid terminal ID. Since there is only one occurrence of the Printer Terminal ID special attribute, the execution of a PRINTER TERMINAL IS action destroys its previous contents.

3.   The PRINTER TERMINAL IS action statement is actually available when building action diagrams during Business Area Analysis, but it should not be used there.

EXIT STATE IS sets the value of the special attribute Exit State.   The format of the EXIT STATE IS action is:

EXIT STATE IS exit-state-value

Notes:

1.   Exit State is used to indicate the outcome of a process. During BAA, it is most often set as a result of the failure of an entity action.

2.   A description of exception handling using exit states is found in the "Advanced Topics" section of Chapter 14.

CONDITIONAL ACTIONS

IF tests the truth of an assertion. The format of the IF action statement is:

```
┌── IF condition-1
│        action-statement-list-1
├── [ELSE IF condition-2
│        action-statement-list-2]...
├── [ELSE
│        action-statement-list-3]
└──
```

Notes:

1. *Condition-1* and *condition-2* are any expression that can be judged either true or false.

2. Any number of ELSE IF clauses may appear in a single IF statement.

3. Only the *action-statement-list* associated with the first condition evaluated as true is performed. If none of the conditions in the IF action prove true, *action-statement- list-3* following the ELSE is performed.

CASE is a special purpose condition used to perform actions based on the value of an expression. The format of the CASE action statement is:

```
┌── CASE OF expression-1
├── CASE constant-1
│        action-statement-list-1
├── [CASE constant-2
│        action-statement-list-2]...
├── [OTHERWISE
│        action-statement-list-3]
└──
```

Notes:

1. *Expression-1* is most often a single attribute view whose value is to be evaluated, although it can be more complex.

2. *Constant-1* is a single possible value for *expression-1*. If the value of *expression-1* equals the value of *constant-1*, the actions in *action-statement-list-1* are performed. If the value of *expression-1* does not equal the value of *constant-1*, the constant associated with the next CASE clause is evaluated. This activity is repeated until either:

   a. The value of *expression-1* equals a constant in a CASE clause, in which case the actions in the associated *action-statement-list* are performed.

      or

   b. The CASE clauses are exhausted and none of their constant values equal *expression-1*. If the OTHERWISE clause is present, the actions in its *action-statement-list* are performed. If not, process execution continues at the next action statement following the CASE action statement.

REPEATING ACTIONS

READ EACH is shown in the section entitled "Entity Actions."

FOR EACH processes elements of a repeating group view. The format of the FOR EACH statement is:

```
FOR EACH repeating-group-view-1
    [TARGETING repeating-group-view-2 [FROM THE BEGINNING]
     [UNTIL FULL]]
    [AND TARGETING repeating-group-view-3 [FROM THE BEGINNING]
     [UNTIL FULL]]...
        action-statement-list
```

Notes:

1. *Repeating-group-view-1* must be either an import or a local view.

2. *Repeating-group-view-2* and *repeating-group-view-3* must be either a local view or export view.

3. The behavior of the TARGETING clause is exactly the same as for the READ EACH.

WHILE repeats a series of actions as long as a condition holds true. The format of the WHILE action statement is:

```
WHILE condition-1
    [TARGETING repeating-group-view-1 [FROM THE BEGINNING]
     [UNTIL FULL]]
    [AND TARGETING repeating-group-view-2 [FROM THE BEGINNING]
     [UNTIL FULL]] ...
        action-statement-list
```

Notes:

1. The WHILE action statement is primarily useful when dealing with explicitly subscripted repeating groups.

2. If *condition-1* is false when the WHILE is first encountered, the IEF never performs the *action-statement-list*.

3. The behavior of the TARGETING clause is exactly the same as for the READ EACH.

REPEAT...UNTIL repeats a series of actions until a condition is true. The format of the REPEAT...UNTIL action statement is:

```
REPEAT
    [TARGETING repeating-group-view-1 [FROM THE BEGINNING]
        [UNTIL FULL]]
    [AND TARGETING repeating-group-view-2 [FROM THE BEGINNING]
        [UNTIL FULL]] ...
        action-statement-list
UNTIL condition-1
```

Notes:

1. The REPEAT...UNTIL action statement is primarily useful when dealing with explicitly subscripted repeating groups.

2. The IEF does not test *condition-1* until the *action-statement-list* completes. Thus, when the IEF encounters the REPEAT, it always performs the actions in *action-statement-list* at least once.

3. The behavior of the TARGETING clause is exactly the same as for the READ EACH.

FOR repeats a series of statements until the value of a loop control variable reaches an established limit.

```
FOR attribute-view-1 FROM expression-1 TO expression-2
    BY expression-3
        action-statement-list
```

Notes:

1. *Attribute-view-1* is set to the value of *expression-1* before the first execution of *action-statement-list*.

2. Prior to each execution of *action-statement-list*, *attribute-view-1* is compared with *expression-2*. If *attribute-view-1* is equal to *expression-2*, or if *expression-3* is a positive number and *attribute-view-1* is greater than *expression-2*, or *expression-3* is a negative number and *attribute-view-1* is less than *expression-2*, the FOR loop is terminated and control is passed to the next action.

3. The value of *expression-3* is added to *attribute-view-1* after each execution.

4. *Attribute-view-1* is either a local attribute view or a subscript.

5. *Expression-1, expression-2* and *expression-3* must be of the primitive domain Number.

CONTROL ACTIONS

USE invokes a subordinate action block. Information can be passed to the import view of the action block and retrieved from its export view. The format of the USE statement is:

```
USE action-block
    [WHICH IMPORTS: view-1 [view-2]...]
    [WHICH EXPORTS: view-3 [view-4]...]
```

Notes:

1. During Business Area Analysis, the *action-block* cannot be the Process Action Diagram of an elementary process. Rather, it refers to a business algorithm (Common Action Block).

2. During Business System Design, the *action-block* can be the Process Action Diagram of an elementary process, or a business algorithm (Common Action Block). It cannot be the Procedure Action Diagram of a procedure step.

3. The views in the WHICH IMPORTS list are sent to the import view of the *action-block* before it begins execution.

4. The views in the WHICH EXPORTS list are returned from the export view of the *action-block* after it completes execution.

5. The WHICH IMPORTS and WHICH EXPORTS lists are built using the IEF View Matching facility. This insures the compatibility of views that exchange data.

ESCAPE terminates the execution of an action group. The format of the ESCAPE action statement is:

 ESCAPE

The arrow indicates the bracket of an action group. The action statement following the closure of that action group will be executed immediately after the ESCAPE.

NEXT bypasses action statements in a repeating action. The format of the NEXT action statement is:

 NEXT

The arrow must always point to a repeating action group (that is, a bracket enclosing a repeating action: READ EACH, FOR EACH, WHILE or REPEAT...UNTIL). NEXT causes the IEF to bypass subsequent actions and begin the next repetition of the repeating action.

MISCELLANEOUS ACTIONS

MAKE dynamically sets the video properties of onscreen fields and special fields from within an action diagram. The format of the MAKE action statement is:

MAKE export-attribute-view   ┌─ ERROR
                               │ video-attribute-list ─┘

Notes:

1. The MAKE action statement is valid only in a Procedure Action Diagram that represents a procedure step. It cannot appear in subordinate action blocks. MAKE has meaning only in online procedures.

2. The ERROR option causes the field associated with the export attribute view to be set to the Error Video Properties specified for that field. In general, the use of the ERROR option is preferred over the *video attribute list* option because it provides a degree of standardization.

3. The *video attribute list* option allows the designer to explicitly specify video attribute properties within the action diagram.

NOTE is used to add a comment to the action diagram.

The format of the NOTE action statement is:

NOTE text

Text is a free-form description up to 2000 characters in length.

APPENDIX E
VIEW MATCHING RULES

- View matching can take place between two entity views of the same entity type.

- View matching can take place between two group views with congruent structures. Two group views are said to have congruent structures when:

  — The entity views and group views that compose each group view to be matched correspond exactly in meaning and relative position.

  — Corresponding component group views have the same cardinality in both group views to be matched.

  — Each component group view is congruent with its corresponding group view.

  In other words, the two group views must look exactly alike except for the list of attribute views they contain.

- View matching causes the values of attribute views in the source view to be copied to the corresponding attribute views in the target view. Attribute views are said to correspond when they implement the same attribute.

- When matching dialog flows, export data views of the source procedure step may be matched to import data views of the target procedure step.

- When matching Procedure Action Block data requirements:

  — Import views of the USEd action block may be matched to the import, local or entity action views of the USEing action block.

  — Export views of the USEd action block may be matched to the export or local views of the USEing action block.

APPENDIX F
SPECIAL ATTRIBUTES

The following matrix identifies the special attributes available during Business System Design.

Special Attributes	Type	Screen	PAD
Command	Text	I/O	T/S/M
Current Date	Date	O	T/S
Current Time	Time	O	T/S
Exit State	n/a	-	T/M
Printer Terminal ID	Text	I/O	T/S/M
Program Function Keys	n/a	O	-
System Error Message	n/a	O	-
Terminal ID	Text	O	T/S
Transaction Code	n/a	O	-
User ID	Text	O	T/S
Scroll indicator message	Text	O	n/a
Scroll amount message	Text	I/O	n/a
Scroll line message	Text	O	n/a
Panel ID	Text	O	n/a
Local System ID	Text	O	n/a
Next Transaction ID	Text	I	M
Subscript of	Number	n/a	T/S/M
Last of	Number	n/a	T/S/M
Max of	Number	n/a	T/S

I   = Data can be entered into a field implementing this attribute

O   = Data can be displayed in a field implementing this attribute

T   = The value of this attribute can be tested in a Procedure Action Diagram

S   = The value of a view of a compatible type can be set to the value of this attribute in an action diagram

M   = The value of this attribute can be modified in an action diagram

APPENDIX G
PROTOTYPING USING THE IEF

Prototyping is a means by which the external behavior of a system being developed can be simulated before the system is actually installed. This technique allows potential users to evaluate their interaction with the system before development is completed.

The IEF supports two levels of **evolutionary prototyping** for online procedures. An evolutionary prototype is one for which the elements of the prototype can actually be used in the construction of the system. In a non-evolutionary prototype, the prototype is discarded after an agreement has been reached on system behavior; the subsequently built system must be designed to reflect the behavior of the prototype.

The two levels of prototyping available are:

- **Online conversation prototyping.**
- **Full procedure prototyping.**

ONLINE CONVERSATION PROTOTYPING

The IEF supports the prototyping of elements of an online conversation at the workstation during Business System Design. An online conversation prototype is used to show the user how screens will appear and how flows between screens will be implemented.

When the workstation based Online-Conversation Prototyping feature is used, screens are displayed in the same manner as using the DISPLAY feature of the IEF Screen Design tool. Flows between screens are simulated for dialog flows based on autoflows to which function keys have been associated. Thus, online conversation prototyping can take place prior to procedure logic design (that is, before the construction and refinement of action diagrams).

This variety of prototyping is limited in that no data can be entered into the fields on the screens displayed. However, it can be used to demonstrate the general appearance of screens and the general behavior of online conversations to users before any time is invested in constructing action diagrams.

Additionally, since this feature is actually part of the IEF Design Toolset, chaining to the Dialog Flow Diagram and Screen Design to modify them and re-run the prototype is supported. Thus, the prototype can be modified almost instantaneously during a prototyping session with the user.

The workstation prototyping feature is described in detail in the *IEF Design Toolset Guide*.

FULL PROCEDURE PROTOTYPING

The second level of prototyping involves the actual generation of selected procedures and procedure steps into a TSO environment prior to the completion of Businesss System Design. This facility can be used to show a user exactly how procedures and procedure steps will interact prior to their installation in the target teleprocessing environment. Full procedure prototyping can only be used after the procedure logic for the procedures under consideration is fully defined. Additionally, it requires that test databases be created.

The vehicle used for full procedure prototyping is the TSO Testing Facility, described in detail in the *IEF Construction Toolset Guide*.

APPENDIX H
TRANSPARENT DENORMALIZATION

Transparent denormalization is a technique used during Technical Design to optimize database retrieval. However, in order to take advantage of this particular kind of optimization, the action diagrams built during Business Area Analysis and Business System Design must be properly formed. In this appendix, the concept of denormalization, the transparent denormalization facility of the IEF, and the implications for action diagramming during BAA and BSD are discussed.

DENORMALIZATION

The result of the data modeling activity during Business Area Analysis is a fully normalized entity relationship model of the business (the notion of normalized and unnormalized entity types is covered in Chapter 16). From the standpoint of the business model, the absence of normalization obscures the meaning of the business reality being modeled and leads to a number of update anomalies in the detailed process logic. However, when it comes time to implement a database which represents the business model, the database designer may identify some performance issues which can best be solved by **denormalizing** the database.

For example, consider the fully normalized Entity Relationship Diagram in Figure H-1. If this model were used as the basis of a database design, one would likely find that each entity type was implemented as a record, that each attribute was implemented as a field, and that each relationship was implemented as some kind of linkage (in the case of IEF-produced DB2 tables, as a foreign key field).

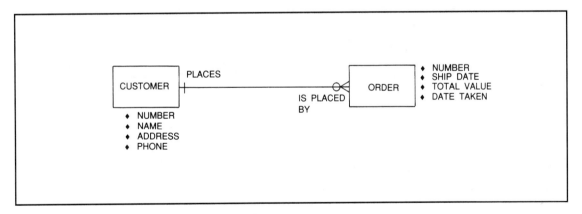

Figure H-1. A Fully Normalized Data Model

However, imagine that in most cases, whenever an ORDER is accessed from within an action block, the Name, Number and Address of the CUSTOMER who placed it are also accessed. Further, imagine that once a CUSTOMER's Name, Number and Address are established, their values are rarely changed.

This situation would lead most designers to conclude that the most efficient design of the ORDER database record would include the Name, Number and Address of the CUSTOMER who placed it. Thus, the Name, Number and Address stored in each CUSTOMER record would be duplicated in (or **denormalized to**) each ORDER record associated with the CUSTOMER. This would make it possible to obtain all information normally required when accessing an ORDER (that is, the details of ORDER and the Name, Number and Address of CUSTOMER) by accessing a single database record.

However, such a database design leads to some additional complexity. In this example, if a CUSTOMER's Address should change, the new address would have to be reflected not only in the CUSTOMER record, but in all of its related ORDER records as well. Thus, in a traditional development environment, a designer is required to make a trade-off between run-time efficiency and development-time complexity.

IEF TRANSPARENT DENORMALIZATION

Using the IEF, however, it is possible to denormalize for efficiency *without changing the Business Area Analysis or Business System Design specifications*. This is accomplished by means of the transparent denormalization feature of the IEF's database design tool, the Data Structure Diagramming Tool. A detailed account of use of this tool appears in the *IEF Design Toolset Guide*.

Given the Entity Relationship Diagram in Figure H-1, above, the IEF's default database transformation algorithm would yield the record definitions presented in Figure H-2 for the CUSTOMER and ORDER tables (assuming that the identifier of CUSTOMER was Number):

CUSTOMER Record Fields	ORDER Record
Number	Number
Name	Ship Date
Address	Total Value
Phone	Date Taken
	Customer Number (foreign key)

Figure H-2. Field Definitions for the CUSTOMER and ORDER Records

The database designer can denormalize fields of CUSTOMER into the ORDER record to yield the record definitions in Figure H-3. (Note that fields can only be denormalized across one level of a one-to-many relationship.)

CUSTOMER Record Fields	ORDER Record
Number	Number
Name	Ship Date
Address	Total Value
Phone	Date Taken
	Customer Number (foreign key)
	Customer Name (denormalized
	Customer Address (denormalized)

Figure H-3. Field Definitions for the CUSTOMER and ORDER Records

When code is generated using the IEF Construction Toolset, the generated system takes advantage of denormalization and resolves all update anomalies.

For example, consider the following action diagram READ statement:

```
┌── READ    order
│              customer
│              WHERE DESIRED order number IS EQUAL TO import order number
│                  AND DESIRED customer places DESIRED order
└
```

For the database definition appearing in Figure H-2, the following pseudocode represents the IEF generated program logic used to implement the READ (assuming that the only attributes of CUSTOMER in the Customer entity action view are Number, Name and Address):

```
GET ORDER RECORD FOR ORDER NUMBER = import order number
SET ENTITY ACTION VIEW order number
    TO ORDER RECORD Number
SET ENTITY ACTION VIEW order ship date
    TO ORDER RECORD Ship Date
SET ENTITY ACTION VIEW order total value
    TO ORDER RECORD Total Value
SET ENTITY ACTION VIEW order date taken
    TO ORDER RECORD Date Taken
GET CUSTOMER RECORD FOR CUSTOMER NUMBER =
    ORDER RECORD Customer Number (foreign key)
SET ENTITY ACTION VIEW customer number
    TO CUSTOMER RECORD Number
SET ENTITY ACTION VIEW customer name
    TO CUSTOMER RECORD Name
SET ENTITY ACTION VIEW customer address
    TO CUSTOMER RECORD Address
```

The following psuedocode represents the IEF generated program logic used to implement the same READ using the denormalized database definition presented in Figure H-3:

```
GET ORDER RECORD FOR ORDER NUMBER = import order number
SET ENTITY ACTION VIEW order number
    TO ORDER RECORD Number
SET ENTITY ACTION VIEW order ship date
    TO ORDER RECORD Ship Date
SET ENTITY ACTION VIEW order total value
    TO ORDER RECORD Total Value
SET ENTITY ACTION VIEW order date taken
    TO ORDER RECORD Date Taken
SET ENTITY ACTION VIEW customer number
    TO ORDER RECORD Customer Number (denormalized)
SET ENTITY ACTION VIEW customer name
    TO ORDER RECORD Customer Name (denormalized)
SET ENTITY ACTION VIEW customer address
    TO ORDER RECORD Customer Address (denormalized)
```

Note that only the ORDER record is retrieved because all of the attribute views requested for CUSTOMER are available on it.

Likewise, for any UPDATE action which SETS one of the attributes of CUSTOMER which has been denormalized to ORDER, the IEF generated program logic will find and replace each affected ORDER record field as well as the CUSTOMER record fields.

Action Diagram Implications of Denormalization

The IEF always ensures the accuracy of the contents of denormalized fields; any time a field value is changed on a database, all denormalized fields based on it are changed, too.

However, the IEF can only take advantage of denormalization in a READ or READ EACH statement under the following conditions:

- The entity action views of the entity types implemented as a "denormalization pair" must be populated by the same READ action.

  For example, the following pair of READ actions accomplish the same result as the single READ action above. However, even if the database design appearing in Figure H-3 is implemented, the IEF generated program logic will still issue a database access for both the CUSTOMER and ORDER records:

  ```
  ┌── READ order
  │      WHERE DESIRED order number IS EQUAL TO import order number
  └──

  ┌── READ customer
  │      WHERE DESIRED customer places CURRENT order
  └──
  ```

- The entity action view of the entity type implemented as a record whose fields have been denormalized (CUSTOMER, in the above example) must only contain attribute views of denormalized fields.

  For example, if the entity action view of CUSTOMER in the multiple-view READ appearing earlier had contained a view of the attribute Phone (which was *not* denormalized to ORDER), the IEF generated program logic would still issue a database access to retrieve its value because it is not available from the ORDER record.

INDEX

J

K